Physical Education
for
Elementary Schools

A Bulletin of

IOWA STATE TEACHERS COLLEGE

CEDAR FALLS, IOWA

By

MONICA R. WILD, Ph.D.
Head of the Department of Physical Education for Women

and

DORIS E. WHITE, M.A.
Associate Professor of Physical Education for Women

12th Edition, 1944

Published by

IOWA STATE TEACHERS COLLEGE

CEDAR FALLS, IOWA

INTRODUCTION

The immediate and enthusiastic reception of the first edition of this bulletin rendered necessary the issuance of a second edition. New material was added: A Course of Study in Physical Education for Elementary Grades, and Daily Progressive Plans in Physical Education for Rural Schools. An eleventh edition of the bulletin is now offered.

Acknowledgment is made of permission given by the following publishers to use copyrighted material: A. S. Barnes & Co., New York; Benjamin H. Sanborn & Co., Chicago; Clayton F. Summy Co., Chicago; Laidlaw Bros., Chicago; The John Church Co., Cincinnati; Theodore Presser Co., Philadelphia; and Milton Bradley Co., Springfield, Mass.

Especial recognition is given to the valuable assistance of Miss Grace Van Ness, of the Department of Physical Education, who so painstakingly arranged the music herein included. This assistance has added much to the possibility for usefulness of this bulletin.

       IRVING H. HART,
        Director of the Extension Division,
        Iowa State Teachers College.

Copyright 1924
by
EXTENSION DIVISION
IOWA STATE TEACHERS COLLEGE
Cedar Falls, Iowa
IRVING H. HART, Director

TABLE OF CONTENTS

General Considerations . . . . p. 5-20
    The Physical Education program: Aims, Needs, Objectives, Definition, Scope. Big Muscle Activity Program, Objectives. Time Allotment. Space. Equipment. Method of Using Signals. The Relief Period. Suggestions for Rural Schools.

Games and Athletics . . . . p. 21-112
    Classification. Teaching of Games. List of Hunting Games. Classification of Athletic Games. Games for Primary Grades: Schoolroom, Playground. Games for Intermediate Grades: Schoolroom, Playground. Track and Field Events, Motor Ability Tests: Plan I, Plan II. Directions for Conducting Motor Ability Tests. Class Athletics.

Rhythmical Activities . . . . p. 113-282
    Types, Significance, Dance Steps and Use of Music, Teaching, Formations, Type Lessons. Rhythmical Activities for Primary Grades; for Intermediate Grades.

Posture Education . . . . p. 283-307
    Significance, Criteria of Good Posture. The Preventive Phase. Exercises, Triple Test. Developing Mental Responses. Special Corrective Exercises.

Marching . . . . p. 308-315

Movement Fundamentals . . . . p. 316-358
    Movement Fundamentals leading to Softball, Basket Ball, Soccer, and Track and Field. Mimetic Exercises. Story Plays. Rhythmical Jumping Exercises.

Stunts and Contests . . . . p. 359-371
    Appendix I Pageant: The Conflict of the
        Seasons . . . . p. 372-398
    Appendix II. County Play Day . . . . . p. 399-
        Purpose. Organization.

Supplement . . . . p. 421
    Course of Study in Physical Education for Elementary Grades. Rope Jumping Skills. Ball Bouncing Skills (O'Leary).

Index . . . . p. 445

College Elementary School Playground

GENERAL CONSIDERATIONS

The Physical Education Program

I. General Statement of Aims: Social Adjustment, Good Citizenship.

Three social standards involved: Happiness, health, character traits essential to good citizenship.

II. Need.

A. General Statement of Need: Our nation needs physical Education.

Specific example: During our recent military struggle, three outstanding truths were unfolded regarding the physical stamina and fighting fitness of the best America could offer its men between 21 and 30 years of age. These three things were:

First: The presence of handicapping physical defects, so handicapping that military service was impossible. This led to the rejection for regular military service of and consequently the reduction of our fighting strength by one-third of the draftees. In studying the list of defects as causes of rejection, few were of the kind that could not have been remedied by early detection, or prevented by control of illness or contagion. Some of these are defective eyesight, hearing, teeth, hearts, and musculature (particularly feet).

Second: The prevalent condition of physical inefficiency; that is, the inability to handle effectively, according to the needs of modern warfare, the body. One particular regiment over in France illustrates this inefficiency. Twenty-eight per cent of the regiment failed to jump over a six-foot trench in a standing broad jump; seventeen per cent of the regiment failed to qualify in running the 220 yard dash in 30 seconds. Such being the case, to faulty human mechanism can easily be prescribed the cause of a large percentage of casualties.

Third: The lack of knowledge of applied hygiene. Many neither knew nor practiced the simple laws of personal hygiene, so essential for effective living.

If we were to describe this general condition of our men between 21 and 30, we would say that their education up to 21 was not the kind that developed capacities which made adjustment of themselves possible at the time of a crisis. Yet, if we review the points in which they were weak, we readily see that the development of such capacities is necessary for adjustment to any kind of living in adulthood, for the pursuits of war or the pursuits of peace, if effective citizenship is expected.

Major General Wood, during the war in giving a talk to a body of Physical Education teachers, said in substance: "You and your scheme of education are to blame for this situation. Not one of these things which we have to spend time on now in this short period of preparation but that could and should have been done by the school." It was a harsh indictment, but the burden of the guilt was manifest, and undoubtedly because of this recent experience in military operations and the disclosure of truths regarding our national vigor, the responsibility has been accepted by the public and a definite step for the prevention of the future lack of this power of adjustment to social needs has been taken by the American people through their legislative bodies.

B. Specific Statement of Need: The child needs physical Education.

1. Education of the child must go on without physical handicaps.

2. Hunger for big muscle activity is the most outstanding characteristic of child-life and is vital to all phases of his development.

III. Specific Statement of Objectives.

1. To prevent and remove handicaps through health supervision and control:
   (a) By detection and correction of physical defects.
   (b) By control of illness and contagion.
   (c) By administration of proper sanitation.

2. To set an ideal of health through:
   (a) Health instruction.
   (b) Guidance in formation of health habits.
   (c) Offering of proper incentives and ideals.

3. To organize and guide big muscle activity.

4. To seek the fulfillment of the possible objectives in development found in big muscle activity which are:
   (a) Development of citizenship qualities which result from the satisfaction of instinct tendencies.
   (b) Development of organic power.
   (c) Development of the psycho-motor mechanism, including posture education.
   (d) Development of habits of exercise.

IV. Definition: Physical Education is that part of the educational process which employs health supervision and control, instruction in applied hygiene, and organization and leadership of big muscle activity as the means to secure development of inherent powers needed to reach the aim of education which is social adjustment. The word "physical" then relates more to the means employed than the end sought.

V. Scope of the Physical Education Program.
1. Health Supervision and Control.
2. Instruction in applied Hygiene.
3. Big muscle activity (commonly known as exercise or physical training).

Bibliography on Health Education:
"Health Education for Elementary Schools." State Department of Public Instruction. H. A. Phillips School Service, Mason City, Ia.
"Health Education." Joint Committee, A.M.A. & N.E.A. National Education Association, Washington, D. C., 1941.

VI. Scope of this bulletin.

The present work will include one phase only of the Physical Education program: Big muscle activity for Elementary (1st through 6th) Grades.

The content of activities has been a result of selection based on:
1. The objectives.
2. Age incentives and capacities.
3. Common conditions of space and equipment.
4. Limitations of leadership.
5. Muscular activities which are natural to children.

The selection consists mainly and under all but few conditions of natural activities, those which grow out of instinct tendencies, and which appeal to the child directly as worth while. Furthermore such activities should form the main content of the physical activity program because the possibility of reaching the objectives in Physical Education is inherent in the nature of the activities and is therefore real if properly guided.

Formal devised physical training work is of less importance in the program of activities because of the character of its appeal, since no deep-rooted inherent instinct tendency except the desire to move is satisfied. Furthermore, devised exercises, as gymnastics, offer no direct appeal to the child as worth while; they offer no possibility of the development of the emotions or of character traits; they do not develop the neuro-muscular mechanism in ways related to adjustment needs; often there is not sufficient amount of big muscle activity for organic needs; and, although the exercises may be enjoyed, the enjoyment comes from the desire to be moving rather than sitting still, and not because of the satisfaction of other strong important native impulses which find satisfaction in the natural activities. Therefore, it is not necessary to include much work in formal gymnastics, except that which is essential for posture education (see page 283) and for Relief Drills (see page 15). It is believed that sufficient work of this kind for such purposes is given in this bulletin, and if well directed and purposefully given, it is adequate for reaching desired results.

Outline of Activities to be included:
A. Natural Activities.
  1. Games and Athletics including Track and Field (measurable).
  2. Rythmical Activities.
  3. Stunts and Contests (not measurable).
  4. Movement Fundamentals: Games Fundamentals, Story Plays, etc.

B. Posture Education, including limited but adequate amount of formal gymnastics, with some special remedial exercises.

C. Appendices.
  1. May Day Pageant for town schools.
  2. County Play Day Plan.

VII. Statement of Objectives of the Big Muscle (Physical) Activity Program.

A. Organization and Leadership of Child-Life in respect to Big Muscle Activity.

The following questions are pertinent:
  1. What is the immediate aim of our educational scheme? (To take the various activities characteristic of childhood, organize them into what is termed a curriculum and guide their procedure for the purpose of development and thus reach the remote aim of education: Social adjustment).
  2. What are some of the activities of childhood?
  3. Which is the first and most strikingly characteristic activity of childhood?
      (Big muscle activity).
  4. Is it vital to the child?
  5. Is it important to physical growth?
  6. Is it important to learning or mental development?
  7. What does the baby learn first?
      (To kick with legs, roll with trunk, thrust with arms).

8. Is this necessary for later learning, as sitting, standing, walking?
9. Is learning to stand, walk, etc., necessary to other learning?
10. Does big muscle activity cease when child enters school?
11. Does it still remain a vital activity?
12. How does it compare with the other activities of childhood in respect to its functioning in the life of the child?
13. Why then has it not long since been organized into a curriculum as other activities have been organized and given a place in the educational program?
14. Why has this most fundamental activity been left to haphazard guidance and leadership?
15. Is not then one of the purposes of Physical Education in the school program to organize childhood's most fundamental activity and place it under adult leadership to reach the objectives in development possible in this activity?

B. Development in directions which lead towards social adjustment: good citizenship.

The lines of development are the following:

1. The development of deep-rooted, important instinct tendencies, with which muscle activity is always associated, into right habits of emotional response, which result in fundamental character traits which in turn have a direct relation to one's fellows (society).

Examples of such habits and traits are: obedience, cooperation, loyalty, spirit of fair play, self-reliance, perseverance, courage, initiative, etc., Habits of human behavior are a result of emotional response to instinct tendencies, but their quality is good or bad, depending upon the leadership. Therefore, the importance of the leadership must be emphasized if this phase of development is to be desirable and possible of proper social adjustment.

2. Development of organic power; that is, good functional activity of vital organs. Big muscle activity is the only natural means by which vigorous and reliable functions of heart, lungs, nerves, nutritive and eliminative organs can be stimulated and thus normally developed. This development is essential in childhood because it stimulates to proper growth. It is important in the adult because it keeps him in condition. Organic power is the basis of health and endurance. Upon it depends much of the capacity of earning a living. Lack of organic vigor results in economic dependence, yet the good citizen must be economically independent.

3. The development of the psycho-motor mechanism resulting in (a) strategic judgment, (b) good posture.

(a) The physical "ego" is the body and upon the mastery of its use depend all physical relations and adjustments. The development of muscular coordination then is necessary to properly suit our movements to the needs of situations that arise in daily life. These neuro-muscular coordinations must be learned. We can not leave them to haphazard learning through life situations. We must plan for equivalent situations which involve no risks. These are found in play activities of the large muscle variety. Such activities, besides strengthening fundamental coordinations, give opportunity to rapidly size up a situation, judge quickly and clearly what the muscle response should be and accurately make that response. Such reaction, called "strategic judgment", is the final goal in psycho-motor education, and finds practical application in the daily situations of life. Lack of this much needed physical efficiency was one of the disclosures of our war. Loss of life by accident is as a rule traceable to inefficient human motor mechanism. But one activity in our educational process can give this development in skill and strategic judgment as related to adjustment needs and that is big muscle play activity.

(b) Another phase of the development of the psycho-motor mechanism is related to posture education. Physically this is a process of learning the right use of muscle groups in order to maintain proper body relations previously learned. More especially applied exercises must be planned to develop these coordinations, if they have not been already unconsciously learned.

4. Development of a knowledge of human nature.

The experimental station for learning and judging human nature is the play field, for contacts in play unfold as do no other means the responses and attitudes of individuals to given or unexpected situations. This knowledge leads into determining how to deal with one's fellows, and is essential to social adjustment.

5. To develop habits of physical activity, ideals of recreation and right use of leisure time. This objective lies in close connection with the standards of life which are necessary for social adjustment, i.e., happiness, health, good citizenship. Our avocational efficiency is a social need and therefore should be an educational objective with the existing eight-hour day and our congested population.

VIII. Suggestions as to Time Allotment.

1. General consideration.

PHYSICAL EDUCATION

Dr. Hetherington, after much research with and study of children, makes the following significant statement, "Up to 10 years of age, a child needs 4 to 5 hours of big muscle activity daily to meet his educational needs; beyond 10 years of age, 2 to 3 hours daily." The past generation, and the adults of this generation undoubtedly received 4 to 5 hours of big muscle activity in childhood, if not in the form of play, then in the form of work, or of getting from one place to another. The children of today, however, have little work of the big muscle variety and modern means of locomotion reduce daily activity. The play time of the child then is his most important means of securing his needed daily quota of muscular exercise. The school can not take on all this needed time, yet, recognizing the fundamental educational importance of big muscle activity, it must plan for sufficient instructional periods in physical training with proper selection of materials so that what is taught will carry over into the extra-curricular play periods and be practised there. Two things rise to importance in this connection. First: the recess and before school periods become significant as times when daily needs in muscular activity can be in part filled. Conscientious leaders of child-life should so organize children in their class period in physical training into self-directing groups with leaders, and there lead them into group undertakings which will carry over into the recess and before school play periods. Second: The home play periods should be provided for, by the teaching of games which can be played or practised at home by one or two or a small neighborhood group.

2. Specific consideration of time allotment.

(a) The instructional period.
15 minutes daily (minimum).

Time used as follows:

(1) For instruction of the more important phases of the program without hurry.

(2) For group organization, with carry-over plans.

(3) For discussion of organization and its relation to conduct and moral standards.

(4) For correlation of applied hygiene to the closely associated incentive, exercise.

(5) For teaching of relief period exercises, games or dances.

(6) For drill in games technique with carry-over purposes.

(b) The relief period.

Two minute relief periods at end of each academic hour—(minimum).

(See page 15).

(c) Time given at the beginning of every session for such necessary survey of children as to determine presence of disease.

IX. Space.

Problems of space are not as great as they would seem without thought, and we must not allow ourselves to believe that because of physical conditions of space, vigorous muscular activity must be cut to a minimum. We are fortunate to live in a climate where during practically all of the fall months and most of the spring months, the physical activity program can go on out-of-doors—the natural, presupposed situation for big muscle play activity, and the most important laboratory of the whole school plant. Effort must be made in communities for good surfacing and care of these health and character building laboratories, in order that the limitation to their use may be at a minimum.

The school room, however, must often serve as this laboratory, but never unless absolutely essential, and should always be considered a make-shift and far from ideal. Yet, on the other hand, physical exercise should not be omitted just because it is impossible to go out-of-doors, for from the natural activities outlined in this bulletin much can be selected which is readily adapted to the school room with excellent results. Among them are rhythmical activities, games fundamentals, relief drills, many games, some simple team games, stunts, and contests. The school room games are classified separately, and suggestions are otherwise given as to specific materials or methods of adaptation.

X. Equipment.

The following is a list of minimal equipment for one town school building.

1 Soccer ball
1 Volley ball
1 Volley ball net and standards
2 Softball
2 Softball bats
2 Basket balls
1 Pair baskets and back stops
1 Dozen bean bags
Victrola
10 Records
1 Pair jumping standards and cross bar

PHYSICAL EDUCATION

1 Climbing rope
1 (or more) Chinning bars
2 Mats (5x7)
1 75-foot cloth measuring tape
1 Stop watch
1 Jumping pit with take off board
1 Jumping pit for high jump
  First aid material
  Tongue depressors
  Eye chart
  Scales (with height attachment)
  Library of physical education books

Ten best records are as follows:

1. One march record
   - (Victor 35804
   - (Victor 20132 Stars and Stripes Forever (but slower tempo)
   - (Victor 20400 Tenth Regiment March
2. One American country dance record
   - Old Zip Coon   Victor 20592
   - Soldier's Joy
3. One English country dance record
   - Sellenger's Round
   - Gathering Peascods   Victor 20445
4. Norwegian Mountain March
   - Pop Goes the Weasel   Victor 20151
5. Danish Dance of Greeting   Carrousel
   - I See You, Kinderpolka   Victor 20432
6. Gustof's Skoal
   - Lott'ist Tod   Victor 20988
7. Tantoli
   - The Wheat   Victor 20992
   - Cshebogar
8. Shoemaker's Dance
   - Klapp Dance   Victor 20450
9. Ace of Diamonds
   - Bleking   Victor 20989
10. Come Let Us Be Joyful
    - Broom Dance   Victor 20448
    - Bummel Schottishe

Bibliography

"Iowa Plan of Physical Education for Use in Elementary Schools of Iowa." Department of Public Instruction, Des Moines, Iowa, 1941.

Method of Using Signals

The use of signals or commands is necessary for Marching, for Gymnastics (as found under section on Posture Education), for Movement Fundamentals and for Relief Drills.

1. How to give the Signals.

Each signal is divided into three parts: The explanatory part, the pause, the executive word.

   a. The explanatory part describes or names the movement to be executed. It should be spoken distinctly and clearly with voice comparatively low, and in a more conversational manner, not in a stilted, mechanical, sing-song fashion.

   b. The pause must be sufficiently long to permit the pupils to analyze and understand the explanatory part, and thus be ready to act. It is the most important single factor in insuring unison of response.

   c. The executive word is the final signal for execution, and consists usually of one word. It must be distinctly given and must indicate the manner of executing the movement. If the exercise is to be done quickly, forcefully, or with large, vigorous movements, the executive word must be given to stimulate such response. If care and slowness are desired as in breathing exercises the executive word must correspond.

Examples:

Arms bending forward..Bend!
   (Preparatory)   (Pause)   (Executive word)
Bending the Knees..One!
   (Preparatory)   (Pause)   (Executive word)
West Point breathing..One!
   (Preparatory)   (Pause)   (Slow executive word)

2. Three common signals necessary for class work.

   a. Class—Attention!

   This is the signal given to unite the class at the beginning of the lesson and after "in place rest." The position assumed on this signal is the correct fundamental standing position, which is explained in detail on page 284. See also page 297.

   b. Class—Position!

   This signal is used to bring class back to fundamental standing position from any other position reached during an exercise.

   c. In Place—Rest! See picture on page 297.

   This is given to relax the attention, and is executed by placing the left foot sideways and the hands behind the back.

3. Method of Rising from Seats.

Signals:
Class—Attention!
This position in seats is that described on page 287 with hands grasping corners of desks, and shoulder blades together.

Ready to rise—One! Two!
On "One," put right foot in the aisle and right hand at side. On "Two," stand in aisle in correct standing position.

Signals for Sitting:
Ready to sit—One! Two!
On "One," place left foot under desk. On "Two" take hold of corners of desk and sit.

The Relief Period

I. The relief period should come at the end of every hour of academic work, should be short, about 2 minutes in length, and should have the following purposes: For relief from poor study position; to stimulate sluggish circulation and overcome mental fatigue; to recreate; to give frequent outlet to desire for activity and thus relieve restlessness.

Note: Windows should be open during the relief period. Pupil leaders are responsible for opening them.

II. Characteristics of good relief period activities.
Activity should be vigorous.
All children should take part within the period. Activity must be done in aisles of schoolroom with no time needed for organization.
Activity must be learned and organized during instructional period.
Activity should be completed within two minutes.

III. Types of relief period activities.
1. Games of the relay type. Running is the activity and all have an opportunity to play. Games are most desirable because they are more enjoyable.

Examples: Indian File Relay
Bean-bag Circle Carry
Auto Race
Tag the Wall Relay.

Note: When games are used, the period should begin with a posture exercise (Page 293) and end with deep breathing.

2. Rhythmical Activities.
a. Folk Dancing and Singing Games which can be adapted to the schoolroom are excellent, after they are learned.

Time should not be taken to go after a victrola. Children should sing or hum own music.

   Examples: Shoemaker's Dance
        Danish Dance of Greeting
        Looby Loo.

  b. Learned Dance Steps, page 115.
  c. Rhythmical Jumping Exercises, page 354.

  Note: When these exercises are given, the period should begin with a posture exercise (page 293) and end with a breathing exercise.

  3. Exercises. If well chosen these make good relief work from the standpoint of activity, but will be less recreative. Samples of Relief Period Drills are given below. Other orders can be arranged by choosing from

   (1) Posture Exercises (page 293).
   (2) Movement Fundamentals for various athletic games.
   (3) Mimetic Exercises (page 341).
   (4) Dance Steps (page 115).
   (5) Rhythmical Jumping Exercises (page 354).

  Each relief period drill should contain (1) an arm or posture movement, (2) a trunk exercise, (3) a leg exercise, (4) breathing.

IV. Samples of Relief Period Drills.
 I.
  1. Posture Exercise I., page 293.
  2. Mimetic Exercise: Chopping, page 343.
  3. Movement Fundamentals for the Standing Broad Jump, page 337.
  4. West Point Breathing, page 300.

 II.
  1. Posture Exercise II, page 293.
  2. Mimetic Exercise: Rowing, page 342.
  3. Step-hop in Place, Page 116.
  4. Raising Arms Sideways—Deep Breathing.

 III.
  1. Arm Stretchings, Triple Test Exercises, Set I, Exercise 3, page 298.
  2. Mimetic Exercise: Paddling, page 342.
  3. Stride Spring Jump, page 354.
  4. West Point Breathing.

 IV.
  1. Arms Flinging Forward Upward and Sideways Downward, page 299.

PHYSICAL EDUCATION

    2. Swimming Movement, page 305.
    3. The Bleking Step, page 122.
    4. Breathing, Rising on Toes.

V.
    1. Posture Exercise III, page 293.
    2. Mimetic Exercise, Climbing a Ladder, page 343.
    3. Forward Cut Step, page 355.
    4. West Point Breathing.

VI.
    1. Triple Test Exercises, Set I, Exercise 1, page 296.
    2. Mimetic Exercise, Screw Driver, page 343.
    3. Running in Place, Triple Test Exercise, Set I, Exercise 6, page 299.
    4. Blowing up a Balloon.

VII.
    1. Posture Exercise IV, page 293.
    2. Triple Test Exercises, Set I, Exercise 5, page 299.
    3. Jumping Jack, page 344.
    4. Popping Bags.

VIII.
    1. Mimetic Exercise, Shaking Limb of Tree, page 342.
    2. Game Fundamentals for Throwing Softball, page 320.
    3. Mimetic Exercise, Riding a Bicycle, page 344.
    4. West Point Breathing.

IX.
    1. Mimetic Exercise, Windmill, page 341.
    2. Side Cut Step, page 355.
    3. Triple Test Exercises, Set II, Exercise 2, page 302.
    4. Popping Bags.

X.
    1. Triple Test Exercises, Set II, Exercise 3, page 302.
    2. Game Fundamentals for Basket Ball, Over Arm Throw, page 326.
    3. Mimetic Exercise, Teamster Warming Up, page 344.
    4. Arms Raising Sideways—Breathing.

Suggestions for Rural Schools

Activities especially adaptable:

I. Schoolroom Games
    1. Relief Period Games

Tag the Wall Relay   Indian File Relay
Beanbag Circle Carry   All-over Relay
Auto Race   Over-head Beanbag Relay

2. Recess Period Games

Potato Race Relay
Run and Pass Relay
Hoop Relay
Beanbag and Basket Relay
Last Man
Meet Me at the Switch
Teacher and Class
Going to Jerusalem
End Ball
Schoolroom Basket Ball Relay

Pursuit Relay
Line Ball
Zigzag Relay with Goals (Use Beanbag and Waste Basket)
Partner Tag (For Schoolroom)
Schoolroom Snatch
Leader Spry
Newcomb

3. Noon-period Games

Teacher and Class
Beanbag and Basket Relay
Newcomb
Beanbag Ring Toss

Leader Spry
Beanbag Board
End Ball
Ball Exercises

II. Out-door Games

Hen and Chickens
Center Base
Brownies and Fairies
Center Catch Ball
Circle Dodge Ball
Black and White
Midnight
Indian File Relay
Stealing Sticks
Newcomb
Bat Ball
Punch Ball
Circle Strike
Simplified Soccer
Handkerchief Tag

Three Broad
Three Deep
Snatch
Partner Tag
Hound and Rabbit
Maze Tag
Most of the Tag Games
Prisoner's Base
End Ball
Long Ball
Progressive Dodge Ball
Simplified Volley Ball
One-old Cat
Work-up
Ante Over

Out-door Games and Activities for Noon Periods:

Playing Catch
Basket Ball Goal Throwing
Horseshoes
Wall Ball Bounce

Beanbag Board
Simplified Volley Ball
Newcomb
End Ball

The more strenuous games should be omitted at least for some 20 to 30 minutes after the noon lunch.

III. Track and Field Athletics.

The first scheme (see page 98) of Motor Ability Tests is especially recommended for Rural School use.

IV. Stunts and Contests.

Selection is possible for every age and for both girls and boys, and many can be worked out in the schoolroom during the winter months. (See page 359.)

V. Movement Fundamentals.

Selection from the "Games Fundamentals" can be made in accordance with the team games taught. Much of this work can be done in the schoolroom.

Movement Fundamentals for Track and Field offers material which can be worked out in the schoolroom preparatory to the use of the school play-ground in the spring.

Story Plays for the younger children are schoolroom possibilities.

VI. Rhythmical Activities.

*Looby Loo	and Toes
*Danish Dance of Greeting	Rabbit in the Hollow
Chimes of Dunkirk	*Yankee Doodle
Tucker	Farmer in the Dell
*Shoemaker's Dance	*How d'ye Do My Partner
Swedish Ring Dance	Kinderpolka
Cshebogar	Ace of Diamonds
German Hopping Dance	Seven Jumps
Tantoli	Swedish Klapp Dance
*Heads and Shoulders, Knees	

*Those starred can be easily played in the schoolroom.

VII. Relief period work, as outlined on page 15, is as applicable to rural school work as to grades and all is recommended.

See Daily Progressive Plans for Rural Schools, p. 446.

Organization of Children in the Rural School

For the simple tag and "it" games, which appeal to all ages, children can be grouped together if need be—also for some of the folk dances which are easy enough for the primary children, yet attractive enough for the older ones. Yet simple team games and track and field athletics should not be left out just because the younger children can not take part. Here division into at least two groups becomes necessary. If the school is large enough children should be divided into three groups as follows: Ages 5 to 7 inclusive, ages 8 to 10 inclusive, ages 11 to 15 inclusive. It is suggested, however, that such groupings be approximate and that the teacher should consider the size and ability of the individual pupils in making the division. To make possible the carrying on of work in all groups at once, the pupil leader plan is used. The two older groups have their own leaders as appointed by the teacher, or selected by the group, and one of the older children is appointed by the teacher as leader for the youngest group. The teacher must help these leaders in the activities so that their leadership will be effective. She then can divide her time between the different groups, and as she teaches one group a new game or dance the other groups can work under their leader on an activity previously learned. This plan must be very carefully worked out and supervised by the teacher, and, if this be the case, the plan should be very successful. Track and Field work (Motor-Ability Tests) and Stunts lend themselves particularly well to group organization and pupil leadership, even in the small school.

Minimal Equipment for the Rural School

The following is a list of the minimal equipment for a one room rural school:

6-8 Beanbags filled with beans, corn or oats
4 Horseshoes
1-2 Softballs (14-inch)
1 Softball Bat
1 Volley Ball
1 Volley Ball Net and Standards (standards can be home made).
1 Soccer or Basket Ball
1 Climbing Rope (about 1½ inches in diameter)
Chinning Bar
1 pair High Jumping Standards with 2 to 3 cross-bars (fishing poles)
Pit with take-off-board
Hoop (iron) attached to schoolhouse 10 feet from ground. This can be used for Basket Ball goal.
2 large rubber balls (5-inch) for younger children
1-75 foot tape
1 stop-watch (if possible) This can be omitted.
Victrola
5 Records. The following are suggested as the first 5 to buy:
  1. Good march record
  2. Danish Dance of Greeting Kinderpolka
     I See You   Victor 20432
     Carrousal
  3. Shoemaker's Dance
     Swedish Klapp Dance   Victor 20450
  4. Ace of Diamonds
     Bleking   Victor 20989
  5. Looby Loo   Victor 20214

GAMES AND ATHLETICS

The types of games and athletics taken up in this bulletin are those which it is believed will reach best the objectives of physical education under the common conditions existing in our schools at the present time.

I. Hunting Games (chasing, fleeing, tag or "it" games)
II. Athletics
    A. Individual events (Events that are definitely measurable as contrasted with stunts and contests taken up in another part of this bulletin).
        1. Track Events.
        2. Field Events
        3. Events involving elements of athletic games.
    B. Athletic games (Team games):
        Relays, Soccer, Volley Ball, Indoor Baseball, etc.

I. Hunting Games

(a) This class of activities occupies a large part of this bulletin because it occupies so large a part of the life of the primary and elementary school child. The hunting type of game is gradually decreased as the child nears adolescence and is supplemented by the simple team games, but its use is never entirely lost even in adult recreation since it gives a freedom of expression and a spontaneity of action that cannot be duplicated by other forms of activity. Because of their simple organization these games are usually quickly learned and therefore require that a greater variety and number be taught than of those more highly organized. This does not mean, however, that any given game should not be frequently repeated. In choosing games for any age of children it is essential that those be chosen that have the greatest instinctive appeal for that age. In the First Primary and Kindergarten the instinct tendencies are mostly toward activities for activity's sake and for imitative and dramatic plays. From the Second to the Seventh grades the child grows less and less dramatic and imitative in his play and tends toward cooperative activities of simple organization. The whole period, however, is strikingly individualistic and competitive.

(b) Teaching the Games—In teaching a game with a certain set form such as a circle or two lines that are close together it is best to get the children into the required formation first and then, using the names of the actual players instead of impersonal terms such as "The Runner" and "The Chaser" the description and explanation of the game should be given briefly but clearly. No explanation should be given until the full attention of every child is secured. If the game is played in a circle formation the teacher should stand at one side of the circle and not inside the circle to make the explanation. Sometimes it is well to have one or two children go through the movements of the game slowly before the actual game is started.

Ways of getting into various formations are as follows:

A. A circle.
    1. As class marches to playground or gymnasium from their room in double file the lines are halted and told to face each other. The children then join hands with the children beside them and the end children join hands across and then all spread out into a circle.
    2. If in single file the leader may lead the group around into a circle.
    3. If in a disorganized group after having played another game the teacher may just hold out her hands sideways as a signal for the rest to join her in a circle.
    4. (a) If a double circle is wanted as for "Three Deep" the double file column marches around in a circle or
        (b) After having formed a single circle all count off by twos and No. two is asked to step behind the No. one on his right.
    5. If a permanent circle is wanted on the playground as for circle dodge ball each player makes a mark in front of him with his foot or a stick.

B. In lines.
    1. If two lines are wanted and class comes in double file formation teacher indicates where each leader is to lead line.
    2. It is well to have classes divided into permanent teams from the Fourth grade through the Sixth for all activities. There should be two main captains and two sub-captains and the sub-captain should be in charge of one-half of the team. If four lines are wanted the teacher indicates where the sub-captains should lead their lines. If girls and boys play together in 5th and 6th grades the sub-captains should be girls and lead the girls. They can then compete against each other instead of against the boys.
    3. If the lines for a game are to be formed after another free running game the teacher should blow her whistle (which should always mean attention) and then indicate where each captain and sub-captain

PHYSICAL EDUCATION

are to stand and which way to face and whether their teams are to line up beside them or behind them.

(c) List of Hunting Games (Alphabetical).

Games and Grades where best used.

Animal Chase 1-2-3
Ante Over 3 to 6
Ball Stand 3 to 6
Big Black Bear Kg. 1-2-3
Black and White 1 to 6
Bombardment 5-6
Bronco Tag 5-6
Brownies and Fairies Kg. 1-2-3
Bull in the Pen 1-2-3-4
Butterflies and Daisies Kg. 1-2
Cat and Rat Kg. 1-2-3
Cats and Rats Kg. 1-2-3
Center Base 3 to 5
Center Catch Ball 3 to 6
Crows and Cranes 3 to 6
Dodge Ball (Simple) 1-4
Every Man in His Own Den 4 to 6
Farmer in the Dell (If chasing) 1-3
Ghosts and Witches 1-4
Going to Jerusalem 4 to 6
Have you Seen my Sheep 2 to 6
Hen and Chickens 2 to 6
Hindoo Tag 3 to 6
Hot Ball Kg. and 1st

Hound and Rabbit 2 to 5
Huckle Buckle Bean Stalk 1 to 3
Jack Be Quick 3 to 5
Jump the Shot 4 to 6
Kitty White Kg. to 3
Last Couple Out 2 to 6
Last Man 2 to 6
Midnight 1 to 6
Musical Indian Clubs 4 to 6
New York 2 to 4
Partner Tag 1 to 6
Pom Pom Pullaway 2 to 6
Rabbit in the Hollow 1 to 3
Red Light 3 to 6
Snatch 2 to 6
Squirrel and Nut 1 to 4
Squirrels in Trees 1 to 3
Street Car 1 to 3
Streets and Alleys 4 to 6
Stores 3 to 6
Tag Games 1 to 6
Third Man 2 to 6
Three Deep 2 to 6
Three Broad 2 to 6
Touch Off 2 to 6
Tucker Kg. to 6
Whip Tag 3 to 6

II. Athletics

By athletic activities is meant all vigorous physical competition between two or more individuals or groups of individuals where the results are definitely measured or the score automatically registers skill. These fall under the two heads. "A" Individual Athletics and "B" Athletic Games.

A. Individual Athletics.
   See Track and Field Events, page 98.

B. Athletic Games.
   (1) There is no means in the educational program for

teaching social adjustment or citizenship equal to athletic games properly supervised. Besides giving broad organic and psycho-motor development they give opportunity for the development of character in its social relationships. They call for self subordination to the group welfare, and give an opportunity for the teaching of fair play and sportsmanship. Because of their great value in reaching the main end in education they should not be restricted to the use of a few individuals for the purpose of self exploitation or the exploitation of the school. As the skill of those participating in the activity increases the joy derived from this participation is also increased, therefore much opportunity should be given for self improvement especially for the least efficient. The cooperative instinct appears in a mild form as early as 9 years and may be exercised by the use of simply organized team games that will also give opportunity for the development of skill in the fundamentals of the later and more highly organized games. A list of such games and the games they lead to follows.

(2) Simple Team Games leading to Basket Ball in the order of difficulty.

1. Catch Ball, p. 80
2. Newcomb, p. 79
3. End Ball, p. 80
4. Goal Keep Away, p. 78
5. Captain Ball, p. 81

Relays and games aiding in developing skill in the above games are:

1. Teacher and Class, p. 27
2. Leader Spry, p. 32
3. Zig-Zag Pass, p. 72
4. Ten Trips 2-3-5, p. 73
5. Basket Ball Shuttle Relay, p. 75
6. Keep Away, p. 77
7. Pass for Points, p. 78
8. Pivot and Pass, p. 74
9. Dribble and Bounce Pass, Shuttle Relay, p. 75
10. Bounce Pass Keep Away, p. 78
11. Bounce Goal Relay, p. 74
12. Dribble and Take Away Relay, p. 77

(3) Simple Team Games leading to Softball.

1. Triangle Ball, p. 82
2. Punch Ball, p. 86
3. Long Ball, p. 88
4. Foot Ball Baseball, p. 85
5. Box Ball, p. 88
6. Circle Strike, p. 90

PHYSICAL EDUCATION

Games and relays aiding in developing skill in the above games are:

1. Fongo, p. 85
2. One Old Cat, p. 83
3. Work Up, p. 83
4. Grounders Shuttle Relay, p. 84
5. Baseball Pivot and Throw, p. 85
6. Ten Trips 1-4-5, pp. 73-74

(4) Simple Team Games leading to Soccer.

1. Soccer Drive, p. 67
2. Corner Kick Ball, p. 68
3. Simplified Soccer, p. 69
4. Square Football, p. 68

Relays and Games aiding in developing skill in the above games:

1. Soccer Dribble Relay, p. 65
2. Soccer Dribble and Shoot, p. 66
3. Simple Soccer Keep Away, p. 64
4. Double Soccer Keep Away, p. 65
5. Soccer Pass, p. 67
6. Soccer Pass and Shoot, p. 67
7. Shuttle Kicking Contest, p. 68
8. Soccer Target Kicking Relay, p. 66

(5) Simple Team Game leading to Volley Ball.

1. Simplified Volley Ball, p. 92
2. Serve and Return, p. 91

Methods of Forming Teams and Carrying on Tournaments

For the purpose of playing team games each grade from the fourth through the sixth may be divided into permanent teams and frequent contests may be held. Every child in the grade should belong to these teams. If the Iowa Plan of Physical Education procedures are followed teams could be made up of the play groups in each grade or teams might be chosen by two, three or four captains elected by the grade. The captains will choose in rotation from a list of names representing the whole grade. The choosing would be done in secret.

Reference: "Iowa Plan of Physical Education for use in Elementary Schools." Department of Public Instruction, Des Moines, Iowa, 1941.

GAMES FOR PRIMARY GRADES
SCHOOL ROOM GAMES

Kaleidoscope

Six or eight of the pupils stand in a row across the front of the room and are named after colors, each child choosing a different color from the rest. The other players who are seated close their eyes while the colors change places. Then volunteers are called for to name the colors in their new positions and put them back into their original positions. The names of flowers, birds or trees may be substituted for the colors. This may be simplified by using no names. Pupils are simply changed back into original positions.

Lost Child

This is a quiet game designed to test the memory. The players are all seated and one player is chosen by the teacher to come up in front and stand facing her and with his back to the rest of the room. When he has closed his eyes the teacher beckons one of the players to leave the room or hide some place in the room. The rest of the players change seats, and the one who had his eyes closed turns around and tries to guess what child is missing. If he finds it very hard the teacher or pupils may give him some hints, but these must not be too leading. If the child is not successful in guessing who is gone, he must be seated and a new player chosen to hide his eyes; but if he succeeds he may hide his eyes again.

Huckle, Buckle, Bean Stalk

Several players are chosen to leave the room, while one player with the aid of the rest of the class hides some object agreed upon before the others left. The place of hiding should be inconspicuous yet visible. After the object is hidden the players are called in and as they see it they give no sign of the fact until they have taken their seats, then they call: "Huckle Buckle, Bean Stalk." This continues until all have found the object when a new group is sent from the room and the player who first called "Huckle Buckle, Bean Stalk" is allowed to hide the object for the new game.

Have You Seen My Sheep?

This may be played in circle formation or in seats. One player is chosen as shepherd. He goes around the room or up and down the aisle and stops by a player and asks, "Have you seen my sheep?" The player asks, "How is he dressed?" The shepherd then tells something of the dress of someone in the room, being careful not to look at the person being described. The player questioned tries to guess as details are added to the description; when he guesses correctly the shepherd says "yes", and the guesser chases the one described. If the chaser catches the runner before the latter has returned to his place the chaser becomes the shepherd; if he does not the runner becomes shepherd.

Street Car

This game is played in the schoolroom and represents the scramble for a seat which is not uncommon in our street cars. Only every odd row will play at one time, two extra people being chosen to stand, one in front and one behind each row of seats. Upon a signal all the pupils playing, stand and circle around their own row of seats. On another signal each one tries to get a seat. The two unsuccessful ones must stand in the front and rear of the car until the signal for rising is given again. After these rows have played for a few minutes, the other rows should be allowed to take part while these watch them.

Squirrel and Nut

All the pupils but one sit at their desks with eyes closed and each with a hand outstretched. The odd player, who is the squirrel and carries a nut (a piece of chalk), runs on tiptoe up and down the aisle, and drops the nut into one of the hands. The player who gets the nut at once jumps up from his seat and chases the squirrel. Should he fail to catch him before he reaches his seat, the squirrel carries the nut again, but if the chaser catches the squirrel he may become squirrel and carry the nut next time. The other players should open their eyes when the chase begins.

Do This, Do That

All the players stand facing a leader. The one who is leader assumes any gymnastic position or imitates any action, at the same time saying, "Do this!" and the others immediately imitate. Should the leader at any time say "Do that!" any player who imitates the action must be seated. The movements should be performed rapidly so the players will be compelled to be on the alert. The object of the game is to see who can stand up longest. Any member of the class may be the leader but the teacher should be leader frequently especially if time is short, in order to show the children new exercises that may be done. A very good imitative gymnastic lesson may be given in this way if the teacher is careful in choosing her exercises.

Teacher and Class

This game may be played with either beanbags or balls, and is one of the simplest and earliest tossing games, being generally used when pupils are first acquiring skill in handling a ball. With very rapid play and greater distance between the "teacher" and the "class", it may become very interesting, however, for older players.

One player is chosen for the "teacher". The others stand in line side by side, facing her at an interval of from five to twenty feet. Where there are many players, there should be several groups of this kind, with a distinct interval between groups to avoid mistakes or confusion. It is desirable to have from six to ten players for each "teacher".

The teacher starts the game by tossing the ball to each pupil in turn, and it is immediately tossed back to her. Each pupil missing goes to the foot of the line. If the teacher misses, the player at the head of the line takes her place, the teacher going to the foot. The action should be as rapid as possible. This is an excellent game to use in teaching the various catches and throws used in the simple team games leading to basket ball.

Ball Exercises

These exercises have two purposes, first to develop rhythm with and without music, and second to develop skill in handling balls as a preparation for later ball games.

Line Bounce Ball
Use music "Playing Ball," page 133

Formation as for "Line Ball", i. e., pupils seated in rows with a leader facing each row with his back to black board. First child in row rises from his seat and toes a line drawn across front of his aisle. Leader bounces ball to first child, who bounces it once to himself and then back to the leader and takes his seat. Leader bounces ball to himself while second child in row rises and toes mark. The leader continues thus bouncing the ball to each child in turn until the music stops, when he chooses a new leader from his own row.

Circle Bounce Ball
(With music)

From two to four balls may be used according to the number and skill of the players. Balls should be distributed about equal distance about circle. On the first emphasized beat the child holding the ball bounces it once to himself. On second emphasized beat he bounces it to his neighbor on his right and so on around the circle.

Note: Both of the above games may be played without music and whether with or without music the difficulty of the games may be increased by the following progressions:

1. Bounce and catch with one hand, right, then left, palm up.
2. Bounce and catch with one hand, right, then left, palm down.
3. Bounce and hit to rebound one or more times, catch with one hand, right, then left.

Wall Ball Bounce

This may be played as a contest for two players or between teams of several players and will be especially suitable for children in rural schools where semi-active games of long duration are needed at the noon hour or when a modification of the work is needed when pupils are physically unable to do the regular work. If there is a suitable wall surface indoors or out of doors the ball is bounded against the wall and allowed to rebound on the floor with the following variations. If there is no suitable wall a bounce from the floor will be sufficient. Each child in turn starts on the series of following stunts and continues as long as he is successful. When he fails he gives the ball over to his opponent or a member of the opposing team as the case may be. When he receives the ball again he continues from where he left off.

1. Throw the ball against the wall, let it bounce once, and catch it; repeat three times.
2. Clap hands three times before catching without bouncing.
3. Twirl the hands around each other before catching.
4. Throw three times with right hand and catch with same hand.
5. Throw three times with left, and catch with left hand.
6. Clap hands three times and slap right knee and catch.
7. Same as six but slap left knee.
8. Bounce the ball and throw the right leg over it and catch it on rebound.
9. Same as eight only throw left leg over.
10. Bounce, turn around, and catch.

Partner Tag
(Schoolroom)

One player is chosen to be runner and another chaser. The remaining players are seated. The game starts with quite a distance between runner and chaser. The object of the game is for the chaser to tag the runner before he can save himself by sitting down in a seat with someone. If the runner does this without being tagged, the one he sits down with must get up and run to save himself by doing the same thing. If, however, the chaser tags the runner before he can save himself, they exchange places, runner becoming chaser.

Last Man

One player is chosen to be runner, another chaser. The remaining players are seated. The game starts with some distance between runner and chaser. Should the chaser succeed in tagging the runner, they immediately change parts, the previous chaser having to flee instantly for safety, with the previous runner now chasing after him. The runner may save himself at any time from being tagged by standing at the rear of any row of seats and calling "Last Man". As soon as he does this the one sitting in the front seat of that row becomes runner. As soon as he has left his seat the entire line moves forward one seat, leaving a seat at the rear for the "Last Man". The seated players must keep their feet under the desks. The runner is never considered as having taken refuge when he stands behind a row unless he calls "Last Man" at the same time.

Auto Race

This game is played in the schoolroom, the children remaining seated in rows. The leader of each row decides what automobile he wishes his row to represent. The rows should be numbered. At a signal from the teacher, the first player in each even-numbered row leaves his seat on the right side, runs forward and around his seat, and then to the rear of the room, completely encircling his row of seats, until his own is again reached. As soon as he is seated, the child next behind him encircles the row of seats, starting to the front on the right side and running to the rear on the left side. This continues until the last child has encircled the row and regained his seat. The row wins, whose last player is first seated. The odd-numbered rows then play, and finally the two winning rows may compete for the championship.

Tag the Wall Relay

The players are all seated, an even number in each row. At a signal, the first player in each row runs forward, tags the front wall, and returns to his seat by the same aisle. As soon as this player is seated, the second player runs forward in the same manner, then each player in turn. When the last player in the line is seated, that line has finished. The line finishing first wins. Seated players must always keep their feet under the desks.

This game may be varied in the following manner and is then called "Blackboard Relay". The first player has a piece of chalk and carries it forward with him placing a mark upon the board. After he is seated he passes the chalk with both hands overhead back to the next player who repeats the play, the game continuing as described above. The teacher or class

PHYSICAL EDUCATION

can think out various things to be put upon the blackboard. Here are a few suggestions:

1. The teacher draws a rough outline of a flag for each row. The children put in the stars on flag.

2. The teacher draws a rough outline of a Christmas tree. The children put the candles on. One tree for each row.

3. She draws a pussy willow stalk, one for each row. The children put on the buds.

4. Each row draws a Jack-o-Lantern, each child putting in one part of it.

All-over Relay

Arrange children so there are an equal number of players in each row. On the floor in front of each row mark 2 12-inch circles. In one circle of each group are placed three objects (erasers, stones, or beanbags, etc.).

At signal to "go", 1st player in each row runs up to circles in front of his row. With one hand behind back, he moves the objects one by one from the one circle to the adjacent circle. This done, he runs back to his seat. As soon as he is seated with feet out of the aisle, the next player runs up, and repeats the process, changing the 3 objects back to original circle, and then runs back to his seat. This then continues until all have run once. The line finishing first wins.

Note: On playground this game is played in same way. Formation in teams of equal numbers of players, standing in single file, one behind the other. The runners run to the circles, change the objects from circle to circle, and as a runner returns to his line, he "tags off" the next runner, and then himself drops to rear of line. Each runs once, and line finishing first wins.

Beanbag Circle Carry

Circles are drawn on the floor in the front and at the back of the class room, at the ends of the aisles. One beanbag (two or more, as desired) is placed in the circles at the front of the room. At a signal from the teacher the children in the front seats run to the front, take the beanbags from the circles at the end of their aisles, and carry them to the circles at the other end of the aisle in the back of the room, then return to their seats. The beanbags from each circle are carried one at a time if there are more than one. When the first runners have returned to their seats, the children in the second seats carry the bags from the back to the front of the room, and so on. A row has finished when each player has run and returned to his seat. The row finishing first wins. The bags must be placed accurately inside the circles.

Line Ball

A line is drawn across the front of the room a foot or more from the blackboard. A second line is drawn across the front of the room in line with the front row of desks.

A leader is chosen from each row, who stands toeing the line nearest the blackboard while he faces his row. There should be an even number of pupils in each row. At a signal, the first pupil in each row rises, stands toeing the line by the desk, and the leader tosses the ball to this player who tosses it back to the leader and immediately sits. The last is a signal for the next pupil to run forward, toe the line, and continue the tossing. This goes on until the leader has thrown to all in his row. As soon as this has occurred, he runs to the line by the desk and holds up the ball. The line to do this first, wins the game. The teacher may designate what kind of a throw is to be used such as, the chest throw, the underhand or overhand pass etc., thus giving skill in the various passes used in basket ball.

Leader Spry

Place even groups on each side of the room standing side by side. Two captains stand in the center, facing their groups, each having a ball or beanbag. At a signal, each captain tosses the bag to the first player of his group who returns it to the captain. It is passed in this way to all the players, and when it reaches the last one the captain calls "Leader Spry," at which this player runs out with the beanbag, and becomes captain, all the players move down one place, and the former captain takes the first place and is first to receive the beanbag when next thrown. Each player then is captain in turn, and each tosses the bag to all the players before calling "Leader Spry." The team whose original captain comes to the captain's position and receives the ball first after all the rest have served wins the contest.

Beanbag Ring Toss

Have an equal number of players in each row. Mark off a starting line even with front row of seats. Near the wall in front of each row should be drawn a circle 12 to 18 inches in diameter. Game starts with an equal number of beanbags upon each front desk. At a signal the first pupil in each row steps to the throwing line and throws the bags in succession to the circle in front of his line. Each beanbag falling completely within the circle scores one point for him. He then steps to the blackboard, writes down his score, collects beanbags, places them on front desk, and seats himself. When he is seated, next player in his row steps forward and repeats the play. Row having highest score when all have thrown wins.

Meet Me At the Switch

Divide class into two teams as they sit.

The teacher (or some pupil) stands in front with an eraser (or other object) in each hand. She gives signal to "go", and immediately the first player in each outside row runs to the front of room. As they reach the one in front each takes an eraser and turning about runs entirely around the room. As they pass at the rear, each goes to his own right like cars at a switch and continues on to the front of the room. The team wins whose runner first succeeds in giving his eraser back again to the one in front.

The next one in each row then runs. Play till all have had a chance to run. Count one point each time for the team which won, then add up the individual scores to get the total final score.

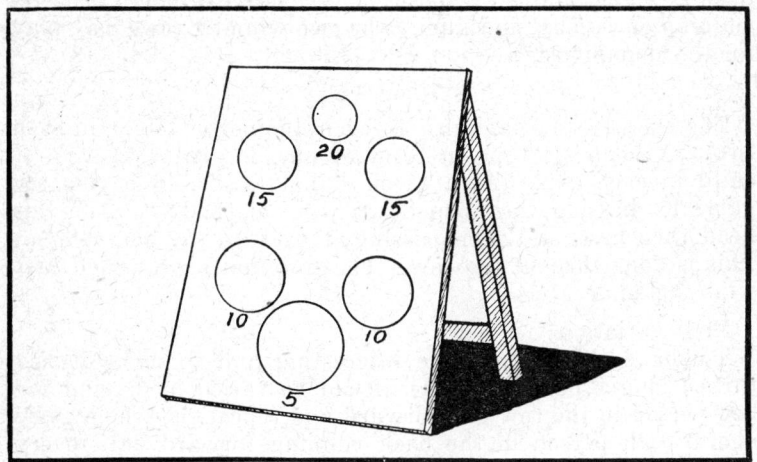

Beanbag Board

Beanbag Board

Players are divided into two equal teams. To each team is given two or three beanbags. These beanbags may be made of strips of ticking 5 inches by 10 inches, folded in the middle and stitched on three sides. They should be filled with one-half pound of corn or beans. In front of each team a line is drawn and from 10 to 20 feet in front of this (depending on size and skill of players) a beanbag board is set up. (See illustration). This board may be made of wood with holes cut as per diagram. A member of one team steps up to the line and takes three throws at the board with his three beanbags and scores for his team as many points as are painted beneath the holes he could throw through. He then recovers his bags and gives them to the next player on his team while the first player on the second team is taking his turn at throwing. This continues until a certain score decided upon at the beginning has been reached by one team. Numbers below holes should be small for primary grades so they can do their own adding.

Indian File Relay
(Schoolroom)

The children are seated, the same number in each row, only every other row playing at the same time. At a signal, all players get out of their seats on the right hand side, run forward and around their row, completely encircling that row of seats back to their own seats, the entire row running one behind the other at the same time. The row having all its players seated and up in position first is the winner. The remaining rows play, and finally the two winning rows may play for the championship.

Hoop Relay

The class is standing with an even number of pupils in each row. A hoop, or rope in form of one, is given to the first child in each row. At a given signal this child begins the game by passing the hoop down over his body, putting his head thru first, and then passing it back to the next player. This is done thruout the row. The row that has finished first wins the game.

First variation:

To make this game more interesting and to make it last thru a longer period of time, it can be varied by having the last person in the row run forward and repeat the whole game again, each person in the back running forward until every person has returned to his own place. In this case only every other aisle may be used as the odd aisle will be needed for running.

Second variation:

This game may be varied also by passing the hoop back as in the first description and then when the last person has gone thru it, she says "change", and the whole row turns in an opposite direction, and she immediately begins going thru and passing the hoop back to the front as was done at the beginning. The row finishing first, wins.

Third variation:

This game may also be done without turning around, but by just passing the hoop to the front again, in the same manner as it was passed to the back.

Schoolroom Basket Ball Relay

Have an equal number of pupils in each row. Mark off a starting line with chalk at the side of each front desk. Mark another line about six feet or more directly in front of this. One child in each line is chosen as a basket and stands back of the line farthest from the seats with his arms held shoulder high in front, and forming a circle. At a signal the first pupil rises, toes starting line and tries to throw ball into basket, then runs and gets ball and passes it, after having seated himself, to next child behind, who immediately rises and runs to line and throws. Thus the game continues until the last person in same line has thrown for basket, secured ball and returned to his seat. Each "basket" made scores 2 points and the row finishing first scores five points. One child representing each team records scores of his team on the blackboard. A beanbag or indoor baseball should be used for a ball.

Schoolroom Snatch

The children are in their seats. One-half the room is playing for points against the other half of the room. A clean handkerchief is placed on the teacher's desk or chair placed in the middle of the front of the room. The last child in each outside row goes to the rear corner of the room nearest him. A signal such as "Go!" or "Run!" is given by the teacher. Two things occur upon this signal. In the first place, the two players in the corner run to the front of the room, using the outside aisles, then each attempts to snatch the handkerchief from the desk and get back to his corner without being tagged, the player failing to get the handkerchief giving chase. Should a player reach his corner with the handkerchief in safety, a point is scored for his side. Should he be tagged before reaching the corner, a point is scored for the other side. The handkerchief is then returned to the desk (if two handkerchiefs are on hand it will save time) and the two players take their seats. In the meantime, after the signal "Go!" has been given by the teacher, the next to the last child in each outside row by way of his inner aisle moves to his rear corner, ready for his turn to play. While he waits he extends one hand to be touched by the present player as an indication that this player has reached his corner. The play continues between new members from each side moving up in the manner described until all have run. Points are recorded on the blackboard and the winning side is announced at the end of the play. Players should be cautioned not to be in too great haste in snatching the handkerchief. Wait for a good opportunity to take it and get away. In case the runner drops the handkerchief it can be picked up by either player as at the beginning of play.

PRIMARY PLAYGROUND GAMES

Hot Ball

Players sit on floor in circle. One player has a ball. He holds his hand over the ball to warm it. When it is hot he hits it away from him and when it comes to other players they hit it away so it will not burn them.

Variations:
(1) This may be played by standing in a circle and kicking the ball away.
(2) A tower of blocks or some Indian clubs may be placed in the center of the circle and an effort made to knock these down when the ball is kicked.
(3) For older children guards are stationed about the clubs to protect them from the ball. Any child succeeding in kicking a club down or destroying the tower of blocks becomes a guard in place of the guard who allowed him to do it.

Slap Jack

Players stand in a circle. One player runs around outside and touches some member of the circle. This person immediately runs in opposite direction around the circle in an effort to beat the tagger to the vacant place. The unsuccessful one must tag next time. When players meet they must obey traffic rules and keep to the right.

Note: Very small children may skip to music as they play this instead of running. Then no especial effort is made to beat.

Squirrels In Trees

Class in circle. Count class off in threes. Numbers one and two join both hands to form a hollow tree. Numbers three stand between the joined hands of one and two and are the squirrels. There is an extra squirrel standing in the center of the circle. When the teacher claps her hands all squirrels must change trees and the extra squirrel trys to get a tree.

Cat and Rat

Players stand in circle with clasped hands. One player, the rat, stands inside the circle. Another player, the cat, stands outside the circle. The rat is allowed to run in and out of the circle as the cat tries to catch it but the players try to keep the cat from passing through them either into or out of the circle. When cat catches rat new players are chosen for these parts.

Midnight

One player is the fox and the others chickens. The fox may catch the chickens only at midnight. The game starts with the fox standing in a den marked in one corner of the playground and the chickens in a space marked in the diagonally opposite corner. The chickens come out and scatter around, approaching as close to the fox as they dare. They keep asking him, "What time is it?" and he answers with any hour he chooses. Should he say "Three O'clock" or "Eleven O'clock," etc., they are safe, but when he says, "Midnight!" they must run for their goal as fast as they can to avoid being tagged by the fox. All that are tagged return to the fox's den and help him tag the next time. Only the first fox may tell the time of night.

Center Base

All the players but one form a circle with considerable space between each two. The odd player stands in the center, holding the ball. He tosses it to any player in the circle and immediately runs away outside the circle. The player to whom the ball is thrown must catch it, place it on the ground in the center of the circle, and at once chase the one who threw it. The one who threw the ball tries to get back to the center of the circle and touch the ball before he can be tagged. If the first center player is not tagged before returning to the ball, he throws again, and the one who chased him returns to the circle.

In a very large circle, two or three people may be placed in the center, using the same ball. This makes the game faster.

Dodge Ball
(Simple)

Players stand in a circle. An extra player stands in the center. Players in circle try to hit center player with a soft ball. He may run and dodge but must stay within the circle. When he is hit he exchanges places with the person who hit him.

Bull In the Pen

All but one of the players stand in a circle with hands firmly clasped. The odd player stands in the center and is the bull. The bull tries to break through the ring by parting the hands of any of the players. If he breaks through, the two players whose hands he parted immediately give chase to him, and the one catching him becomes the bull.

Animal Chase

Two pens are marked off in distant corners of the playground. One player, called the chaser, stands at one side of one of these pens. The other players stand within the pen that is nearest the chaser. All of the players in the pen are named for different animals, there being several players of each kind. Thus there may be a considerable number each of bears, deer, foxes, etc. The chaser calls the name of any animal he chooses as a signal for the players to run. For instance, he may call "Bears!" whereupon all of the players who represent bears must run across to the other pen, the chaser trying to catch them.

Any player caught before reaching the opposite pen helps the chaser.

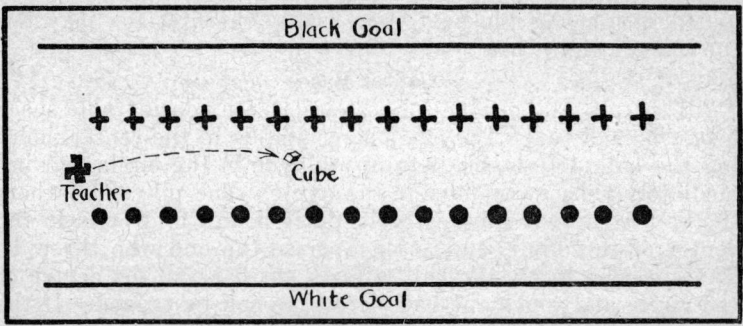

Black and White

Black and White

Two parallel lines, about 60 feet apart, are drawn to form the goals. The players are divided into two teams, the Blacks and the Whites, who stand facing each other and about five feet apart, near the center of the field. A cube, which has been painted black on three sides and white on the remaining three sides is rolled on the floor between the two teams, by the teacher. If the black side is uppermost when the cube stops, that team chases and tries to tag the other team, who dash immediately to their goal of safety (beyond the line). All those who are tagged must join the opposing team and assist them in tagging. The teams come back to the center and the game is repeated. The side which has caught the greatest number of opponents in a stated length of time is the winner.

Variation:

This game may be varied by giving points for the tagging of opponents, one point being given to the chasers for each player tagged. The side having the greater number of points, gained in a given length of time is the winner.

Ghosts and Witches

As a Hallowe'en Game, Black and White may be called Ghosts and Witches. Then the white faces represent the ghosts and the black faces the witches.

Crows and Cranes

This is played like Black and White only that the players are named Crows and Cranes instead of Black and White. The leader calls whichever name he desires but he should trill the "r" in order to deceive them as to which is going to be called.

Tag Games

Most tag games are played in the same way; i.e., one person is "it" and tries to tag someone who is not meeting certain requirements, and when that person is tagged, he becomes "it" in place of the original tagger. The following is a list of such games:

1. **Wood Tag**
   Anyone not touching wood may be tagged.
2. **Squat Tag**
   Anyone not squatting may be tagged. Players may squat but three times in saving themselves and then must flee to be safe.
3. **Hang Tag**
   Body must be suspended by arms and feet off ground to be safe.
4. **Sidewalk Tag**
   Must be touching a sidewalk to be safe.
5. **Hindoo Tag**
   Must kneel down and touch head to ground to be safe. If a player has taken refuge in this way and the tagger moves away 25 feet and the person down does not get up, the tagger may return and tag him, even if he is down.
6. **Ostrich Tag**
   Played as above, only to be safe the player must be standing on one foot with opposite arm under knee of same side, hand grasping nose.

Poison Snake

One or more Indian clubs, blocks of wood or any other objects are placed in the center of a circle. The circle of players then try by pushing and pulling to make their comrades touch one of the clubs. Should they do this, or unclasp hands to avoid doing it, they are out of the game.

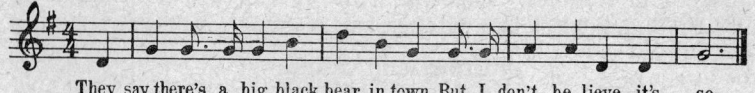

Big Black Bear

They say there's a big black bear in town, But I don't be-lieve it's so.

Big Black Bear

Play like Hide and Seek only the one player hides and the rest of the players seek. The one player who hides is the bear. While all the rest of the players close their eyes, the bear hides away some place. After a sufficient time has elapsed the seeking players sing or chant "They say there's a big black bear in town, but I don't believe it's so," and while singing it they hunt for the bear. The bear remains hidden until the seekers are close to him then he jumps out at them and tries to catch as many as he can before they reach home. Since to be the bear is a choice position, the teacher or the previous bear should choose the next bear from the children who were not caught. The object is to see which bear can catch the most children.

Brownies and Fairies

Two equal groups of players, one group called the Brownies, the other the Fairies. Each group has a goal, the goals being 40 to 60 feet apart. The Fairies stand behind their goal with their backs to the Brownies who come stealing up. One Fairy, the Queen, keeps watch and, when ready, calls, "Look out for the Brownies!" The Fairies then chase the Brownies to their goal and tag as many as they can. All caught are Fairies. Then the Brownies turn their backs behind their goal and the Fairies come up. The King of the Brownies warns them and they tag the Fairies. The side having the greatest number at the end of the time wins.

Snatch

Place two equal groups of players in line formation, one line facing the other, behind goals marked forty feet or more apart. Midway between the two lines is placed a handkerchief or something easily snatched. At a signal the diagonally opposite end players, one from each line, run toward the handkerchief. Each tries to get possession of the handkerchief and to return to the goal line without being tagged. If a player returns with the handkerchief without being tagged, or if he succeeds in tagging the player who takes the handkerchief, it counts one point for his side. On another signal the next two players come out to snatch the handkerchief and so the game proceeds. Caution the players to not snatch the handkerchief at once, but to make false moves for it until a good opportunity comes to snatch it and get away without being tagged. At the same time players must be on the alert to tag the other player, should that player snatch it and attempt to get away. In case the handkerchief is dropped, the other player should snatch it and flee for his goal. The team having the most points at the end of the game is winner.

Pom Pom Pullaway

The playing space is limited by two lines from thirty to fifty feet apart. All the players but one stand back of one of these lines, while the one who is "it" stands in the middle between the two lines and calling one of the players by name says "Pom pom pullaway; come away or I'll fetch you away." Whereupon the player named tries to run across the open space and the tagger tries to touch him. If he is touched, he also becomes a tagger and helps catch the next player called. This may also be played by having all the players run across when the tagger says the little jingle and he catches whom ever he can.

New York

Players are divided into two equal groups. Each group has a goal. After deciding among themselves what occupation they will dramatize, one group starts toward the other calling, "Here we come." The other group answers, "Where from?" the dialogue continues thus: "New York." "What's your trade?" "Lemonade." "Show us some if you are not afraid." Whereupon the advancing side stops and acts out such things as making a cake, freezing ice cream, building a wall, etc. When the other side guesses what is being acted, the actors must run for their goal to be safe. All caught must stay with the chasing side.

As a Christmas game the dialogue may be: "Here we come," "Where from?" "The North Pole", "What's your trade?", "Santa Claus", "Show your toys if you are not afraid", whereupon they act out some toy.

Stores

Players are divided into two groups as for New York. One side decides upon the kind of store, and the article from that store they will have, then they advance to the other group and say, "My father owns a grocery store (or any other kind of store) and he keeps 'L' ". The other side then proceed to guess what the "L" stands for by such guesses as "lemons", "lettuce", "loaf sugar", etc., until they hit upon the article chosen by the first side. As soon as this is accomplished the first side must flee for safety behind the goal for all that are tagged must stay with the guessing side.

A Christmas variation of this might be: "Santa came to our house and he left 'T' "—the "T" to stand for some toy. Otherwise the game is as above.

Run for Your Supper

Players in a circle. One player chosen by teacher goes around inside, holds out his hand between two players and says, "Run for your supper." The two run around opposite ways outside, being careful to go to the right when they meet. The one who first returns to the vacant place wins, and may start the next runners.

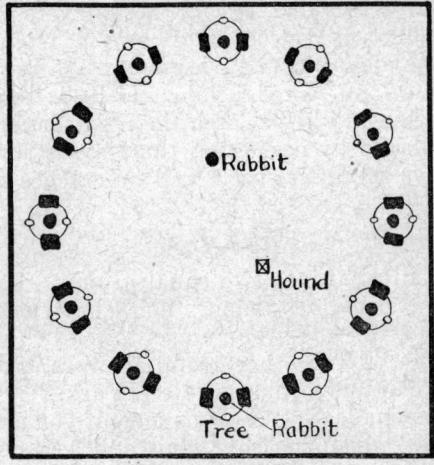

Hound and Rabbit

Hound and Rabbit

A considerable number of the players stand in groups of two with their hands joined, each group clasping hands to represent a hollow tree. In each tree is stationed a player who takes the part of rabbit. There should be one more rabbit than the number of trees. One player is also chosen for hound.

The hound chases the odd rabbit who may take refuge in any tree, always running in and out under the arms of the players forming a tree. But no two rabbits may lodge in the same tree; so as soon as a hunted rabbit enters a tree, the rabbit already there must run for another shelter. Whenever the hound catches a rabbit, they change places, the hound becoming a rabbit and the rabbit a hound. Upon a signal from the teacher a player forming the tree changes places with the rabbit. This change is made a second time in order that each may take the part of a rabbit during the game.

Aeroplane Relay

Players are divided into two or more equal teams. Each team stands in file formation and the leader of each file toes a line drawn across the ground. Upon a signal the leader of each line, with arms stretched out sideways, runs to a given goal, which should be marked by a cap or stake or Indian club, and passing it on the right side, sails around it and back to the next player in the line who has moved up to the starting line. He then takes his place at the back of the line. As soon as the second player is touched by the runner, he runs in the same manner as the first and so on until each player in the team has run and the leader is back again at the head of the line. The team whose leader first accomplishes this wins.

Tag the Line Relay

Players line up in two or more equal lines in file formation. On signal the first player in each line runs forward about 100 feet and places his foot on a line or some mark that has been previously made and runs back, touches off the next player in his file and takes his place at the back of his line. The file whose players have all run the course and got back in original formation first wins.

Indian File Relay

The players are divided into teams of equal number. The players of each team stand one behind the other in file formation, with hands on the shoulders of the one in front. At a distance of about fifty feet in front of each file some object is placed on the ground for the teams to run around. At the word "Go!", the teams drop their hands, run forward, keeping their places behind each other in Indian file, turn around the object, race back to their original positions behind each other, each runner placing his hands upon the shoulders of the next in front of him, thus finishing as they began. The team first to get in this position wins.

Butterflies and Daisies

Children are divided into two groups—one group are the daisies and one the butterflies. The daisies take a squat position about four or five feet apart like flowers in a bed. When soft music is played the butterflies with arms outstretched as wings run softly among the daisies. When ever the music stops the butterflies must also stop and the daisies reach out and try to touch them. All who are touched must squat and become daisies. This is continued until all have been touched. The daisies are butterflies the next time.

GAMES FOR INTERMEDIATE GRADES
SCHOOLROOM GAMES

Note: Most of the Schoolroom Games for Primary Grades are suitable for the Intermediate Grades.

See also adaptations of the following Playground Games for use in the Schoolroom:
Run and Pass Relay
Zig Zag Pass
Ten Trips
Simplified Volley Ball
Newcomb
End Ball

Posture Tag

One player is chosen to be "It". He has two beanbags and throws one to any player, and immediately gives chase; each player balancing the bag on his head as he runs. "It" endeavors to catch the runner before he can return to his seat, and if successful the chaser takes both bags again and throws as before. If not successful the runner takes the bags and becomes chaser for the next time. When the bag falls off the runner must stop to put it on.

Going to Jerusalem

The class is divided into sections of two rows each. Each player gets out of his seat on the right side. Music, preferably a good march, is used for the game. If it is not convenient to have music, one of the children or the instructor may clap for a signal to stop. Every other row faces the back of the room, and, as the music starts, each group of two rows marches around the row of seats between them. One seat out of every two rows of seats is marked in some way and called the "poison" seat. When the music stops each group rushes for seats in their own section, all avoiding the "poison" seat. The players who are forced to sit in the "poison" seats are, therefore, out of the game, and remain seated. Another seat in each section is marked and the game continues as before. It adds much to the enjoyment of the game if the speed of the music and the stops are varied.

Variation 1: This game may be played in the Gymnasium by using chairs placed in a long row, or rows, there always being one less chair than there are players. The players march around the chairs to the music, and when it stops, rush for the chairs and are seated. The one who is left without a chair is out of the game and takes a chair with him, after which the game is continued as before.

Variation 2: A circle of chairs is arranged with one less than the number of players. An extra chair is placed in the center of the circle, on which one of the players stands, while the rest walk or skip around the circle of chairs, while a march is played. When the music stops, all the players, including the one who is "It," run for the chairs and try to sit down. The one who is left without a chair is "It" for the next game, and takes his place on the chair in the center. The music begins and the game is continued, as before.

Beast, Bird, or Fish

Players may be seated in the schoolroom or in a circle. One player is chosen to be "It" and stands by his seat or in the center of the circle with a beanbag or a soft ball. This he throws at one of the players and says quickly, "Beast, Bird or Fish;" then repeats one of these classes and immediately counts ten, whereupon the player who has been hit, must name some beast or bird or fish, according to the class called for by the thrower, before the thrower has finished counting. There must not be a repetition of an animal previously named in the game. Should the player hit by the bag fail to meet the requirements, he changes places with the thrower. Should he succeed, the thrower repeats the game by hitting some other player. The throwing of the beanbag may be substituted for by the pointing of the finger.

Beanbag and Basket Relay

Each player is provided with a beanbag or one beanbag for each row will do. A waste paper basket or a box is placed on the floor near the blackboard in front of each aisle or one for two aisles will be sufficient in case more cannot be secured. At a signal from the teacher, the first pupil in each row stands back of a throwing line near the front desk and throws for the basket. If the bag goes into the basket it scores five. Should it lodge on the edge of the basket it scores three; if outside, there is no score. As soon as the first player has thrown he walks forward (in case there is but one bag for the row) secures the bag and hands it to the player back of him and sits down. The second player does the same as the first has done and returns the bag to the third until all have thrown; whereupon the score for the row is added up and the row getting the highest wins. There should be one score keeper for each row and he should keep score on the blackboard. The room may be divided into two teams instead of rows, each team occupying the seats in one-half the room. Each player then comes to a designated spot to throw.

Pursuit Relay

Players in two teams of equal number line up on opposite sides of the playing space. The running course is around the square formed by the teams, runners passing outside of both lines. Mark the corners of the course with a chair or stake if played on playground or gymnasium. If played in the schoolroom the outside aisles and front and back space of the seats are the running course. The team on the right faces the back of the room in file formation and the other the front. The first player in each line holds a basket ball, stick, handkerchief or

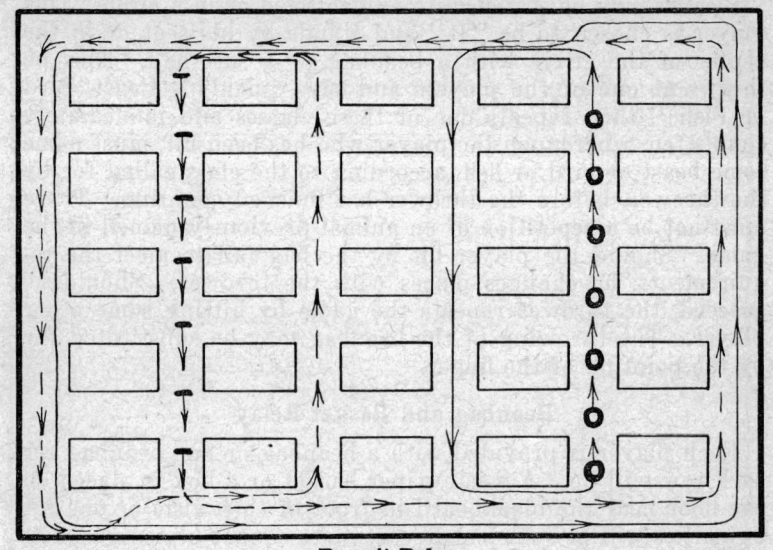

Pursuit Relay

(Dotted line indicates course of one team; solid line, course of other team.)

any other object and at a signal these two players run to the left around the course, each trying to catch up with the other. On reaching his starting point, each runner hands the ball to the next player of his team and then goes to the foot of the line. This next player runs in like manner, and so on, until all have run. The team finishing first scores. Should one runner overtake another at any time during the game the team wins whose player succeeded in overtaking the other. To make the game longer if there are few players, it may be played through 2 or 3 times without stopping and ends with the players in original position at the end of the third round.

Potato Race Relay

At the back of each aisle a box or square, about 12x8 inches, is placed. About 24 feet from this box a cross is marked on the floor and on the cross a block, a beanbag, or an eraser is placed. About eight feet on from this block and in line with it another cross is marked and a block placed on it. At a signal to go the person sitting in the last seat in the row takes his place by the box and then runs forward in the aisle and brings in one of the potatoes and immediately runs out again after the second potato. He touches the box or square with this and immediately replaces it on a cross, then goes

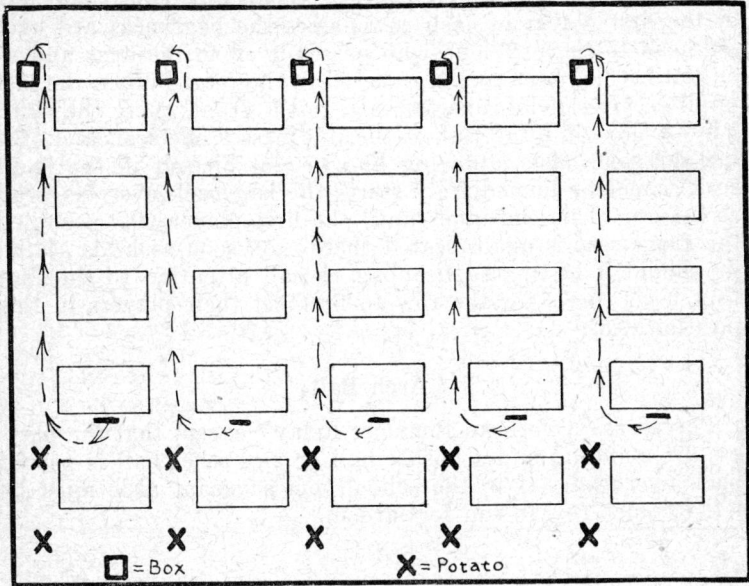

□ = Box   X = Potato

Potato Race Relay

back and gets the other potato and places it on a cross and runs to his seat. As soon as he is seated the next person in front of him does just what he has done and so on down the row until all have run. The row having all of its members through first wins. Care should be taken that each player takes his place by the box before he starts to bring in the blocks.

A simplified form and one that should be played first follows:

When the teacher claps her hands each player sitting in the back seat of his row takes his place beside the box or square and upon a signal "Go!" runs forward and picks up the blocks or potatoes as described above and finishes by sitting in his seat. The player first seated wins the race. The players in the next to the back seat take their places when the teacher claps her hands and upon the signal "Go!" run as the others did. This is continued until all have run. The row having the largest number of winners is the winning row.

Overhead Beanbag Relay

Players are all seated with an equal number in each row and with a beanbag on each front desk. At a signal from the teacher the first player in each row passes the bag backward over his head to the next one who passes it on to the next and so on until it has been quickly passed to the rear. When the last pupil receives it he runs forward to the front, using the right hand aisle, while the rest of the line passes one seat back, using the same aisle, allowing him to seat himself in the front seat, where he immediately starts the bag back over his head as before. This continues until the first player who occupied the front seat is again seated there. As soon as he is seated he should hold up the beanbag to call attention to the fact that he is there, for the row to first get their players in this position wins.

Arch Ball

Played as "Overhead Beanbag Relay" except that the players are standing and a basket ball or any other ball is passed back overhead. If in the schoolroom a vacant aisle must be left for each row to run forward in.

INTERMEDIATE PLAYGROUND GAMES
Hop Scotch

Hop Scotch is an interesting individual hopping game that develops balance and muscle control. It is a valuable game to teach in a physical training period because it can be played by one or two players and with almost no equipment. For this reason it makes a good home game.

There are many varieties of the game. Some very simple and some quite complicated. A complicated variety good for children from 10 to 14 will be described here but by taking out some cross lines this may be simple enough for children as young as 7 years.

With chalk draw the diagram given here, on a cement sidewalk or scratch it with a stick on the ground. The first player throws a flat piece of wood or stone into the square marked 1

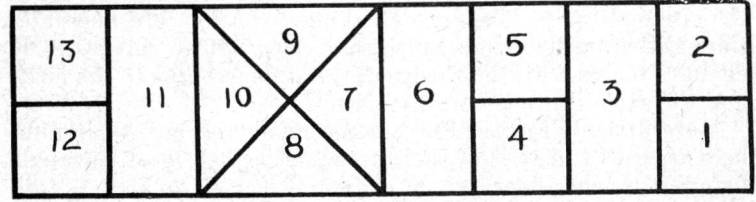

Diagram for Hop Scotch

and then hops into this square and without putting the other foot down or stepping on a line, picks up the block and hops out again. The block is then thrown into the square marked 2 and the player must this time hop first into 1 and then into 2, pick up the block as before and hop out again through square 1. This continues, each space being taken in order, until the player fails either to throw the block in to the proper space or violates a hopping rule. Then the next player proceeds as above until a rule is violated. When the first player again resumes play she begins with the space failed in before. The player first to successfully hop into all the spaces and return in the way prescribed wins.

Variations:

In returning, after the player reaches space 3, she may be required to hop and land so the right foot goes in space 1 and the left foot in space 2. Likewise when in space 6 she must land so the right foot is in 4 and the left foot in 5 at the same time, then jump and land on one foot in space 3 and again with one foot in 1 and the other in 2. In other words, in returning, whenever there are two spaces side by side these spaces must be taken simultaneously with both feet and each single space must be taken with only one foot.

Hens and Chickens
(Fox and Geese)

One player is chosen to be fox and another to be the hen. The remaining players all stand in single file behind the hen, each with his hands on the shoulders of the one next in front. The hen tries to protect her chickens from being caught by the fox by spreading her arms and dodging around in any way she sees fit. Only the last chicken in the line may be tagged by the fox. Should this chicken be tagged he becomes fox and the fox becomes hen.

If there be a large number of players several groups should be formed as it is better if the line of chickens is not too long.

Ring Call Ball

The players form a circle with one in the center who throws the ball in the air, at the same time calling the name of one of the circle players. The one called must run forward and catch the ball before it bounds more than once. If he catches it, he changes places with the thrower; if not, he returns to the circle and the same thrower throws again.

More difficult form: Players are numbered and their numbers are called instead of their names. The ball must be caught before it touches floor.

Ante-Over

Ante-over may be played by children of widely varying ages and is, therefore, a splendid rural school game. It requires a rather low building or a high board fence with openings at two places. A rural school building, a coal house, or a low barn are most satisfactory although a low part of a larger building may also be used.

The players are divided into two teams and these teams take their places on either side of the building. One team has a small ball which is thrown over the building to the other team. As a warning to this team that the ball is being thrown the thrower calls, "Ante-over." If the ball fails to go over and rolls back to him he calls "Pig tail." If it goes over, the other team attempts to catch it and if successful takes the ball and runs around to the other side of the building, players taking different courses so as to deceive the other team as to who has the ball. As soon as the members of the other team see them approaching they try to escape to the opposite side of the building without being tagged by the ball, either in the hand or thrown. Any player tagged must stay with the team that tagged him. The team having the larger number of players when play ceases or succeeding in getting all players on its side wins.

Jack Be Quick

Mark as many places on the floor as there are players, less one, these marks being here and there in different parts of the room. A circle is drawn about one mark which designates it as the leader's mark. There is an odd player who stands in the middle of the room. When the music begins the leader leads all the players except the odd one, anywhere about the room. When the music stops, all run for the marked places, including the odd player. The one reaching the leader's mark becomes the new leader, and the one left without a mark becomes the odd player, and must stand in the center of the room as the game is repeated.

Musical Indian Clubs

This may be substituted for "Going to Jerusalem," when there are no seats or chairs to sit on as is the case in many gymnasiums and on the playground. All players but one are given Indian clubs (or any other objects as sticks or blocks of wood) and after forming themselves into a circle these clubs are placed on the floor one beside each player toward the inside of the circle. Upon a signal (or the playing of music) the players march around the circle. Upon another signal (or the stopping of the music) all grab a club, but one player of course, will be left out. He leaves the circle and takes an Indian club with him.

Remarks: If a player stoops to pick up a club or stops before the signal is given he is out and must take an Indian club with him.

Variation: A club or ball may be passed from player to player as they stand in a circle. When the music stops or a signal is given the player having the object in his possession is out of the game.

Three Broad

All players, but two, form a circle of couples facing inward. Couples have arms joined. The two odd players, one of whom is runner and other chaser, run outside the circle. The chaser tries to tag the runner before he can save himself by catching hold of the arm of some couple, thus forming three broad. The person farthest from the runner in this group of three becomes the new runner and the game proceeds. If at any time the chaser tags the runner, the chaser then becomes the runner, and the runner, the chaser.

Three Deep

This game may be varied by having players standing facing inward in a double circle or partners standing one back of the other. In this case the runner saves himself by stopping in front of some couple, the last person in the row of three deep becoming runner.

Third Man

The players forming the circle may stand face to face, one good step apart. In this formation the runner saves himself by stepping between the two forming the couple, the one toward whom his back is turned becoming the third man or runner.

Center Catch Ball

The players stand in a circle with from six to eight feet between each two and with one player in the center. The circle players throw a ball from one to another, the object of the game being for the center player to catch the ball or knock it to the floor. The circle players may throw the ball across the circle or make sudden feints of throwing it in one direction, turn suddenly and throw it in another, to deceive the center player.

Any player in the circle who last touched the ball, changes places with the center player whenever the latter touches or catches the ball.

Whip Tag

Apparatus: Towel with one end knotted. Description: All but one of the players stand in a circle with hands behind backs facing center of circle. The odd player runs around outside circle, carrying towel, which he drops into the hands of a player, and then joins the circle. The player receiving the towel immediately turns to chase his right hand neighbor, beating him as much as he can find opportunity for, while he chases him around the circle and back to his place. It is obviously to the interest of the neighbor to outrun the beater and escape a beating. The towel is then delivered into the hands of some other player and the game proceeds as before.

For the schoolroom, the person carrying the beater lays it on the desk of some player and this player chases the player sitting ahead of him. Children should be cautioned to avoid hitting each other on the head or face.

Bronco Tag

Players stand in a circle in groups of three, one behind the other, the second clasping the first and the third clasping the second around the waist. The first of each group of three represents the head of the bronco, the second the body, the third the tail. Two players are chosen who chase each other around the circle. The one who is being chased, to avoid being caught, tries to catch hold of the tail of the bronco, but the bronco turns away from him and tries to keep him off by dodging first one way and then another. If he should succeed in keeping hold of the bronco, the player who is the head must then run and be chased, and so the game continues. If the chaser tags the runner before he catches hold of a bronco's tail, then the runner becomes the chaser and must try again to tag him.

Remarks: This is a very lively and amusing form of the game, "Three Deep", and players must be warned to keep tight hold of one another when the bronco is "bucking". The game may be too rough for younger children so it may be wiser to restrict its use to older ones, especially in the case of boys.

Partner Tag

All of the players but two hook arms in couples. Of the two who are free, one is "It" or chaser, and the other the runner. The runner may save himself by locking arms with either member of any couple he chooses. Whenever he does so, the third party of that group becomes runner and must save himself in like manner. If the runner be tagged at any time, he becomes "It" and the chaser becomes runner.

The couples should run and twist and resort to any reasonable maneuver to elude the runner. For large numbers there should be more than one runner and chaser.

Last Couple Out

Players are lined up in couples, about eight couples in a line. One player stands in front of the line as "caller". When he calls "last couple out," the two who are at the end of the line separate and run up to the front, and try to get together again before he catches either one. If he does tag one of them, he may be the caller again. If he fails, he may choose one of the two to take his place, and he becomes the partner of the other, with whom he takes his place at the beginning of the line, the game proceeding as before.

Remarks: Emphasize the fact that those who are called out must come very quietly and use various methods of getting up to the front without being caught. The one who is calling must also be warned not to look to either side until the couple is in sight, so that they will have a fair chance to get together.

Streets and Alleys

Players stand in parallel ranks or files, the number in each file depending upon the number playing. All the players join hands in horizontal lines across the files, thus forming aisles for the runners to pass through. Two are chosen; one to be

"It," the other to be chased. These two run in the aisles between the files, until the leader (previously chosen) periodically gives the command "Streets" or "Alleys" whereupon everyone turns to the right (or left) and clasps hands again in the new formation. This makes new aisles through which the runners must go. These frequent changes in the running course often save the one who is being chased from being caught. The leader should often change the direction of facing, so that the excitement will be maintained. He must also see that the same two runners do not run too long and so monopolize the game.

Players may not break through the lines nor tag across the hands. As soon as the runner is tagged, each player chooses another to take his place.

Every Man In His Own Den

If a comparatively small number are playing, have each player choose some well defined spot which is to serve as his den. When there is a large group, have three or four use the same den, and have the dens scattered about the playground, at least 20 feet apart.

The object of the game is for the player or players from each den to catch or tag as many other players as possible. One player starts the game by leaving his den, and the others try to catch him. The player who leaves his den last has precedence over any other player on the field and may tag anyone who does not belong to his den. As soon as a player is caught he becomes a member of the den into which he has been caught and must thereafter affiliate himself with, and try to catch others for, that den. The game ends when all are brought to one den. If time is called before this is done, the den in which there are the greatest number, wins.

Jump the Shot

Players stand in a circle with one in the center who is the "Swinger". A beanbag is tied to the end of a long rope, and the one in the center swings this around on the floor, so that it comes just in line with the feet of the players. As the bag approaches any player he jumps into the air to avoid it. If he is hit he must drop out of the game. The player who stays in the longest wins, and becomes "swinger" the next time.

Remarks: The one in the center must be warned not to swing the bag above the floor for otherwise it might hurt someone. Nothing heavier than a beanbag should be used, because when it swings around with great speed the force is likely to hurt ankles if a hard object is used. Since the position of "swinger" seems to be a coveted one, it is better not to have the one hit become the swinger because, it has been discovered that, when this is done, the players will not try very hard to jump.

Spud

The players group themselves in a small circle. One player is chosen to toss the ball up at the same time calling out a players name, or a player's number, where numbers have been given each player beforehand. The one whose name or number is called must run in and catch the ball before it strikes the ground, while all the other players run as far as possible in the opposite direction. If the one called catches the ball, he shouts "Stand", and the others must stop wherever they are. He then throws the ball at them and if he hits someone, this places a "Spud" on the player hit. The thrower then recovers the ball and all go back to the original circle where the game is played again as before. If the thrower fails to hit anyone, he then has a "Spud" on him. The player takes the ball to the circle and starts the game again. When a player has three "Spuds" on him he must stand facing a wall or fence and after bending forward lets each player throw a ball at him from a distance of about thirty feet behind him.

Touch Off

Class is divided as for "Snatch" (see p. 40). The first child in one line advances to the other line where each child is holding out his hand palm up. As he goes down the line he gently touches each hand until he comes to a player he wishes to have chase him. He then gives this hand a hard slap and immediately tries to run back to his place in his own line before the player slapped can tag him. If he is tagged he becomes a member of the tagger's line, but if he returns safely the tagger becomes a member of his line. The first child in the other line then advances in the same manner as the other child did and each child in each line takes his turn in similar manner until all have given a dare; then a count is taken of each line and the one having the greatest number is declared the winner.

Red Light

One player, who is chosen to be "It," stands at the extreme end of the field or gymnasium with his back to the center. All other players are grouped at the opposite end. The one who is "It" counts up to ten as rapidly but as clearly as possible, then shouts "Red Light" and turns around quickly. While he is counting, the other players are running toward him, but as soon as he says "Red Light" they must stop at once and must not move while he is looking at them.

If he should see a player moving, he sends him back to the starting line to begin again. Then he turns around again and the game proceeds as before. The first player who reaches the goal line on which the one who is "It" is standing wins the game, and may be "It" the next time.

Remarks: The game is a variation of "Ten Steps" in which game the players are supposed to go somewhere and hide, and it can be played either on the playground or in the gymnasium. It gives practice in quick action and quick muscular control; it encourages timid children to take chances; and it affords continuous exercise.

Caution: Be sure to emphasize the fact that a child who is seen moving must go all the way back to the starting line and not merely make a feint at going. Make it plain that this is a point of honor and exclude any child from the game who is found not to be fulfilling the requirement. Be sure that the one who is "It" counts to ten without skipping any numbers, and speaks loudly and distinctly enough to be understood.

Push Ball Relay

Formation is the same as in simple form of relay.

Each team is provided with a wand and a basket ball or a medicine ball. The object of the game is to have each player in turn push the ball with the wand to a designated spot and return. The team getting back to their original position first wins.

Remarks: The ball may not be hit—it must merely be pushed, the wand being kept close to the ball all the time and a sort of "scooping" motion used. The same rules as apply in other relays apply here.

Push Club Relay

This relay is played in the same way as "Push Ball Relay," except that an Indian club replaces the ball, and the club may be hit, as well as pushed.

Remarks: Owing to the shape of the club it is very difficult to make it go straight so that amusing situations constantly arise. This is therefore a very interesting game to use in a gymnastic meet of any kind, as the audience enjoys it almost as much as the participants.

Driving the Pig to Market

Played as the two above games except that a dumb-bell is used in place of a ball or Indian club.

Shuttle Relay

Players divided into 2 or more teams of equal numbers. Each team is then divided into 2 divisions, which form single lines one player behind the other. These two divisions line up at either end of the room and face each other. One leader is appointed for each team, and toes a starting line. There should be 50 to 150 feet between the two divisions. At a signal to "go" all the leaders on one side of the room run forward across the room to the other divisions of their team. As the leader reaches it, he "tags off" the 1st runner in that group, and then takes his place at the back of the line, while the

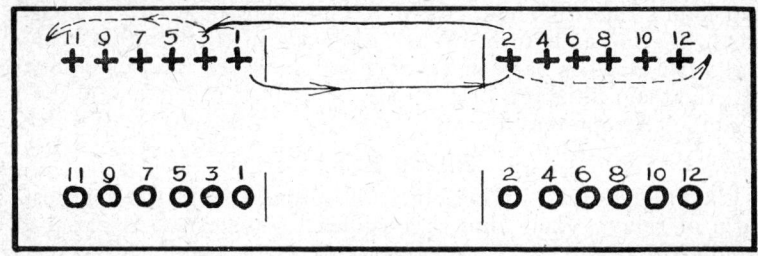

Shuttle Relay

one whom he has "tagged off" runs down to the opposite end and in turn tags off the next player there who has moved up to the starting line. Each time the player, as he is "tagged off," runs to the opposite group and tags off the first one there. This is continued until all have run once, and the team whose last runner first crosses the finish line wins the race. The runners must never step over their starting line until tagged. To do so constitutes a foul. A scoring system may be used giving 5 points for coming in first, and 3 points for second, and subtracting 1 point for each foul. Thus, if the team finishing first has 3 fouls and the team finishing second has none, the latter would actually win because its score is 3, while that of the team finishing first, but having 3 fouls, would be only 2. This effectually prevents fouls, but its use is optional.

Partner Shuttle Relay

This is played much like shuttle relay with these exceptions. The first player instead of tagging off the player opposite him, grasps his hand and runs back with him to the first player's original place. The first player then takes his place at the back of the line and the one whom he took over grasps the hand of the next in line and runs with him back across the field. This continues until the lines are in original position again. The line first to accomplish this wins.

Jump Wand Relay

Players are divided into teams of equal numbers, who stand one behind the other as in the usual relay formation. Each team is provided with a wand about 3½ feet in length. At the signal to start, the first and second players in each team take the wand between them, and run the length of the team, one on each side, dragging the wand along under the feet of the others, each of whom jumps as the wand comes near him. When the two with the wand reach the end of the team, No. 1 lets go of his end of the wand and takes his place at the end of the team. No. 2 runs back to the front carrying the wand, and hands the other end to No. 3, and then these two proceed down the line as before. When each one in the team has run, and when No. 1 is back in his original place, the relay is ended, and the team finishing first wins.

Note: A rope may be substituted for the wand.

All Up Relay

Players are lined up in single file columns as in the simplest form of relay. Each line is considered a team and is given a number or letter as 1, 2, etc., or A, B, etc. About thirty feet from the first player in each team two circles are drawn, side by side, and in one of these three Indian clubs are placed. On the signal, the first one in each team runs to the clubs, and transfers each club separately to the adjoining circle, being sure that each club is standing before running back to the team. He tags the hand of the next one in line who has moved up to the starting line, and the game continues as in the simple form of relay until one team has finished. The team finishing first wins.

Remarks: This game is excellent in training children in self-control while hurrying, and it is one of the tests in the American Playground Association for developing speed and accuracy.

Figure Eight Relay

Formation is the same as in "All Up Relay" except that the clubs are in a line about 5 feet apart. On the signal, the first player in each team runs to the clubs, and weaves

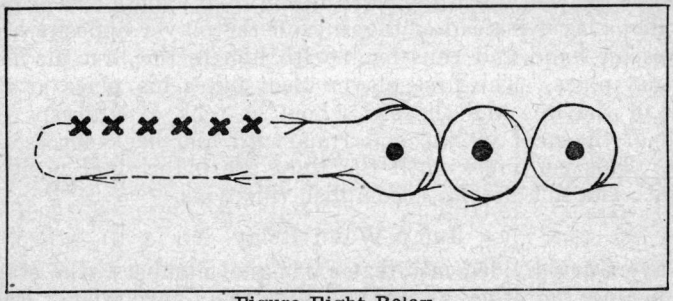

Figure Eight Relay

his way between them describing a figure eight, both going and returning. He then runs back to his team, touches the hand of the next one in line, who proceeds in the same way, and so on, the race continuing as in other relays. If a player knocks a club down, he must stop and set it up again.

Fifty or Burst

This game is played as "Beanbag Board" described in the Primary section, page 33, with the following addition. Whichever team scores just fifty points (or any other number agreed upon) first wins, but if either team scores even one more point than fifty it bursts and must begin all over again.

Ten Pin Contest

In place of the beanbag board, six Indian clubs are set up in the form of a triangle with the apex pointing toward the players, clubs to be set about a foot apart. Each player takes his turn at bowling a basket ball or indoor baseball at the clubs and each club knocked down counts one point for his team. The game may be ended with a certain score agreed upon or played as "Fifty or Burst" described above.

Bombardment

The ground is divided into two equal fields by a line across the center. The players are divided into two teams. Some distance, about 25 feet from the dividing line, in their own field, each team sets up a row of Indian clubs, at least 2 feet apart, one for each player. The players stand between their clubs and the dividing line. Balls of all kinds are used. If there is a large number of players, use several balls. The object of the game is to knock down the opponents' clubs. Each player therefore serves as guard to protect his or his neighbor's club, and as thrower. He can throw whenever he can secure a ball there being no order in which throwers should throw. No player may step across the center line. Each club overturned scores one point for the side which knocked it down. Every club overturned by a player on his own side scores one point for the opponents. A time limit of from ten to twenty minutes is given. The side wins which has the highest score at the end of that time. Clubs should be set up as soon as they are knocked down.

Circle Dodge Ball

Any number of players, divided into two equal teams, may take part. A circle about 25 feet in diameter is marked out and one team takes its place within this circle, the other one on the outside. The object of the game is for the outer or circle team to hit the players of the inner team with a basket ball or other ball, thus putting them out of the game as fast as it succeeds in hitting them. The game is played in two halves of several minutes each. Each team is within the circle during one half. The team having the greatest number of players left in the circle at the end of a half is the winning team. The ball can be thrown only by a person outside of the circle. In case the ball stops in the circle, a player from outside may recover it, throwing it to another outside player or carrying it outside the ring before throwing it. Only one player (the first one hit) may be put out by one throw of the ball and this must be by a direct hit. Caution players to throw at lower part of body and not too hard.

Stealing Sticks

A large playing space is divided across the middle by a well-defined line. The players are divided into two teams, A and B, with a captain for each team. At the extreme back end of each side, in the middle, three sticks of wood or Indian clubs or beanbags are placed, which are called the "booty." Over in one corner on a line with the booty is marked off a space about 4 feet square which is the prison.

The object of the game is to steal the sticks, or booty, of the opposite team. As soon as any player crosses the center line he is in enemy territory and is liable to be caught, but if he can succeed in capturing a stick, club, or beanbag, or whatever is being used as booty, he may then return to his own side in safety. If he is caught before he gets the stick, he must go to prison and wait there until a player from his own team comes to get him. As soon as the one who rescues him touches his hand, they may both return to their own side without being tagged, as in the case of the capturing of a stick. The game ends when one team has all the booty and none of its men in prison. If time is called, the team having the greater number of sticks or prisoners wins.

Rules:
1. The game must not start until a definite signal is given.
2. Only one stick (beanbag, ball, etc.) or one prisoner may be taken at a time by any player.
3. Not more than one player may guard either the sticks (booty) or the prison.
4. The guard of the sticks (booty) may not sit or stand upon the sticks, but must leave them well exposed.
5. The last prisoner caught at any time during the game, must stand with at least one foot in the prison; the other prisoners may then stretch out from him, but must keep their hands or feet touching, all of the time, in one continuous line. The rescuer then takes the first one in the line each time, until all are freed.

PHYSICAL EDUCATION

6. No prisoner may run out to meet a rescuer who is coming toward him.

Remarks: Coach players to use strategy in making advances for booty; as, for example, by having several make a concerted attack and thus confuse their opponents. Urge them to take risks and thus keep up the interest of the game. In cold weather it is suggested that prisoners either be allowed to escape or else be exchanged in order to avoid having them stand still too long.

Sometimes in the midst of the game, if action seems somewhat slow, the leader calls out: "Prisoners may escape." Allowing prisoners to escape creates great excitement and makes everybody move.

This game is practically a universal favorite, affords much exercise, holds the interest of the players, and tends to encourage timid children to be less afraid.

Bat Ball

The size of the field depends upon the number of players, the average size being about fifty feet long and thirty feet wide. The ground is divided so that one-fourth of it at the end is used for the batters and the remaining three-fourths for the fielders. On the batters' side, about three or four feet back of the line, a batting line is drawn. See diagram. Near the center and back of the larger territory, there should be a tree, post, Indian club, or some such object around which the batters must run.

The players are divided into two teams, A's and B's. The game starts with the A's batting, lined up behind the batting line. The B's are scattered about the larger division. The batters try to bat an inflated ball (volley ball) with the hand across the division line, and run thru the enemy's territory, from right to left, around the object, and back across the division line. The team fielding secures the ball and tries to hit the player who is running. If the runner is hit, he is out.

Details of the game: Number one of team A stands back of the batting line, bats the ball and runs around the object, as described above. A member of team B secures the ball and, if he is near the runner, he throws it and tries to hit him. If he is not near the runner, the ball should be rapidly passed to a player who is, and the ball then thrown at the runner. The player who throws the ball may not hold it longer than three seconds, neither may he step with the ball. The runner may dodge the ball in any manner, as long as he stays within the boundaries. Should the batter fail to get the ball over the line on the first serve, he may have a second serve. If he fails on the second serve he

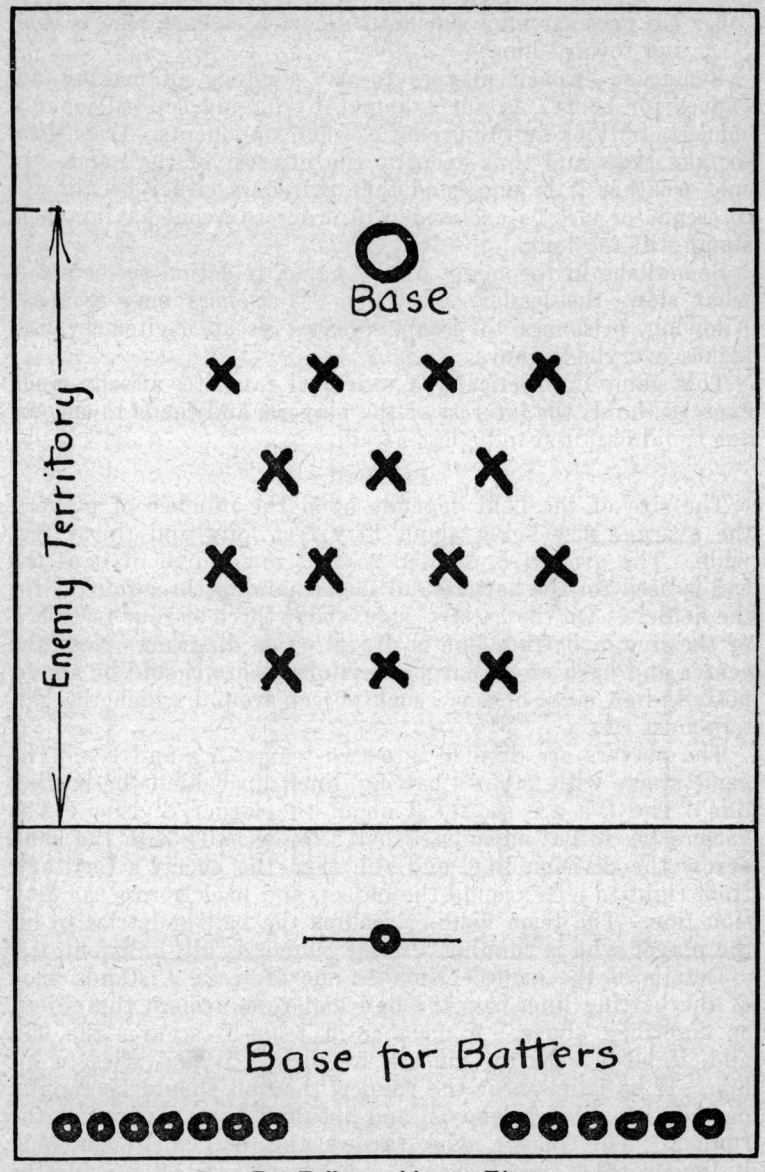

Bat Ball o=A's x=B's

loses his turn, is declared "out," and does not bat again until all on his side have batted. If a runner is hit, he is out and no score is made. When three men are out the sides change. An inning is completed when both sides have been at bat. The number of innings should be decided upon at the beginning of the game.

Score: If a run is made by a batter (if he crosses the division line without being hit) one point is scored for his side. Should a fielder walk with the ball or hold it more than three seconds, a point is given to the batting side for each foul thus made. The only side scoring is the batting side.

Progressive Dodge Ball

The ground for this game is divided into three equal parts, each about 30x30 feet. The players are divided into three equal teams which for convenience we will designate as A, B, and C. As the game starts Team B occupies the center space and Teams A and C occupy the spaces at either end and stand with a foot on a division line. The playing time is divided into three innings each of five minutes duration. The object

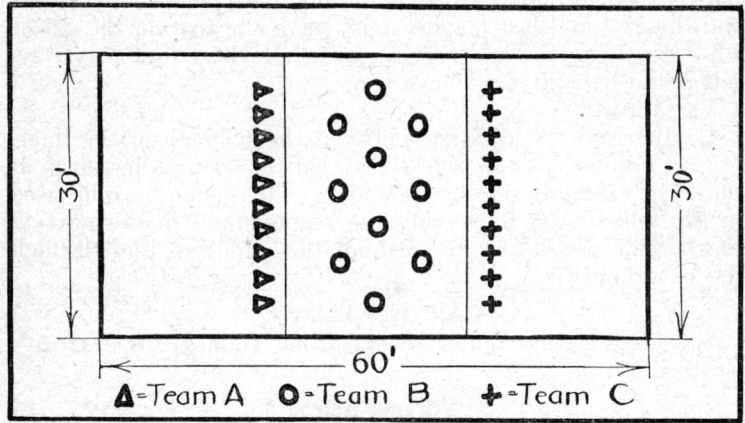

Progressive Dodge Ball

of the game is for the two end teams to hit the members of the center team with the ball before it has bounced or hit any object and for the center team to hit any member of the two teams in the same way. Any member hit in this manner must step out of the game for that inning.

The ball is put in play by the referee tossing it to some member of the center team who immediately throws it at some one in either of the end teams. As soon as the ball is thrown teams A and C may run from the line to safer places. After the ball has hit the floor, or any obstruction, it may be picked up by any player near it and thrown at the center team. Should the center team succeed in hitting a member of either of the other teams the ball starts in the center again as at first. Should a player be hit by a ball thrown by an opponent who was over the line with one or both feet he is not out, or if someone steps over a line to avoid being hit he is out.

At the end of the first inning one of the two end teams occupies the center court while the center team occupies one end court and play is resumed as before. Team having the lowest score, i.e., the fewest men hit during all three innings, wins the game.

Run and Pass Relay

Players are divided into two teams of equal numbers, and stand on two parallel lines about 30 feet apart, facing each other. The first player at the right end of each line is given a ball and on the leader's command runs around the opposite line and gives the ball to the last player at the end of his team line; the ball is passed up the line, each player touching it; the player at the head of the line runs as soon as he receives the ball. The ends of the lines should be marked by stones and the first and last players must leave one foot on the stones when receiving the ball. The team wins whose first player receives the ball after all have run.

Variations:
1. Increase the distance between the players on the line.
2. Permit the runner to throw ball as soon as he turns at the head of the opposing team line. This game may be used in the schoolroom by having the teams stand in the next to the outside aisles and run behind the opposing line through the outside aisles.

All Over Relay

See description under Schoolroom Games for Primary Grades.

Pursuit Relay

See description under Schoolroom Games for Intermediate Grades.

Simple Soccer Keep Away (See Diag. I)

Class stands in two parallel lines facing each other and about 20 or 30 feet apart. If possible have more than one ball. Upon a signal a player from line 1 dribbles (advances with small kicks) a ball toward an opposite player in line 2 and this player runs out to meet him and tries to take the ball away from him and kick it back across line 1. If he succeeds in this he scores a point for his team but if the player from line 1 kicks it across line 2, line 1 scores one point. The ball is then taken out again by the second player in line one and so on until all in this line have taken it out. The game is played in two halves and in the second half line 2 starts with the ball. The team having the highest score after each member of each team has taken the ball out wins.

Remarks: The hands must not be used in any way in this game. All the "taking away" is done by the feet. Pushing and tripping are fouls and give a point to the other side.

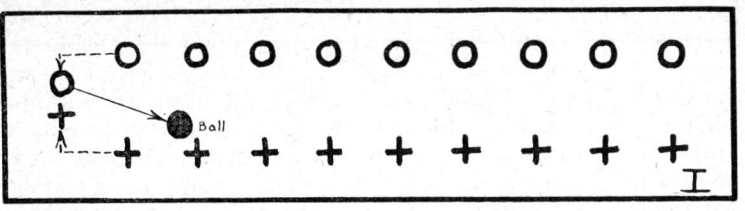

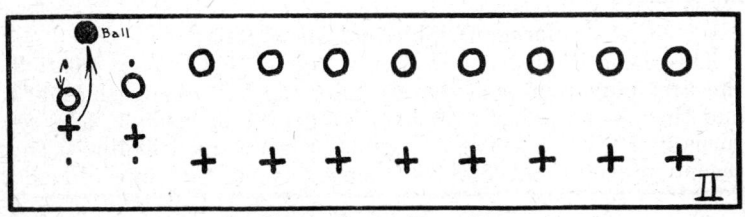

I. Simple Soccer Keep-Away
II. Double Soccer Keep-Away

Double Soccer Keep Away (See Diag. II)

Teams are lined up as for "Simple Soccer Keep Away," but in this game when the first player from line 1 comes out with the ball a second player from his line follows him out and backs him up; that is, receives the ball and feeds it to him should he lose it. Likewise after the opposing player from line two has come out to meet the first player from line one, a second player from line 2 follows him and backs him up. In order to score a point the players from either line must get the ball across the opponents' line between two given marks about 18 feet apart. These spots may be marked by jumping standards, bricks, or two players. The scoring and order of the game is the same as in "Simple Soccer Keep Away."

Soccer Dribble Relay

Teams are lined up as for simple relay. About 30 or 40 feet from the head of each line a jumping standard or any other mark is placed. Upon a signal the first player in each line dribbles (carries with the feet by a series or short kicks, keeping the ball always under control) a soccer ball down

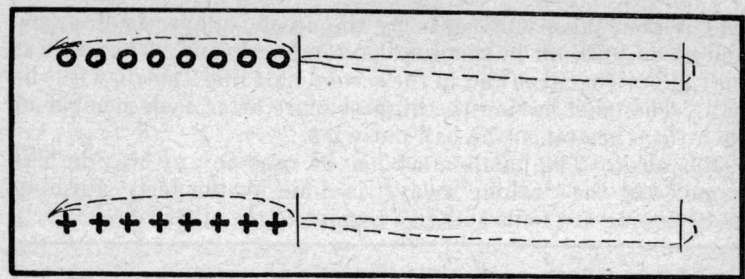

Soccer Dribble Relay

around the standard and back to the next person in his line. This player must stop the ball with his feet and then dribble around the course as the first player has done. The team first having all its players do this, wins, provided none of its players has fouled. A foul is touching the ball with the hands or making a long kick.

Soccer Dribble and Shoot Relay

This game is played as "Soccer Dribble Relay," except that the first player in each line dribbles the ball out to the mark and then kicks it back to the next person in his line, and returns and takes his place behind the last person in line. The second player then dribbles it down as the first one did and

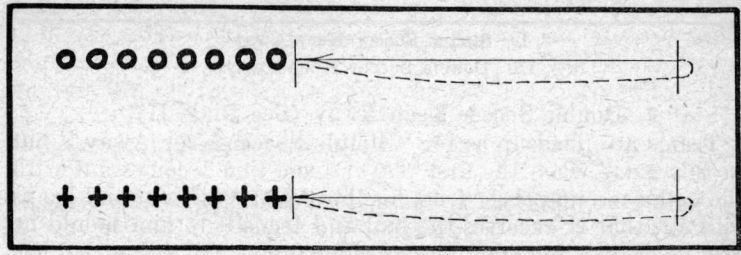

Soccer Dribble and Shoot

(Dotted line indicates course of player dribbling ball; solid line, course of ball after kicked.)

after kicking it back takes his place behind the first player. This continues until all have dribbled and kicked. When the first player in line receives the kick from the last player the game is over. The team to accomplish this first wins.

Soccer Target Kicking Relay

Teams are lined up as for regular shuttle relay. The first player in each team has a soccer football or an old basket ball on the ground in front of him. Upon a signal from the teacher this player kicks the ball to the first player in the line opposite, and then takes his place behind his own line. If the ball lands right at the feet of this player, 5 points are scored for this team. If it lands within three feet on either side, 2 points are scored. The next kick is made by the player who received the ball and this continues until all in the team have kicked. The team with the highest score wins. No points are given for speed as this is a contest of accuracy. The length of the kick should depend upon the skill of the players.

Soccer Drive

The members of each team line up in front formation, (standing side by side). The lines face each other about 30 feet apart. A soccer ball is given to one line and they attempt to drive it through the other line lower than the players' heads. The other team, without touching the ball with their hands, try to drive it back through the other line. Whenever a team succeeds in this it is a point for them. Game is played for time. Team scoring most points wins.

Variation: A feeder from each line may stand between the lines and try to recover the ball for his team, with the use of the feet only. A kick made from any point between the lines cannot count for score.

Soccer Pass

Class is divided into two teams and each team is divided into two parallel lines facing each other. A soccer ball (or an old basket ball) is given to each team which they pass between their lines in the manner prescribed by the teacher, i.e., the inside of the left or right foot, the outside of the left or right foot or the instep. The team making the most passes at the end of the playing time (2 minutes) wins.

Remarks: Practice in the various passes should precede this game.

Variation: The ball is started at one end of the two lines of each team and is passed to each member of the team in succession. The team through first wins.

Soccer Pass and Shoot

Each team is divided into two lines and these lines stand side by side in file formation. Upon a signal the first two players in each team take a soccer ball which is lying upon the ground in front of them and start running down the field passing the ball between them using the feet only. They run to a designated spot, return and give the ball, without the use of the hands to the next two players in their team, who proceed in the same manner, and so on through the whole team.

The object of the game is to see which team can finish first and which can make the best use of their feet in passing, that is, pass to the left with the inside of the right foot or the outside of the left, etc.

Variation: When the players have reached the designated spot the player in possession of the ball shoots (kicks) it back to the next two players in line. This develops accurate placing of the ball.

Shuttle Kicking Contest

This is a team event and may be played with a soccer football or a Rugby football.

Teams line up in file formation facing each other. The space between teams will depend upon age and skill of players. The team securing the toss (team A) mark a line in front of them and, standing behind this line, kick the ball in the direction of the other team. Wherever the ball first strikes the ground the first member of the team "B" makes a line and kicks from behind this in the direction of team "A." The second player in team "A" then secures the ball, where it first touched the ground, and kicks from behind the spot to team "B." This continues until all members of each team have kicked. The teams must be even in numbers so this will give the last kick to team "B." If this last kick strikes the ground beyond the first line marked by team "A," team "B" is the winner. If, however, it falls short of this line, team "A" is the winner.

Square Football

The players are divided into two teams, one team occupying the two adjacent sides of a large square with clearly marked boundary lines. A soccer football is placed in the center of the square. At the leader's command the player at the right end of each team runs to the center and endeavors to kick the ball thru the opposing side. The players on the lines stop the ball, with hands or body, throwing or kicking it back to the center, or if possible through the other team, the two center players assisting. If the ball is kicked over the heads of the players on the line, the opposing center player is given a free kick from the center of the square, the other center standing back of him. After a team scores a point, the center players take their places at the foot of their teams, and two new players enter the square. One point is scored each time the ball is kicked through the opposing team. The team wins that first scores 21 points.

Corner Kick Ball

Soccer ball used. Any number of players divided into two teams. Playing space about 70 by 40 feet, but may vary according to number and age of players. At each end of the playing space is an end zone from 6 to 8 feet wide. A team lines up in each end zone. The ball is placed in the center of the field and upon a signal from the referee four players (one from each end of each team line) run to the center and endeavor to kick the ball through the opposing team. The players in the end zones stop the ball with any part of their bodies but their hands and kick it back into the central area so that their center players may kick it again. Two points are scored every time a ball passes completely through the end zone of an opposing team, not higher than the defenders' heads. One point is scored for each foul. The fouls are pushing, tripping, holding, or touching ball with hands.

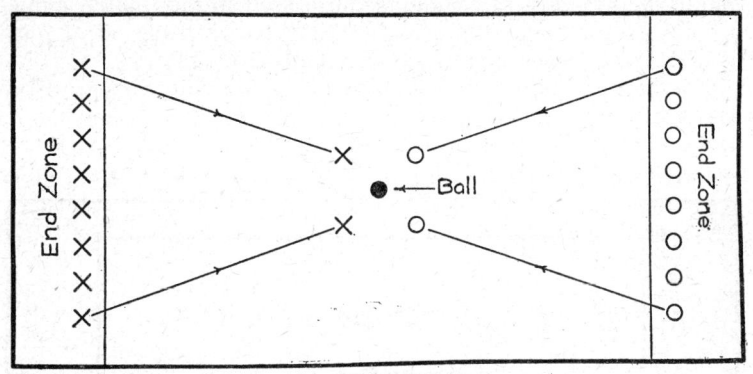

Corner Kick Ball

Playing time may be ten minute halves. The center players return to their end zones after each goal has been made and take their places in the center of their teams. Those at the end of the team line come out when the game starts again as at the beginning. Whenever ball goes out of bounds or over the heads of the defending team it is kicked in by a player on the team opposite the one that kicked it out, at the point where it went out.

Note: Game may be varied by having more than four players play in the center, especially in case of a large number of players.

Simplified Soccer Football

Playing Space: (Changed to suit conditions) 240 feet long by 90 feet wide (may be smaller if necessary—150 by 160). The length of the field is divided into four equal sections by tennis tapes or by whitewashed lines. Goal-posts are placed at either end of the field, 18 feet apart and 6½ feet high. The lines dividing the field are designated as center-line, half-back-line, and goal-line.

Number of Players in Playing Space: Each team has eleven players: one goal-keeper, two full-backs, three half-backs, and five forwards, (number of players may be varied to accommodate a smaller field, or a smaller or larger class.)

Ball: A twenty-seven-inch Soccer Football.

Time: Two 15-minute periods with five to eight minutes rest between.

Scoring: Every time the ball is kicked across the goal-line between two goal-posts, whether it be on the ground or in the air, one point is scored by the attacking team.

Umpires, Referees, Time-keepers, Scorers: The rules for appointing these are the same as those used in any match game. Choice of goals and change of goals after each period of play is done in the same manner as in other match games.

Position of Players and Restriction to Playing Space: Five forwards lined up on their own side of the center-line facing their opponents' goal. The two taking the outside positions are called "Outsides," the one taking the center position is

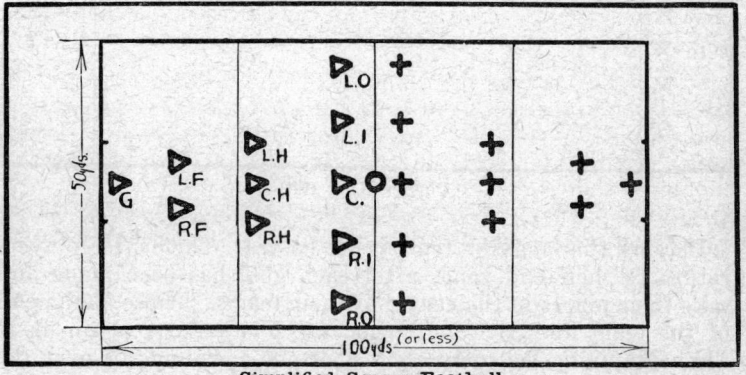

Simplified Soccer Football

Field and players placed, ready for game: △ players play toward + goal: + players play toward △ goal.

called "Center," those taking the positions between are called "Insides." The words left and right are used along with those positions to designate the side of the field the player is on and this is always in relation to his own goal, and he always stands with his back to his goal. These five forwards may go only as far as the center-line in their own territory and to the goal line of their opponents' territory. They must keep to the outside, inside, and center of the field as their names indicate.

Three half-backs; center, left, and right may play only between the half-back-line and the center-line of their own territory. Full-backs; two, left and right, may play only between the half-back-line and the goal line. Goal-keeper plays between the goal-posts and 19 or 20 feet in front, or to the left or right of the goal. No penalties are attached to the crossing of these dividing lines, but if a player continually plays out of his place, especially if he be a forward or a half-back, he is taken out of his position and put into goal-keeper or fullback's position. The same can be done for players on the forward-line who continually cross into center, inside, or outside positions.

Duties of the Players: Forwards attack their opponents' goal. Half-backs keep the ball in the possession of their forwards. Full-backs and goal-keepers protect their own goal and keep their opponents from scoring.

The Start: The ball is placed on the center-line between the two center players of each team. When the whistle sounds, these two players touch in unison, the ball and the ground alternately three times with their foot. At the finish of the third time, each player tries to kick the ball to one of his inside forward men.

Rules: No one may touch the ball with his hands or arms. A ball may be kicked with the foot or bunted with the knee, thigh, or body. A foul is called for touching with the hands or arms, even if accidental and the opposite side from the one making the foul receives a free kick at the point where the ball was touched. At any time when a free kick is given, all players must be at least five feet away from person taking a free kick. If the ball goes out of bounds, either at the side or ends, the player opposite the one last kicking it is given a free kick from the point on the side lines where the ball passed out.

No holding, pushing, kicking, or tripping of players shall be allowed. A foul must be called immediately and a free kick given to the other side.

Suggestions: Teach the forward players to play the ball to each other rather than straight ahead, also, that it is absolutely necessary for the forwards to be in a nearly straight line across the field when attacking their opponents' goal. When nearing the goal-lines, the outside players should begin to close in towards the center and inside players and always be ready to drop back and get the ball, should it be played out by their opponents' full-backs or goal-keeper. They should also be taught that hard kicks are usually unprofitable ones, and short well-placed kicks with every kick followed up is the idea. Never interfere with the ball if one of your own players is fighting for it—either cover the ground in front of him or drop a little behind him so that if he loses the ball, you can be ready for it.

Weak players may take full-back or goal-keepers' positions, as there is comparatively little running to be done. Stronger and more active players should be put into forward and half-back positions.

For official rules of Soccer, refer to Sports Library "Soccer and Speedball Guide", A. S. Barnes Co., New York. For coaching helps see "The Coaching of Soccer", H. E. Coyer, W. B. Saunders Co., Philadelphia.

Zig Zag Pass

Class is divided into four lines. Each two lines is a team. A basket ball is given to the first player in lines 1 and 3. Upon a signal the ball is passed between the lines of each team using the kind of pass indicated by the teacher. The team completing its course first wins, provided no fouls have been made. Fouls consist of throws made that were not prescribed by the teacher and failure to pass to some member of the team.

Basket Ball Goal Games

1. Each contestant is allowed 30 seconds in which to shoot as many goals as he is able. He may shoot in any manner and from any position. As a team game the individual scores are added together as the team score.

2. Each contestant is allowed five shots from the foul line. The number of goals he makes is added to those of his other team mates or he may compete as an individual to see what percent of his throws are good.

3. Around the Town.

This may be played with scores or without. In either event circles are placed at varying distances and positions of difficulty from the goal. If scores are used numbers are placed in these circles, the higher numbers in the circles from which a shot would be most difficult. One contestant starts at the circle with the lowest score and shoots for goal. If successful he goes to the circle next in point of difficulty and so on until he fails to make his goal from some circle. Then he retires and an opponent starts at the beginning and goes as far as he can go, then retires. This continues until all contestants have gone as far as possible, then the first contestant begins where he was forced to stop and continues again until he fails to make his goal. The player who throws from all the circles first wins.

If scores are used the other players may count as their score the added points of the circles from which they have made successful shots.

As a team game the same system as above is used, but the members of the team contest in order by turns and the team having the highest score or having all its members through first wins.

Arch Goal Ball

The players are divided into groups, and line up in single file in two or more lines facing a basket ball goal. Each line has a basket ball. At a signal each leader passes the ball backward overhead, the next player catches it and passes it in the same way, and so on to the end of the line. When the last player receives the ball, he runs forward and tries to throw it into the basket, standing on a line marked from five to ten feet from the goal. He is allowed but one throw, when he quickly takes his place at the front of his line (which moves backward one place to make room for him), and at once passes the ball backward overhead. The last player, in turn, runs forward, throws for goal, etc. This is repeated until each player in a line has thrown for the goal. Each goal made scores two points for the team. The team wins which has the highest score when all of the players have thrown. This may also be played for time. Then each player throws until he succeeds in getting the ball into the basket. The team wins whose last man finishes first.

Ten Trips

1. Players in groups of threes, with the three in a straight line ten to twenty feet apart. Each group has a ball. The center player has the ball, and at the signal he throws it to another of his group, who must throw it to the third, over the head of the first player; the third returns it to the one in the center. When he receives it the center player says, "One Trip," and begins as before. The group completing ten trips first wins.

This game is especially good for practice in throwing and catching an indoor baseball as it necessitates catching from in front and throwing to the rear.

2. Class is divided into two equal circles. Upon a signal the ball is passed from player to player around the circle. When it reaches the first thrower he says "one trip," etc.

3. Players stand in a double circle with a wide space between players. Each circle numbers off by two's. All the Nos. 1 are one team, the Nos. 2 another. Two basket balls are started around the circle, one by a No. 1 player, the other by a No. 2 player and are passed across to each player on each

team. Each time the ball gets back to the one who started it, he calls out the trips. The team to first reach the required number of trips wins. The last two games are especially good for preliminary practice in basket ball as different methods of passing the ball may be used. The side arm throw is good for the single circle game while the chest, under arm, over head, and shoulder throws may be used in the double circle.

4. Class divided into groups of four. Each one of each four stands on the corner of a square and each four has a ball (indoor baseball). The ball is thrown around this square and the trips are called as above.

5. Players are lined up as for Shuttle Relay with not more than six players to a team. The space between the two divisions of the teams should be from 20 to 50 feet according to the skill of the players. Upon a signal the first player in one line throws across to the first player of the other half of the team and then takes his place at the back of his own line. The player receiving the ball throws it back to the next player in line one and goes to the back of his line. When the player who started this game throws again he says "one trip," etc.

Remarks: This should be played first as a simple relay and the trips added after skill is developed.

Pivot and Pass

Class is in two or four lines. The first player in each line holds a basket ball. Upon a signal from the teacher this player pivots and passes the ball to the next player in line, who catches, pivots and passes to the next and so on down the line and back to the leader again. The team whose players accomplish this first without making fouls wins.

Fouls consist of: 1. Stepping around instead of making a pivot on one foot. 2. Turning with both feet on the floor and finishing with legs crossed. 3. Throwing the ball while making the pivot.

Remarks: The reverse turn which is a turn to the right on the left foot or a turn to the left on the right foot may be substituted for the pivot as the teacher desires. The word pivot here means a turn to the right on the right foot or a turn to the left on the left foot.

Bounce Goal Relay

Teams are lined up in file formation about 15 or 20 feet away from the basket ball goal. The first player of each team has a basket ball. Upon a signal this player bounces the ball and recovers it, after having proceeded toward the goal, then shoots for goal, recovers ball, and bounce passes back to the next in line. The team whose members all accomplish this first wins. Substitute other passes for the bounce pass.

Variations:

1. The game may be played for numbers of goals shot instead of speed.

2. The teacher may designate the kind of shot to use or the kind of pass to make.

Dribble and Bounce Pass Shuttle Relay

Teams lined up as for the common shuttle relay. First player in each team is given a basket ball. Upon a signal this player makes one dribble to cover space and then bounce passes to the first player in the opposite line. This continues until the teams are back in their first formation. The first to accomplish this wins. Combine other passes with the dribble.

Basket Ball Shuttle Relay

Players are lined up in teams as in "Shuttle Relay" (see p. 57). On a signal the first player in one half of each team throws a basket ball to the first player in the other half of his team lined up just opposite, and then runs across to the back of this half. The player who caught the ball throws it across to the player facing him on the opposite side and runs across to that side as the first player did. This continues back and forth until all the players on a team are back in their original places. The team on which the last player reaches the opposite side first wins.

Zig Zag Goal Ball

Played with basketballs like Zig Zag Pass p. 72 except that each team stands about 10 feet away from the goal. Balls start with the rear player in line one and in line four. When the balls reach the first player in line two and in line three, after all other players in his team have had it, this player shoots for goal, recovers his own shot and passes it with an overarm pass to the last player in lines one and four. After the pass is made and shooters are returned to their lines, the lines move around thus: line one and line four move forward while line two and line three move back. The last player in line two and

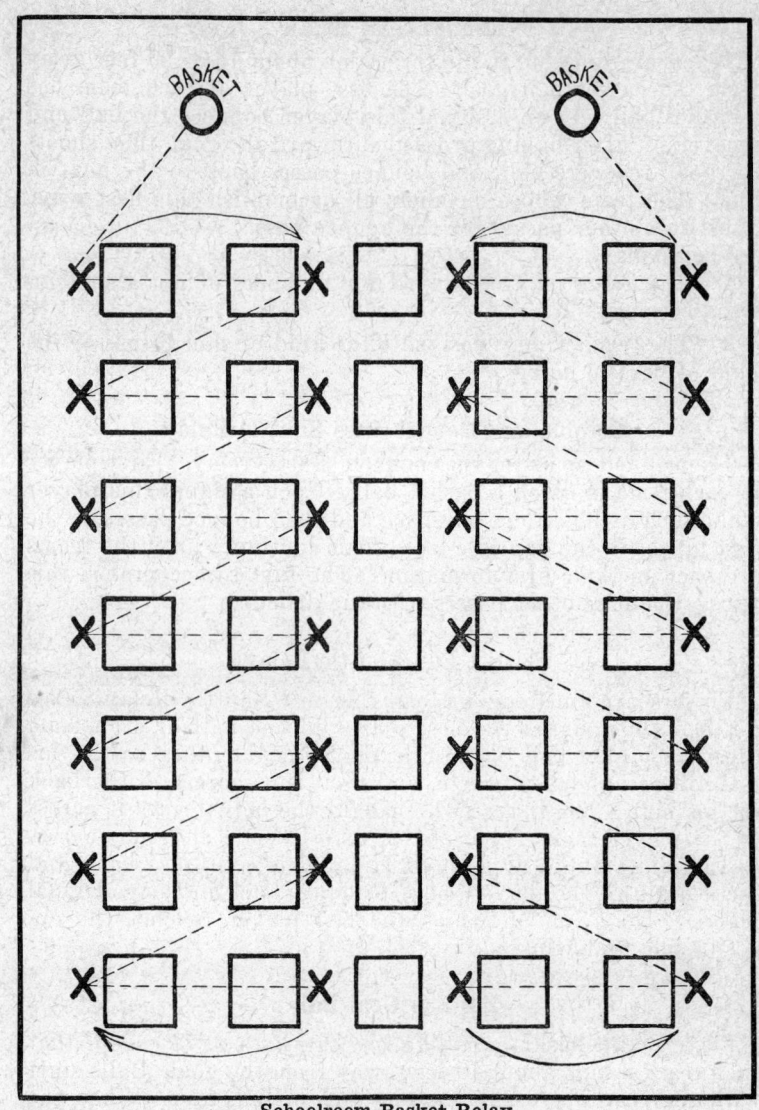

Schoolroom Basket Relay

(See Zig-Zag Goal Ball)

in line three move across into line one and line four. The last shooters move over to the front of line two and line three. This continues until all players have shot for goal. The team completing this first wins.

This game may be played in the schoolroom by using bean bags and two waste baskets and starting bean bags as in diagram p. 76.

Dribble and Take Away

Two teams are standing at opposite ends of the gymnasium in file formation. Teams facing each other. The first player of one team is given the ball. Upon a signal this player with the ball starts dribbling toward the other team and at the same time the first member in the opposite team runs toward him. When they meet the player with the ball stops his progress, grabs the ball with both hands and pivots to rear

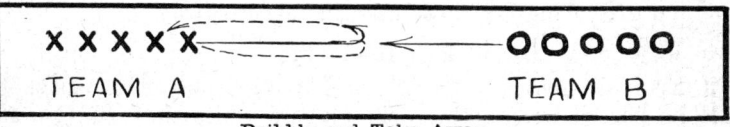

```
x x x x x─────────⇀      ←──── o o o o o
              ⇐─────
TEAM  A                          TEAM  B
```

Dribble and Take Away
(Solid line indicates course of players; dotted line, course of ball).

and passes the ball back to the next member of his team. Before he can do this, however, the opposing player tries to snatch the ball from him. If he is successful in this he passes the ball to the next member of his team, who would dribble down upon the next signal. In the first event, team "A" would make a score. In the second, team "B" would make it. The game should be layed in two halves, the team being given the ball at the beginning of the second half that did not have it at the start of the first half. The team with the highest score at the end of the game wins.

Keep Away

Sides are chosen and the ball is thrown up between two players as in basket ball to start the play. Playing space is unlimited. The side having possession of the ball attempts to pass it about among their players without letting the other side get possession of it. Tripping or catching hold of a player is not allowed. The person in possession of the ball can not take more than one step before throwing it or allow more than three seconds to elapse before sending it to another player. In any of the above offenses the ball can be taken from the player and given to an opponent and the play continued, or each offense may count a point for the opposite side. Play may be continued for a specified time and score is kept by counting the number of successful passes made by each team during that length of time. If the ball is dropped during a pass it does not count as a score.

Goal Keep Away

There are an equal number of players on each side. The field is any playing space at each end of which a goal is marked by means of a stone, board, circle, or cross. The game is started by tossing the ball up between the two opposing captains at a mark in the center equidistant from the two goals. These players endeavor to bat the ball to one of their own side. The team thus securing it tries to pass it back and forth until it is successfully caught by a player who can at the same time touch the goal with some part of his body. Such a play scores one point for that team. The ball is started in the center after each score. The rules enforced with the exception of the method of scoring are those used in "Keep Away."

Pass for Points

Class is divided into teams of six or nine players. A basket ball is passed among these six players while they run about a limited area in any direction. A point is counted every time a successful pass is made. A successful pass means that the ball must be caught not muffed. The catcher must be running when the ball is caught and must throw it again without taking a step with the ball. The game is played for 1 or 2 minutes and the scores counted. The next team then competes and the scores are counted. The team having the high score wins.

Bounce Pass Keep Away

Class is in four equal lines, equal distance apart. A basket ball is given to the first player in line 1 and the last player in line 2. Preliminary to the "keep away" game the players are instructed in making a bounce pass past one player and

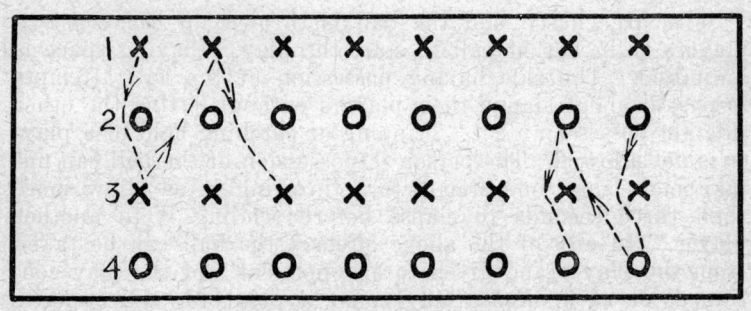

Bounce Pass Keep Away

to another and this is practiced without interference from the intervening lines. When the real game is started lines 2 and 3 are allowed to intercept the balls passing them; i.e., 2 intercepts a ball passed from 1 to 3 and 3 one passed from 2 to 4. The players of lines 2 and 3 may move only one of their feet in intercepting. The object of the game is to make a complete unintercepted series of passes from one end of the team to the other, each player bouncing it once. Whenever a line succeeds in intercepting a ball they of course throw it to the head or foot of their line so a new series of passes may be started. The team first completing a series of passes wins.

Newcomb

Players in two teams not necessarily of equal number. The playing space may be a basket ball court or a volley ball court. Stretch a rope or a volley ball net across the middle of the court at a height of five or six feet. Use a basket ball, volley ball, or soccer ball. Send one team to each side of the net and give the ball to one side. The referee should have a score board or score card right at hand as scores are usually net and give the ball to one side. The umpire should have a made rapidly. Unless there is a clock in plain view a timekeeper should be appointed to call time at the end of half the

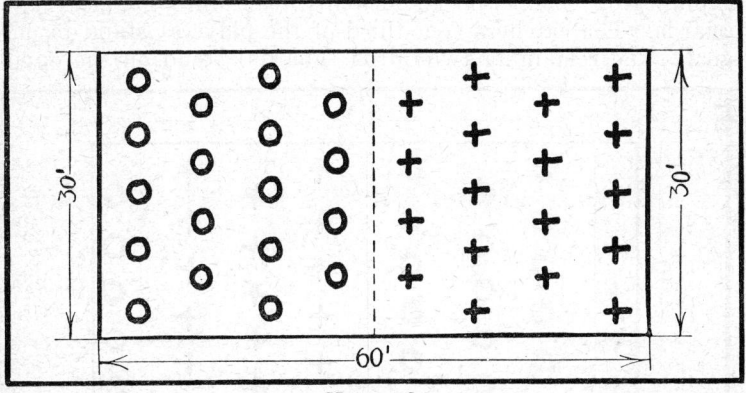

Newcomb

time set for play. When the referee calls "play," one player of the side having the ball throws it over the net with the object of making it strike the floor in the opponents' court. The opponents try to catch the ball before it strikes the floor, and then throw it back over the net. If the ball hits the floor in the opponents' court it is a score for the throwing side. Players should be stationed about the floor so as to leave no part unprotected. Smaller players should be stationed near the net, strong throwers and good catchers near the back. It is a foul to walk with the ball, to throw the ball under the net and to throw it outside the opponents' court in any direction unless the opponents touch the ball on its way out. A foul gives a score to the other side. Only about two or three minutes will be needed for rest between halves during which time the players may change courts. The side that held the ball when time was called starts the ball again in the second half. The side having the largest score at the end of the second half wins.

Note: This game may be played in the schoolroom by using a rope held by two pupils.

Catch Ball

Played like Newcomb but with a neutral place, 10 to 15 feet in width between the two playing courts, instead of a rope or net.

End Ball

The ground should be about sixty feet by thirty feet, with a line drawn through the center dividing the field into two equal parts thirty feet square. A division for goal is made at each end by drawing a line four feet from and parallel to the boundary. The players are divided into two teams with a captain for each, who divides his team into catchers and guards. The catchers (one-third of the players) stand in one goal. The remaining two-thirds (guards) stand on the oppo-

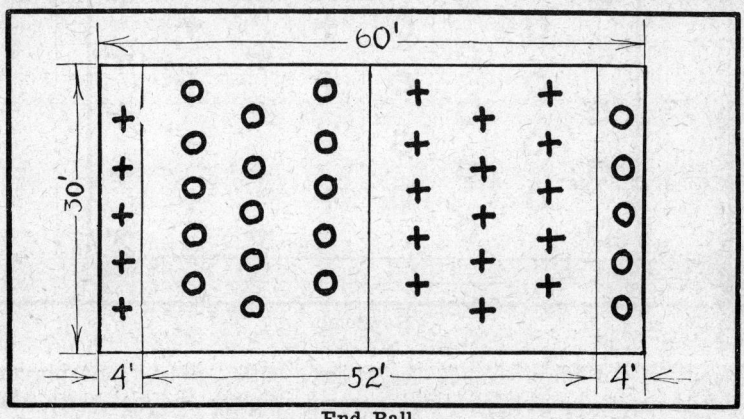

End Ball

site side of the center line facing their catchers and in front of the enemy's goal. The order of players on the field should be as follows, considering the teams as A and B; catchers for team A; guards for team B; guards for team A; catchers for team B.

The game is started by the teacher tossing the ball up in the center between the two guards who try to catch it. The man who catches it throws it to a guard on his side, and returns at once to his place. The guard throws the ball over to the catchers. Should they succeed in catching the ball, a point is made for that side. The guards of the opposing side try to secure the ball and throw it to their catchers. Whether or not the ball is caught, it is picked up by the catcher and thrown over to his guards. The ball caught by the guards scores nothing for that team. The guards simply throw it back to the catchers again.

Fouls: 1. Stepping over any of the division or boundary lines. 2. Walking with the ball. 3. Handing (not throwing) the ball to a player. 4. Holding the ball more than three seconds.

The penalty for a foul is a point for the opponent.

The game is played in eight to ten minute halves. Courts are changed at the end of the first half.

The side having the largest score at the end of the second half wins the game.

Ball going out of bounds is recovered by the player nearest where it went out of bounds, but is recovered only by permission of the umpire.

Captain Ball

The Team: The players are divided into two teams, each consisting of three basemen, three guards, and one or more fielders. One of the basemen is a captain and stands in the base at the end of the ground. Each team has a guard sta-

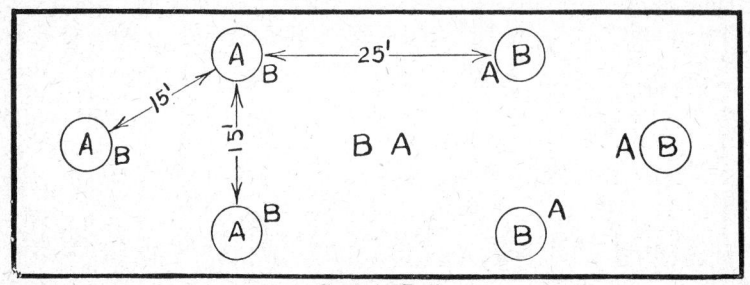

Captain Ball
A: Players of one team.   B: Players of other team

tioned near each of its opponent's bases and one or more fielders who may run to any part of the ground. See diagram for field of play. Each base is a circle 3½ to 4 feet in diameter.

Object of the Game: The object of the game is to have a captain catch a basket ball from one of his basemen. (A ball caught by the captain from anyone beside the baseman does not count). The guards try to prevent the basemen from throwing to the captain and try to secure the ball so that they may throw it to their own basemen or fielders.

Start: The ball is put in play by being tossed up in the center of the ground between the two fielders who try to hit it. Rules in basket ball governing the toss up in center apply here. The ball is put in play at center at start of game, between halves, and after each point is scored.

Rules: When the ball is thrown outside the boundary lines of the field of play it is thrown in by a guard or fielder of the opposite team from that throwing it out. Basket ball rules govern here. The basemen may put one foot outside of their circles but at no time both feet. The guards must not step inside the basemen's circle at any time.

Fouls: It is a foul to transgress any of the rules given above; to snatch or bat the ball from an opponent's hands, to bounce the ball more than once, to run with the ball, to kick it, to hand it instead of throw it or to hold it more than three seconds.

Penalty: A free throw from the basemen of the opposite team without interference of his own guard, to the captain. The captain's guard may try to prevent its being caught.

Score: The ball scores one point whenever a catch is made by a captain from one of his basemen. The game is played in equal halves.

Triangle Ball

Ground: Triangle for home plate, three feet on each side. One base about fifteen feet from the triangle. The pitcher's box about fourteen feet in front of the triangle. Any size of field may be used for players.

Players: The players, any number from two to one hundred, are divided into two teams. One team is at bat, while the other fields. The outs have just a pitcher and fielders, no catcher. The fielders are scattered about any place on the field.

Object of the game: The object is for the batter to hit ball pitched by pitcher, and to run on anything he strikes, to the base. He must not stay on the base and let another batter knock him in, but he must run from the triangle to the base and immediately back to the triangle (as in one-old cat) to make a score. The players try to get the hit and as soon as they get it, whether caught or picked from the ground, they must throw it to the pitcher who throws it into the triangle before the batter runs home. It is not counted if the ball hits the line of the triangle; it must light within or roll across the

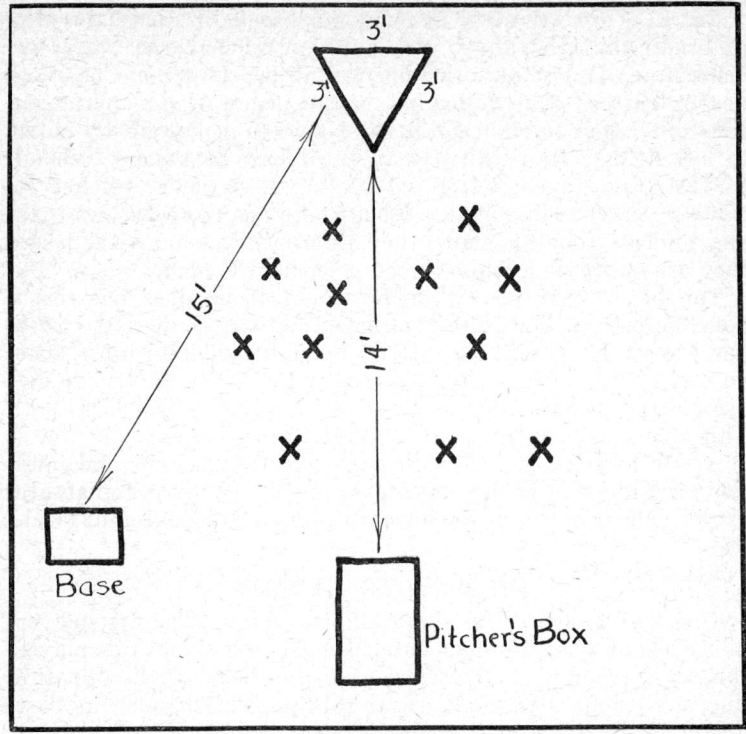

Triangle Ball

triangle. When the batters have three out they exchange places with the ones in the field. The ones who receive most scores at end of playing time win. When only two play, they exchange places at each "out."

One-Old Cat

One-Old Cat is like "Work Up" in many ways, but it may be also played by two teams. It is suitable for a smaller number of players, as there is only one base besides the home base. The batsman runs to first base and without waiting runs back again to make a run. As more players enter the game, two batters are used, but only the first and home bases.

Work Up

The Field: The baseball diamond unless very few are playing. In this case just home plate and first base are used.

Players: One, two or three batters according to number of players; the rest all out at field.

Object of the Game: Each player tries to get into bat and to remain a batter or baserunner.

Rules: Outs are made as in indoor baseball. Baseball rules of baserunning, stealing, etc., apply. Whenever a batter or baserunner is put out, the players all work up one position nearer batter. The following is the order of advancement: An "out" goes to right field; right field to center field; center to left field; left to third base; third base to second; second to first, first to short-stop; short-stop to pitcher; pitcher to catcher; catcher in at bat. When there are more batters than one, and an "out" is made, they stay in at bat or on the bases they are occupying, while the advancement is made.

The baserunner nearest home is out if he does not reach home before the ball is held on home plate after the last batter has batted, it being a forced run home in order to have some one in at bat. It is the object then of every batter to get around the bases as fast as possible in order to stay in at bat. This encourages stealing, and taking big risks.

A few local rules such as, a man who catches two flies and two grounders, or even who catches one fly, comes in to bat, are made. The order of advancement differs also in different localities.

Grounders Shuttle Relay

Teams arranged as for simple shuttle relay. The first player in each team has an indoor baseball. Upon a signal this player throws a grounder and then runs to the back of the opposite line. As soon as the ball leaves this player's hands, the first player in the line opposite runs forward, recovers the grounder and while still running throws it to the second player in line

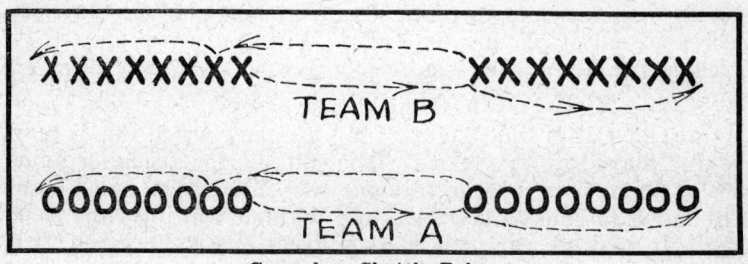

Grounders Shuttle Relay

one and takes his place behind line one. This continues until all have run twice and are back in their original positions. The team through first wins.

Remarks: The player who is to recover the grounder must be impressed with the fact that he must not run until the ball leaves the thrower's hands.

Baseball Pivot and Throw

Class in four lines with lines 2 and 3 standing quite close together. All face forward. Lines one and two are one team and lines three and four are another. An indoor baseball is given to the first players in line one and three. Upon a signal these players throw the ball to the first players in lines 2 and 4. These players throw the balls to the second players in their own lines and these throw to the second players in lines 1 and 3. This continues down the lines until every player has received it. The lines then face the back of the room and the last one to receive it throws it again to the player who threw it to him and he to the one from whom he received it, until it reaches the original starter again. The team first to accomplish this wins, provided no fouls have been made. The fouls are: 1. Not making the proper pivot on the right foot and transferring the weight to the left foot in the direction of the throw. 2. Not holding the hands properly for the catch of the ball.

Football Baseball

Refer to Softball rules. Use a soccer football. Use Softball diamond. The following rules are unlike Softball:
1. Batter kicks ball instead of batting.
2. Pitcher rolls ball instead of throwing it.
3. A "ball" is one that does not roll over home plate or is thrown through the air.
4. A "strike" is a ball that rolls over the base.
5. A base runner is out only when hit with ball off base.

Fongo

Any number of players, boys and girls, from ten years up. Apparatus: Bat and Ball.

One player, standing 20 to 30 feet from the other players, bats the ball toward them as they stand at random in various parts of the field. If a ball is caught on the fly or two grounders are stopped the player succeeding in catching it now takes the batter's place, while the batter takes his place in the field with the others. If nobody catches the ball the same player bats again.

Sometimes the following is added to the game. If, when the batter hits the ball, nobody succeeds in catching it, the first one to pick it up is allowed to roll the ball from where he picked it up toward the bat which the batter must now lay on the ground so that it is parallel to the front and rear walls. If the "thrower-in" succeeds in hitting the bat he becomes the batter. Should he miss, the same batter remains at bat.

For more skillful players, the "thrower-in" must roll the ball at the bat held upright on the ground.

Variation: fist Fongo.

A volley ball or basket ball is batted out with the fist. A player catching it on the fly is up. If missed the player having the ball is allowed to roll or throw it at the batter who must not move his feet but may duck his head or body. If the batter is hit he changes places with the "thrower-in". The ball may be thrown at an Indian Club instead of the batter.

Punch Ball

Apparatus: Volley ball

The Ground: Diamond similar to that of baseball diamond, square in shape and measuring from 30 to 40 feet on each side. A larger or smaller space may be used, according to the avail-

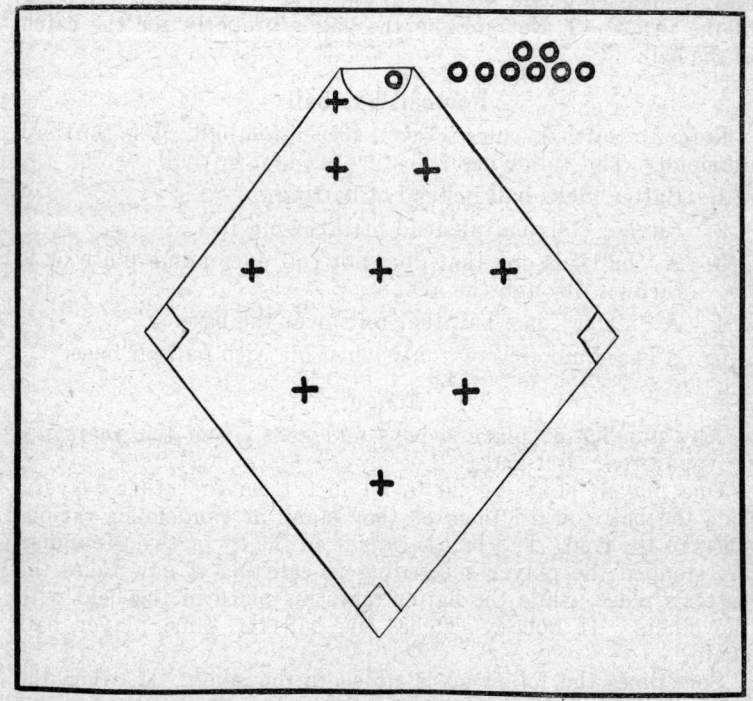

Punch Ball

able space and size of the children. At each of the four points of the diamond a base, one foot square, shall be marked out, except in the case of the home plate where a semicircle three feet in diameter shall be marked out. A line shall be drawn from the home plate to first base and extending beyond it on the right hand side of the diamond, and one from the home plate to third base and extending beyond it on the left hand side of the diamond. These lines constitute the foul lines.

Players: The players shall be divided into two equal teams; any number from three to twenty may play on each team. One team shall be in the field while the other team is at bat. The players shall have a batting order; namely, shall be numbered off as one, two, three, etc., the catcher being number one. The players shall always bat in consecutive order, that is, if number five is the last at bat in a given inning number 6 shall be the first at bat in the next inning of that team. The team at bat shall stand at one side of the home plate, out of the way of the runner and catcher, while waiting to bat. The players in the field, with the exception of the catcher, shall spread out to cover the field. Crosses may be marked on the diamond to indicate location of each player; but this does not mean that the player shall not move about. The catcher stands close to the home plate. The game shall be started by a command from the referee to "Play ball". The catcher who is then holding the ball, shall toss it to the first batter on the opposing team. The first batter on the opposing team shall stand on the home plate and shall bat the ball, with his closed fist, into the field and run to first base.

Object of the game: The object of the batter is to hit the ball in such a way that it may not be caught by the fielders, and to run to first base. The object of the fielders is to return the ball to their catcher, who shall stand on the home plate and while holding the ball calls the batter's name before he reaches first base. If the fielders muff the ball and are slow in returning it to home plate, the batter who has reached first may continue on to the second and third base or as far as in his judgment he can get before the ball reaches home plate. The player running the bases may always advance a base whenever the opportunity occurs and the ball is in play. The final object of the player running to bases is to touch each base and to reach home plate without being put out, thus scoring one run for his side.

An Inning: An inning consists of each team having a turn at bat. When each team has been at bat nine times, nine innings shall have been completed and the game ended. The score at the end of these innings is the final score for the game, except in case of a tie at the end of the ninth inning. In this case the game continues until one team at the end of one or more innings has scored against the other. Each inning lasts until each team in turn has made three outs, and has been retired. When the first team batting has made three outs, it goes into the field and the team that has been in the field takes its place at bat.

An Out: The player is out: 1. If the catcher with ball in hand and foot on home plate calls his name before he reaches first base. 2. If the ball he bats is caught on the fly, whether fair or foul, that is, if the ball is caught by the fielders before it touches the ground. 3. If he is at any time off base when the ball is in play, and the catcher is able to hold the ball with one foot on the home plate and call his name. 4. If running the bases he neglects to touch each plate. 5. If he fails to accept a chance to run to next base, causing two players to be caught on the same base.

A Fly Ball: If, when the ball is hit out by a batter, any player in the field catches it before it touches the ground, the ball shall have been caught on the fly; the batter shall be out; and any player running between bases shall return to the base he was on before the ball was batted and may be put out in so doing.

A Foul: If when the ball is batted it falls outside the foul line, stretching from home plate through first base or from home plate through third base, the ball is foul and is out of play, the batter receives another chance and he is allowed to try until he hits a fair ball. Any player running between bases shall return to the base he held before the foul was made.

The Score: When a player has successfully run from base to base, first, second, third, and reaches home plate, he has made a run and scores one for his side. At the end of each inning the number of runs made in that inning shall be marked upon a score board.

Box Ball

Played same as Punch ball only that there is a pitcher and catcher. An indoor baseball and bat are used in place of a volley ball.

Long Ball

Played with softball and bat and two bases.

Place the bases from thirty to sixty feet apart, depending on the size and skill of the players. All of the pupils may play.

Divide the players into two groups as nearly equal as possible. Number the players in each group, 1, 2, 3, 4, etc. One team takes turn at bat; the other team takes the field. The team taking the field selects a pitcher who stands half way between home and second base and pitches the ball always underhand to the catcher who stands immediately behind home base. The remaining players of the side taking the field arrange themselves in an elongated semi-circle about the field.

Players of the side at bat come up to bat in order of their numbers. Each inning after the first is begun with the player whose number follows the number of the player who made the third out of the previous inning.

The batter stands on either side of home base (not on the base) as is most convenient in batting the ball.

There are no fouls in this game. Every time the batter standing in his position touches the pitched ball with the bat, it is a hit and batter attempts to run to second base and if possible to return to home base.

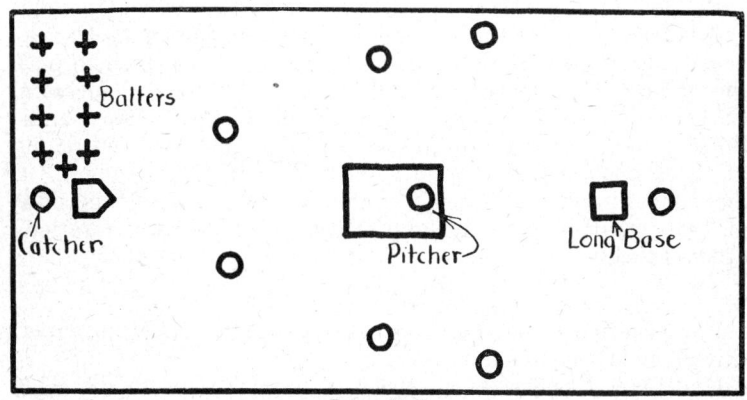

Long Ball

The base runner may take any path he chooses in running to and returning from second base.

More than one base runner may remain on second base at the same time.

A pitched ball, passing over home base while the batter is in his position not higher than the batter's shoulders or lower than his knees counts one strike against him whether or not he strikes at it.

If the catcher catches a third strike it puts the batter out. If a third strike is not caught the batter becomes a base runner.

A pitched ball which does not pass over home base, or which goes higher than the shoulders or lower than the knees of the batter and is not struck at by him is called a ball. Four balls entitle the batter to take his place on second base. After the batter becomes a base runner he may be put out in the following ways: 1. By the catching of the ball he batted before it touches the ground. 2. By being hit by a thrown ball while attempting to run to or return from second base. 3. By being touched, by the ball in the hands of an opposing player while running to or returning from second base. 4. By being struck by a batted ball.

Each base runner returning safely to home base after touching second base counts one score for his team. More than one player may run home from second base at the same time. No player may score on the play which results in the third out. After three outs the teams change positions. Nine innings constitute a game. The captains may decide at the opening of the game on some other number of innings that is to constitute a game.

Points to emphasize in teaching the game of Long Ball: 1. Diagram the position of the various players on the blackboard and explain the duties of each before attempting to play the game out of doors. 2. Pitching must be done underhand. Catcher and fielders may throw overhanded. 3. Any additional number of players necessary to accommodate the pupils of the school may be added to the semi-circle of fielders. 4. Someone should be chosen to act as umpire, giving decisions on balls, strikes, outs, and any other necessary interpretations of the rules.

Circle Strike

For practice in batting and fielding, catching and pitching, this game is recommended.

One team forms a large circle, (about 60 feet in diameter for sixth grade boys). The players are numbered off around the circle and number one acts as catcher, while the player opposite him in the circle acts as the pitcher. The pitcher steps into a position of about 30 feet from the catcher.

The other team lines up in a line and counts off. Number one of the team is the first batter and steps in front of number one of the other team. Four or five strikes are pitched to this batter and he attempts to hit them outside of the circle. Each ball thus batted counts a score for his team. If he bats a fly, however, and a boy from the circle is able to run back and catch it, no score is made.

When the first batter has had his four strikes the next batter steps into his place and the circle shifts one place to the left so that No. 2 is the catcher and the player opposite him is the pitcher. This continues until all on one team have batted, then the teams change places and the second team bats as the first one did. The scores are recorded and compared at the end of the game.

Softball

For official rules of Softball, refer to Sports Library—"Official Softball—Volley Ball Guide", A. S. Barnes Co., New York.

For coaching, refer to "Softball", A. T. Noren, 1940, A. S. Barnes Co., New York.

For Movement Fundamentals leading to Softball see page 318 of this bulletin.

For games leading to Softball see list, pp. 24-25.

Serve and Return

A contest in serving and returning in Volley Ball.

Teams are arranged on either side of the net and in rotating order. The ball is given to a girl who is in the server's position on team "A". If the relayed service is being taught she is given two trials to get the ball over the net by the relayed service. If she is successful she is given two points; if she makes one and fails on the other she scores one point and one 0. If she fails on both she is given two zeros. Then her team and the team on the opposite side of the net rotate one position and the second player on team "A" is given two trials and her scores checked up as before. This continues until all of the team "A" have had two trials at serving. Every time a ball is successfully served over the net the opposite team must try to return it. If this team makes a successful return they score one point; if they fail they score a zero. This much constitutes one-half the game and the ball is then given to team "B" and this team serves as did "A" in the first half. When the game is finished the serving and returning ability of the teams may be compared by percentage of successful serves and returns. For example: Supposing team "A" has ten players. This team then had twenty chances to serve and if they succeed in getting ten of these serves over their score would be expressed as 10-20 or 50 per cent. Team "B" then had ten chances to return the ball back over the net. If they were successful in six of these chances their score would be 6-10 or 60 per cent.

If team "B" had twelve players they then had twenty-four chances to get the ball over and if they succeeded in eighteen of these serves their score would be 18-24 or 2-3 or 66⅔ per cent and if out of these eighteen chances team "A" returned 16 their returning score would be 16-18 or 8-9 or 88 2/9 per cent. In serving then team "A" was defeated by a score of 50 per cent against team "B's" 66⅔ per cent. But in returning team "A" was victorious by a score of 88 2/9 per cent against team "B's" 60 per cent.

Simplified Volley Ball

1. May be played in schoolroom, on playground or gymnasium.

2. Any number of players.

3. Use a volley ball and a light rope or string in the schoolroom. A volley ball net may be used in the gymnasium or on the playground. In the room two children may stand in chairs or in the seats and hold the ends of a rope that is stretched across the room.

4. Players are divided into two even teams and one team stands in the aisles on one side of the rope while the other team takes its place on the opposite side. The ball is given to any player in one of the teams and that player bats the ball with the open hand over the rope in an attempt to make it hit the desks or floor in the opposite court. The players in the opposite court however try to bat it back before it has hit the floor or desks and thus make it return over the rope to the opposite court. Should they fail in doing this it counts a point for the side who served it. In other words a point is scored for a team each time the ball is allowed to touch their opponents' floor or desks or any of the players in any way except their hands in the act of batting it.

In the gymnasium or on the playground definite boundary lines about 30 by 60 feet should be made but in the room the walls are usually the boundary. Should a team bat the ball over these boundaries or hit the wall in the room it counts a score for the team that did not touch it last. The ball should be put in play by any player who secures it in his own court. There is no formal way or place for serving the ball as in regular volley ball.

It is a foul to hit the ball more than twice in succession or to touch the rope or net or run into the opposite court. A foul gives one point to the opposite side.

Games may be played for ten minute halves or for twenty-one points. This is a particularly good game to give practice in returning balls in volley ball.

Volley Ball

Court: The court shall be 35 ft. by 60 ft. in size with a net 6 ft. 6 in. or 7 ft. 6 in. high stretched across the middle from side to side. (The former is recommended for grade use).

Ball: The ball shall be a regulation volley ball weighing not more than nine ounces.

Teams: Teams shall be composed of an equal number of players. Nine is recommended as a good number for contest use though a much larger number may play in regular classes.

Substitutes: Substitutions may be made only when the ball is dead. A player who has left the game may not re-enter it.

The Game: The ball is put in play by one member, the server of serving side, who bats it with open hand from behind rear line of his court, over the net into opponents' field.

The ball is kept in play by returning ball back and forth over net without violation of rules.

Definition of Terms

1. Serving order: The order in which players are to serve.

2. Service: The putting of a ball in play by an eligible player, by batting it into the opponents' court in any direction with one or both hands, while standing with both feet behind any part of the end line of the court.

Note: The play ceases to be a service as soon as the ball is played by a player other than the server.

3. Fault: A service which puts the side out because of one or more of the following violations:

(a) Strikes the net and bounds back into the court from which it was batted or out of bounds.

Note: Any ball other than a service may be recovered from the net.

(b) Strikes the floor in the court from which it was served.

(c) Goes over the net and out of bounds.

(d) The server steps on or over the service line in the act of service.

4. Point: When the team receiving fails to legally return the ball to the opponents' court.

5. Side out: When the team serving fails to win its point or plays the ball illegally.

6. Net Service: One which strikes the net and falls into the opponents' court.

7. Out of Bounds: The ball is out of bounds when it touches any surface, object or part of the floor outside of the court, or if it strikes any of the boundary lines.

8. Dead Ball: Whenever the referee's whistle blows calling a decision or when the timekeeper's whistle blows at the end of halves.

Note: A ball striking an official who is in the court shall be declared dead, and shall be served again by the same player.

9. Delaying the Game: Committing any act which in the opinion of the referee slows down or interferes with the game unnecessarily.

10. Playing the Ball: A player touching or being touched by the ball.

11. Catching or Holding: Allowing the ball to momentarily come to rest in the hands or arms. It must be batted.

12. Dribble: To hit the ball more than twice in succession.

13. Rotation: The shifting of players over the floor so that a different player is server each time the team secures the ball after side out.

Length of Halves: Fifteen minute halves with five minutes between halves.

Tie Games: In case of a tie game an extra five minute period shall be played.

Courts and Service: Shall be determined by a toss of a coin. The winner of the toss may have choice of service or courts for the first half.

Time Out: Shall be called by the referee. It may be called for not more than 2 minutes in case of injury and except in case of an injury it may be called only when the ball is dead.

Server: At the opening of the game the ball shall be put in play by the first player on the serving order of the team. At the beginning of the second half the ball shall be put in play by the player eligible when time was called at the end of the first half.

Each server shall continue to serve until the referee calls side out. The other team shall then put the ball in play by a service.

Service: A service which strikes any object or surface (other than the net) which deflects it from its course, shall put the side out. No point shall be scored on a net service, but it shall be served again. If the second attempt is a net service it shall put the side out. A net service cannot be played but must be taken again.

Playing the Ball:

1. The ball may be batted by one or both hands but it must not touch the floor or go out of bounds or under the net.

2. The ball may be played by any number of players before being batted over the net provided no attempt is made to delay the game.

3. A ball except a service, striking the net or dropping over, is still in play.

4. A fault shall put the team out.

5. If a player on either team bats the ball out of bounds, it shall count against her team. This does not prohibit the recovery of a ball by the team batting it outside the court,

provided the player does not advance beyond the net or the ball go out of bounds.

A player shall not:
1. Strike the ball with her fist.
2. Strike the ball while supported by any player or object.
3. Bat the ball against the ceiling so that it bounds into the opponents' court.
4. Dribble.
5. Throw the ball.
6. Catch or hold the ball.
7. Reach over the net to strike the ball.
8. Hold or push the ball against the net.
9. Kick the ball in an effort to return it.
10. Serve out of regular order or change places on the field so as to receive the relay or change in any other way except when a substitution is made.
11. Touch the net.

Note: If two players on opposite sides touch the net simultaneously no point or side out shall be called and the ball shall be served again by the same player.

12. Interfere with the play of the opposing team by entering their court.

Note: Due allowance shall be made for a player who is unable to stop and who gets back to her own court as soon as possible without interfering with the play.

13. Touch an opponent who is in her own court.

Penalties: Side out shall be called by the referee for violation of the above 13 rules by the team serving. Point shall be called by the referee for violation of the above 13 rules by the team receiving.

14. Address an official.

Note: Captains only may address the officials.

15. Delay the game.
16. Make remarks or commit actions derogatory to the officials or tending to influence their decisions.
17. Make personal or derogatory remarks about opponents.
18. At any time pull the net with intent to lower it.
19. Re-enter the game after being disqualified.

Penalties: A point or side out may for the first offense, and shall for the second offense, be given the opponents for the violation of 14 to 17 inclusive.

The referee may disqualify for a violation of 16 or 17.

A team shall forfeit the game for violation of 18.

20. There shall be no coaching from the side lines during the progress of the game by any one officially connected with either team, nor shall any person go on the court during the progress of the game, except by permission of the referee.

Penalty: For the first offense the side shall be warned by the referee, and for the second offense a point shall be awarded to the opposing team by the referee.

Scoring

1. Failure of the receiving team to legally return the ball over the net into the opponents' court shall count one point for the team serving.

Note: A point cannot be made while the ball is "dead".

2. No point can be scored on a ball that strikes an official, but must be served over by the same player.

3. A game shall be decided by the winning of the most points in the playing time.

Duties of an Official

I. (a) The referee shall be the superior officer of the game. He or she shall decide when the ball is in play; when it is "dead"; when a point has been made; when side is out, and shall impose penalties for any violation of the rules.

(b) The referee shall blow a whistle when he or she puts the ball in play at the beginning of a half, and whenever necessary to make a decision.

(c) The referee shall have power to make decisions for violation of the rules committed at any moment from the beginning of the play to the call of time at the end of a half, or game. This includes the periods when the game may be momentarily stopped for any reason.

II. (a) The timekeepers shall note when the game starts and shall deduct time consumed by stoppage during the game on order of the referee, and shall sound a whistle at the expiration of the actual playing time of each half. They shall compare timing after each stop and any discrepancy shall be at once referred to the referee who shall decide the correct time. For failure to notify the referee at once, she shall decide in favor of the longer playing time.

Note: Time deducted for stops during the game shall be reckoned from the time the referee blows the whistle calling time out, until she again blows it on resuming play.

(b) If the ball is in play when time out is called on account of injury, play is resumed by a service by the player serving, when time out was called.

(c) The timekeepers shall blow their whistles immediately up on the expiration of the playing time of the half of game, and the ball shall be "dead" whether in play or not.

III. (a) The linesmen shall station themselves at opposite ends of the court and on the side opposite the referee, so that each has two lines in plain view, and whenever the ball strikes the ground near a line the linesman nearest the point of contact shall call "good" or "out."

(b) Upon the referee's request they shall report to the referee on any play about which the referee is uncertain.

(c) Before the game the linesman shall secure from the Captain the serving order of the team, and shall see that the players serve in rotation.

IV. (a) The scorers shall be placed in the center of the court beside the referee, where they can readily hear the points as called by the referee.

(b) The scorers shall record the points as called by the referee and shall check every five points. If at any time there is a discrepancy in the score, it is to be referred to the referee at once, who shall decide what the score shall be. If the referee is unable to decide which is the correct score, she shall make her decision in favor of the smaller score.

The score as kept by the scorers shall constitute the official score.

Bibliography

Games for the Playground, Home, School and Gymnasium—Jessie H. Bancroft—Macmillan Co.

Active Games and Contests—Mason and Mitchell—A. S. Barnes Co., New York, 1935

Social Games for Recreation—Mason and Mitchell—A. S. Barnes Co., New York, 1935

Hospital and Bedside Games—Boyd Fitzsimons Co., 23 E. Jackson Boulevard, Chicago, Ill.

Games and Game Leadership—Smith Dodd, Mead and Co., New York

TRACK AND FIELD EVENTS
Motor Ability Tests

By motor ability tests is meant a contest in which each individual has the opportunity of testing himself in relation to some accepted standard for his age, and a grade or school competes against another grade or school, through the combined efforts of all its pupils instead of by a picked team.

The superiority of this kind of contest over the time honored "track meet" where a few stars are trained at the expense of the rest of the school to represent the school is obvious to everyone. A school where every girl and every boy is taught to run, jump, and throw is a school that is really physically trained.

The great difficulty in the individual efficiency contest is to determine a just scheme of classification. Many methods have been used and are being used but none of them have yet proved entirely satisfactory. One need only glance at any grade of children to realize that any contest in physical ability on equal terms within the grade would be unfair to many children. Perhaps the best method of classification would be one that takes into consideration the child's age, height, weight, and grade in school and such a scheme will be included in this discussion. But this method is too complicated as a rule for the average teacher, so a simpler plan, based on age alone, is recommended for convenience and simplicity in handling records. Such a plan follows:

Plan I. Motor Ability Tests. The Pentathlon.
BOYS

	Age Aim	Excellence
8 Years		
50 Yard Dash	9 sec.	8⅘ sec.
Standing Broad Jump	3'4"	4'4"
High Jump	2'2"	2'8"
Playground Ball Throw	38'	71'
Rope Climbing or	8'	10'
Chinning	1 time	6 times
9 Years		
50 Yard Dash	8⅘ sec.	8⅗ sec.
Standing Broad Jump	3'8"	4'10"
High Jump	2'5"	2'10"
Playground Ball Throw	47'	86'
Climbing or	10'	12'
Chinning	1 time	6 times

PHYSICAL EDUCATION

10 Years
- 75 Yard Dash .... 13 1/5 sec.   9 4/5 sec.
- Standing Broad Jump .... 4'   5'4"
- High Jump .... 2'8"   3'2"
- Playground Ball Throw .... 57'   104'
- Climbing or .... 12'   13'
- Chinning .... 1 time   8 times

11 Years
- 75 Yard Dash .... 12 3/5 sec.   9 4/5 sec.
- Running Broad Jump .... 8'3"   9'1"
- High Jump .... 2'10"   3'4"
- Playground Ball Throw .... 67'   113'
- Climbing or .... 13'   14'
- Chinning .... 1 time   8 times

12 Years
- 100 Yard Dash .... 15 2/5 sec.   15 sec.
- Running Broad Jump .... 9'3"   10'8"
- High Jump .... 3'   3'6"
- Playground Ball Throw .... 77'   120'
- Climbing or .... 14'   15'
- Chinning .... 2 times   9 times

13 Years
- 100 Yard Dash .... 15 sec.   14 2/5 sec.
- Running Broad Jump .... 10'   12'2"
- High Jump .... 3'1"   3'9"
- Playground Ball Throw or .... 88'   141'
- Basket Ball Throw (Single Arm) .... 37'   70'
- Running Hop Step and Jump .... 19'9"   26'

14 Years
- 100 Yard Dash .... 14 1/5 sec.   13 3/5 sec
- Running Broad Jump .... 10'2"   13'5"
- High Jump .... 3'2"   4'2"
- Playground Ball Throw or .... 102'   151'
- Basket Ball Throw (Single Arm) .... 42'   73'
- Running Hop Step and Jump .... 21'7"   29'

15 Years
- 100 Yard Dash .... 13 2/5 sec.   13 sec.
- Running Broad Jump .... 10'5"   14'7"
- High Jump .... 3'3"   4'5"
- Playground Ball Throw or .... 108'   187'
- Basket Ball Throw (Single Arm) .... 47'   73'
- Running Hop Step and Jump .... 23'   29'5"

GIRLS

                       Age Aim   Excellence

8 Years
- 50 Yard Dash .... 9 3/5 sec.   8 4/5 sec.

Standing Broad Jump	3'	4'4"
High Jump	2'2"	2'6"
Playground Ball Throw	23'	45'
Knee Raising or	4 times	8 times
Trunk Lifting	4 times	8 times

9 Years

50 Yard Dash	9 2/5 sec.	8 sec.
Standing Broad Jump	3'2"	5'
High Jump	2'5"	2'8"
Playground Ball Throw	26'	56'
Knee Raising or	8 times	12 times
Trunk Lifting	6 times	10 times

10 Years

50 Yard Dash	9 1/5 sec.	7 sec.
Standing Broad Jump	3'6"	6'5"
High Jump	2'8"	2'10"
Playground Ball Throw	30'	60'
Knee Raising or	12 times	16 times
Trunk Lifting	8 times	12 times

11 Years

50 Yard Dash	9 sec.	7 sec.
Standing Broad Jump	3'8"	6'6"
High Jump	2'9"	3'
Playground Ball Throw	35'	68'
Potato Race (224 feet)	25 sec.	21 sec.

12 Years

50 Yard Dash	8 4/5 sec.	7 sec.
Standing Broad Jump	3'10"	6'7"
High Jump	2'10"	3'2"
Playground Ball Throw	43'	75'
Potato Race	23 sec.	20 sec.

13 Years

50 Yard Dash	8 3/5 sec.	7 sec.
Standing Broad Jump	4'	6'9"
High Jump	2'11"	3'3"
Playground Ball Throw	48'	82'
Potato Race	22 sec.	20 sec.

14 Years

50 Yard Dash	8 3/5 sec.	6 3/5 sec.
Standing Broad Jump	4'4"	7'2"
High Jump	3'	3'4"
Playground Ball Throw	53'	90'
Potato Race	22 sec.	19 sec.

15 Years

50 Yard Dash	8⅗ sec.	6⅖ sec.
Standing Broad Jump	4'6"	7'3"
High Jump	3'1"	3'5"
Playground Ball Throw	57'	97'
Potato Race	22 sec.	19 sec.

Note: The Potato race used in this test is the 224 foot test as described on page 106.

Scoring

For team or inter-grade competition the following point system of scoring may be used. For accomplishing the age aim or average standing in one event, 2 points are given; for accomplishing the age aim in all five events, 15 additional points are given, making a total of 25 possible points to gain.

If one accomplishes the excellent standard in any event he receives 5 points; and if the excellent standard is reached in all events, 50 additional points are given, making a total of 75 possible points.

These points added to the points previously earned make a possibility of 100 points for each age.

In competitions between grades or teams the points of all the members of the grade or team are added together and divided by the number of children competing. This gives the grade or team standing. Other schemes of mass competition will be described later.

Badge Award

In addition to competition in teams, individuals may have incentive added by the awarding of a button or ribbon for attaining the first 25 points or an average standing in all events. Then a ribbon or button of a different color can be awarded for excellent performance in all events or for the 100 points. If a child attains either average or excellent standing two years in succession some additional insignia should be awarded.

Plan II. Motor Ability Tests

Classification for Boys and Girls

Junior Division—Pupils in the 5th and 6th school grades

Exponents	4	5	6	7	8	9	
Grade		5A	5B	6A	6B		
Age—up to	10	10'1-11	11'1-6	11'7-12	12'1-13	13'1	or over
Height—up to	4'2	4'3-5	4'6-8	4'9-11	5'-5'2	5'3	or over
Weight—up to	64 lbs.	65-74	75-84	85-94	95-104	105	or over

Senior Division—Pupils in the 7th and 8th school grades

Exponents	4	5	6	7	8	9
Grade		7A	7B	8A	8B	
Age—up to	12	12'1-13	13'1-6	13'7-14	14'1-15	15'1 or over
Height—up to	4'4	4'5-8	4'9-5	5'1-3	5'4-6	5'7 or over
Weight—up to	74	75-89	90-104	105-119	120-129	130 or over

Class
Same for Senior or Junior Division

	A	B	C	D	E
Sum of Exponents up to	21	22-25	26-29	30-33	34 or over

EXAMPLE—Boy in 5B   Exponent for Grade   6   (See grade)
           Age 10'6   Exponent for Age   5   (See age)
           Height 4'10   Exponent for Height   7   (See height)
           Weight 84 lbs.   Exponent for Weight   6   (See weight)

Sum of Exponents   24   (See Class B)

This classification system is applied to both boys and girls. At this period of development, the fifth to the eighth year of school the girls, maturing earlier, average practically the same as the boys in height and weight. This does not hold true earlier or later in life.

Note: One feature of this plan is that it automatically provides a sliding scale by which the boy or girl must go on improving his performance term after term or fall down on his rating. As he grows older, taller, heavier, higher in school, he must meet progressively higher standards. And this is determined by his reclassification at the beginning of each term, an operation which takes about twenty minutes for a class of forty.

The standards proposed include a minimum (A) which is low enough to be reached by nearly all pupils after a reasonable amount of practice, and a maximum (E) beyond which no credit is given. The effect of the first is to center attention on the weaker pupils. The more active pupils will take an interest in coaching the weaker, so that they may score at least five points, and so help the average. The effect of the maximum is to discourage specialization, making it necessary to work for all-around development in order to score high.

Standards for Boys

		Min.	Max.	Class	A	B	C	D	E
1.	Potato Race								
	Min. 5 pt., 3 pt. added for every sec. under standard	5	20	Junior	26 sec.	24	22	20	18
				Senior	32 sec.	30	28	26	24
2.	50 Yard Dash								
	Min. 5 pt., 3 pt. added for every fifth second under standard	5	20	Junior	9 sec.	8⅗	8⅖	8⅕	8
				Senior	8 sec.	7⅗	7⅖	7⅕	7

PHYSICAL EDUCATION

3. Standing Broad Jump
Min. 5 pt., 3 pt. added
for every 3 in. over — 5 20 Junior 4'6" 4'9 5   5'3 5'9
                                Senior 5'3" 5'6 5'9 6   6'6
4. Chinning the Bar
Min. 5 pt., 3 pt. added
for every 2 pull-ups
over — 5 20 Junior 3 times 4 5 6 6
              Senior 5 times 6 6 7 7
5. Goal Shooting (30 sec.)
Min. 5 pt., 3 pt. added
for every goal over or
Basket Ball Far Throw
(Overhead) Min. 5
pt., 3 pt. added for
every foot over — 5 20 Junior 1 time   1 2 2 3
                         Senior 3 times 4 5 5 6

                         Junior 21' 23 25 27 30
                         Senior 24' 27 30 33 36
                    25 100 points

Standards for Girls

Min. Max. Class A   B   C   D   E

1. Potato Race
Min. 5 pt., 3 pt. added
for every sec. under — 5 20 Junior 28 sec. 26 24 22 20
                              Senior 34 sec. 32 30 28 26
2. 50 Yard Dash
Min. 5 pt., 3 pt. added
for every fifth second
under standard — 5 20 Junior 10 sec. 9⅗ 9⅕ 9   8⅘
                        Senior 9 sec.   8⅗ 8⅕ 8   8
3. Standing Broad Jump
Min. 5 pt., 3 pt. added
for every 3" over — 5 20 Junior 3'6" 3'9" 4   4'3" 4'9
                           Senior 4'3" 4'6" 4'9 5   5'6
4. Knee Raising
Min. 5 pt., 3 pt. added
for every two over — 5 20 Junior 4 times   6   8   10 12
                            Senior 10 times 12 14 16 20
5. Goal Shooting (30 sec.)
Min. 5 pt., 3 pt. added
for every goal over or
Basket Ball Far Throw
(Overhead) Min. 5
pt., 3 pt. added for
every foot over — 5 20 Junior 1 time   1 2 2 3
                         Senior 2 times 3 4 4 5

                         Junior 16' 19 21 23 25
                         Senior 18' 22 23 28 30
                    25 100 points   o

NOTE: The 224 foot Potato Race is used by the Juniors, the 304 foot Potato Race by the Seniors. See description on page 106.

Equipment Needed

Stop watch, spade, rake, jumping pit, jumping standards, cross bar, 14 inch playground ball, four two inch wooden cubes, two paper or wooden boxes about a foot square and eight inches deep, tape line 50 to 75 feet long, basket ball and a horizontal bar, rope.

Directions for Making Equipment

Jumping Pit: Spade up a lot fifteen or sixteen feet long and four feet wide. Smooth it over with a rake or remove the dirt and fill the pit with sand. A joist eight inches wide should be sunk level with the ground as the take-off at the near end of the pit.

Jumping Standards: Uprights may be made of two by two inch sticks six feet in height. Beginning two feet above the ground the holes are bored one inch apart. The uprights should be placed on bases or set in the ground so they will stand straight. They should be twelve feet apart. The cross bar should be one-half inch thick and one inch wide by 14 feet long. A bamboo fishing rod may be used for the cross bar. This bar rests on five inch spikes placed through the holes of the upright, and is always on the pit side of the uprights.

Horizontal Bar: Place a wooden bar or iron pipe across a doorway or between two uprights set in the ground from 8 to 10 feet high.

The rungs of a ladder set at an angle against a building may serve the purpose.

Dash: On your marks; Get set; Go!

Directions for Conducting Motor Ability Tests

For organization and methods of instruction in form, see pages 335 to 341.

Dashes: Mark off a starting line, then measure from this line the varying distances to be run in your school, i. e., 50 yards, 75 yards, and 100 yards. If stakes are placed in the ground to mark these distances they will not need to be measured each time. Since the "start" of a dash position is so important this should be thoroughly taught first. The crouching position is most popular and effective. The front foot is placed about six inches behind the line, the rear foot is placed so that when kneeling the knee is opposite the instep of the front foot. When the starter says "Get on your marks," the boy kneels on the knee of his rear leg and places his hands just back of the line. On the command "Get set," this knee is raised and straightened slightly and the body is pushed forward keeping the back flat. On the word "Go" the boy springs forward with a sharp upward swing of the arm opposite the foot that comes forward, keeping the body well forward until he has run several feet. The arms should continue to swing straight forward and back in opposition to the feet throughout the race and the feet should toe straight ahead with the knees brought well up in front. A clap of the hands or of two boards may be substituted for the word "Go." Should a boy start before this signal he should be brought back and told that this is a foul with a penalty of being set back 1 yard for the first offense and 2 yards for the second, with disqualification for the third offense. Carelessness in this respect may cost him the race in a regular meet. Each boy should be coached to keep going at top speed until the finish line for his race is crossed and that if a string is held at the finish he must not touch this with his hands. In determining the individual times in the various weight classes only one boy's time can be taken at one time but it is much better to have one or more boys run with him as few boys run their fastest when running alone, e. g., you wish to see how fast John can run seventy-five yards. You ask James to run with him and ask some other boy to act as starter. You stand at the finish line, watch in hand, and when the starter says "go" he throws up one arm and you start your watch. When John crosses the finish line you stop your watch even though James may have crossed it sooner.

Potato Race: A starting line is drawn and the boxes are placed on this line. For the 224 foot test the first potato (or block of wood) is placed twenty-four feet from this box and the second thirty-two feet from the box and in line with the first potato. The spots where the potatoes lie should be marked by something that is easily seen—chalk dust, lime, or paper fastened down. For the 304 foot test the first potato is thirty-four feet out and the second forty-two feet from the box. In the race the runner starts back of the starting line, and on a signal to go she runs out and brings in one potato, drops it in the box. Goes out and brings in the second, touches the box with it and replaces it on the mark, comes back, takes the first one out of the box, replaces it on the mark and returns to the starting line. Failure to drop block in box or place it on the mark constitutes a foul for which the runner has one second added to his time. As in the dashes the person being timed should have someone running against her so that she will do her best. She should keep up her speed until she has crossed the starting line after replacing the blocks on the marks.

Running High Jump: The bar is placed at the lowest limit of the weight class and is raised one inch at a time. Each boy is allowed three jumps at each successive height and takes his jump in turn. Those who fail on their first trial take their second trial in turn and those who fail on their second trial take their third in proper order. When a boy fails on his third trial at any height he is declared out of the test and is given credit for the last height which he cleared. Knocking down the bar is counted as a trial. Running under the bar is a "balk." Two balks are counted as one trial. The boy may run any distance and from any direction before making his jump but he should be encouraged to shorten his distance as this allows more spring into the air.

Running Broad Jump. A board eight inches wide is sunk level with the ground at the near end of the jumping pit and a run away of not less than 100 feet should be allowed leading to this pit. The boy should practice his run so that he will land on the same foot on the take-off board each time. He should be encouraged to draw his knees well up after he takes off and jump high as well as broad. He lands on both feet and as he does so throws both arms forward and up so that his body will fall forward. The measure of the jump is taken from the edge of the take-off board to the last mark he leaves on the pit. If he falls backward or lets his hand drop behind him the measurement is taken to that point where his body or hands touched which is nearest the take-off board, but if he falls forward and his feet are his last marks the measurement is taken to the back of the heel mark of the foot print nearest the take-off board. Should the boy over-step the take-off board so that his toe touches the ground beyond it this is a foul and counts as one trial. Each boy has three trials and the best jump out of the three is recorded. The ground should be kept soft and level after each jump so that there will be no mistakes about foot prints and so that there will be no sprained ankles.

Standing Broad Jump: This is conducted much the same as the running broad jump although if the ground is reasonably soft no pit is necessary. The boy stands with his toes on a line with the far edge of the take-off board or behind a line drawn on the ground. After rising on his toes and lifting hands high, and then bending his knees and lowering hands,

Standing Broad Jump

First preparatory position

Second preparatory position
(Weight should be more on toes than picture indicates.)

he throws his arms forward quickly and jumps forward with both feet at once. To get a good jump he must bend his knees well up in front while he is in the air and land with his weight forward as in the running broad jump. Measurements are taken as in the running broad jump.

Playground Ball Throw: A line is marked on the ground back of which the thrower must stand. He is given three trials and his best throw is recorded. Should he step over the line on any throw it is a foul and counts as a trial without any measure being taken. It will save much time and trouble in measuring if some permanent stakes are driven in the ground at varying intervals from the throwing line, then the individual throw may be measured from these stakes provided the throw has been made in line with the stakes. The measurement is made from the point where the ball first touched the ground.

Basket Ball Far Throw (Single Arm): A circle six feet in diameter is drawn on the ground. The contestant (if right handed) stands with his left side toward the direction of the throw and with his left foot forward; the weight is on the

Fig. 1   Fig. 2
Basket Ball Single-arm Throw
Fig. 1: Beginning of throw   Fig. 2: Finish of throw

right foot, right knee bent. The ball is held in the right hand which is extended to the rear. When the throw is made the right foot is brought forward as the right arm swings over the head. In throwing, the contestant shall not touch outside the circle with any part of the body until the ball has struck the ground. If any part of the body touches outside the circle, the distance made shall not be recorded but the throw shall count as one trial. Three trials are allowed. The measurement of each throw is taken at the circle from the point where the ball first touched the ground to the circumference of the circle on a line from such point to the center of the circle.

Basket Ball Far Throw (Overhead): Contestant toes the line with both feet and throws the ball from overhead with both hands. The feet must not be moved (except to raise the heels) until the ball touches the ground, and the contestant must not cross the scratch line until the throw has been recorded. The throw is measured from where the ball hits the ground in a perpendicular line to the scratch line. Two trials are taken and the best one recorded.

Chinning: Jump to a straight-arm, still-hang position on the horizontal bar. Either over or under grip may be used. From this position pull up slowly until the chin is slightly above the bar. Lower slowly to the straight arm hang, and repeat as many times as possible. The legs should hang straight, and the feet should be together, and the toes pointed toward the ground.

Knee Raising: Hang by the hands at full length. Raise the knees to a level with the hips, knees bent at right angles; hold them there for an instant, and extend them at full length before raising again. Any swing or kick constitutes a foul.

Trunk Lifting: Lie flat on the back, arms folded across the

Fig. 3—Trunk Lifting

chest, then rise to a sitting position keeping the head in line with the trunk. The feet may be held by another person or may be hooked under a support. This movement is repeated slowly for as many times as it is possible. Whenever the head comes forward the contestant has failed and is given credit for the number of trunk lifts completed to this point.

Climbing: The standard rope for this event is one and one-quarter inches in diameter though a smaller rope may be used provided it does not have any assisting devices of any kind such as knots and balls. It must not be fastened at the bottom. The climb using the feet and hands is made to the height required. This is decided by the hands touching the highest point.

Hop Step and Jump: The equipment for this event consists of a take off line or board and a level stretch beyond it about 15 or 20 feet long, at the end of which is a jumping pit 12 to 15 feet long.

With a good running start, take off with either foot and hop (landing on the same foot) then step forward with the other foot, following with a broad jump, landing on both feet. Fouls consist of stepping over the take off line and failing to hop, step or jump in proper order.

Class Athletics

There are many different ways of conducting mass contests in Track and Field Events known as "Class Athletics" in which all members of a class compete against all the members of another group. One such scheme was described under the Pentathlon where points were used in determining the class standing. Another scheme which takes no measuring or recording of points is called the "Shuttle Method." The teams must be equal for this kind of contest.

I. **Shuttle Broad Jump:** Team "A" draws a line on the floor and the first jumper from this team toes this line and jumps. A mark is placed at this jumper's heels and the first jumper from the team "B" toes this mark and jumps in the opposite direction. This continues until all on both teams have jumped. The last jumper will be from team "B" and if by his jump he crosses the original line drawn by team "A" his team has won. If he falls short of this line team "A" has won.

II. **Shuttle Basket Ball Throw:** Conducted as the broad jump.

III. **Mass Running:**
    a. If teams are even they line up behind the starting line, the first member of each team crouching ready to start.

Two starters, one for each team, stand at the finish line. One starter begins the race and holds a handkerchief high. When he brings the handkerchief down this is a signal for the first runner of each team to start. As the runners near the finish line each starter raises his handkerchief and when the runner of his team crosses the line he lowers his handkerchief as a signal for the next runner in that team to start. The team whose last runner crosses the finish line first wins.

b. If teams are uneven just one team lines up behind the starting line and one starter stands at the finish line with a stop watch. When he lowers the handkerchief to start the race he starts the watch and when the last runner of this team crosses the finish line he stops the watch and records the time and the number of runners. This process is then repeated for the other team and then the total time of each team is divided by the number of runners on each team and the result will be the average running time for each team. That team whose average running time is the lower wins. All runners are started by the handkerchief as in "a."

IV. Mass Potato Race: If teams are even the event is conducted just as a regular relay as described on page 47. If teams are uneven the total time for each team is taken and divided by the number running, as in III. b above.

V. Chinning, Trunk Lifting and Knee Raising: Take the total number of lifts of each team in either of these events and divided by the number of each team. If the teams are even no division is necessary and the total will represent the score.

Bibliography

New Rational Athletics for Boys and Girls—Reilly—D. C. Heath & Co.

Track and Field—Ray Conger—A. S. Barnes Co., New York, 1939

Official Recreational Games and Sports Guide, Official Sports Library for Women—A. S. Barnes, New York

RHYTHMICAL ACTIVITIES

I. **Types.**
 1. Rhythmical Interpretations.
    a. Simple rhythms with dramatic content, for example, "The train."
    b. Dramatization with music of various things from child's environment, as "See-Saw" and "Birds Flying."
 2. Singing games.
    a. Traditional, as "Looby Loo."
    b. Mother Goose.
    c. Miscellaneous.
 3. Folk Dances.
    a. All traditional and of various countries.

II. **Significance of Rhythmical Activities.**

In this field we have an opportunity for the expression and satisfaction of inherent instinct tendencies through the rhythmical use of big muscle activity, which will contribute largely to the development of emotional conduct and manners.

The satisfaction comes first from the rhythmical responses made possible. Rhythm which is a strong instinct tendency in man is a law of the universe; it is an astronomical and biological principle, as evidenced by the seasons, and by rhythms of growth and reproduction in plants and animals; it is a physiological principle, as evidenced by the heart beat and respiration; it is a law of hygiene, as evidenced by the importance to health of regularity in habits of living; that it is a deep-seated physical tendency is shown by the fact that our natural movements developed during childhood take on rhythmical characteristics, for example, walking and running. Rhythm, then, is a fundamental law of life and it is to be expected that rhythm should offer a very strong appeal to man, and its responses give great satisfaction. When satisfying responses are made to instinct tendencies, doing is in harmony with being, and normal development results.

The satisfaction comes, however, not only from the rhythmical responses made possible through the big muscle activity, but also through the responses in expression made possible. These responses in expression are evidenced in joy, in dramatization of emotions or ideas inherent in the dance itself, or in interpretation of the thought or feeling of the music. Much of the material is traditional, has lived with the race, is a part of the race, because it has grown out of the feeling, thought, and customs of people for many generations. It is therefore sound material to be used as a means of emotional education. Other material is taken from child life, and with music sympathetic to the thought, the child has opportunity for self expression through bodily movement, which is the first, most fundamental, most integrally associated, and most universal mode of human expression.

The content of rhythmic work centers around big muscle activity, which is favorable to the securing of the objectives of Physical Education. It is surprising how many singing games, folk dances, and rhythmical interpretations can be done in the aisles of the schoolroom with all the children active. Large returns in development can be expected from this type of big muscle play activity.

III. Dance Steps and Use of Music.

A. Elemental Rhythmical Activities are those which have as a rule been learned before the child comes to school. They arise out of instinct tendencies and their development usually proceeds without instruction. These elemental rhythmical activities are walking, running, hopping, skipping, galloping, sliding, jumping, leaping, stamping, clapping.

These elements combined in various ways make up the common dance steps used in folk dancing, as the polka step, for example, which is a combination of hopping, and galloping. Folk dancing employs the elemental activities, plus their simple combinations, almost wholly. Each dance is characterized by its particular pattern which is a result of the manner in which it utilizes these steps and makes changes with the phrasing of the music.

B. Importance of Music.

    a. Rhythm or Time: 4/4; 6/8; 2/4; 3/4.

By the rhythm of the music, we mean the recurring beats or pulses which are felt, and, because of an emphasized pulse occurring at regular intervals, the music takes on a particular rhythm and is divided into measures of so many beats, resulting in 4/4 time, 2/4 time, etc.

Children naturally respond to the feeling of pulse in music and can readily pick out the accented beats. A part of the foundation work in teaching folk dancing is this listening and responding, by means of hand clapping or tapping, foot tapping, and experimentation with elemental activities. The learning of the steps of a dance follows rapidly the preliminary study of the rhythm of the music.

    b. Phrasing.

By "Phrasing" we mean the grouping of measures into units of melody. The number of whole melodies is first determined.

Then one melody is listened to and, wherever in it there seems to be a break where a change in the dance could logically come, such a break is determined. The melody is thus divided into its breaks or half or quarter units. We call these units phrases. Children readily pick out these breaks and determine the number of times changes can be made in the dancing. This is also a matter of rhythm, for these breaks occur at regular intervals.

The learning of the pattern of a dance follows rapidly the study of the phrasing of its music. When a dance is worked out in this manner it becomes unnecessary for the teacher to state the number of steps taken. The music determines this wholly for the child. The learning of the dance then is not a memory drill, but a thinking out process by the child. Dancing taught in this manner is a decidedly educational activity.

In dances having a traditional form, as the folk dances and many singing games, this traditional form must be adhered to. Therefore, after the class has determined rhythm and phrasing, the teacher gives the exact changes to be made in accordance with the traditional form, and because of the previous attention to the music, the class rapidly fits these changes to the music.

C. Derived Dance Steps.

1. **Polka** | step together | step hop 2/4 or 6/8 time
   Counts: | 1 and | 2 and

(a) The manner of developing the polka step is a matter of employing an elemental step and the process of phrasing.

a. Use a 6/8 rhythm (page 126) or music for Tantoli, (page 235); galloping or sliding will be one elemental activity which the children will wish to do with this music. (2 gallops or 2 slides to a measure)

b. Work out long phrase. Ask children to mark phrases by changing feet as they slide. (This makes a change at every 8 slides)

c. Can break be observed more frequently? Where? (Clap) Can a change of feet be made that frequently? Try it. (This makes a change every 4 slides)

d. Can we change still more often? Listen and clap when. (Children clap first beat of each measure) Try with feet. A change is made every 2 slides, or every measure, and the result is the polka step, step-together-step hop)

(b) Polka Series. For drill purposes in learning the polka step and in phrasing, series of steps can be used.

The numbers suggested are not to be stated to the children, but are given here for convenience in noting a phrase.
    a. 4 Polka steps forward
       4 Polka steps back to place
       4 Polka steps across to right
       4 Polka steps across to left
       Repeat.
    b. 4 Polka steps followed by
       8 skip steps—Any direction
       Repeat.
    c. Same as a, but 2 polkas in each direction
    d. 2 polkas
       4 skips turning in place
       Repeat turning other direction
       Repeat all

Any combinations of the above can be used or harder ones devised. Plan a series that can be done in the aisles of the schoolroom. For the gymnasium, series working with partners can be planned.

This kind of drill appeals to girls, and can lead into the selection of a fairly difficult series, which can be given as a "Rhythm Test" along with other "Motor Ability Tests." When used as a test, the child is graded and awarded points on (a) accuracy of phrasing (b) correctness of rhythm (c) accuracy of dance step.

  2. **Heel-toe Polka.**
      Step: Touch heel forward | touch toe back — hop
      Counts: 1 | 2   and
          step together | step |
            1   and | 2 |

2/4 or 6/8 time. Trunk bends in opposite direction to touch of foot. Note sequence and count of polka, with hop first.
    a. Develop Polka as above
    b. Class claps rhythm (2 beats to measure)
       Class claps phrasing (short phrases—2 measures each)
    c. Show class how the beats of each measure can be utilized in a short phrase of two measures by doing a "heel-toe polka"
    d. Class works on it. Can be done in schoolroom
  3. **Step-Hop**.

	Step right	hop right	step left	hop left
Polka 2/4 time:	1	2	1	2
Schottische 4/4 time:	1	2	3	4

Use 2/4 music as Tantoli or 4/4 music as Highland Schottische.

      a. Listen to music to clap beats

      b. Class can be allowed to experiment to see what elemental activities can be combined to fit with music, or

      c. Teacher shows how step hop is done with the beats of the music

      d. All drill on it, bringing knee of free foot up in front on the hop

Note: For a more detailed method see Type Lesson I, page 122, in relation to developing the "Hop Waltz."

4. **"Hop Waltz."**

This can be developed as the step-hop. It differs in execution in that the free leg is raised sideways on the hop, instead of forward. It is usually done turning around at the same time progressing forward, and is done with a partner.

See Type Lesson I, page 122.

5. **Bleking Step.**

See Type Lesson I, page 122 and page 236.

6. **Schottische.** 4/4 time.

Step forward r.	bring l. foot up and step on it	step forward r.	hop r.
1	2	3	4

(a) Use March page 125 or Schottische page 261.

When repeated, begin with left foot.

      a. Listen to music, tapping out beats

      b. Teacher shows use of beats to make a schottische step

      c. Class drills on it. On beat 4 (the hop) swing free foot forward and knee up in front

(b) Schottische Series.

      a. 1 Schottische forward, r.

      4 Running steps in place, l, r, l, r, bringing feet up behind.

      1 Schottische forward, l
      4 Runs in place, r, l, r, l
      Repeat

      b. Repeat "a", but turn in place with running steps

      c. 2 Schottische steps forward, r and l
      4 Step hops, r, l, forward
      Repeat

      d. 1 Schottische step forward r.
      2 Step hops, l, r, turning in place
      1 Schottische step forward l.
      2 Step hops. r, l, turning in place
      Repeat

The above can be done in the aisles of the schoolroom. Other combinations can be made, and for use in the gymnasium a series for couples can be worked out.

Girls will enjoy drill work in these dance steps, and a series can be arranged as a "Rhythm Test," as explained under the Polka.

7. Mazurka.

Step: Slide r. | Bring l. to r. and take weight | Hop on l.
| | lifting r. forward | bend r. knee up
Counts: 1 | 2 | 3

(a) 3/4 Mazurka time, with a decided accent. Use music for "Bounding Heart." The step is always performed with same foot, unless other steps intervene.

  a. Listen to music, and clap out rhythm
  b. Teacher shows how beats are used to make a mazurka step
  c. Practice with one foot several times; then with other
  d. Practice with both feet can be given by taking Series "a" below

(b) Mazurka Series
  a. 3 Mazurkas forward, r. (3 measures)
   3 stamps in place, r, l, r. (1 measure)
   3 Mazurkas forward, l. (3 measures)
   3 stamps in place, l, r, l. (1 measure)
  b. 3 Mazurkas forward, r. (3 measures)
   Step forward, r., jump forward on both feet. (1 measure)
   3 Mazurkas forward, l. (3 measures)
   Step forward, l, and jump on both feet. (1 measure)
  c. 1 Mazurka forward, r. (1 measure)
   Slide forward right foot and hop twice on it. (1 measure)
   1 Mazurka, left. (1 measure)
   Slide forward left foot and hop twice on it. (1 measure)
   Repeat.
  d. Repeat "c" turning about in place on the slide, hop, hop.

8. Bob (peasant) Courtesy.

(a) Step sideways right (Ct. 1); bring left toe to right heel and bend right knee (Ct. 2)
  For drill in it the following series may be used. Use March, page 125.

a. Four steps forward, beginning r. (1 measure)
2 courtesies (step r, and bend; step l, and bend) (1 measure)
Repeat
b. Four skips forward, beginning r (1 measure)
2 courtesies (1 measure)
Repeat
c. Two polka steps forward, r, l.
2 courtesies
Repeat

(b) In folk dances this courtesy is done as follows:
Place left toe to right heel, and bend right knee. (Ct. 1)
Straighten knee (Ct. 2). See Swedish Klapp Dance.

IV. Teaching a Folk Dance.

1. The music is main guide in learning a dance (See page 114).

(a) Listen to music:
Clap out rhythm
Clap out phrasing
Become familiar with music; whistle or hum melody

(b) Suggestion and experimentation as to types of rhythmical steps which can be done to the music

(c) Teacher follows this with final dance structure in its traditional form. If possible teach the entire dance in one lesson.

2. The teacher's main aim should be to get a spontaneous expression of joy in the dancing. Therefore, too great emphasis should not be placed upon perfection of execution. Review the dance often when learned, for then it becomes "play for play's sake."

3. Have groups demonstrate for each other. Much can be learned by observing, and greater effort at proper phrasing can thus be stimulated.

V. Formations.

Formations used in Folk Dancing are found on pages 120 and 121 and for schoolroom on page 312.

The usual line of direction, called forward line of direction when speaking of a moving circle, is counterclockwise, which is moving to one's right when facing center. The reverse line of direction is clockwise, or to one's left.

The position of the boy when dancing with a girl is always at left side.

120

Diagram I — Single circle facing center.

Diagram II — Single circle facing to move counter-clockwise. (clockwise—backward—left; counter-clockwise—forward—right)

Diagram III — Single circle. Partners facing each other.

Diagram IV — Double circle facing center.

Diagram V — Double circle facing to move counter-clockwise.

Diagram VI — Double circle. Partners facing each other.

Formations for Folk Dancing

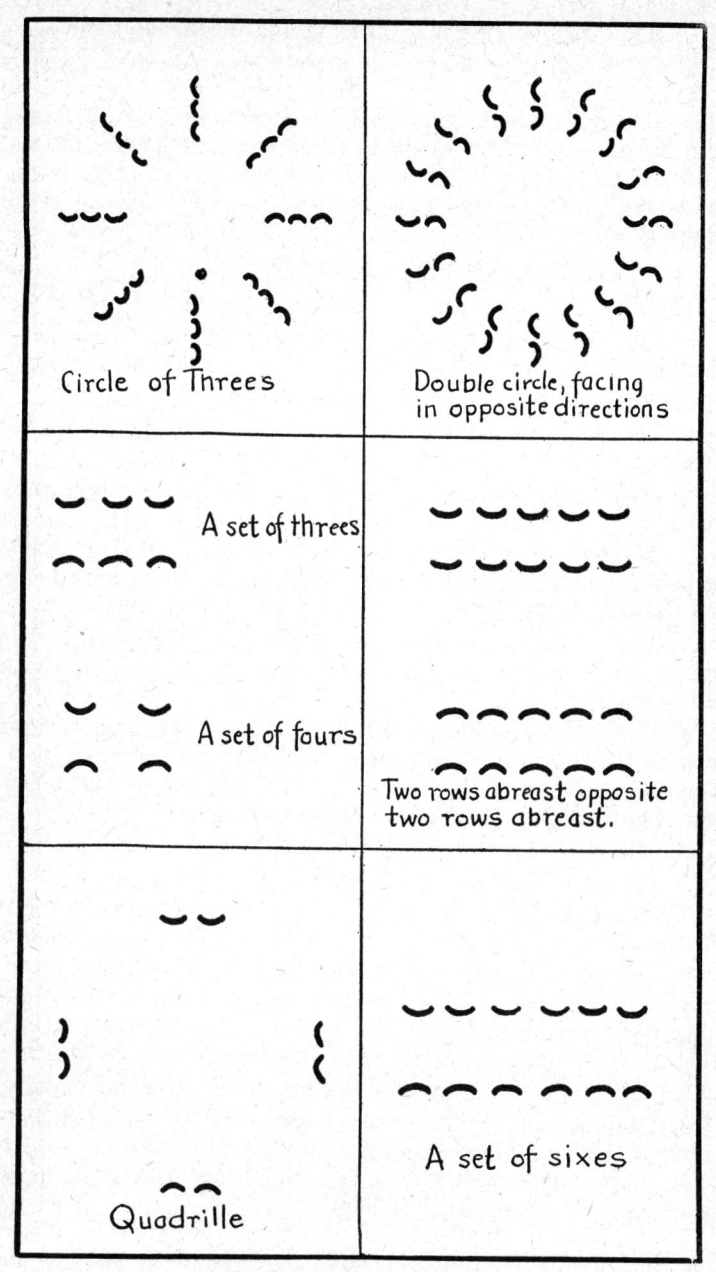

Formations for Folk Dancing

Type Lesson in Folk Dancing for the Schoolroom

Note: While there are some dances that can be done in their complete original form in the schoolroom there is almost no dance that cannot be taught there in its parts and then be taken to an open room or out of doors to be put together in its final form. Even though the weather is cold most dances are strenuous enough to keep the dancers warm out of doors after the dance is once learned.

Bleking (See p. 236)

Formation: Class seated at desks.

1. Play music once through and ask the class to notice if there is an introduction and if there is more than one melody.
2. Ask class the answer to above questions.
3. Play music again and ask class to raise hands at change in melody.
4. Play music and ask class to clap rhythm any way they wish.
5. Repeat and see if any one can clap it differently. (The probable result here will be the clapping of the whole beats and the half beats).
6. Ask if they can combine the two ways of clapping so that one measure will be clapped with whole beats and one with half beats.
7. When this has been accomplished have class move right hand forward and left hand backward then reverse their positions to one measure then reverse 3 times to the second measure. Continue this throughout the first melody.
8. Still sitting try the same with the feet.
9. Repeat with hands and feet.
10. Stand and move right foot and right hand forward and left foot and left hand backward and reverse slowly, then 3 times quickly throughout melody. This is the Bleking Step.
11. Every other person in each row faces backward and joins both hands with person standing back of him. Both starting with right foot and right hand repeat above.
12. Sit again and clap the rhythm for the second melody.
13. Repeat same but turn the hands over on each two half beats (if they suggest beating half beats first time.)
14. Repeat by tapping desk two half beats with right hand then two half beats with left hand.
15. Have class stand and do with feet what they have just done with hands (Step hop on right foot then on left.)
16. Partners face again and join hands outstretched side-

ways. All facing front of room start with left foot and all facing back of room start with right foot and repeat above.

17. Still facing and with hands joined repeat dance from beginning. Warn those facing front to change feet when second melody begins.

18. Have all but one row sit down. Have this row come to front of room and with partners repeat the dance but try turning around when the step hop of the second melody is done.

19. Repeat and see if they can progress from right to left (considering those facing front of room) as they turn around on second melody.

20. Have this row sit and have each other row do in turn as this row has done.

21. The dance is now ready to be done in circle formation so should be taken to the playground or gymnasium for this.

Type Lesson in Folk Dancing for the Gymnasium
Cshebogar (See p. 229)

Formation: Class standing in a single circle facing inward.

1. Play record through and ask class to observe the following points:
   1. Is there an introduction?
   2. How many melodies are there?
   3. Are any of these melodies repeated?
2. Ask for answers to above questions.
3. Play record through again and ask class to raise hands on the first beat of the music after the introduction, and at beginning of second melody.
4. Play the first melody only and ask the class to mark the breaks in it by holding up their hands. (They will probably note the four big phrases).
5. Repeat the first melody and ask class to think which ones of the simple steps they could do to this music.
6. Call for suggestions. Whatever suggestion is offered either have the person offering it demonstrate the step suggested or have all of class try it. After several suggestions have been made and tried including slide, skip and walk, have class try marking the breaks (phrases) by skipping forward to end of first phrase then turn around and skip back to end of second, etc.
7. Have class join hands and try sliding to right to first break and sliding back to left to second break.
8. Whistle or hum the third phrase (which is a repeat of the first one) and ask them to raise their hands where they

would start out if they were to walk into center of circle and out again on that one phrase.

9. When some have accomplished this let them try walking in and out on the one phrase and see if they get back where they started from and have all music used up. Keep trying this until someone gets it just right.

10. Have whole class try walking in and out.

11. Ask what there is left of the first melody—(one phrase). Tell them to face their partners and with outstretched and joined hands skip around in place turning right, to the end of this phrase.

12. Repeat the first melody and see if all can do it from beginning.

13. Play second melody and clap the emphasized beats raising the right hand high at the end of each phrase.

14. Play just the first phrase, and, with partners facing and hands joined, with sides toward center of circle step toward the center of the circle on the first emphasized beat. Draw the other foot up to this foot on the next unemphasized beat.

15. Play second phrase but this time step toward outside of circle on first emphasized beat thus returning to the starting point.

16. Whistle or hum the third phrase and mark the center of it. Ask class to use the same step as above, but go in and out on the one phrase.

17. Skip with partner, turning right in place on rest of melody (one phrase).

18. Repeat all of second melody.

19. Repeat whole dance.

RHYTHMICAL ACTIVITIES
FOR
PRIMARY GRADES

March

HOLLAENDER *

* By permission of Theodore Presser Co.

Skip

From Sorrentina - LACK *

★ *By permission of Theodore Presser Co.*

Birds Flying

This music can be used for different interpretations where swift, yet soft noiseless action is to be expressed, as snow falling, leaves dropping, butterflies, etc. Fast yet very quiet steps on the toes, with arms moving down and up would suggest "Flying Birds."

Rocking Dolly

BRAHMS

Slow 3/4 rhythm.

The manner of expression, whether dollies are held in the arms or rocked in a cradle is left to the children. Uniformity should be a result of selection by the class.

Raindrops

Raindrops *(Continued)*

The quick light patter of the falling rain can be interpreted by the quick light patter of little feet.

The Train

The Train*

Much opportunity for variety and detail in expression can come from the study of the train. The starting, full speed ahead, stopping; the train of cars, with engine and caboose; the sound of the engine by the scuffling of feet; the piston and drive-wheel, by the movement of the bent arms at the side, etc. From the standpoint of the music, note values, rhythm, acceleration and retard can be expressed by movement.

PHYSICAL EDUCATION 131

*Music from Crawford's "Rhythms of Childhood." Copyright 1915, A. S. Barnes Co., Publishers.

Rolling a Hoop

Use a 3/4 rhythm. The children run, following out the beats of the measure in their run, that is, run three steps to the measure. While running they swing their right arms to strike a real or imaginary hoop on the accented beat or first beat of each measure.

Use music for "Birds Flying."

Jumping the Rope

Jumping Rope*

Use 6/8 rhythm, or 2/4 where note values are dotted 8″ and 16″. Without or with ropes. Children perform the various modes of rope jumping according to their desires. If in a schoolroom, no ropes are used and all must decide upon uniform interpretations.

*Music from Hofer's "Music for the Child-World," Vol. II. Used by permission of Clayton F. Summy Co., Publishers.

Jumping Jack

Rhythm—4/4 time

On the accented beats of the measure (1st and 3d) a high jump from both feet may be made, bringing knees well up and out. All joints are loose and arms flop in various directions, and sometimes stick in some position to which they have flopped.

The interpretation should be free, the children responding according to their experiences.

This music is good for leaping, and for the Schottische.

Playing Ball

Use 3/4 rhythm or 6/8 rhythm. With or without ball.

When done without ball, children can freely, according to their own pleasure, dramatize playing ball, bounce and catch, throw into the air or across to a playmate.

When balls are used, certain definite stunts may be set to be performed by all at the same time, as bouncing with right hand and catching with left. Plan progression from lesson to lesson. Refer to Ball Exercises on page 28.

Playing Soldier

Playing Soldier*

Music: Any good lively march. The players are in a circle or, if in schoolroom, arranged as in Diagrams, page 312.

Various soldier activities are dramatized; at each new strain of the march rhythm, a change to a different activity is made. Suggested activities are:

1. March very erect through one strain of music, saluting at the end as heels come together in the halt.
2. Form soldier caps with hands on head, march again as erect as ever, around circle.
3. Continue marching, beating snare drum.
4. Beat bass-drum.
5. Blow bugle.
6. Blow fife.
7. Skip, waving the flag. Standard bearer.
8. Charge with guns. Run forward; kneel on next to last measure of strain; aim; and fire with a loud "bang" on last beat.

* Music from Crawford's "Dramatic Games and Dances." Copyright 1908, by A. S. Barnes & Co.

The Swing I

Arr. G. V. N.

How do you like to go up in a swing, Up in the air so blue? Oh, I do think it the pleas-ant-est thing ev-er a child can do.

I. Formation: Children in groups of threes; two are facing each other, with crossed hands joined; (they represent the swing) the third, who pushes the swing, faces their joined hands and grasps them with both of his hands. The swinger pushes the swing forward on the first part of the first measure and lets it swing back on the second part of the same measure.

PHYSICAL EDUCATION 135

The swinging is continued until the last swing, when the swinger runs under the swing and goes on to the next swing. After a time children change places.

Swing Song II

Arr. G. V. N.

Swing high, swing low Up in the air we go, We touch the leaves of the ma-ple trees; Swing-ing high and low.
Swing high, swing low Like lit-tle birds we fly, We fly so high that we touch the sky; Let-ting the old cat die.

II. Another interesting swinging game is played with music II. The game is played using the same formation as the above. The swinger swings all through the song swinging more slowly toward the end as "the old cat dies." Then those forming the swing hold hands high in an arch as the swingers run under all the way around the circle and back to place with running steps. The music is repeated for the running but is not sung; the tempo being a little more lively and without the retard at the end. For succeeding repetitions of the game the children change places.

See-Saw

Arr. G. V. N.

A slow swinging 3/4 rhythm is needed. The following different interpretations are possible:

1. Partners in double file or double circle facing each other, both hands joined. One child bends knees way down on the first measure. As he straightens on the second measure his partner fully bends his knees. They continue to alternate. They thus interpret the children at each end of the board.

2. Each child by himself interprets the action of the one who stands on the center of the board. With arms held out at side he steps far over sideways upon the right foot, raising

the left leg sideways, then transfers weight to left foot, raising right sideways. One measure for each step.

3. This is a combination of 1 and 2. The formation of 1 is used. The movement of 1 is done through one phrase of music (4 measures). Then the movement of 2 is used, each child going in the same direction, that is, one right and one left as they face each other—for one phrase (4 measures). The two movements are repeated in alternation through the music, phrase by phrase.

4. This is still another combination of 1 and 2. The line or circle is divided into threes. Each set of threes form a line, the two ends facing the center child who represents both the board and the child who stands in the center of the board. His arms are stretched sideways and each end player takes hold of one of his hands. These players then execute movements of 1, while the center player executes movements of 2. After having played once through, the children exchange places.

All of the above forms can be adapted to the aisles of the schoolroom.

Since the bending and stretching of knees quickly tires the children, the teacher is cautioned not to carry this activity on too long. A good plan with the music given is to perform the movement for 8 measures, then rest 8 measures, and so on.

Elephants

Free expression should be sought. A possible interpretation is a heavy slow lumbering step, taken more or less sideways, body swaying with step. Trunk is relaxed far forward, and the arms which hang down relaxed swing as the elephant's trunk.

March on page 125 may be used played slowly and heavily.

The Butterfly

I wish that I could float thru the air And cir-cle round and round I wave my arms and hop and skip But can-not leave the ground. Do not go but-ter-fly but-ter-fly but-ter-fly.

poco rit.   *pp*

Butterfly*

I. Without using words, work for freedom of interpretation. The smooth easy flying of the butterfly, its soaring up, then down, and its flitting from flower to flower.

II. With singing the words, the thought and feeling of the words are expressed in movement.

*Song from Alys Bentley's "Play Songs," used by permission of Laidlaw Bros., 1922 Calumet Ave., Chicago.

Examples of Rhythmical Interpretations with Thought Sequence

I. The Snow Storm

1. Trees blown by the wind, 3/4 rhythm. Music on page 133 can be used.
2. The snow falling quickly but softly. Fast running movement, preferably 3/4 time. Music, page 127 or 129.
3. Children happily skipping out to play in new-fallen snow, 6/8 rhythm. Page 126.
4. Walking through deep snow. March, page 125.
5. Shoveling the walk. March, page 125.
6. The snow-birds who live out-doors all winter. 3/4 time, soft and fluttering. Page 127.

II. Christmas Rhythms

1. Children tip-toeing in to hang up stockings. A soft, mysterious, or a sleepy rhythm. Page 39 of reference No. 2 below.
2. Santa Claus driving Reindeer. A galloping rhythm. See page 203.
3. Santa Claus coming in carrying a heavy pack. Slow, heavy march. See page 125.
4. The various toys left by Santa Claus.
    a. Mechanical Doll. Stiff accented march. Page 51 of reference 2 below is excellent.
    b. Jack-in-the-box. Any rhythm with sharp, accented phrases. Page 55 of reference 2. Also page 107 of reference 1, Vol. II.
    c. New Dolly—rocking it to sleep. Page 128.
    d. A Train of Cars. Fast run. Page 130.
    e. Elephant. See page 137.
    f. Top. Page 23 of Reference 3.
    g. Ball. Page 133.
    Others, ad libitum.

Suggested subjects for more studies in rhythmical interpretations with thought sequence:
1. The Carpenter
2. The Farmer
3. Helping Mother
4. On the Play-ground
5. The Circus Animals

6. Picnic in the Woods
7. A Day on the Farm

Reference books with excellent music for Children's Rhythms:

1. Hofer—"Music for the Child-World," Vol. I, II and III. (Especially valuable is Vol. II)—Clayton F. Summy Co., Chicago.

2. Crawford—"Rhythms of Childhood"—A. S. Barnes Co., N. Y.

3. Bentley "Play Songs"—Laidlaw Bros., Chicago.

The Gallant Ship

Arr. G. V. N

Three times a-round went the gal-lant ship, And three times a-round went she; And three times a-round went the gal-lant ship, And she sank to the bot-tom of the sea.

Formation: Single circle, all facing center with hands joined. Slide around the circle sideways to the left, during first three lines of stanza. On the fourth line, "and she sank," etc. the players stop sliding and jump in place three times on the words, "sank," "bottom," and "sea." On the last jump all finish in a deep knee bend position.

Repeat all sliding right.

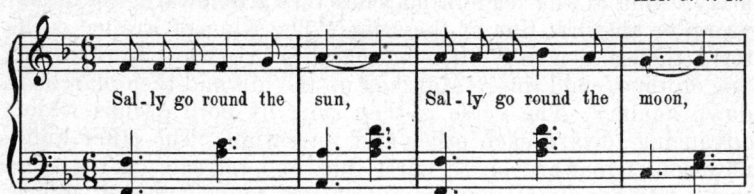

Sally Go Round the Sun

Arr. G. V. N.

Sal-ly go round the sun, Sal-ly go round the moon,
Sal-ly go round the chim-ney pot, On a Sun-day af-ter-noon. *Spoken* Whoo!

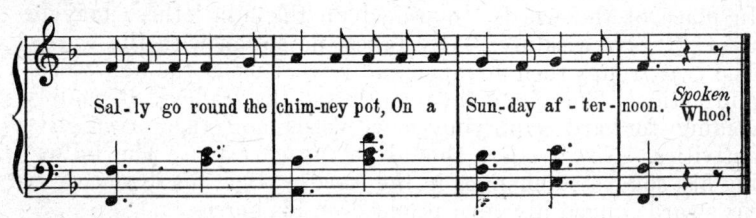

English.

Formation: Children in a circle, hands joined. One player in the center.

The circle skips around to the left. On the whoop at the end, all jump high in the air, then land in a low squat position. The player in the circle watches to see who is last one down. The game is repeated.

The King Of France

Arr. G. V. N.

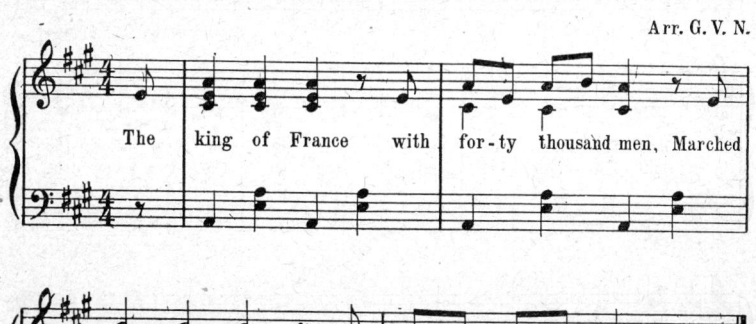

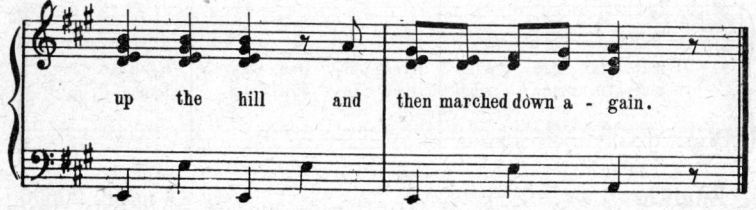

The king of France with for-ty thousand men, Marched up the hill and then marched down a-gain.

The players stand in two rows facing each other, each row having a leader who stands in the center and is king of his army. One of the leaders marches forward toward the other group on the first line of the song, "The King of France with forty thousand men;" then he marches backward toward his line on the second line, "Marched up the hill and then marched down again." The verse is then sung by both groups while advancing toward each other and retreating. The other king now comes forward on the first line, and retreats on the second. He, however, changes the words replacing such other words as indicate soldier activities as he chooses. For example: In place of the words "marched up the hill," these may be used: "gave a salute." He takes the action with the words. The two groups then advance and retreat using the new words and action. The game thus continues, the leaders alternately coming forward supplying new words and their respective activities. New leaders should be chosen often. The following are suggested changes in the words: Beat his drum; drew his sword; aimed his gun; pranced on his horse.

The Muffin Man

Arr. G. V. N.

Oh do you know the muf-fin man, the muf-fin man, the muf-fin man? Oh do you know the muf-fin man who lives in Drury Lane?

Oh yes, I know the muf-fin man, the muf-fin man. Oh yes, I know the muf-fin man who lives in Drury Lane.

English.   Victor: 20806

Formation: Single circle, facing center with one or more in the center.

Those in the center skip four steps forward and four steps back two times each before a player in the circle, as they sing the first verse.

The circle players before whom they dance answer by skipping four steps forward and four steps back two times toward the center players, as they sing the second verse. The remaining circle players during this verse jump up and down in place, hands joined around the circle or on hips, and sing "Oh, yes, we know the muffin man, etc."

A third verse is then sung by the center players and those addressed, who, clasping hands, skip around inside the circle with the words "Now we both know the muffin man, etc." The circle players at same time skip in the opposite direction around the circle.

The game is now started from the beginning, all of those in the center now advancing each toward a circle player.

The game is repeated until all players have partners and are skipping around the circle, when they sing "Now we all know the muffin man," etc.

At Christmas time, the words "Muffin man" can be replaced by "dear Santa Claus," and "that lives in Drury Lane" by "who comes at Christmas time."

In the schoolroom "The Muffin Man" may be played as follows: Four or five children are selected who leave their seats as the first verse is sung and walk or skip up and down the aisles stopping at some child's seat. The child chosen by each player is taken by the hand and during the singing of the second verse, the two skip forward to the space in front of the room where all form a small circle. The circle then dances around singing the third verse. As the game is repeated, the first verse being sung again, the partners chosen select new partners, while the original players take their seats. The game is thus continued until all have had a chance to play.

Rabbit in the Hollow

Arr. G V N

Rab-bit in the hol-low sits and sleeps
Hunt-er in the for-est near-er creeps.
Lit-tle rab-bit have a care, Deep with-in the hol-low there,
Quick-ly to your home you must run, run, run.

One child crouches asleep in the center of the circle while the children in a single circle holding hands walk about him singing the words. Another child outside of the circle walks about pretending to be looking for a rabbit. On the words "Run, Run, Run", the children stop, drop hands and the hunter

PHYSICAL EDUCATION   145

on the outside gives chase to the rabbit. After the rabbit is caught, a new rabbit and hunter are chosen.

The Farmer In The Dell

Arr. G. V. N.

Victor: 21618

English.
2. The farmer takes a wife
   The farmer takes a wife
   Heigh-o! the cherry-oh!
   The farmer takes a wife

The succeeding verses vary as follows:
3. The wife takes a child, etc.
4. The child takes a nurse, etc.
5. The nurse takes a dog, etc.
6. The dog takes a cat, etc.
7. The cat takes a rat, etc.
8. The rat takes a cheese, etc.
9. The cheese stands alone, etc.

Formation: Single circle, all facing center with hands joined. One child within the ring represents the farmer.

During the first verse the players walk or skip around the circle to the left. During the remaining verses the circle continues moving. On the second verse, the center player or farmer chooses another child to join him in the center. This continues with each verse, the wife choosing a child, the child a nurse, the nurse a dog, etc., down to the cheese. When the ninth stanza is sung everyone jumps up and down and claps hands, as the others within the ring join the circle. The cheese now stands alone and is farmer for the next game.

When played out of doors, the ninth verse can be omitted and on "the rat takes the cheese," the rat points to the cheese who leaves the circle, and after the completion of the stanza all chase after the cheese. The one catching him becomes the new farmer.

Another form of playing this game is to sing through the eighth stanza, then add eight more, the first one being "The farmer goes away," after which the wife, child, nurse, dog, cat and rat go away in turn, the sixteenth stanza being "The cheese stands alone." During the singing of these verses each player joins the ring until the cheese is left alone in the center. Upon the singing of the last stanza the children jump up and down and clap hands.

1. The farmer plants the corn

The Farmer Plants the Corn

Music: Farmer in the Dell, page 145.
  The farmer plants the corn
    Heigh-Ho the cherry-o,
  The farmer plants the corn.
2. The wind begins to blow
  The wind begins to blow
    Heigh-Ho the cherry-o
  The wind begins to blow.
3. The rain begins to fall, etc.
4. The sun begins to shine, etc. ⎱ Play music for these
5. The corn begins to grow, etc. ⎰ verses slowly.
6. The farmer cuts the corn, etc.
7. He binds them into sheaves, etc.
8. We all are happy now, etc.

Formation: Part of the players, the seeds of corn, are in a single circle, standing apart, facing center. Other players stand outside the circle—the farmer, the wind (three to four players), the rain (several players) and the sun (one player).

1. The farmer skips into the circle and plants the corn. He touches lightly the heads of the circle players, who bend to a deep-knee bend position; the farmer returns to his place.
2. The "wind" group with hands joined in a line run into the circle and in and out among the seeds. They bend forward as they run. They then return.
3. The "rain" group run lightly in and out, using arms and fingers as falling rain.
4. The sun walks in tall and erect, with arms forming a circle overhead.
5. The corn slowly grows until at full height, arms stretched upward.

PHYSICAL EDUCATION 147

6. The farmer skips in again, moves around the circle on the inside and with a cutting movement of his right arm, cuts the corn. As each circle player is passed, he bends forward dropping trunk and head.

7. The farmer skips around circle collecting players quickly into circles of threes. They raise trunks.

8. The sun, wind, and rain come in and with the farmer form a small circle and skip around within the large circle. The circles of threes—the sheaves—jump up and down on both feet and move around their own small circle with these little jumps.

Looby Loo

Arr. G. V. N.

English.

Victor: 20214
Columbia: A-3148

Introduction and chorus:
　Here we dance looby loo,
　Here we dance looby light,
　Here we dance looby loo,
　All on a Saturday night, Whoop!

Verses:
1. I put my right hand in,
　I put my right hand out,
　I give my right hand a shake, shake, shake,
　And turn myself about. Whoop!
2. I put my left hand in, etc.
3. I put my right foot in, etc.
4. I put my left foot in, etc.
5. I put my head 'way in, etc.
6. I put my whole self in, etc.

Formation: Single circle, all facing left with hands joined.

Introduction and Chorus (after each verse): Players dance around the circle, with skipping, sliding, walking or running steps, first to left for four measures, then to right.

Verses: Players stand facing the center. The action suggested by the words of the verses is given in pantomime. The children should be encouraged to make large and vigorous movements. For line 3 of each verse the movement is made only three times, that is, on the words, "shake, shake, shake." On line 4, clap hands four times as a complete turn with 4 running steps is made. In verse 6 the players jump with both feet together into the circle, then out, then three times fast in place. This game can be played in the aisles of the schoolroom, two rows of children dancing around one row of seats.

Shoemakers' Dance

Arr. G. V. N.

Danish.

Victor: 20450
Columbia: A-3038

Formation: Double circle. Partners face each other.

Measures 1-2: With arm shoulder-high and hands clenched, roll one arm over the other three times. Reverse and roll three times. "Winding and unwinding the thread."

Measure 3: Pull hands apart and jerk elbows backward twice. "Pulling thread tight."

Measure 4: Hammer the fists three times. "Driving the pegs". Repeat measures 1 to 4. On measure 4 clap hands three times.

Measures 5-8 and then repeat: Join inside hands, outside hands on hips. Skip around the ring counter-clockwise. The simple polka step may be used. Repeat from beginning.

When done in the aisles of the schoolroom, two rows of children face each other for the first part. For the skipping all turn right and skip down the aisles and around the row of seats between them for measures 5 to 8; then face about and skip back to place as the same measures are repeated.

London Bridge

Arr. G. V. N.

Lon-don bridge is fall-ing down, Fall-ing down, fall-ing down,

Lon - don bridge is fall - ing down, My fair la - dy.

English.   Columbia: A-3148
                                            Victor: 20806

Build it up with iron bars,
Iron bars, iron bars;
Build it up with iron bars,
  My fair Lady!
Iron bars will bend and break,
  Bend and break, bend and break;
Iron bars will bend and break,
  My fair Lady!
Build it up with gold and silver, etc.
Gold and silver'll be stolen away, etc.
Get a man to watch all night, etc.
Suppose that he should fall asleep, etc.
Get a dog to bark all night, etc.
Suppose the dog should meet a bone, etc.
Get a cock to crow all night, etc.
Here's a prisoner I have got, etc.
What's the prisoner done to you? etc.
Stole my watch and broke my chain, etc.
What will you take to set him free? etc.
One hundred pounds will set him free, etc.
One hundred pounds we have not got, etc.
Then off to prison you must go, etc.
  Two players stand facing each other with both hands clasped and arms raised so that an arch is formed. The remaining players form a long line and walk under the arch. At the end of each stanza as the word "Lady" is sung, the players forming the bridge lower their arms and capture the player

who is passing under the arch at the time. This player is then taken aside and asked to choose between two valuable articles, such as a gold crown or silver slippers. The two players have previously decided privately what they will represent. The prisoner then stands behind the player of his choice. The game goes on until all players have been captured and have chosen the article they wish. A tug of war then takes place. The two players representing the bridge grasp hands tightly and the remaining players take hold around each others' waists. Each line pulls. The side which holds fast without breaking away or which is not pulled across a given line wins the game. Sometimes only the first and last stanzas are sung.

Bean Porridge Hot

Arr. G. V. N.

Victor: 20621

Formation: In double circle, or in two lines, partners facing each other.

Measures 1-2: Clap own thighs with both hands; clap own hands; clap partner's right hand. Repeat clapping left hands.

Measures 3-4: Clap thighs; clap own hands; clap partner's right hand; clap own hands; clap partner's left hand; clap own hands; clap both of partner's hands.

Measures 1-4, repeated; Repeat clapping as above.

The pleasure from this rhythmic study comes from the clapping mainly, but the music can be repeated during which the partners may slide around the circle or down the line and back before starting over, if this is desired. Players can change partners as they finish sliding. This form could be adapted to the schoolroom.

The clapping part can also be done with children sitting in their seats, and clapping hands of those across the aisle.

The Snail

Arr. G. V. N.

Hand in hand you see us well, Creep like a snail in-to his shell. Ev-er near-er, ev-er near-er, Ev-er clos-er, ev-er clos-er, Ve-ry snug in-deed you dwell, Snail with-in your ti-ny shell.

2. Hand in hand you see us well
Creep like a snail out of his shell.
    Ever farther, ever farther.
    Ever wider, ever wider.
Who'd have thought this tiny shell
Could have held us all so well.

Description: The players all stand in line holding hands; while singing the first verse they wind up in a spiral, follow-

PHYSICAL EDUCATION 153

ing the leader, who walks in a circle growing ever smaller until all are wound up, still holding hands. The leader then turns and unwinds, until all are again in one long line.

In place of the unwinding the following can be done: The leader draws the line out by going from the center straight out through the rings, under the raised arms of the players in the several rings around him, as though passing through a hole in the side of the shell. Hands must always remain joined.

Kitty White

Arr. G. V. N.

Kit - ty White so sly - ly comes To catch the mous - ie gray; But mous - ie hears her soft - ly creep, And quick - ly runs a - way. Run, run, run, lit - tle mouse, Run all a - round the house For

Kitty White (continued)

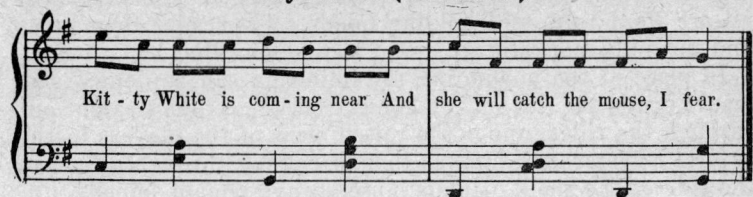

[musical notation with lyrics: "Kit-ty White is com-ing near And she will catch the mouse, I fear."]

One player is chosen for the mouse and stands in the center, and another for Kitty White, who stands outside of the circle. The other players join hands in a ring and move softly around while singing the first four lines. Meanwhile Kitty White is creeping around outside of the circle, peeping in at little Mousie Gray. When the fourth line is reached, "And quickly runs away," the circle stops moving and drops hands while the mouse runs out and in through the circle, chased by Kitty White. For the last four lines while the chase is going on, the players in the circle stand in place and clap their hands while singing "Run, run," etc.

When the mousie is caught both return to the circle, and another mouse and kitty are chosen.

I'm Very, Very Small

[musical notation with lyrics: "I'm ver-y, ver-y small, I'm ver-y, ver-y tall; Some-times small, some-times tall, Guess which I am now." May-be played an octave higher]

I Am Very, Very Small*

No. I. The music and song can just be used as a study in pitch, i.e., whether the music speaks "high" or "low." The children are in a circle or in the aisles of the schoolroom. As they sing, and in accordance with what the music speaks as well as what the words say, the children stoop very low making themselves very small, or they stretch away up high, making themselves very tall. On the last two measures, the teacher may play the music as written or an octave higher. The children not knowing which way it is to be played then suit the movement to the pitch of the music, stretching tall if the music is high, or being very small if the music is low.

No. II. As a game this is played as follows:* The children are in a circle with one child in the center who covers her eyes. Some member of the circle is chosen to tell the rest what they are to do—whether to be tall or small—at the end of the game. As they sing, they stretch up tall or make themselves very small according to the words, until the last two measures (last line of the song) are reached. After a short pause, while the one named at the beginning of the game gives the signal for them all to be either tall or small, they sing quickly, "Guess what I am now," and take that position. The center player guesses which it is. The game is repeated with a new child in the center. The music is always played the same for the last two measures.

* No. I is an adaptation from the No. II which is taken from Crawford's "Dramatic Games and Dances." Copyright, 1908, by A. S. Barnes & Co., Publishers.

Tucker

Formation: A circle of partners, facing to move around the circle. An odd player is in the center.

With music (any march or skipping rhythm): While the music plays the circle players skip (or march) around the circle, and the center player must wait. But when the music stops, all players must rush to the center and secure a new partner, forming the circle again immediately. This gives the center player an opportunity to secure a partner. The one left without a partner when the music begins again must stay in the center alone until it stops and all change partners once more.

Without music: When played without music, the odd player in the center calls "Tucker" whenever he wishes, and all must run to the center and change partners as before, the odd one securing one for himself then, and the game is repeated.

Here We Go Round the Mulberry Bush

Arr. G. V. N.

Here we go round the mul-ber-ry bush, The mul-ber-ry bush, the mul-ber-ry bush, Here we go round the mul-ber-ry bush, So ear-ly in the morn-ing.

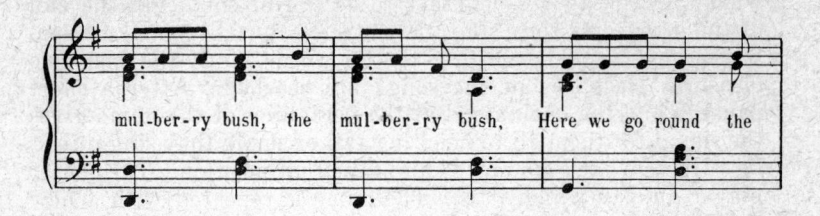

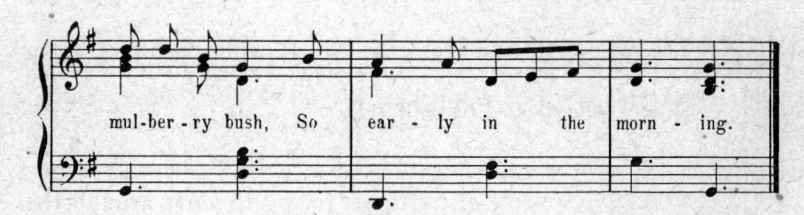

Columbia: A-3149
Victor: 20806

2. This is the way we wash our clothes,
   We wash our clothes, we wash our clothes;
   This is the way we wash our clothes,
   So early Monday morning.
3. This is the way we iron our clothes,
   Etc., so early Tuesday morning.
4. This is the way we sweep the floor,
   Etc., so early Wednesday morning.
5. This is the way we mend our clothes,
   Etc., so early Thursday morning.
6. This is the way we scrub the floor,
   Etc., so early Friday morning.
7. Thus we play when our work is done,
   Etc., so early Saturday morning.
8. This is the way we go to church,
   Etc., so early Sunday morning.

Players form a circle. All join hands and during the first stanza walk around from right to left, swinging the arms in and out in time to the music. In the second and following stanzas the players go through the movements which are indicated by the lines. On the last line of each stanza the players release hands and turn rapidly about in their own places. The first verse is sung and danced after each verse.

Here We Go Round the Christmas Tree

(Adaptation of Mulberry Bush. Music on page 156)

1. Here we go round the Christmas tree,
    Christmas tree, Christmas tree,
   Here we go round the Christmas tree,
    So early Christmas morning.
2. What do you wish that Santa should bring, etc.
3. I should like a big red drum, etc.
4. I should like a nice new doll, etc.
5. I should like a top to spin, etc.

New stanzas can be added according to the suggestions of the children.

Formation: Single circle, facing center. Hands joined. During stanza 1, children skip around an imaginary Christmas tree. During the second stanza they walk into center of circle, then out. In the remaining stanzas suit the action to the words.

This can be done around the seats in the aisles of the schoolroom.

Nuts in May

Music: "The Mulberry Bush," page 156.

The children join hands and form two straight lines about 12 feet apart. The second line stands in place, while the first walks or skips toward the second (meas. 1 to 4) and retires (meas. 5 to 8), singing:

1. Here we come gathering nuts in May,
    Nuts in May, nuts in May;
   Here we come gathering nuts in May,
    On a cold and frosty morning.

The first line stands, while the second advances and retires singing:

2. Whom will you have for your nuts in May,
    Etc.

Those in the first line agree among themselves upon the child in the second line whom they will choose, and advance and retire as before, singing:

3. We will have (child's name) for nuts in May,
    Etc.

The second line advances and retires singing:

4. Whom will you have to pull her away,
   Etc.

Those in first line choose one from their own side and advance and retire, singing:

5. We will have (child's name) to pull her away,
   Etc.

The two children chosen advance midway between the two lines, join right hands and each one tries to pull the other across a line scratched on the ground between them. The losing child goes with the winner to her side. The winning side begins the game again, or the sides may take turns. The children should be urged to choose those who are nearly equal in size and strength.

Let Us Wash Our Dolly's Clothes

Arr. G. V. N.

Let us wash our Dol-ly's clothes, And wring them out to dry, And then we'll turn them in-side out, And hang them up so high.

Formation: Couples facing each other with both hands joined, in line or circle.

Move hands up and down as if rubbing clothes on a board.

At the word "wring," twist hands, still joined around each other, first one pair on top, then the other.

On words "Turn them inside out," turn under hands joined by raising arms on one side high and partners turning under them away from each other, then on around toward each other under the other arms. (This is often called "wring the dish-rag"). Make two such turns.

On words "Hang them up to dry," stretch up on toes with hands high.

I Want to Go to London

Music: Tune to "Pop Goes the Weasel," on page 238.
Formation: Single circle, one player in center.
All sing.

"I want to go to London town;
 How shall I get there?"

Center player sings: "Go the way the ———— go (es)," filling the blank with some word as horses, auto, boat, aeroplane, bicycle, rabbit, elephant, etc. "That's how to get there."

Then the rest of the music is played and all imitate movement of vehicle or animal suggested. Center player then chooses one to take his place.

Cock-a-doodle-doo

[Musical notation with lyrics: "Cock-a-doodle doo! My dame has lost her shoe, My master's lost his fiddle stick And don't know what to do."]

Cock-a-doodle-doo*

Formation: A single circle in line of direction, dancers with hands on hips.

Measures 1-2: Bend right knee upward waist high (count 1); straighten knee straight forward slowly (count 2); step right foot forward raising left heel (count 3); hold (count 4). This should represent the way the rooster walks.

Measures 3-4: Repeat this step with left foot.

Measures 5-8: The Rooster run. Run forward on toes, beginning with right foot, bringing feet forward with stiff knees, and taking long steps. With hands on the hips the elbows may be moved forward and back to imitate the movement of wings.

*From Moses: "Rhythmic Action Plays and Dances." Published by Milton Bradley Co.

Thorn Rosa

Arr. G. V. N.

German.
1. Thorn Rosa was a princess fair, princess fair, princess fair.
Thorn Rosa was a princess fair, princess fair.
2. She lived up in a castle high, castle high, castle high.
She lived up in a castle high, castle high.
3. One day there came an ugly witch, ugly witch, ugly witch.
One day there came an ugly witch, ugly witch.
4. She touched her with her magic wand, magic wand, magic wand. She touched her with her magic wand, magic wand.
5. Thorn Rosa slept a hundred years, hundred years, hundred years.
Thorn Rosa slept a hundred years, hundred years.
6. The thorny hedge grew giant high, giant high, giant high.
The thorny hedge grew giant high, giant high.
7. But brave Prince Charming cut the thorns, cut the thorns, cut the thorns.
But brave Prince Charming cut the thorns, cut the thorns.
8. Thorn Rosa wakened at his touch, at his touch, at his touch.
Thorn Rosa wakened at his touch, at his touch.
9. Oh, all our hearts are happy now, happy now, happy now.
Oh, all our hearts are happy now, happy now.
10. Tra la la la la la la la—etc.

Formation: Two concentric circles facing center, outer representing hedge, inner the castle.

Characters: Prince, Princess and Witch.

1st verse: Princess stands inside inner circle. Prince and witch outside outer circle. Circle join hands and walk around, outer circle to left, inner to right.

2d verse: All stand still, inner circle raising hands high to represent high castle.

3d verse: During singing Witch comes into castle.

4th verse: Witch waves her wand over the Princess who falls asleep at the end.

5th verse: Princess sleeps and Witch leaves circles.

6th verse: Players representing hedge take squat position and rise slowly, stretching arms up with fingers stretched, representing the growth of the hedge.

7th verse: Prince skips around outside circle, touching the upraised arms which fall at his touch. (Cutting the thorns with his sword).

8th verse: Prince enters castle, touches the Princess who rises and they stand with joined hands.

9th and 10th verses: All join hands. Outside circle skips to left, inside to right. Prince and Princess skip around inside inner circle. Reverse directions on 10th verse.

Repeat, choosing new characters.

The Thread Follows the Needle

The thread fol-lows the nee - dle, The thread fol-lows the nee - dle, In and out the nee - dle goes, As moth - er mends the chil - dren's clothes.

The Thread Follows the Needle*

Children form lines and stand side by side hands joined. The players in a line will be numbered from 1 to 10 for convenience. No. 10 is the knot and always stands in place; No. 1 is the needle. The line in between is the thread. No. 1 leads the line down to pass under the arms of Nos. 10 and 9. Nos. 10 and 9 then face in the opposite direction as the line passes under, and as they keep hands joined, they stand with the arms crossed across the chest forming a chain stitch with their crossed arms. The line continues around and the next time

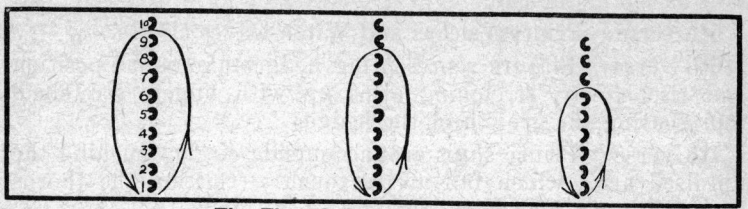

The Thread Follows the Needle

passes between Nos. 9 and 8. This continues until all the players in all the lines are turned in the opposite direction with arms all crossed in front and sewed together. At a signal or chord on the piano, the children turn under top arms, unravelling the chain.

Care should be taken not to drop a stitch or break the thread. The first is done by turning under arm too soon; the second, by letting go of hands.

While the children are learning the song at their seats, they can sew with an imaginary needle and thread and watch the thread grow shorter. They then direct the formation of one group, placing the knot and needle, and help plan the using of the thread.

*From Crawford's "Dramatic Games and Dances," Copyright, 1908, by A. S. Barnes & Co., Publishers.

PHYSICAL EDUCATION 163

Pussy Cat

Arr. G. V. N

Pus-sy cat, pus-sy cat where have you been? I've been to Lon-don to vis-it the queen Pus-sy cat, pus-sy cat what did you there? I fright-ened a lit-tle mouse un-der her chair.

Victor: 20621

Formation: A double circle, partners facing each other.

Nos. 1 (the inside circle) sing first. On, "Pussy Cat, Pussy Cat" they stamp annoyingly and shake forefingers twice. On, "Where have you been?" they clap own hands demandingly four times.

Nos. 2 (outside circle) reply on "I've been to London," etc., with a deep courtesy.

Nos. 1 then ask "Pussy Cat, Pussy Cat, what did you there?" in the same manner as above.

On the answer "I frightened," etc., partners take hold of hands, and slide around rapidly in place to right.

The game is repeated. Nos. 2 asking the questions.

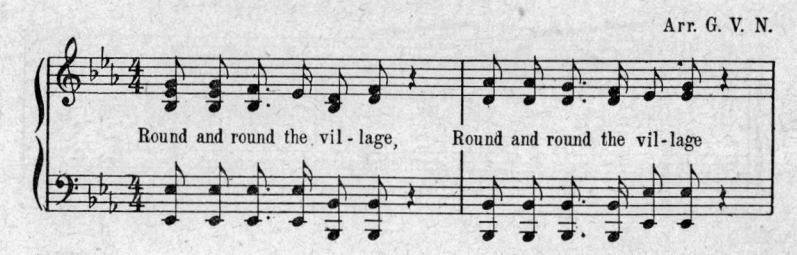

Round and Round the Village

Arr. G. V. N.

Round and round the vil-lage, Round and round the vil-lage, Round and round the vil-lage, As you have done be-fore.

Columbia: A-3148

English.
2. In and out the windows,
   In and out the windows,
   In and out the windows,
   As you have done before.
3. Stand and face your partner,
   (Repeat this line twice more)
   And bow before you go.
4. Follow me to London, etc., (as stanzas 1 and 2).

The children join hands and stand in a ring. One child skips around outside of the circle, as all sing the first stanza. On the second stanza, the children in the circle raise their joined hands as high as possible, and the outside player goes in and out under the arches. Thus winding in and out around the circle. On the third stanza this player stands inside the ring and faces another child, each bowing on the last line. On the fourth stanza the player again skips around outside the circle followed by the child chosen. This part can be made a chasing game; the verse is then repeated until the runner is caught. The runners may wind in and out. In either case the child chosen becomes the leader for the next game. When large numbers are playing, several players may begin at the same time.

How D'ye Do, My Partner

Arr. G. V. N.

Lyrics: How d'ye, do my part-ner, How d'ye do to-day. Will you dance in the cir-cle? I will show you the way. *repeated twice*

Swedish.

Columbia: A-3153
Victor: 21685

Formation: Double circle, partners facing each other.

Measures 1-2: Children in the inside circle make bow or courtesy to partners.

Measures 3-4: Children in outside circle return courtesy.

Measures 5-6: Partners offer first the right hand, then the left to each other.

Measures 7-8: Then with crossed hands joined they turn ready to move forward side by side.

Measures 1-8, repeated twice; sing "Tra la la la la la, etc., with these repeats. Partners run around circle counter-clockwise, three running steps to the measure for eight measures. They then turn in toward each other to face opposite direction and run clockwise in the same manner for eight measures.

Music: For verse, play once through slowly; for chorus, play twice through rapidly.

Note: Boys should use a bow in place of the courtesy, and when girls are their partners the boys are in the inside circle.

This folk dance can be done in the aisles of the schoolroom. Rows face each other for the courtesy, but do not join hands across. The running is taken around the seats, two rows of children around one row of seats. On the change of direction in the run, they will return to their seats.

Old Roger is Dead

Arr. G. V. N.

Old Rog-er is dead and gone to his grave; Hm, ha, gone to his grave.

English.

The children join hands and walk around in a ring, singing verse 1. One child representing Old Roger lies in the center of the ring flat on his back; children, one representing the old woman, one representing the apple tree, two to plant the tree, and one to be the East Wind, stand outside the ring.

2. They planted an apple tree over his head,
   Hm Ha—over his head.

The circle stops moving, the players forming the circle standing still through the rest of the game.

The child representing the apple tree is led into the ring by the two who plant it and stands at Old Roger's head with arm outstretched for branches.

3. The apples were ripe and ready to drop,
   Hm Ha—ready to drop.

4. There came an east wind a-blowing them off,
   Hm Ha—blowing them off.

The East wind enters and blows on the outstretched arms of the Apple Tree. The tree sways and twists from side to side, the branches dipping and swinging.

5. There came an old woman a-picking them up,
   Hm Ha—picking them up.

During this verse the old woman limps into the ring and walks round Old Roger pretending to pick up the apples.

6. Old Roger jumped up and gave her a knock,
   Hm Ha—gave her a knock.

During this verse Old Roger jumps up, slaps the old woman on shoulder and chases her around the ring.

7. Which made the old woman go hippity hop,
   Hm Ha—hippity hop.

During this verse Old Roger continues to chase the old woman in and out of the ring who, limping as she goes, tries not to be caught until the end of the song is reached. Each then chooses a new player, and the game is repeated.

Snowball Game

Arr. G. V. N.

Formation: Single circle with partner.

1. Ho! Ho! Ho! So! So! So!   All join hands and slide
   Ready for frolic and fun.   around circle to left

   We pick up snow
   and roll it so   Make up snowballs
   Into snowballs round.

   Here's one for you
   and one for you   Throw them in various di-
   And one for you and you.   rections

One child who is to be snow man takes his place in center of circle.

2. Big snow man! You must
   go!   Point fingers at snow man
   We will knock you down.

   Your right arm off,   Children t h r o w balls at
   Your left one, too;   snow man who drops arms,
   Pop! Now goes your head.   head, body, etc., as words
   Your body falls,   suggest. At end he falls to
   Your big legs, too!   floor and children cover him
   Now you're surely dead.   with snow, stepping into cen-
                                ter. He joins the circle at end
                                of verse.

3. Ho! Ho! Ho! Fingers cold!   Face partner, shake or rub
   Toes are frozen, too!   fingers and stamp feet

A slap, slap, slap,	Slap own arms 3 times
And a clap, clap, clap,	Clap partner's hands 3 times
Whirling round so, so.	Join partner's hands and whirl around
A tramp, tramp, tramp,	
A stamp, stamp, stamp,	Stamp feet six times
Scampering home we go.	Join hands with partner and skip off breaking circle.

Note: At end of each verse, except the last, music for last six lines is repeated and all join hands and skip to left for three lines and back to right for three lines.

PHYSICAL EDUCATION 169

Three Little Mice

Arr. G. V. N.

Three lit-tle mice went out to see what they could find to have for tea, For they were naugh-ty sauc-y mice and liked to nib-ble some-thing nice But the big round eyes of the wise old cat, See what the three lit-tle mice are at Quick-ly she jumps, but the mice run a-way, And hide in their snug lit-tle holes all day.

Victor: 20621

Formation: Circle of groups of threes. The threes stand

abreast, hands joined facing to move around the circle counter-clockwise. See page 121.

Measures 1 and 2: The three little mice walk gayly forward around the circle.

Measures 3 and 4: They skip gayly forward.

Measures 5 and 6: Threes join hands to form a small circle, and skip around it to left.

Measures 7 and 8: They pretend to nibble on something which they much enjoy.

Measures 9 and 10: Played more slowly. All forming a single big circle now become the cat. They steal forward holding up hands to form "big round eyes."

Measures 11 and 12: Crouch down to watch.

Measure 13: Jump forward.

Measures 14 to 16: They all become mice and each group of threes run outward into a small circle, and crouch down close to each other to hide in their holes.

The following is an adaptation of the above:

Formation: Circle of groups of threes. The threes stand abreast, hands joined, facing to move around the circle counter-clockwise. Within the circle there are as many cats as there are groups of threes.

Measures 1 and 8 are played as in the first description.

Measures 9 and 10; the cats in the center steal out while the mice still nibble.

Measures 11 and 12: The cats crouch to watch the mice.

Measure 13: Cats jump forward.

Measure 14: Mice run away outward from circle in threes.

Measures 15 and 16: Mice crouch down in a small circle of threes, very close together, hiding in their holes.

To Market, To Market

Arr. G. V. N.

To mar-ket to mar-ket to buy a fat pig;
To mar-ket to mar-ket to buy a plum bun;
Home a-gain, home a-gain rig-gi-ty jig; Home a-gain, home a-gain, mar-ket is done.

Formation: Children in a single circle, facing center.

Measures 1 and 2: Skip or gallop forward toward center. On the words "fat pig," each makes a large circle with arms in front of body.

Measures 3 and 4: Turn left about and skip or gallop back to place, turning to face center again on "riggety jig."

Measures 5 and 6: Skip or gallop forward toward center again; make a big circle with the fingers of both hands in front of chest on "plum bun."

Measures 7 and 8: Turn left about and take 2 skips and 4 slow walking steps back to place, turning to face center at the end.

Repeat music.

Measures 1-4: Join hands in the big circle. All gallop to right.

Measures 5-8: Change directions and gallop to left, slowing down to a walk on "market is done."

This can be arranged for the schoolroom.

Danish Dance of Greeting

Arr. G. V. N.

Danish.

Victor: 20432
Columbia: A-3039

Formation: Single circle. Partners face center, hands on hips. Boy on left side of girl.

Measures 1 and 2: Clap hands twice, turn to partner, bow and courtesy. Turn to center. Repeat, bowing to neighbor.

Measure 3: Stamp right, stamp left.

Measure 4: Turn around in place with four running steps. This turn can either be made away from partner, or all may turn in the same direction, as, all turn right.

Measures 1-4 repeated. Repeat from beginning.

Measures 5-8: Join hands in circle. Run to the right for 4 measures (16 steps); four running steps to each measure.

Measure 5-8 repeated: Turn and run to left.

This dance can be done in the aisles of the schoolroom. Two rows of children face each other and form an elongated circle. During the running steps, the rows run around the row of seats between them and then return to places.

These words can be sung:
   Clap, clap, courtesy; clap, clap, courtesy;
   Stamp, stamp.
   Turn yourselves about.

Hickory, Dickory, Dock

Arr. G. V. N.

[musical notation]

Victor: 20621

Formation: Single circle, facing center.

1. "Hickory Dickory Dock"—Children with arms high above heads bend trunk sideways right, left, right.

"Tick tock"—Arms are lowered to sides or placed on hips while the feet are stamped twice, right, then left.

"The mouse ran up the clock"—Skip forward toward center of circle.

"The clock struck one"—Listen, then clap hands sharply on "one."

"The mouse ran down"—Run back to place with quick little running steps.

"Hickory Dickory Dock"—With arms again stretched overhead, bend trunk sideways right, left, right.

"Tick tock"—Stamp right, left as before.

2. Repeat Music.

With hands on hips or joined in the circle, slide (3 slides) to the right around the circle and stamp twice, right, left, facing out, back to center of circle (2 measures). Repeat the slides in same direction around circle which will be now to the left. Stamp left, right, and face in (2 measures). Repeat all again (4 measures).

This game can readily be adapted to the schoolroom by skipping up and running back in the aisles in Part 1, and sliding sideways right and left down the aisles in Part 2. The turn in Part 2 can be omitted, each child will then be brought back to his place at the end.

The circle game can be varied using partners as follows: Partners face each other in a single circle. Each bends right, left, right, then they exchange places in the skip and run of Part 1. In Part 2, they take hands out at side, slide toward the center, then out, using the same steps as before described but without turns.

A-Hunting We Will Go

Arr. G. V. N.

English.

Formation: Two straight lines, facing each other. Six to eight in a set.

Measures 1-4: The first head couple join crossed hands and slide down the center between the lines. At the same time the other players clap and stamp on the first beat of each measure.

Measures 5-8: The head couple slide back to the head of the set.

Measures 1-8 repeated: The head couples drop hands upon reaching their places, go outside of their own lines and skip down to the foot of the line, each followed by his line. The head couple meet at the foot and join hands for an arch. The rest of the players pass under the arch, returning to the former formation. A new couple is now at the head. The game is repeated until all have been head couples.

For the third grade, the following method may be used. Formation the same.

Measures 1 and 2:. Head couple slides down the set between the lines with crossed hands joined.

Measures 3 and 4: Head couple slides back to place.

Measures 5-8: Head couple drop hands, each skipping down the outside of his line to the foot where they remain. During the eight measures the players in the lines clap and stamp on the first beat of each measure, progressing sideways a little with each stamp down the set. The music is repeated and the new head couple now slide down and up the set and skip down the outside to the foot. The set, however, during this repetition stamp to move sideways up the set (in opposite direction). The game continues until each couple has played; the set reverses its direction for each repetition. When all have played, the set forms a circle, and with hands joined, players slide around the circle to the right and on the last measure jump up into the air and clap hands above head.

Three Little Kittens

Three Little Kittens*

Formation: In groups of threes around a big circle, each group facing into center of group.

Song
1. There were 3 little kittens
   Put on their mittens
   To eat some Christmas pie.

Action

Put on imaginary mitten on one hand; then on the other.

Mew, mew, mew, mew,
Mew, mew, mew.

Turn around in place to right with 6 leaps (right, left, right, etc.) heels together on last count.

2. These three little kittens
They lost their mittens,
And they began to cry.

Look over one shoulder to find mittens. Look over the other shoulder. Put fists in eyes.

Mew, mew, etc.

Sadly turn right in place with 6 walking steps, holding fists in eyes. Music slower.

3. Go, go naughty kittens,
And find your mittens
Or you shan't have any pie.

Shake right forefinger at one kitten. Shake left forefinger at the second. Shake right forefinger again.

Me-ow, me-ow, etc.

Put fists in eyes and turn with six melancholy steps.

4. These 3 little kittens,
They found their mittens,
And joyfully they did cry.

Hold up one hand to show mitten. Hold up the other hand to show mitten. Shake hands with delight.

Mew, mew, etc.

Turn in place with joyful leaps.

5. Oh, granny dear,
Our mittens are here,
Make haste and cut the pie.

Hold an imaginary pie in the left hand and cut it with 3 slicing movements of the right.

Purr, purr, etc.

Turn in place with easy leaps purring contentedly. Hold up one hand, astonished.

6. These 3 little kittens,
They soiled their mittens,
While eating Christmas pie.

Hold up the other hand, astonished. Hide hands behind back.

Mew, mew, etc.

Turn with six jerky steps, agitated and distressed.

7. These 3 little kittens
Then washed their mittens
And hung them up to dry.

Rub mittens on an imaginary wash board. Pin mittens on line with 2 imaginary clothes pins.

Mew, mew, etc.

Turn with quick leaps, mewing with a busy expression.

PHYSICAL EDUCATION 177

8. These 3 little kittens
   Then ironed their mittens
   And all sat down close by.

   Purr-rr, purr-rr, etc.
       or
   And smelled a mouse close by.

   Mew, mew, etc.

Left palm for ironing board, pass palm of right hand over it, back and forth. Sit down and raise right arm and rub it over face as though washing face, purring contentedly. Same for chorus.

All turn and form single circle, facing in line of direction, sniffing from side to side. Hurry off, moving around circle after an imaginary mouse, by long leaps.

* From "Rhythmic Action Plays and Dances"—Moses. Published by Milton Bradley Co.

Cats and Rats

Arr G. V N.

{ Now here comes sly old pus - sy cat }
{ You'd best be - ware, you lit - tle rat! }

Pus - sy wants with you to play, So you'd bet - ter run a - way!

This is a chasing game. The players are arranged in two lines side by side facing in opposite directions. Players opposite are partners.

```
    ( ( ( ( (  Cats        ( ( ( ( (
Rats ) ) ) ) )           ) ) ) ) )
```

Fig. 1   Fig. 2

178   IOWA STATE TEACHERS COLLEGE

After making sure as to who are partners, the lines separate as in Fig. 2. The lines then march forward toward each other. On the word "away" the rats scatter and run, each pursued by his own partner (cat), until tagged. When tagged the cats and rats both return to places in the lines. When all are caught the rats become cats for the next game.

Away We All Go

We follow our leader and a-way we all go a-way we all go a-way we all go We follow our leader and a-way we all go Far a-way, far a-way we go.

Away We All Go*

Formation: Children in a circle with alternate ones facing inward and outward. Both lines take one step backward which places them as in the diagram. They join hands across as indicated by the dotted lines, the circle being broken at one place.

The leader passes under the arch made by the joined hands with the players all following her. This will take the circle once around in passing under the arch. When all have been pulled through the players still keeping hold of hands step back into their original formation except that the leader is at the other end of the circle. The situation is like pulling a stocking inside out. The stocking can be put right side out again by the leader turning and leading under again, this time in opposite direction. Or the dance may be finished by all dancing around the circle.

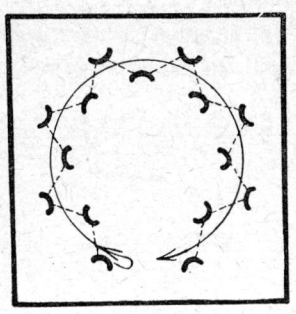

Away We All Go

* Adapted from Crawford's "Dramatic Games and Dances." Copyright, 1908, by A. S. Barnes Co., Publishers.

Yankee Doodle

Formation: A single circle facing in line of direction with backs of hands on hips, or held in front of body as if holding reins. In schoolroom, two rows of children, facing each other, play around one row of seats.

"Yankee Doodle went to town riding on a"—Seven galloping steps forward in line of direction—"pony"—Halt and face center of circle.

"He stuck"—Raise right hand and point right forefinger toward head.

"a feather"—Point forefinger upward to represent a feather.

"in his cap"—Salute.

"and called him"—Bow head and place tips of fingers on chests.

"Macaroni"—Step back on right foot and courtesy, bowing well forward and extending arms sideways shoulder-high.

"Yankee Doodle, ha, ha, ha, Yankee Doodle"—Circle to right with slides, hands joined.

"Dandy"—Stamp right, stamp left.

"Yankee Doodle, ha, ha, ha, Buy the girls some"—Circle to left with slides.

"candy"—Clap twice.

(The music for this can be secured from any songbook)

My Son John

Arr. G. V. N.

Diddle, diddle dumpling, My Son John
Went to bed with his stockings on.
One shoe off; One shoe on;
Diddle, diddle dumpling, My Son John.

Victor: 20621

PHYSICAL EDUCATION 181

Formation: Single circle, facing center. Hands joined.

Measures 1 and 2: Take two slides right around circle and run in place, left, right, or stamp three times.

Measure 3: Make pillow with arms by taking each elbow in the other hand and lay head on it to right. "Went to bed."

Measure 4: Lift right foot behind and slap it with right hand. Repeat with left foot and left hand "Stockings on."

Measure 5: Step on right foot and kick left foot sharply forward. "One shoe off."

Measure 6: Step on left and stamp right foot in place, "one shoe on."

Measures 7 and 8: Join hands in a circle again and take two slides left and stamp left, right, left.

Measures 9-16: With hands still joined slide or skip to the right (4 measures). Same to the left (4 measures).

Draw a Bucket of Water

Arr. G. V. N.

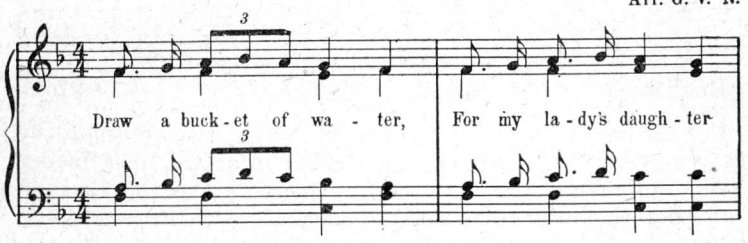

[musical notation with lyrics: "Draw a buck-et of wa-ter, For my la-dy's daugh-ter, One in a rush, two in a rush, Please lit-tle girl, bob un-der the bush."]

Formation: Sets of fours in a small square. Players across from each other join hands. Arms are stretched; those of one couple cross the arms of the other.

Music once through singing verse: With one foot forward, couples sway back and forth with a pulling movement. On "bob under the bush," players all raise their unclasped arms and put them around their companions, who stoop to step inside.

Music played through again: Children humming or singing, "Tra, la, la." All skip to left (2 measures) then skip right (2 measures).

Note: This singing game is for very young children, or for girls only.

The Roman Soldiers

Arr. G. V. N.

Have you an-y bread and wine? For we are the Ro-mans;

Have you an-y bread and wine? For we are the Ro-man sol-diers.

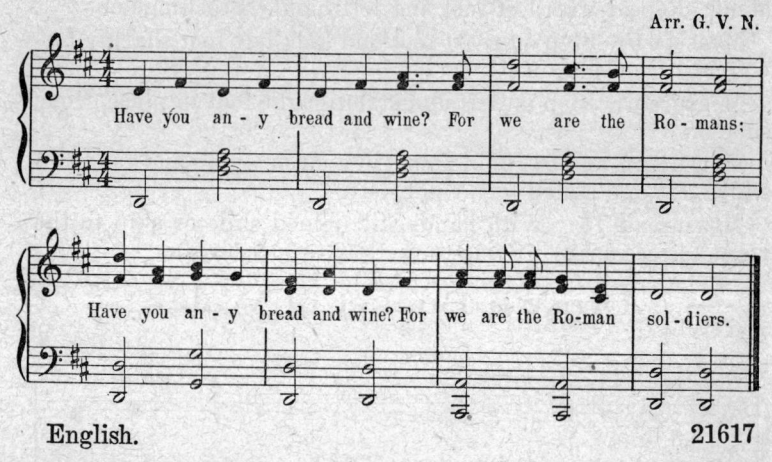

English. 21617

Formation: Players in groups of ten to twelve (more or less) players. The groups are divided into two lines facing each other about ten feet apart. One line are the Romans who sing the first verse and advance toward the other line during the first two lines, and retire during the last two; the other line are the English who sing the second verse, advancing toward the Romans, and retiring. This alternation between the Romans and English in the singing of the stanzas with the advancing and returning continues through twelve stanzas.

2. Yes, we have some bread and wine.
   For we are the English
   Yes we have some bread and wine
   For we are the English soldiers.

In all the verses which follow the 2d and 4th lines remain unchanged, the first and 3d being changed as follows:

3. Then we will have one cupful
4. No you won't have one cupful
5. We will tell the King of you
6. We don't care for the King or you
7. We will send our cats to scratch
   (Pretend to scratch like cats)
8. We don't care for your cats or you

9. We will send our dogs to bite
   (Some bark and growl)
10. We don't care for your dogs or you
11. Are you ready for a fight?
    (Make fists)
12. Yes, we're ready for a fight
    (Also make fists)

The lines now cease moving forward and back. A mark is drawn or scratched midway between them. The players from each line move forward to this division mark and each carries on a tug of war with the player opposite him, to draw him over the line. When each couple in the group has finished the tug of war, all the players form a circle and the singing again proceeds, each one singing "Romans" or "English" according to which group he belongs to.

13. Now we've only got one arm,
    For we are the Romans (English)
    Etc.
  (Each player supports one elbow with the other hand).
14. Now we've only got one leg
    (All limp around as if lame).
15. Now we've only got one eye
    (Each covers his eye with his hand).
16. Home we heroes all must go
  (Each has a different injury, one arm, one leg, or one eye, etc.).

Santa Claus and Reindeer

Jin-gle, jin-gle, ring the bells, Snow is on the ground. The hors-es prance, the sleigh-bells ring, Hark, the mer-ry sound! Jin-gle, jin-gle, jin-gle on the frost-y air Jin-gle, jingle, jingle, sleigh-bells ev-'ry-where Jin-gle, jin-gle, jin-gle hear the mer-ry cry Jin-gle, jin-gle, jin-gle, see the sleighs dash by.

Santa Claus and Reindeer*

Victor: 19791

2. Jingle, jingle, ring the bells,
   Happy throngs dash by,
   The air is full of noisy shouts,
   See the cutters fly!

Chorus:

Formation: In groups of threes; two players representing the reindeer, take hold of inside hands, and hold in outside hands the end of a string. The third person, who is standing back of the two, and who is the driver (Santa Claus), holds the strings in each hand as reins.

Measures 1-4: All take 8 galloping steps or skipping steps, forward.

Measures 5-8: The two players representing reindeer drop hands, take eight skipping or galloping steps away from each other, making a half circle outward to bring them around to face in the opposite direction. The driver skips in place turning to the left but under his own right arm, and, when facing in the opposite direction, he pulls the player who has hold of his left rein under the rein in his right hand, thus making him pass behind the other reindeer. All now face in opposite direction, the reindeer joining inside hands again. There has been no change in hold on reins and neither reindeer goes under his own rein.

Measures 9-24: Repeat the above two times, three times altogether.

*Song used by permission of John Church Co., Cincinnati.

Kinderpolka

Arr. G. V. N.

German.

Columbia: A-3052
Victor: 20432

Formation: Single circle. Partners face each other, join hands with arms extended at sides, shoulder-high.

Measures 1-8: Take two slides (slide together, slide together) toward center, followed by three running steps in place (2 meas.). Repeat moving outward (2 meas.). Repeat in and out again (4 meas.).

Measures 9-12: Clap thighs with both hands; then clap own hands, in slow time (1 meas.). Clap partner's hands three times in quick time (1 meas.). Repeat (2 meas.).

Measures 13-14: Point right toe forward, place right elbow in left hand and shake finger at partner three times (1 meas.). Repeat left (1 meas.).

Measure 15: Turn a complete circle right with four running steps.

Measure 16: Stamp three times.

Ride a Cock-horse

(Music: Ride a cock horse to Banbury cross, To see a fine lady upon a fine horse; Rings on her fingers and bells on her toes, She shall have music wherever she goes.)

Ride a Cock Horse* Victor: 20212

Formation: In single circle, facing to move counter-clockwise, boys and girls alternating. The girls may place hands on the boys' shoulders.

Measures 1-4: Take eight galloping steps forward, starting with the right foot; face partners at the end, forming a double circle, with boys on the inside.

Measures 5-6: Raise the arms over the head, wiggle the fingers, then jump in the air twice.

Measures 7-8: Partners take hands and turn once about with skipping steps.

Measures 1-8: Repeat music from the beginning. Do not sing unless there is no other music. Partners face each other, joined hands raised at the sides to shoulder level. Take three slides to the side with left foot (girl right) and swing the right foot forward. Repeat to the right and swing left. Repeat to the left. Slide once around in a circle, then into first position to repeat the play from the beginning. This time the boy is in the back.

*From Clark's "Physical Training for Elementary Schools." Used by permission of Benj. H. Sanborn Co., Publishers.

Otto and the Crow

Arr. G. V. N.

(Musical score with lyrics: "Ot-to would a rid-ing go, and so he har-nessed up a crow, But could not drive it. Hith-er he'd hitch, and thith-er he'd pitch, Till down in the ditch fell Ot-to.")

Swedish.

Formation: Single circle with hands joined.

Measures 1-4: and repeat. All run around the circle to the right beginning with the left foot, three steps to the measure. Raise feet forward with straight knees with each running step. On measure 4 played the second time, all face center of circle with two stamps, right and left.

Measures 5-8: and repeated. Hands are still joined. On the word "hitch," all make a vigorous lunge diagonally forward to the left with the left foot, letting the shoulders and head drop forward, body relaxed. Resume standing position, ready for a lunge to the right in the same manner, on the word "pitch." Resume standing position again ready to jump to a deep knee bend position on "ditch," body relaxed. Stand on "Otto."

Little Miss Muffet

[Musical score with lyrics: "Lit-tle Miss Muf-fet sat on a tuf-fet Eat-ing her curds and whey; A-long came a spi-der and sat down be-side her, And fright-ened Miss Muf-fet a-way, a-way, And fright-ened Miss Muf-fet a-way." Marked "Faster" and "Play faster 2nd time." Measures numbered 1-10.]

Little Miss Muffet*

Formation: Two rows of children who stand side by side, one row behind the other, facing in the same direction; opposite them, about eight feet away, two other such rows. Those in the front lines are Little Miss Muffets. Those behind them are the spiders, about three feet to the rear.

Figure I.

Music played slowly except last 4 measures, which are played very fast.

Measure 1: Each little Miss Muffet makes a deep bow and points her right forefinger at herself.

Measure 2: She sits down on heels.

Measures 3-4: Holds an imaginary bowl in left hand and eats as from a big spoon held in right hand.

Measure 5: The spiders crawl forward on hands and feet.

Measure 6: Each spider sits on his heels beside his Miss Muffet and looks at her.

Measures 7-10: Miss Muffet suddenly perceiving the spider rises precipitately, catches up her skirts and exchanges places with the Miss Muffet opposite. The two ranks of Miss Muffets now face each other.

Figure II.

Music played in good skipping rhythm.

Measures 1-4: The little Miss Muffets skip forward to meet the one opposite midway between the lines, they take hands and skip around each other, turning right; separate, and skip back to places they just came from.

Measures 5-10: They come forward again, meet, join hands, skip around each other, a turn and a half and skip back to own places, cutting down the spider's thread on first note of last measure.

During these ten measures the spider is rapidly climbing his thread. He takes high skip steps in place, with hand-over-hand motion of arms as if climbing. The spider's thread is cut on first note of last measure, and upon last note he drops down to ground.

* Adapted from Shafter's "Dramatic Dances for Small Children," copyright 1919—A. S. Barnes & Co., Publishers.

Chimes of Dunkirk

Arr. G. V. N.

French.   Columbia: A-3061
Victor: 21618

Formation: Double circle, partners facing each other, inside circle facing out and outside circle facing in.
Measures 1-2: Stamp three times (rt. l. rt.).
Measures 3-4: Clap own hands above head three times.
Measures 5-8: Join hands with partner out at side and turn around in place with eight walking steps.
Measures 1-4: Repeat above.
Measures 5-8: Same as above only skip instead of walk for the turn.
Measures 9-10: With partners' hands joined slide 4 steps counter-clockwise.
Measures 11-12: 4 sliding steps clockwise.
Measures 13-16: 4 sliding steps, each person to his own right pass one and meet next for new partner; stamp three times.
Measures 1-8: Repeat with new partner the steps of measures 1-8, using the skipping steps for the turn.
Repeat from beginning.
Note: This description has been arranged to fit the Victor record.

Carrousel

Arr G V N.

Little children, sweet and gay / Carrousel is running, / It will run till evening / Little ones a nickel, / Big ones a dime, Hurry up, get a mate / Or you'll surely be too late / Ha, ha, ha, / happy are we, / Anderson and Peterson and Henderson and me

Swedish.

Columbia: A-3036
Victor: 20432

Formation: Partners stand in a double circle, facing inward, one behind the other. The inside circle join hands. Those in the outside circle place hands on shoulders of their partners in front of them.

Measures 1-7: Both circles move to right with two sliding side steps to the measure. On measures 6 and 7 these slides become decisive stamps, as the music is somewhat accelerated.

Measures 8-11: The music is played faster for the chorus. The circle continues to move right, but faster, 4 fast slides being taken to the measure.

Measures 8-11: Repeated. Repeat the fast slides, but moving to the left. Partners then immediately change places for the repetition of the whole dance.

This dance represents the Merry-go-round. During the first part the merry-go-round is just starting up, gradually takes on speed, until in the last part it is in full swing.

I See You

Arr G V N.

Swedish.

Columbia: A-3041
Victor: 20988

Formation: Two double ranks facing each other about five feet apart. Those in the front ranks (Nos. 1) place hands on hips; those in the rear ranks (Nos. 2) place hands on shoulders of those in front.

Measure 1: Nos. 2 bend heads right, playing "peek-a-boo" with rear players in the opposite ranks.

Measure 2: Bend heads to left.

Measures 3-4: Bend heads fast three times, right, left, right.

Measures 1-4 repeated: Repeat the above beginning left.

Measures 5-8: All players clap hands once sharply; Nos. 2 skip forward to the right of their partners, meet in the center, grasp hands and swing vigorously around to the right, using skipping or sliding steps.

Measures 5-8 repeated: All clap hands sharply again; then twos grasp own partners' hands and swing around to left with them, finishing in the original formation of double ranks, but with partners having changed places.

Gustaf's Skoal

Arr. G. V. N.

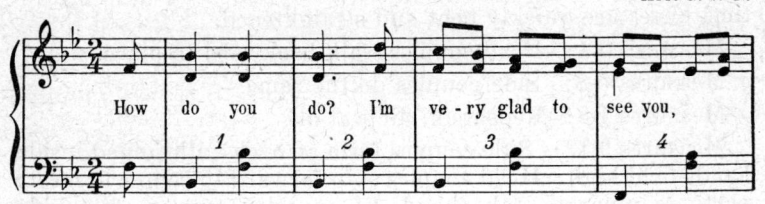

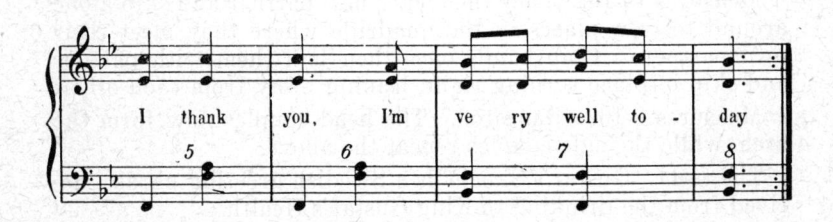

*How do you do? I'm ve-ry glad to see you,
I thank you, I'm ve-ry well to-day
Tra la la la la la la la la la Tra la la la la la
la la la Tra la la la la la la la la Tra la la*

Swedish.

Victor: 21617

Formation: In quadrille formation—sets of four couples on the sides of a square facing center. The two head couples stand opposite each other; the two side couples opposite each other. Partners join inside hands, outside hands on hips.

Measures 1-2: Head couples walk forward three steps toward each other and bob courtesy. For the bob courtesy the ball of one foot is placed close to the heel of the other and at the same time knees are quickly bent and straightened.

Measures 3-4: Head couples walk backward to place.

Measures 5-8: Side couples do the same.

Measures 1-8: Repeated. Repeat all.

Measures 9-12: Side couples form an arch with joined inside hands held high. Head couples skip forward to center to meet; partners separate, take hands of opposite, turn to face side couples and with new partner skip under nearest arch.

Measures 13-16: They then leave new partner and skip alone around to own places in the quadrille where they meet their own partners. Clap hands once then join them with partner and skip in place turning right, leaning away from each other.

Measures 9-16: Repeated. The head couples now form the arch, while the side couples repeat the above.

The term "Gustaf's Skoal" is a Swedish greeting phrase, derived from the drinking to King Gustaf's Health.

PHYSICAL EDUCATION

Indian Dance

Arr. G. V. N.

Indian Dance *(Continued)*

A.
Formation: Seated cross-legged in a single circle.

Worshiping the Four Winds
Measure 1: With arms folded bend forward, lowering the head.

Measure 2: Raise the head and trunk, tipping the head backward slightly at the end of the upward movement.

Measures 3-8: Continue above movements.

Measures 9-10: Bend sideways right and return to erect sitting position.

Measures 11-12: Bend sideways left and return to erect sitting position.

Measures 13-16: Continue the same.

Worshiping the Sun
Measure 1: Unfolding the arms raise them high above the head.

Measure 2: Bring arms down to floor at the same time bending the trunk low.

Measures 3-8: Continue above movement.

Smoking Peace Pipe
Measures 9 and 10: Quickly jerk imaginary pipe from the mouth and puff the smoke three times (once to two beats) and then hand the pipe to the next person to the right.

Measures 11 and 12: The person on the right receives the pipe and puffs three times then passes it on.

Measures 13-16: Continue the above two times more.

Note: Since the pipe is to be passed 4 times the circle should be counted off in fours. Number 1 then smokes first and hands it to number 2, etc.

Looking Out for the Enemy
Measure 1 repeated: Placing the right hand above the eyes as if shading the eyes and looking searchingly to the right.

Measure 2: Repeat using left hand and looking left.

Measures 3-8: Continue the same.

Measures 9-16: All jump up and dance around the circle using the high knee step hop with the arms bent sharply at the elbow and trunk bent forward.

B.

Signalling the Friends

Measure 17: Kneeling on the right knee, slap the ground two times with the right hand.

Measure 18: Using the back of the hand, strike the mouth three times as a call is given.

Measures 19 and 20: Repeat above.

Measures 21-24: Dance around the circle again using Indian step hop.

Measures 17-24 repeated: Repeat above movements.

Three Crows

Arr. G. V. N.

Lyrics: Three crows there were once who sat on a stone; Fa la fa la fa la;— But two flew a-way and then there was one; Fa la fa la fa la.— The oth-er crow felt so tim-id a-lone Fa la fa la fa la That he flew a-way and then there was none; Fa la fa la fa la.

Formation: Single circle, facing in. Three children in center of circle, numbered 1-2-3.

Measure 1: Hop on left foot and touch right toe forward (count 1); hop on left foot and replace right (count 2).

Measure 2: Hop on right foot and touch left toe forward (count 1); hop on right foot and replace left (count 2).

Measures 3 and 4: Jump on both feet three times, arms flapping (move up and down at side) on each hop. A quarter turn right is made during these three hops.

Measures 5-8: Repeat the movements of the above 4 measures, turning right again, to face out. During this, Nos. 1 and 2 fly from the center to the circle.

Measures 9-12: Repeat again, making another quarter turn right. No. 3 in the center droops his head.

Measures 13-16: Repeat, making quarter turn to face in. No. 3 flies out to circle.

Repeat music.

Measures 1 and 2: Join hands in the circle and slide right.

Measures 3 and 4: Drop hands and take 3 jumps on both feet to face out.

Measures 5-8: Join hands again, and slide left. Three jumps to face in. The slide carries circle in same direction as in measures 1 and 2.

Measures 9-16: Repeat the above slides and jumps.

Nest Making

Arr. G. V. N.

Finnish.

Columbia: A-3058

Formation: Partners face each other in a big double circle.

Fig. I.—Measure 1: Walk backward away from partner, clapping hands on first step. Begin with left foot.

Measure 2: Walk forward to partner; clap on first step.

Measures 3 and 4: Take partner's hands held at side shoulder-high; turn with partner around in place to right with light running steps (8 steps).

Measures 1 to 4 repeated: Repeat the above.

Measures 5-8: Inside circle take hands; the outside circle does the same. Each circle moves to its left with running steps (16 steps).

Measures 5-8 repeated: Circles run to their own right.

Fig. II—Measures 1 and 2: Dramatize the motion of chopping wood for the house (4 chops).

Measures 3 and 4: Clap own hands, clap partner's right, clap own, clap partner's left, clap own, clap both of partner's twice, rest.

Measures 1-4 repeated: Repeat steps of measures 1 to 4 in Fig. I.

Measures 5-8 and repeat. Same as in Fig. I.

Fig. III—Measures 1 and 2: Dramatize movements of planing the boards, 4 times.

Measures 3 and 4: Clap hands as in Fig. II.

Measures 1-4 repeated: Take steps of Fig. I.

Measures 5-8 and repeated. Same as Fig. I.

Note: Emphasis must be placed upon which circle a child is in, outer or inner circle, for after the turn with partner on measures 3 and 4, each must finish in his own place and circle, ready to join hands with those in his own circle to slide around the big circle. Confusion may occur unless preliminary care is taken.

Steps may be added to bring in other phases of building a house, as sawing, hammering, etc.

The Hobby Horse

SCHUMANN

Victor: 18598

Music: Schumann's "The Wild Horesman."

Formation: Children in lines facing forward. Each has a real or imaginary hobby-horse and whip.

Fig. I. To come in:
    4 gallops forward (2 measures).
    Stand in place and whip horse 4 times (2 measures).
    Repeat all (4 measures).

Fig. II. Repeat all of Fig. I moving around in a circle to right and face front at end (8 measures).

Fig. III. Leap to the side with right foot and close left to right, as if horse were plunging off to right (1 measure).
    Gallop in place 2 times holding steed with both hands, pulling him back (1 measure).
    Repeat all 3 times (6 measures). (In all 8 measures).

Fig. IV. Six gallop steps to right in a circle; finish facing front (3 measures).

Look off to left under right hand and spy enemy suddenly (1 measure).
Point with right hand toward enemy, slap chest with right hand bravely (2 measures).
Gallop four times in place holding rein with both hands.
Toss head as if to say you are not afraid (2 measures).
Fig. V. Play music for Fig. III.
One big brave gallop step toward enemy (1 measure).
Two small gallop steps moving back (1 measure).
Repeat both measures (2 measures).
Draw sword with right hand, and brandish it in air (2 measures).
Exit forward left with galloping steps, flourishing sword at enemy (2 measures).

Supplementary Material

The following excellent material for Primary children can be found in the books indicated.
Crawford's "Dramatic Games and Dances"-A. S. Barnes and Co.
    My Dolly
    Leaves at Play
    The Ginger-Bread Man
Crawford's "Rhythms of Childhood"—A. S. Barnes and Co.
    Jack-in-the-Box
    Rocking-Horse
    Dolly Goes a-Walking
    Giants
    Elephants
Bentley: "Play Songs"—Laidlaw Bros., Chicago.
    My Top
    Train
    The Toad's Mistake
Hofer: "Music for the Childworld" Vol. II—Clayton F. Summy Co.
    Elephants
    Jack-in-the-Box
    The Swing
    Balls
Moses: "Rhythmic Action Plays and Dances"—Milton Bradley Co., Springfield, Mass.
    Three Funny Old Men
    Peter Pan
Shafter: "Dramatic Games for Small Children"—A. S. Barnes and Co.

RHYTHMICAL WORK FOR INTERMEDIATE GRADES

Foundation work in Rhythm for Intermediate Grades.

1. Review of Elemental Rhythmical Activities as marching, running, jumping, hopping, sliding, skipping, galloping. These should be worked out with some dramatization.

2. If the children of the intermediate grades have not had much work in folk dancing during the primary grades, many folk dances listed under the Primary section, can be taught first. Some of these are:

    Shoemaker's Dance
    Danish Dance of Greeting
    How D'ye do My Partner
    Kinderpolka
    Chimes of Dunkirk
    Carrousel
    I See You
    Gustaf's Skoal
    Tucker
    Nuts in May
    Santa Claus and Reindeer
    Indian Dance
    The Hobby-Horse
    Nest-Making

3. The dance steps employed in the following dances are outlined on page 115.

The method used in developing them is given in that section.

4. For Type Lessons in Folk Dancing, see pages 122 and 123.

The First of May

Arr. G. V. N.

To-day's the first of May, To-day's the first of May, May, May, To-day's the first of May, To-day's the first of May.

Swedish.

Columbia: A-3047

2. Goodbye, goodbye my (little) friend,
We'll meet again some day, day, day.
We'll meet again some day.
Before the first of May.

Formation: Double circle; partners have inside hands joined; outside hands on hips; they face forward to move counter-clockwise around the circle.

Measures 1-8: Begin with outside foot. All polka around circle turning toward partner when using outside foot, and away from partner when using inside foot. Hands swing back then forward.

Repeat music.

Measures 1 and 2: Face partner and shake hands three times.

Measures 3-8: Clap hands, face right and skip away from partner around circle, waving hand in farewell. Outside and inside circles will be skipping in opposite directions. Meet partner at the end. If the circle is large this can be accomplished by skipping just half way around the circle. If small, skip way around the circle taking your partner when you meet her the second time.

If a change of partners is desired, each player passes his own partner and meets the one who is next behind.

Three Little Girls

Arr. G. V. N.

Three lit-tle girls went slid-ing on the ice, Slid-ing on the ice, slid-ing on the ice; Three lit-tle girls went slid-ing on the ice, So ear-ly in the month of May. Swing them all a-round as you bring them in, Bring them in, bring them in; Swing them all a-round as you bring them in, So ear-ly in the month of May.

Note: First eight measures should be played twice in succession.

The first eight measures should be played twice before playing the chorus. The following words are sung on the repetition of these measures.

The ice was thin and they all fell in,
They all fell in, they all fell in.
The ice was thin and they all fell in
So early in the month of May.

Formation: One large single circle, hands joined. One small circle of three dancers (girls) in the center of the large circle, hands joined.

Measures 1 to 8: Circles slide around in opposite directions.

Measures 1 to 8 repeated: Reverse directions.

Chorus: The big circle stands in place. The girls in the center skip out to the circle; each chooses a boy; partners join both hands, skip in to the center, whirling as they go. The girl leaves her partner there and joins the circle.

The game is started again with the three boys forming the small circle in the center. The word "boys" is now sung in place of "girls" in the first stanza.

Nixie Polka
(Nigarepolska)

Arr. G. V. N.

Swedish.

Victor: Nigarepolska—21685

Formation: Single circle, all facing center, with hands on hips. One child stands in the center.

Measures 1-4: All hop on the left foot placing the right heel forward once in measure 1., the change coming on the accented second count of the measure. Change feet with a jump, left heel forward on count 2 of measure 2. Take this single "Bleking'' step twice more in measures 3 and 4. There are four jumps changing heels forward (Bleking Steps) altogther.

Measures 5-8 and repeated: All clap hands on first note. Center player runs with three steps to the measure, around the circle until the last measure, when he finishes with two stamps in front of and facing a circle player. At the same time the circle players run in place and stamp twice at the end.

Measures 1-4 repeated: All take the same steps as previously described for Measures 1-4.

Measures 5-8 and repeated: All clap hands. On the clap, center player jumps left about, and runs again around circle. The player he has chosen follows him, placing hands on his shoulder. They run to another circle player.

Measures 1-4: Repeat the same steps as used above.

Measures 5-8 and repeated: Both players jump left about on the clap. This makes the 2d player the new leader. The third one chosen joins the string.

Measures 1-8: The music and steps are repeated until all have been chosen to join the line. The line then joins ends and dances all steps through once or twice in a circle. When there are many players, the game can begin with two or more center players. The lines join and form a circle at the end. Also the circle may be a double circle. Two will then be added to the line each time.

Variation:

The Bleking Step used in measures 1-4 is sometimes danced as follows:

All hop on left foot placing right heel forward on count 1. Change feet with a jump, left heel forward on count 2. Hold on count 3. (1 measure). Take these **two** changes three more times. (3 measures).

Come Let Us Be Joyful

Arr. G. V. N.

German.

Come, Let Us Be Joyful

Victor: 20448

Come, let us be joyful,
While life is bright and gay;

Gather its roses
Ere they fade away.

We're always making our lives so blue,
We look for thorns, and find them too,
And leave the violets quite unseen
That on our way do grow.
   Repeat first stanza.

Formation: Dancers divided into sets of six, three opposite three. The middle player of each row of three is the boy. Three join hands.

Measures 1-2; The two lines of threes advance toward each other with three steps and bow (girls make a bob courtesy—touch toe of one foot behind the other and bend both knees).

Measures 3-4: The lines walk back to places; bring feet together.

Measures 5-8: Repeat going forward and back.

Measures 9-10: The boy and the right hand girl hook right elbows and turn with skipping steps.

Measures 11 and 12: The boy and the left hand girl hook left elbows and turn with skipping steps. In the meantime the right hand girl skips in a small circle counter-clockwise by herself.

Measures 13-14: The boy and right hand girl skip again. In the meantime the left hand girl skips in a small circle clockwise.

Measures 14-16: The boy and left hand girl skip again with right hand girl skipping in small circle as before. They finish in original lines with hands joined.

Measures 1-8 repeated: The steps of Measures 1-8 are repeated, except that when the lines advance the second time, boys exchange places and retire with opposite girls.

The groups of sixes may be arranged in a circle, and the dance made progressive. In this case, during the last 4 measures (Measures 5-8) when repeated, the lines advance toward each other; then, in place of retiring, they drop hands and pass on through the opposite three, passing right shoulders, to meet the next set.

Snow Storm

Russian.

Formation: Double circle, partners standing side by side but facing in opposite directions to move around circle, outside circle counter-clockwise, inside circle clockwise.

Measures 1-4: Circles move with fast, light, little, running steps in opposite directions around the circle. Their hands are held high above their heads and their fingers are constantly moved. The action indicates the light falling of the snow.

Measures 1-4 repeated: Circles, turning toward each other, face about, and run back in the opposite direction to meet partners.

Measures 5-8: Join right hands high, and, still fluttering fingers of other hand, run around each other with the same little running steps.

Measures 5-8 repeated: Join left hands and reverse the direction.

Measures 9 and 10: Partners face each other in a double circle. The following action is to represent the trees blown by the wind. Arms are held diagonally above head. Step sideways to outside partner's right, close with left, and step sideways again with right. Bend the trunk sideways with each step to the side.

Measures 11 and 12: Repeat the steps and trunk bending to the left.

Measures 13-16: Take hold of both hands, lean back away from each other, whirl around in place with many little side steps. The action is to indicate the blizzard.

Measures 9-16 repeated: Repeat the steps of these measures.

Seven Jumps

Arr. G. V. N.

Danish.

Victor: 21617

Formation: One large single circle is best for children. Hands joined. A number of smaller circles may be used.

"First Jump."

Measures 1-8: The circle moves around to the right with step hops, one to a measure (step on beat one and hop on beat two).

Measures 9-16: Jump up high from the ground and come down with a stamp on both feet on the first beat of Measure 9. Then, step hop around circle to left.

Measure 17: Drop hands, place them on hips, and bend the right knee upward.

Measure 18: Stamp right foot to ground on first note. Join hands on second note.

"Second Jump."

Measures 1-16: Same as before.

Measure 17: Raise right knee as before.

Measures 18 and 19: On first note, stamp down right foot; on second note lift left knee; on third note stamp left foot; on fourth note join hands.

"Third Jump."

Measures 1-16: Same as before.

Measure 17: Raise right knee.

Measures 18, 19 and 20: First note—Stamp right foot; 2d—lift left knee; 3d—stamp left foot; 4th—place right toe backward on floor; 5th—kneel on right knee; 6th—stand and join hands.

"Fourth Jump."

Measures 1-16 and 17: Same as before.

Measures 18, 19, 20 and 21: 1st, 2d, 3d, 4th and 5th notes as before. On 6th note put left foot back, on 7th note, kneel on left knee; 8th, stand and join hands.

"Fifth Jump."

Measures 1-16 and 17: Same as before.

Measures 18, 19, 20, 21, and 22: First seven notes same as before. Eighth note, put right fist to cheek, raising elbow; 9th note, put elbow on floor, cheek resting on fist; 10th note, stand and join hands.

"Sixth Jump."

Measures 1-16 and 17: Same as before.

Measures 18, 19, 20, 21, 22 and 23: First nine notes same as before. Tenth note, put left fist to cheek and raise elbow; 11th note, put left elbow to floor, cheek resting on fist; 12th note, stand and join hands.

"Seventh Jump."

Measures 1-16 and 17: Same as before.

Measures 18, 19, 20, 21, 22, 23 and 24: First eleven notes same as before; 12th note, push body forward; 13th note, touch forehead to floor; 14th note, stand and join hands.

Measures 1-16: same as before.

PHYSICAL EDUCATION   215

Heads and Shoulders, Knees and Toes

The children may be in a circle, or in lines, as in the aisles of the schoolroom. The following verse is sung to the tune of "Here We Go Round the Mulberry Bush," page 156.

Heads and Shoulders, Knees and Toes
Heads and Shoulders, Knees and Toes
Heads and Shoulders, Knees and Toes
Heads and Shoulders, Knees and Toes

As each part of the body is named the players touch with both hands that part. Vary the order, as "Head and Knees, Shoulders and Toes." Also make the game more lively by singing faster. Changes in order or tempo must be stated each time before playing.

Hallowe'en is Here

Arr. G. V. N.

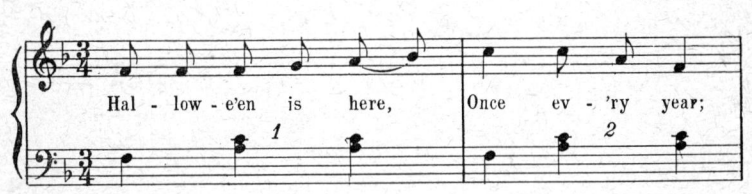

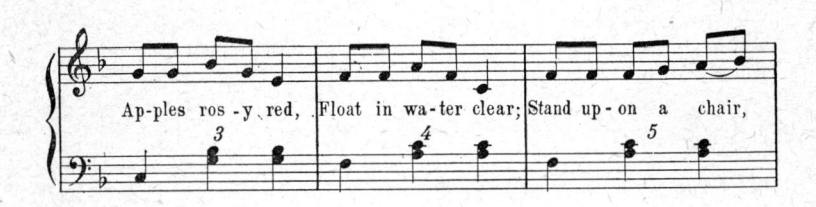

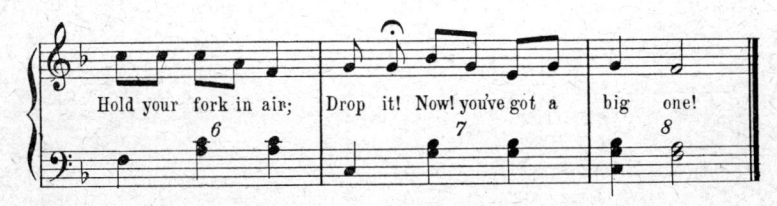

Hal-low-e'en is here, Once ev-'ry year; Ap-ples ros-y red, Float in wa-ter clear; Stand up-on a chair, Hold your fork in air; Drop it! Now! you've got a big one!

Formation: Two rows of children facing each other about ten feet apart, hands joined.

Measures 1 and 2: Both rows advance toward each other 3 steps, and retire 3 steps. They swing their hands back and forward.

Measures 3 and 4: Repeat, walking forward and backward.

Measure 5: Bring both arms forward, shoulder-high, with palms down.

Measure 6: Bring left hand to position, and hold right arm up as if holding a fork.

Measures 7 and 8: Open hands as if dropping fork; look down; clap hands, and run around in place.

Music repeated, singing tra la la.

Measures 1-8: All face up in same direction. Head couples turn outward away from each other and skip down the outside of their line, to the foot. The lines follow. On reaching the bottom, head couples face each other, stand still and join hands; the rest pass under the arch and skip up to places. The couple forming the arch remain at the foot.

Christmas Dance

Arr. G. V. N

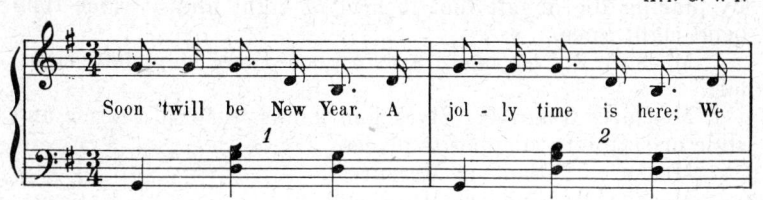

Soon 'twill be New Year, A jol-ly time is here; We wish you all a Mer-ry Christ-mas. Up and down we go, Danc-ing to and fro, We wish you all a Mer-ry Christ-mas

Swedish.

Formation: Players are in two long lines, preferably of 12 each, facing each other about 10 feet apart. The lines are divided into threes. This makes the whole group be divided into four small groups of threes opposite threes. Adjacent hands are joined. Outside hands are on hips. (Diagram I).

Fig. I.

Measure 1: Opposite lines both move forward toward each other with two steps left, right, and bob courtesy, done by placing toe of left foot to heel of right and at same time bend right knee.

Measure 2: Go backward to place three steps left, right, left.

Measures 3 and 4: Sixes join hands to form a circle and slide or skip left to opposite places.

Measure 5: Same as Measure 1.

Measure 6: Same as Measure 2.

Measures 7 and 8: Sixes join hands again and slide or skip on to left back to places.

Chorus: The music is repeated twice. Sing Tra la la la.

The threes in group 1 each in a string, hands joined, follow the route as marked out in Diagram II; down the outside

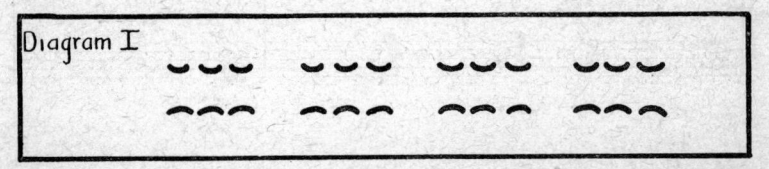

Diagram I

Diagram II

Christmas Dance

of the opposite line, in and out around the groups to the top of the set again, then down the inside of the lines to the foot where they remain. The other groups move up. This is done by a new group after each figure.

Fig. II.

Measures 1 and 2: Same as Measures 1 and 2 in Fig. I.

Measures 3 and 4: Each group of threes joins hands to form circles and slide or skip left around in place.

Measures 5 and 6: Same as Measures 1 and 2.

Measures 7 and 8: Threes join hands again and move left around in place as before.

Chorus: Group 2 takes chorus and finishes at foot of set.

Fig. III.

Measures 1 and 2: Same as in Fig. I.

Measures 3 and 4: Sixes join right hands in center to form a wheel and skip around to opposite places.

Measures 5 and 6: Same as Measures 1 and 2.

Measures 7 and 8: Sixes again join right hands and skip on arriving at own places.

Chorus: Group 3 dances.

Fig. IV.

Measures 1 and 2: Same as before.

Measures 3 and 4: Threes join right hands in center and skip around in place.

Measures 5 and 6: Same as Measures 1 and 2.

Measures 7 and 8: Threes join right hands again and skip around in place.

Chorus: Group 2 takes chorus and finish at foot of set. Group 1 is now in its original place.

The dance can be adapted to any number of groups in the set.

Hansel and Gretel

Arr. G. V. N.

Lit-tle part-ner, dance with me, Both your hands now give to me;
Point your toe and away we go Up and down the mer-ry row. Tra la la la la la la Tra la la la la la la Tra la la la la la la la Tra la la la la la la

With your feet go tap, tap, tap, With your hands go clap, clap, clap, Point your toe; away we go, Up and down the mer-ry row.
With your head go nip, nip, nip, With your fin-gers snip, snip, snip,

German.

Columbia: A-3080
Victor: 21620

Formation: Double circle, partners facing each other.

Measures 1 and 2: Bow and courtesy low.

Measures 3 and 4: Take right hands, then left hands across.

Measures 5 and 6: Outside circle use right foot, inside circle left. Point toe forward then to the side, and take two slides sideways.

Measures 7 and 8: Repeat pointing and sliding with other foot.

Measures 5-8 repeated: Repeat movements of these measures.

Measures 9-16: Face to move counter-clockwise; take partner's inside hand and walk around circle.

Measures 9-16 repeated: Continue around the circle skipping.

Measure 17: Face partner and stand still.

Measure 18: Stamp right, left, right.

Measure 19: Stand still.

Measure 20: Clap three times.

Measures 21-24: Join crossed hands and take steps of measures 5-8.

Measures 17-24, repeated: Repeat the steps for these measures except on Measure 18, nod head three times and on Measure 20 snap fingers three times.

Swedish Ring Dance

Arr. G. V. N.

Swedish.

Formation: Double circle, partners facing to move counter-clockwise, inside hands joined.

Introduction: Wait.

Measures 1-4, and repeated. Walk forward around circle, arms swinging.

Measures 5-8, and repeated: Continue in same direction skipping.

Measures 9-12: Form quickly into a single circle, all hands joined and slide to right 8 slides.

Measures 9-12 repeated: Slide to left 8 slides.

Measures 13 and 14: At end of preceding slides, quickly face partner in a single circle. All dancers then separate from partner and slide to their own right with 4 slides. This carries one partner in toward the center of the circle and the other out away from the center.

Measures 15 and 16: Then both slide 4 slides left, which brings them back to place facing each other again.

Measures 13-16 repeated: Taking partner's right hand, and raising left arm obliquely upward, skip around partner with 8 skipping steps, moving clockwise.

Captain Jinks

Arr. G. V. N.

Victor: 20639

I am Captain Jinks of the Horse Marines,
I feed my horse on corn and beans,
And swing the ladies in their teens,
For that's the style in the army.
I teach the ladies how to dance,
How to dance, how to dance,
I teach the ladies how to dance,
For that's the style in the army.
Salute your partner, turn to the right.
Then promenade your lady right,
And swing your neighbor with all your might,
For that's the style in the army.

Formation: Double circle, partners facing each other. Stand very erect, arms down at side.

Measures 1 and 2: Mark time four steps in place beginning with left foot and salute on last beat.

Measures 3 and 4: Joining crossed hands, face to move forward (counter-clockwise) around circle, and slide forward with left foot 4 slides.

Measures 5 and 6: No. 1, who is left-hand partner, with a strong pull with right hand swing right-hand partner [No. 2] across in front of him over to his left side (1 measure). No. 2 draws No. 1 across to his left side in the same way.

Measures 7 and 8: Face partners and mark time with salute as in Measures 1 and 2.

Measures 9 and 10: March four steps forward past partner, passing right shoulders. Raise right hand high and touch partner's hand lightly.

Measures 11 and 12: March backward four steps to place.

Measures 13 and 14: Give both hands to partner and turn around in place with four steps.

Measures 15 and 16: Face partner, mark time and salute.

Measures 1-8, repeated: Bow to partner (1 measure). Each face right (1 measure). Join crossed hands with new partner facing you, turn to move forward around circle repeating the steps of Measures 3 to 8, as described before.

Pig in the Parlor

Arr. G. V. N.

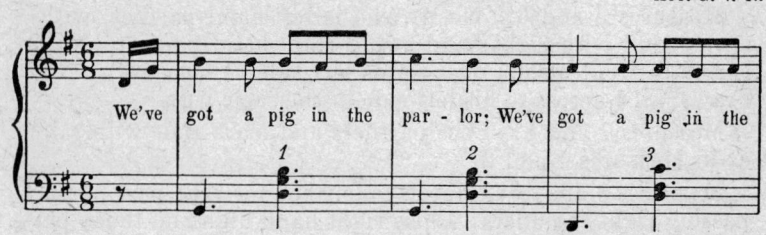

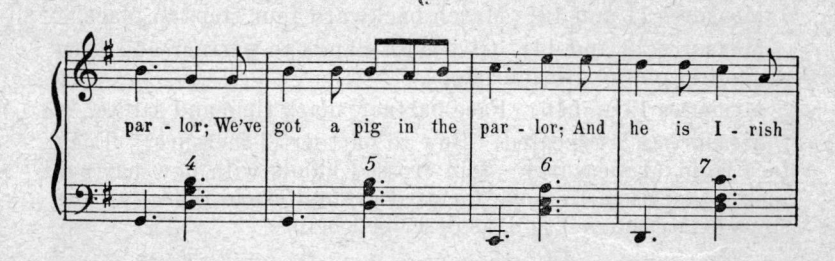

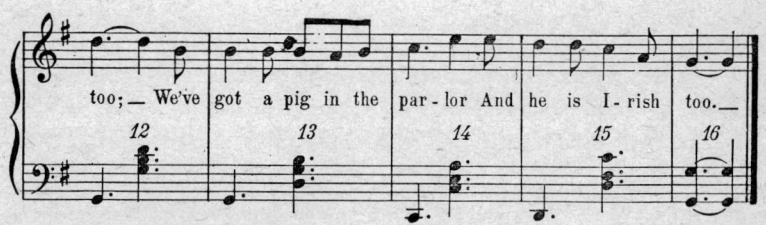

We've got a pig in the par-lor; We've got a pig in the par-lor; We've got a pig in the par-lor; And he is I-rish too. And he is I-rish too; And he is I-rish too; We've got a pig in the par-lor And he is I-rish too.

American Country Dance.

2. Right hand to your partner,
   Left hand to your neighbor,
   Right hand to the next you meet,
   And we'll all promenade.
   We'll all promenade,
   We'll all promenade,
   Swing your partner once and a half,
   And we'll all promenade.

Formation: Double circle partners side by side. Right hands are joined, and left hands are joined (skater's position). One extra player stands within the circle.

First stanza:

Measures 1-16: Walk or skip around the circle counter-clockwise.

Second Stanza:

Measures 1 and 2: The right-hand dancer drops left hand, and turns to face opposite direction. Passing right shoulders, the partners move in opposite directions.

Measures 3 and 4: Each meets a new partner to whom the left hand is given in passing left shoulders.

Measures 5 and 6: Meet another and clasp right hands. Do not pass, but give left hands also, the outside dancer faces forward again and the partners walk forward in the original line of direction.

Measures 7-12: Continue walking around the circle.

Measure 13: Gentleman (left-hand player) draws lady across in front of him and to his left side, without dropping hands on "Swing your partner." The gentleman pulls with right hand.

Measure 14: The lady draws gentleman across and to her left in the same way.

Measures 15 and 16. They continue walking around circle, in same direction as before.

During Measures 1 to 6 while changing hands and singing "Right hand to your partner, etc." the odd one, the "pig," in the center tries to get a partner. If he succeeds he joins the circle and promenades with his partner. The one now without a partner must go within the circle. The dance is repeated. If there is a change of center players, the first stanza is sung, "We've got a new pig in the parlor," etc. If no change of center players occurs, it is sung "Same old pig in the parlor," etc.

Strasak

Arr. G. V. N.

Bohemian.

Formation: Single circle, partners facing each other. Hands are joined and held straight out in front shoulder-high. When girls only are dancing, No. 1 can put hands at partner's waist; No. 2 can put hands on partner's shoulders.

Measures 1-8: Partners move around circle counter-clockwise, No. 1 always moving forward, No. 2 always backward, with following step: Both partners begin with outside foot. The step as explained is for No. 1. Step forward right foot (count 1); bring left foot to right (and); step forward right (count 2); hop on right, lifting leg sideways (and). One measure is needed for each step. Alternate feet are used as step is repeated. This is a form of the Schottische step.

Measure 9: Partners still facing each other stand still in double circle.
Measure 10: Stamp three times, right, left, right.
Measure 11: Stand still.
Measure 12: Clap three times.
Measure 13: Left hand on hip, shake right forefinger three times.

PHYSICAL EDUCATION 229

Measure 14: Right hand on hip, shake left forefinger three times.

Measure 15: Strike partner's right hand and whirl to left on left foot, making a complete turn.

Measure 16: Hands on hips, face partner, stamp three times.

Measures 9-16, repeated: Repeat all the above for these measures, except that on the 15th, when the turn away from partner is done, enough ground is covered to move back around circle to meet a new partner. A complete turn is made as before to do this, and each dancer faces in same direction as before.

Cshebogar

Arr. G. V. N.

Hungarian.

20992

Formation: Couples; single circle, all hands joined, facing center. Measures 1-4: Eight slides to left.

Measures 5-8: Repeat right.

Measures 1 and 2 repeated: Beginning with left foot walk forward 4 steps, body bent forward.

Measures 3 and 4: Repeat, moving backward, heads and arms high.

Measures 5-8: Partners face, right arm around partner's waist, and left arm slightly curved over head. Eight skips in place, turning right, finishing in original positions. The partners may take hold of hands and raise them sideways shoulder-high, rather than placing hands around waist.

Measures 9-12: Partners still facing, and with hands joined and arms extended sideways take four steps inward, the body bending sideways inward with each step. A step and close to each measure.

Measures 13-16: Repeat this step outward with corresponding trunk movement.

Measures 9-12 repeated: Same as Measures 9-12 taking only 2 steps inward and 2 outward.

Measures 13-16: Skip with partners as in Measures 5-8 repeated.

German Hopping Dance

Arr. G. V. N.

Note: First eight measures should be played twice.
German.

Columbia: A-3051

Formation: Single circle. Partners face each other, inside hands joined and held high, outside hands on hips.

Measures 1 and 2: Slide sideways away from center four slides. Bend slightly outward.

Measures 3 and 4: Change hands, and slide inward.

Measures 5-8: Repeat measures 1-4.

Measures 1-8 repeated: Slide outward four slides (2 measures); take four slow running steps in place, with hands on hips (2 measures). Slide inward 4 slides (2 measures). Take the four running steps in place, making a complete turn away from partner (2 measures). On the slides, arms are used as in Measures 1-4. Finish in circle facing center, all hands joined.

Measures 9 and 10: Run sideways right, 8 fast steps.

Measures 11 and 12: Run sideways left 8 steps.

Measures 13 and 14: Slide forward with right foot toward center of circle four slides. Hands still joined.

Measures 15 and 16: Slide backward with left foot 4 times.

Measures 9-16 repeated: Take partner again. Slide outward four slides. Run in place 4 steps. Slide inward four slides. Run in place 4 steps turning away from partner and completely around.

PHYSICAL EDUCATION 233

Ace of Diamonds

Arr. G. V. N.

Danish.

Columbia: A-3001
Victor: 20989

Formation: Double circle, partners facing each other, one with back to center, one facing center. Hands on hips.

Fig. I.

Measures 1-4: Clap own hands sharply, immediately hook right elbows, and swing partner around to right with running or skipping steps (2 to a measure). Start with left foot.

Measures 5-8: Without pausing, clap hands again, hook left elbows and swing partner around the other way. Finish in original positions in the double circle, partners facing each other.

Fig. II.

Measures 9-12: With arms folded in front of chest, take 4 step hops to the center of the circle. The inside dancer moves backward beginning with left foot, and the outside dancer forward beginning with right foot. A step hop is done to one measure of music as follows: step on 1st beat, hop on same foot and raise other knee on 2d beat.

Measures 13-16: Repeat the step hops but moving outward from center. The inside dancer goes forward, the outside one goes backward.

Fig. III.

Measures 17-24 and repeated: Partners face, standing side by side, inside hands joined, to move counter-clockwise around the circle. They take the polka step forward beginning with outside foot, the one away from partner. Inside joined hands are swung backward and partners turn toward each other on this polka step. Polka with inside foot at same time, swing arms forward and turn slightly back to back. Continue polka steps alternating feet. The description of the polka and the method of learning is found on page 115.

Note: Figure III of Ace of Diamonds can be made easier by skipping in place of the polka.

Tantoli

Arr. G. V. N.

Swedish. Columbia: A-3054
Victor: 20992

Formation: Double circle, partner's inside hands joined. Outside hands on hips. Face to move counter-clockwise around circle.

Fig. I.

Measures 1-8: Heel-toe polka forward around circle, beginning with outside foot. A heel-toe polka is done to two measures of 2/4 time as follows: Touch heel of outside foot forward, lean body slightly backward (beat 1); touch outside toe backward, lean slightly forward (beat 2); slide forward with outside foot, bring inside foot up to it (beat 1); slide forward, outside foot (beat 2). This is repeated using inside foot (2 measures). It is repeated with each foot again (4 measures). Or follow description as found on page 115.

Fig. II.

Measures 9-16: Step hop forward around circle until last measure. A step hop is done to one measure of 2/4 time as follows: step on outside foot (beat 1); hop on this foot lifting the other knee high in front (beat 2). On the last measure, both partners jump from both feet high in the air, landing on both feet, in the same formation ready to start the dance again.

Note: The above description is an adaptation for grade use. The following changes can be made when girls are dancing together. In Fig. I, the inside dancer puts right arm around partner's waist, who puts left arm on partner's right shoulder. The steps remain the same. In Fig. II partners face each other, the inside dancer puts both hands on waist of partner, who puts hands on her shoulders. Beginning with forward feet (right for one and left for the other) they "hop waltz" around the circle, turning as they go. The "hop waltz" differs from the step hop just described in that the free leg is raised sideways instead of up in front. On the last measure, one partner jumps the other high in the air and puts her down on her right side ready to dance again from the beginning.

Hands may be joined and held out at side. This may be more suitable for use in some circumstances.

Bleking

Arr. G. V. N.

Swedish. Columbia: A-3037
Victor: 20989

Formation: Double circle partners facing each other, hands joined.

Fig. I.

Measure 1: Jump, placing right heel forward, push right arm forward at shoulder-height and draw left elbow back, twist body slightly left. Change feet, bring left heel forward and left arm—right elbow back. This is called the Bleking step.

Measure 2: Take Bleking step three times quickly, right, left, right.

Measures 3-8: Repeat Measures 1 and 2 three times beginning with the alternate foot each time.

Fig. II.

Measures 9-16: Hold joined hands out at side, shoulder-high. Take "hop waltz" with partner forward around the circle, turning partner. The "hop waltz" is similar to a step hop and is done to one measure of 2/4 time as follows: Step on right foot, lifting left leg sideways and bending trunk right, —1st beat; hop on right foot,—2nd beat. This is then repeated with left foot on next measure.

Note: Fig. II can be adapted by joining inside hands and taking the step hop forward around the circle, beginning with right foot. The step hop then is done by stepping on right foot, bringing left knee high in front, and hopping on right foot; then repeat left foot.

Pop Goes the Weasel

American Country Dance.

Victor: 20151 or 20447
Columbia: A-3078

Although usually not sung, the following words help in producing the spirit of the dance.

    1. All around the chicken-coop
         The monkey chased the weasel;
         That's the way the money goes—
         Pop-goes the weasel.

2. A penny for a spool of thread,
   A penny for a needle,
   That's the way the money goes—
   Pop-goes the weasel.

Formation: Groups of six called a set, three in a line, lines opposite each other, about six feet apart. Girls in one line, their partners opposite them in other line. The couple at one end (in American Country Dances—the couple nearest the music) are called the head of the set.

"Down the Outside and Back"

Measures 1-4: The head couple turn outward, boy to his left, girl to her right, and each skips down the outside of his line toward the foot of the set.

Measures 5-8: They turn in and around and skip back outside of their lines to the head of the set.

"Down the Center and Back"

Measures 9-12: The head couple join hands across and slide down the inside of the set to the foot.

Measures 13-16: They slide back to place.

"Three Hands Around With Lady"

Measures 1-6 repeated: The first couple join hands to form a circle with the second girl and skip around once and a half to left with her, arranging to stop at the end of this time, so that she stands in the circle opposite her original position in the line.

Measures 7 and 8: On the first note of the measure, which suggests "Pop," the head couple raise their joined hands, and forcibly pull the second girl under their arms, popping her into her place in the line, and release her hands.

"Three Hands Around With Gentlemen"

Measures 9-16: The head couple then join hands with second man, and skipping this time to the right, "pop" the second man into place.

Measures 1-16, played a third time. Repeat the above with third lady, and third gentleman. The head couple have now reached the bottom of the set, and they join their respective lines.

"Six hands Round"

Measures 1-4: (Music all repeated a fourth time). All join hands in one circle, and slide or skip around to left.

Measures 5-8. Reverse directions, skipping right to place. Do not drop hands.

"Under the Arch"

Measures 9-16: This is a form of casting off. Without dropping hands in the circle, the original head couple, who are now at the foot hold high joined hands; the second couple, who are now at the head, come down and pass under the arch, the third couple following. When couple 2 has passed under they drop hands between them, the man turns outward back to left, the girl to right, heading back to places. The rest follow. The couple forming the arch turn under their own arms and take their places in the line at the foot. The second couple are now head couple; all drop hands. The dance is repeated until each couple has been head couple.

There can be more couples in the set, if desired.

Swedish Klappdans

Arr. G. V. N.

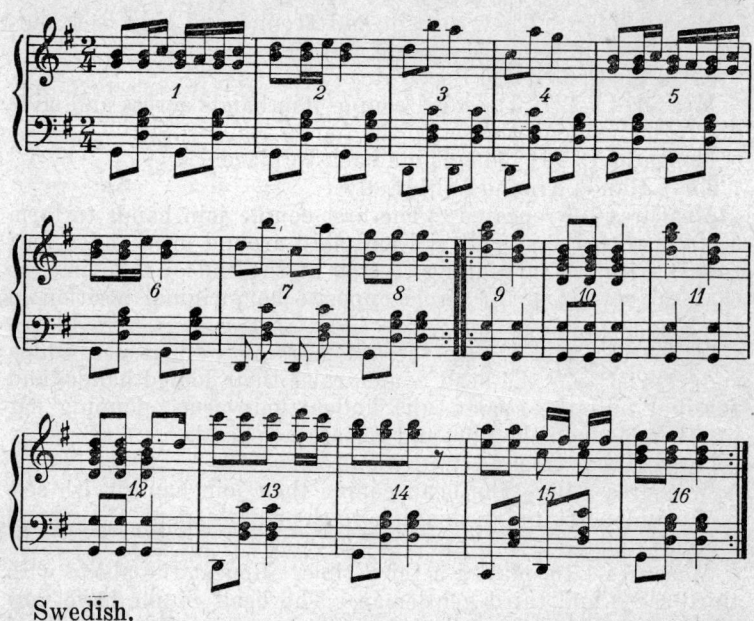

Swedish.

Victor: 20450
Columbia: A-3036

Formation: Double circle, partners side by side facing to move counter-clockwise around the circle, inside hands joined, outside hands on hips.

Fig. I.

Measures 1-8: Partners take polka step forward, beginning with outside foot. Inside joined hands are swinging backward and partners turn toward each other on this polka step. Polka with inside foot; at same time swing arms forward and turn slightly back to back. Continue polka steps alternating feet thru the 8 measures.

A Polka step is done to one measure of 2/4 time as follows: Hop on left foot and immediately slide forward with right foot, bring left foot to right foot (beat 1); slide forward with right foot (beat 2). To repeat left, hop on right foot and immediately slide forward with left foot, bring right foot to left foot (beat 1); slide forward left foot (beat 2). This can be simplified by taking first slide, together, slide with the right foot, and repeat with left, leaving out the hop.

Measures 1-8 repeated. Take heel-toe polka step in same direction beginning with outside foot. A heel-toe polka is done to 2 measures of 2/4 time as follows: Touch heel of outside foot forward, lean body slightly backward, (beat 1); touch outside toe backward, lean slightly forward (beat 2)—1 measure; take polka step forward with this foot—1 measure. This is repeated using inside foot.

Fig. II.

Measure 9: Partners face each other with hands on hips, and bow to each other, the boy makes an ordinary bow, the girl makes a bob courtesy (touch right toe behind left heel and bend both knees). Stand erect.

Measure 10: Clap own hands three times.

Measures 11 and 12: Repeat Measures 9 and 10.

Measure 13: Partners clap right hands across; each claps own hands once.

Measure 14: Clap left hands across, then own hands.

Measure 15: Slap right hands and with a swing of the body turn completely around left facing partner again.

Measure 16: Stamp three times in place beginning with right foot.

Measures 9-12 repeated. Repeat the bow and claps of Measures 9 to 12.

Measure 13: Rest right elbow on left palm and shake right forefinger at partner three times.

Measure 14: Repeat with left forefinger.

Measures 15 and 16: Same as before.

Note: A change of partners can be made for each repetition by each player moving around the circle to his own right on the three stamps, thus meeting the next one for a new partner.

Swiss May Dance

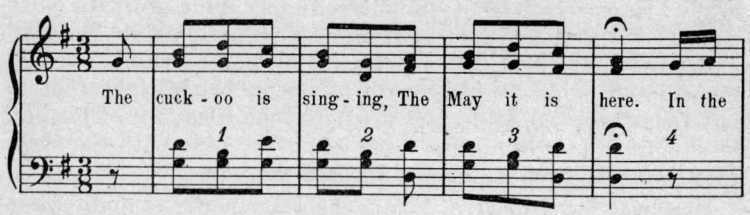

Arr. G. V. N.

The cuck-oo is sing-ing, The May it is here. In the field and the for-est The green doth ap-pear. Then dance chil-dren dance, While the sky it is blue; Turn round and turn un-der, While I go with you.

Swiss.

Columbia: A-3153

Formation: Double circle, partners facing to move counterclockwise around the circle, hands joined. Girls hold skirts with outside hands.

Measures 1-3: Nine running steps forward beginning with left foot.

Measure 4: Partners face each other; put the right foot back and make a deep courtesy, skirts held out at side.

Measures 5-8: Face in toward each other and about, join hands and run nine steps in opposite direction, beginning with left foot. Step right back and courtesy as in measure 4.

Measures 9 and 10: Join right hands; take three running steps forward beginning left foot, changing place with partner. Face partner, put right foot back and courtesy.

Measures 11 and 12: Join left hands and return with three running steps. Put right foot back and courtesy.

Measures 13 and 14: Join right hands. The inside partner beginning with left foot, takes six running steps turning under her right arm. The outside partner takes six running steps in place, beginning left foot.

Measures 15 and 16: The outside partner turning under her right arm takes three more running steps moving forward to meet a new partner; puts right foot back and courtesies. The inside partner continues running three steps in place and courtesies to new partner.

Norwegian Mountain March

Arr. G. V. N.

Norwegian.

Victor: 20151
Columbia: A-3041

Formation. A triangle of threes. One leader (the mountain guide) and two followers. The leader No. 1 holds a handkerchief in each hand. The two following who stand side by side grasp these handkerchiefs in outside hands, and join inside hands. The one on the left hand is No. 2, the one on the right is No. 3.

Measures 1-8, and repeated: Beginning with right foot all run forward three steps to the measure, stamping on the first count of each measure. When the stamp is made with the right foot, sway the trunk to the right. When the stamp is left, sway trunk left.

Measures 9 and 10: No. 1 bending trunk forward runs backward six steps, stamping on first step, passing under the joined hands of Nos. 2 and 3, who run in place.

Measures 11 and 12: No. 2 with six running steps dances across in front of No. 1, and turns inward under No. 1's right arm. The rest run in place.

Measures 13 and 14: All still running in place, No. 3 turns inward once around in place under his own left arm.

Measures 15 and 16: No. 1 turns once around to the right under his own right arm. This brings all back to original position.

Measures 9-16 repeated. Repeat the same.

PHYSICAL EDUCATION   245

Reap the Flax

Arr. G. V. N.

Swedish.

Columbia: A-3001

Formation: Fives in a group standing side by side. Groups can be arranged in a column or in a circle. They face as if to go counter-clockwise if in a circle. Hands on hips.

Step. I. Gathering in the flax. See Fig. I—Diagram.

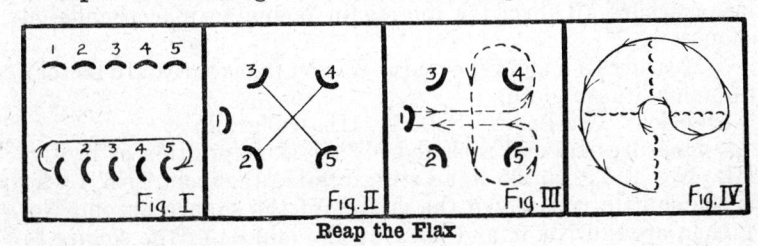

Reap the Flax

Measures 1-4: All reach down to left, to pull the flax. Come to standing position and pull hands to waist, reaping the flax. Throw the flax over the right side. Place hands on hips. One measure for each movement.

Measures 1-4 repeated: Repeat same movements. On last measure all face and stamp, placing hands on shoulders of one in front, leader's hands on hips. If lines are in a column the facing is left. If in a circle the facing is also left to face center of circle.

Measures 5-8 and repeated: Wagons bringing flax in from field to barn. Beginning with right foot each group runs around in a small circle to the right, taking three steps to a measure, and returns to place, facing right with two stamps on last measure, to form original formation.

Step II. Hackling flax.

Measures 1-4: All reach down to right. Return to standing positions as if picking up flax. Place the flax forward around the hackle. Jerk hands back, as if pulling flax from hackle. One measure for each movement.

Measures 1-4 repeated: Repeat same movements facing on the last movement, in the same manner as in Fig. I.

Measures 5-8 and repeated. Wagons bringing flax to house. Repeat steps of measures 5 to 8 in Fig. I.

Step III. Spinning the flax into thread. See Fig. II— Diagram.

Measures 1-4: The dancers in the groups will be numbered 1, 2, 3, 4, 5. No. 1 is the leader, and at the left end. Nos. 2 and 5 step sideways out of line and form a square with Nos. 3 and 4. These four dancers join right hands across in the center, left hands on hips. They are the spinning wheel. They run around to the right, three steps to the measure. In the meantime No. 1 turns about to face the wheel and represents the spinner. He treads the wheel with right foot, and claps his hands, once to each measure.

Measures 1-4 repeated: The dancers forming the wheel, join left hands across and run in the opposite direction, three steps to the measure. No. 1 continues to tread wheel. On the last measure all form the line again facing to place hands on shoulders.

Measures 5-8 and repeated: Wagon takes thread to factory to be made into cloth.

Step IV. The Loom. See Fig. III—Diagram.

Measures 1-4 and repeated: Take same position as in Fig. III. Nos. 2, 3, 4, and 5 stand still, forming the loom. No. 1 who is the shuttle runs down the middle of the square around No. 4, then around No. 5, and back up the middle of the square to place. All face into one line on last measure.

Measures 5-8 and repeated: Wagon takes cloth to train.

Step V. See Fig. IV—Diagram.

Play all the music again and again until all are back to place. This may represent yards and yards of cloth, or may represent a train of cars carrying the cloth to the different stations. The groups are numbered. When done in a circle, Group I starts around the inside of the circle to the left; as it passes Group II this group hitches on, and so on around the circle until all are attached in one long line. The leader then turns back on the line to the left and cutting a large circle leads the line the other way. When each group gets to its original place it breaks off from the line and runs down to form its own line as at the beginning. This represents cars switching off at various stations. Two stamps with a facing complete the dance and dancers are in formation to start, again. When done in a column of lines Group I. at the right-hand end, turns to left to run across in front of the lines. Each group hooks on as the line passes. They cut a circle counter-clockwise, until the leader reaches his place, when he turns left and cuts diagonally across the circle to the far corner, and then turns left again to go in a straight line across the rear to a point opposite his place. He leads his line down to place and as each group arrives opposite its place it breaks off and returns down to original formation.

The Crested Hen

Arr. G. V. N.

Danish.

Victor: 21619

Formation: Circles of threes, hands joined. The dancers are numbered 1, 2, and 3. No. 2 is a man. The step used throughout is a fast step hop, more like a skip step. One step hop is done to one measure of music, stepping on beat 1, and hopping on beat 2. The music is played quite fast.

Measures 1-8: With a stamp on left on the first note, take 8 step hops around circle to left. Lean out from circle and dance vigorously.

Measures 1-8 repeated. Jump high into the air on the first note, and take the same steps around the circle to the right.

Measures 9 and 10: Nos. 1 and 3 drop hands, the dancers forming a line. No. 1 who is on the right crosses in front of No. 2 and dances under the arch formed by the raised joined arms of Nos. 2 and 3.

Measures 11 and 12: No. 2 follows No. 1 turning under his own left arm.

Measures 13 and 14: No. 3 crosses in front of No. 2 and dances under the joined arms of Nos. 2 and 1.

Measures 15 and 16: No. 2 follows, passing under his own right arm. During measures 9 to 16, all step hop in place when not moving forward.

Measures 9-16 repeated. Repeat the same.

French Reel

Arr. G. V. N.

Danish.

Victor: 18600

Formation: Two rows facing each other; boys in one and girls in the other. Couples are numbered 1 and 2. The dance is described for the first two couples. Each set of two couples does likewise.

Measures 1-4: First boy turns to second boy and shakes his right hand four times. Then he shakes his left hand four times. The two girls do the same at the same time.

Measures 5-8: Turn to partner and shake right hands four times, then left hands.

Measures 9-12: Clap own hands, clap partner's right hand, clap own; clap partner's left, clap own, clap both of partner's hands; clap own hands three times in fast time.

Measures 13-16: Take the hop waltz alone in place 4 times (See p. 117).

Measures 9-16 repeated. The two couples join hands to form a circle and beginning with an appel walk around circle counter-clockwise for measures 9 to 12; then with an appel change directions and walk clockwise for measures 13 to 16. An appel is an emphasized step.

Measures 17-24. The grand right and left is taken around the circle of fours with walking steps and an appel is made on the first of every 8 steps. The grand right and left is done as follows: In the single circle each girl faces her partner; gives right hand to partner and passes him by the right shoulder; gives left hand to other girl and passes her by the left shoulder. This continues around the circle, first right hand then left hand until the end of the strain. Finish at end in own place in two lines as at first.

Measures 17-24 repeated. The two boys join inside hands; also do the two girls. The boys raise arms to form an arch. With an appel the two rows change places, the ladies passing through the arch. Keeping the row formation, the dancers drop hands and turn left about, joining inside hands again (4 meas.). Take walking steps. With an appel the rows change places again in the same manner except that the girls form the arch and the boys pass under (4 meas.). Finish with a nod to partner.

Note: Though the form is retained, the above is a slight simplification for grade children.

Sellenger's Round

English Country Dance.

Victor: 20445
Columbia: A-3065

Formation: Single circle facing in. Hands joined.
Step I.
Measures 1-4: All slide 8 steps to left.
Measures 1-4 repeated: All slide 8 steps to right.
Interlude
Measures 5 and 6: All drop hands and do two singles toward center of circle. (Step forward right foot, draw left foot up to right. Step forward left foot and draw right foot up to it).

Measures 7 and 8: Fall back a double. (Walk back three steps and bring the feet together and rise on toes on the fourth count).

Measures 9-12: Turn toward partner and set and turn single. [Step to the right with the right foot and draw the left foot up and rise on toes: repeat left (Set). Each person turns to his own right with four running steps bringing the feet up behind (turn single).]

Measures 5-12 repeated. Repeat interlude.

Step II.

Measures 1-4: With hands joined all move in a double and out a double to place.

Measures 1-4 repeated. Do this again.

Interlude

Measures 5-12 and repeated. Same as before.

Step III.

Measures 1-4: Partners side (Partners face each other and starting with the right foot walk three steps forward passing left shoulders and turn left about on the fourth count without removing feet from floor. Beginning with the left foot walk back to place three steps keeping to the same side, that is, passing right shoulder, and turn right to face partner on fourth count).

Measures 1-4 repeated: Do this again.

Interlude

Measures 5-12 and repeated. Same as before.

Step IV.

Measures 1-4: Partners arm with the right. (Partners meet, link right arms, swing around, separate, and fall back to places.)

Measures 1-4 repeated: Partners arm with the left.

Interlude

Measures 5-12 and repeated. Same as before.

Step V.

Measures 1-4 and repeated: Same as Step I.

Interlude

Measures 5-12 and repeated: Same as before, except at end finish with courtesy and bow facing partner.

Fist Polka

Arr. G. V. N.

Finnish.

Formation: Double circle, partners standing side by side facing forward with both hands joined, skaters' fashion.

A.

Measure 1: Starting with inside feet do step-together-step and leap onto the outside feet. This leap is much as one would go over a hurdle.

Measures 2 and 3: Repeat above twice more.

Measure 4: Stamp three times while turning in place toward each other so as to be facing in the opposite direction.

Measures 1-4 repeated: Repeat all of above but finish facing partner.

B.

Measure 5: With hands on hips, each jumps and turns left so that right elbows are touching. (Partners facing in opposite directions).

Measure 6: Jump and turn about to right so that left elbows are touching.

Measures 7: Jump placing the right foot forward and shake the fist in partner's face three times.

Measure 8: Jump and change feet and shake left fist.

Measures 9 and 10: Partners turn out away from each other to their left and after turning 3 quarters around run on in the same direction they are going to a new partner, at the same time clapping their hands in time to the music (5 claps). On the last step all jump landing on both feet, hands on hips, facing new partner.

Old Zip Coon
(Turkey in the Straw)

Arr. G. V. N.

Victor: 20592

Virginia Reel
Old Zip Coon (Turkey in the Straw)

Victor: 20592
Columbia: A-3077

American Country Dance.

Formation: Long ways for six couples, boys in one line, and girls in the other; head couple nearest the music; boys at girls' left when facing down the hall (toward the music); two lines face each other to dance.

Steps: The usual country-dance step, a springing walk.

The Dance
"Forward and Back"

Measures 1-4: The head (first) girl and foot (sixth) boy advance four steps toward each other, honor each other (courtesy and bow) on the fourth count, and retire four steps backward to their places.

Measures 5-8: The head boy and foot girl do the same.

"Swing with Right Hand"

Measures 9-12: The head girl and foot boy advance, join right hands, swing once around and return to places.

Measures 13-16: The head boy and foot girl do the same.

"Swing with Left Hand"

Measures 1-4: The head girl and foot boy swing once around with left hands joined, and return to places.

Measures 5-8: The head boy and foot girl do the same.

"Swing with both hands"

Measures 9-12: The head girl and foot boy swing once around with both hands joined, and return to places.

Measures 13-16: The head boy and foot girl do the same.

"Dos a Dos"

Measures 1-4: The head girl and foot boy advance, pass each other, right shoulder to right shoulder, go around each other back to back, and retire backward to their places.

Measures 5-8: The head boy and foot girl do the same.

"Right Arm to Partner and Reel"

Measures 1-16 repeated as necessary.

(1) The first couple (head girl and head boy) hook right elbows and swing once and a half around.

(2) The head girl swings the second boy once around, with the left elbows hooked (while the head boy does the same with the second girl).

(3) The head girl and boy swing each other once around with right elbows hooked as before.

The head couple continue the "Reel" in this manner, swinging each couple in turn, until they reach the foot of the set, where they swing each other half around with right elbows hooked so that the girl finishes on the girls' and the boy on the boys' side.

"Up the Center"

The head couple face each other, join both hands, right with right, left with left, and with 8 slide steps dance up to the head of the set, where they release hands.

"Cast off"

Measures 1-16 repeated as necessary.

The head couple separate and "cast off," the girl marching down the outside of the girls' line, followed by all the other girls in single file, and the head boy, at the same time, marching down the outside of the boys' line, followed by all the other boys.

When the head girl and boy meet at the foot, they join hands and march up to the head of the set, followed by all the other couples.

"Down the Center"

When all reach their original places, partners (with the exception of the head couple) join both hands and raise them high, forming a column of arches, under which the head couple, (with both hands joined) dance down to the foot of the set with 8 slide steps.

The "Head Couple" remains at the foot of the set, and now becomes the "Foot Couple," while the original second couple now becomes the "Head Couple." Repeat dance from first. The dance pattern is repeated until each couple has been a head couple.

Variation: The last figure "Down the Center" is often omitted and after "Casting Off" the head girl and boy meet at the foot and join hands to form an arch. The lines as they meet partners join hands and slide under the arch to their positions in the set. The head couple is now at the foot where it remains.

Troika

Polish.

Formation: Players in lines of threes standing abreast, boy in center, two girls on either side, hands joined and arms stretched out. These lines of threes are arranged around a large circle, facing counter-clockwise.

Fig. I.

Measure 1: Run four steps diagonally forward right, outward from circle, starting with right foot.

Measure 2: Repeat the four running steps moving diagonally forward left, inward into circle.

Measures 3 and 4: Run forward around circle 8 steps, the man in advance of the others pulling them along.

Measures 5 and 6: All take eight running steps so that the group turns in place to face opposite direction. This is done as follows: Girls cross in front of boy, who runs in place. Girl on boy's right (outside girl) passes around the left-hand girl. The left-hand (inside) girl passes under arms of boy and outside girl. Boy follows her turning about in place under his own right arm. Keep hands joined all the time.

Measures 7 and 8. Repeat the turning as in Measures 5 and 6; the left-hand girl passes around and the right-hand girl passes under this time. They finish facing in original direction.

Fig. II.

Measures 9 to 12: Each group of threes join hands in a circle; take 16 running steps around to left, with arms stretched out; kick heels up behind on running steps.

Measures 13 and 14: Reverse the direction, running right, with 8 steps. Arrange to place boy in the circle facing in line of direction of the big circle at the end of this run.

Measures 15 and 16: On the first count of measure 15, boy drops hands of girls, claps his own hands loudly, and runs forward under the raised joined arms of the girls with 8 running steps, on to meet next group of girls, with whom he joins hands ready to start the dance from the beginning.

Note: Boy must start on time, clapping hands on first beat of measure 15, and must reach new group within the 8 running steps. Girls must keep their hands joined, and form the arch on the clap.

Minuet

Victor: 17087, 20990, 20440

Music: Minuet-Mozart

Formation: Quadrille;—a set of four couples, each couple standing side by side on one of the sides of a square, facing in. Boy on left side of girl. Girl lays her left hand on boy's right palm.

Steps:

(a) Minuet step. Two measures needed for one minuet step. Step forward three steps, right, left, right (1 meas.); point left foot forward and hold (1 meas.).

(b) Step and point. One measure needed. Step right

foot (ct 1), point left foot diagonally forward (ct 2) and hold (ct 3).

(c) Balance forward and back. Two measures needed. Facing partners and right hands joined, step forward right foot; step left to right and rise on toes; step right (1 meas.). This is balance forward. Step back left foot; bring right foot to left; step left; (1 meas.). This is balance back.

(d) Curtsey and bow. Two measures needed. For the curtsey, the girl steps right, draws left foot back behind right foot, bends both knees, at same time bending trunk and head forward. The weight slowly settles on rear foot as forward knee straightens. The rear knee then also straightens and body is brought to erect position, weight on left foot. For the boy, the boy steps left, brings right foot to left, and bends trunk and head forward from the hips. His right hand comes to his chest. The left arm hangs lightly at side. Bring body slowly back to erect position.

Intro: Face partner, curtsey and bow.

Step I.

Measures 1-14: Turn with partner right and take seven minuet steps, starting with outside feet, moving around the quadrille in a circle counter-clockwise and reaching own places at end; facing in.

Measures 15 and 16: Face partner. Curtsey and bow.

Step II.

Measures 1-4: Still facing partner, and joining right hands, balance forward right foot, and backward left foot. Repeat.

Measures 5-8: With right hands still joined walk around each other with two minuet steps, right, left, changing places.

Measures 9-16: Repeat all moving on around, but finish with boy's back to center, girl facing center.

Step III.

Measures 1 and 2: Curtsey and bow.

Measures 3-6: Move backward away from partner with 2 minuet steps, right, left, the boy goes toward center, the girl outward.

Measures 7 and 8: Take step and point twice, right and left, in place.

Measures 9 and 10: Curtsey and bow.

Measures 11-14: Move toward partner with 2 minuet steps.

Measures 15 and 16: Curtsey and bow.

Step IV.

Measures 1-4: Both face right and move around the quadrille to the corner to meet next partner. Take two minuet steps to accomplish this.

Measures 5 and 6: Take step point twice.

Measures 7 and 8: Curtsey and bow.
Measures 9-12: Take girl's right hand and balance forward right, backward left two times as in Step II.
Measures 13-16: Walk around each other with 2 minuet steps, as in Step II, changing places.

Step V.
Measures 1-4: Pass partner and return to own partner, with 2 minuet steps.
Measures 5 and 6: Take step point twice in place.
Measures 7 and 8: Curtsey and bow, very low; finish music with a retard on the last two measures.

Highland Schottische

Arr. G. V. N.

Scotch.

Victor: 21616
Columbia: A-3039

Formation: Single circle, partners facing each other. Right hand at hip; left arm in half circle cover head.

Measure 1: Touch right toe to right side, hop left. Bring right foot in behind left knee, hop left. Touch right toe to right side again, hop left. Bring right foot in front of left knee, hop left.

Measure 2: Schottische step with right foot, done to one measure of Schottische (4/4 time) as follows: Step right (beat 1); bring left foot to right, changing weight to it (beat 2); step right again (beat 3); hop right, bringing left knee up in front (beat 4).

Measures 3 and 4: Repeat steps of Measures 1 and 2 with left foot and with right hand over head.

Measures 5 and 6: Partners hook right elbows, left hand on hips, and take two schottische steps, turning.

Measure 7: They then hook left elbows, turn around the other way, with one schottische step with right foot.

Measure 8: They leave each other going opposite directions around the circle with three running steps to meet a new partner. Each dancer goes in the direction in which she was first facing at the beginning of the dance.

Bounding Heart

Arr. G. V. N.

Finnish.

Formation: A double circle, partners facing each other, about six steps apart, one has back to center, the other faces center. Hands on hips. The dance has a rather saucy, flirting character. The mazurka step is used. This is done to one measure of the music as follows: Slide forward right foot (first beat); bring the left foot up to the right, changing weight to left foot, and extending right forward (second beat); hop on the left foot and bend the right knee (third beat).

Measures 1-3: Three mazurkas forward, with right foot, toward partner, as if glad to meet him.

Measure 4: Stamp forward right foot (1st beat); and with a toss of head, nose in air, jump to turn left about (2nd beat) and hold (3rd beat); partners are now back to back.

Measures 5-7: Three mazurka steps away from each other, with left foot. The outside circle moves away from and the inside circle toward the center of the circle.

Measure 8: Stamp left foot, and turn right about to face partner, ready to make up with him.

Measures 9 and 10: One mazurka step right; stamp right and turn left about, again back to back. You have changed your mind.

Measures 11 and 12: One mazurka step away; with left foot; stamp left and turn right about. Once again you have changed your mind.

Measures 13-15: Now you go eagerly toward your partner taking 3 mazurka steps with right foot.

Measure 16: Stamp right foot forward, hesitating as to whether to spurn him again or not. Jump to turn left, but instead of turning about as before, make a full turn facing partner.

To repeat the dance, have circles exchange places, repeating the last four measures to make the change. The inside circle moves out and outside circle moves in; they pass left shoulders; and turn to face each other. Partners may be changed during this, by moving diagonally forward right.

Weaving Dance

Arr. G. V. N.

Swedish.

Formation: Six couples in two lines, four steps apart, facing each other; lines hand in hand. The boys are in one line, the girls in the other, partners opposite.

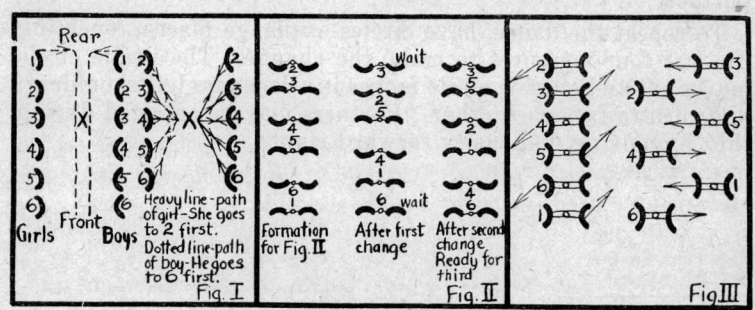

Weaving Dance

The step used throughout the dance is the running step, one to each beat of the music, three to a measure. Occasionally as directed below, the first step of the measure is emphasized by bringing the foot down hard, called an "appel." The music is played over and over again until the dance is completed.

I.

2 measures: With an appel the lines take 6 small running steps toward each other.

2 measures: With 6 steps beginning with appel return backward to place.

4 measures: Repeat forward and back.

4 measures: Boy and girl of first couple with appel run toward each other; boy takes girl's left hand with his right, and they run down between the lines to the front, where they halt, face about, turning toward each other. (See Diagram—Fig. I).

2 measures: Boy takes girl's right hand with his left, and with appel, they run to X. (See Diagram—Fig. I).

2 measures: Link right arms and dance around one turn.

2 measures: With appel, boy runs to girl of couple 6, and his partner to boy of couple 2; they link left arms and dance around one-half turn.

2 measures: With appel they run back to partner, meeting at X, link right arms, and dance around one-half turn.

4 measures: Repeat steps of last 4 measures, but boy and girl of couple 1, dance respectively with girl No. 5 and boy No. 3.

4 measures: Girl No. 1 with boy No. 4; Boy No. 1 with girl No. 4.

4 measures: Girl No. 1 with boy No. 5; Boy No. 1 with girl No. 3.

4 measures: Girl No. 1 with Boy No. 6; Boy No. 1 with girl No. 2.

4 measures: Boy No. 1 takes his partner's left hand in his right and with appel, they run to starting place (rear); both face boys' line.

4 measures: They run, still holding hands, down this line, boy outside, girl inside, the boys in the line leaning down to allow arms of couple 1 to pass over them, and accenting the time of the music by clapping hands.

4 measures: In the same way, couple 1 run down girls' line to rear.

4 Measures: Then run up between the lines to the front and become leading couple in the line.

2 measures: With appel lines take three steps toward each other; at fourth step stop with appel.

2 measures: Boys of odd couples take with left hand their partner's right and turn away from front while boys of even

couples take with right hands their partner's left, and turn toward front.

II. (See Diagram—Fig. II)

1 measure: Odd couples form arches, and with appel take three small running steps forward, while even couples with three steps pass through arches; couples thus exchange places.

1 measure: Even couples, with appel, form arches and odd couples pass through.

26 measures: Dance continues until couples, after ten times alternately forming arches and passing through them, have regained their places. One measure is needed for each going over, and one for each going under. When a couple during the dance reach the extreme front or rear, they face about and remain in place during one measure, then continue the dance; if they have just formed the arch, they pass through one; if they have just passed through one they now form one.

The music continues for this figure until all is completed and every one in place. Couples face each other across and join hands when they have finished, and thus await the end of a refrain before starting the next figure. About 28 measures are needed in all, and the group rest through four measures more.

III. (See Diagram—Fig. III)

This figure represents the movement of the shuttle.

2 measures: The boys of odd couples, drawing their partners with them, take six small steps obliquely backward to right and stop. At the same time boys of even couples, pushing their partners backward before them, take six small steps obliquely forward to left and stop with appel, so that odd couples are now on the right and even couples on the left in a straight line across.

2 measures: The boys of odd couples pushing their partners backward before them take six long steps obliquely forward to right and stop. At the same time boys of even couples, drawing their partners with them, take six long steps obliquely backward to left and stop so that odd couples are now on the left side and even on the right.

20 measures: This exchange of places from right to left and from left to right continues until each couple has reached its starting place. Twenty-four measures of music are needed in all. When a couple during the dance reach the extreme front or rear, they remain in place during two measures; they then continue the dance returning in the same way that they came.

IV.

Each boy keeps his partner's left hand in his right, and with his left hand takes the right hand, crossed under her left arm, of the girl on his left side. Arms are raised to make a continuous row of arches. Through the archway so formed the girl at the extreme rear with appel draws after her all the rest in line. When she reaches front, she turns to the left and draws the line into a semi-circle so large that when she reaches her starting place the last couple will have passed through the arches. She stops; her partner still in line, makes a half turn to the left under her left arm, and resumes his place facing her. Under their raised arms he brings forward the girl at his left hand, who raises her arms above her head and with whole turn to right, resumes her starting position. Dance continues in this way until every one has resumed the starting position of Figure Four. The figure is then repeated.

The music continues until the figure is completed. When the dancers have finished all await the end of the refrain.

V.

Couples raising arms, again form archway, through which the girl of rear couple again draws line as in Figure Four, but into a circle. When all are through the archway, the boy of leading couple (last in line) runs still in line to center of circle and stops. His partner (leading girl) winds the line about him. When winding is complete all raise their arms, and the boy in the center works his way out from the center straight out to outside of circle under arches; he then turns to the right and draws the line again into a circle. All dance to the right until the end of the refrain.

VI.

4 measures: Boys link right arms with partners and dance around two turns.

4 measures: Then link left arms with next girl and dance around two turns.

8 measures: Continue linking right and left arms, alternately around the circle, the boys going counter-clockwise, the girls clockwise, until each boy meets his partner.

To end of Music: With partner turn several times around both hands joined, appel on first beat of each measure, thus finishing the game.

Rufty Tufty

Arr. G. V. N.

Victor: 20446
Columbia: A-3065

English Country Dance.
Formation: Groups of four. Two couples facing each other, man standing on left of lady.
Music consists of 3 parts: A, B and C. Double quick time.
Fig. I.
A. Measures 1-4: Both couples move forward a double and fall back a double* to places (running step).
Measures 5-8: Repeat.
B. Measures 1-4: Partners set* and turn single*.
Measures 5-8: Repeat.
C. Measures 1 and 2: First man, with his left hand, leads* his partner a double toward the left wall; while second man, with his left hand leads his partner a double toward the right wall (running step).
Measures 3 and 4: Both couples turn around and face each other; the men with their right hands lead their partners a double to places (running step).
Measures 5 and 6: All turn single.
Measures 7-10: First man, with his right hand, leads second woman toward end of room, a double, turns and leads her back to her place. Second man does same with first woman, leading her toward other end of room and back.
Measures 11 and 12: All turn single.
Fig. II.
A. Measures 1-4: Partners side* with each other
Measures 5-8: Repeat.
B. Measures 1-8: Same as B in Figure 1.
C. Measures 1-12: Same as C in Figure 1.
Fig. III.
A. Measures 1-4: Partners arm* with the right.
Measures 5-8: Partners arm with the left.
B. Measures 1-8: Same as B in Figure 1.
C. Measures 1-12: Same as C in Figure 1. Bow and courtesy at end.
Play the music through once for each figure.
*Explanation of terms:
Running Step: A slow running step, executed upon the ball of the foot. Arms held loosely, should be slightly bent at the elbows, and allowed to swing naturally.
Double: Three steps forward or backward, followed by "feet-together".
Turn Single: The dancer moves around in a small circle, clockwise, taking 4 small running steps, beginning with right foot.
Single: A step forward or to side is made with one foot, e. g., the right, and weight supported on it. The left foot, heel raised and toe touching the ground is drawn up and the

heel placed in the hollow of the right foot. As the left foot is dragged towards the right, the body is raised upon the instep of the right foot and lowered as the feet come together. (2 counts).

Set: A single to the right followed by a single to the left. 2 measures.

Side: Dancers face each other, move forward a double, passing left shoulders, (begin with right foot). Make a half-turn counter-clockwise on the fourth step. Return to places (beginning with the left foot) passing right shoulders.

Arm: Partners meet, link right (or left) arms, swing around, separate, and fall back to places.

Lead: Dance forward.

Shepherd's Hey

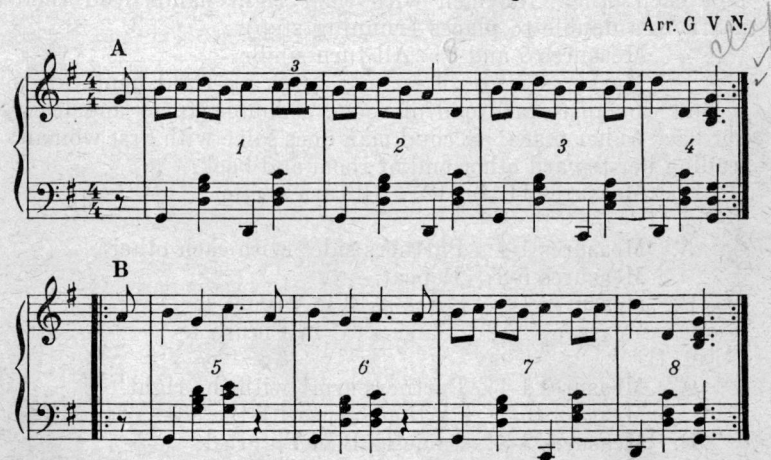

Arr. G V N.

English Morris Dance. 20641

Formation: A group of six boys (the Morris Dances of England were always danced by men). This group of six is called the "side" a term similarly used as the word "set" in English and American Country Dances. The side may be, according to the figure, either in "column" formation facing "up" or "down," or in the "front" formation. See diagrams.

This Morris dance may be done with hand-clapping or with sticks. As described here the hand-clapping is used.

Steps:

The Morris Step: The nature of the Morris step resembles marking time with a straight knee but the heel does not touch the floor. It also resembles running with a straight but relaxed knee, but little space is covered and the leg not raised high. A combination of both running and marking time with a straight knee will bring the characteristic Morris step. When taking a step, be the step in place or moving forward or backward, the leg is swung sharply forward from the hip just far enough to bring the heel off the floor about 3 inches from the ground; then the ball of the foot is brought down in sharp contact with the floor.

The Step Hop: The Morris step as above described is used in combination with a hop; step right on count 1; hop right on count 2, the other leg in same position as in Morris step,—raised a few inches from floor, knee straight; step left, count 3; hop left, count 4.

The 1-2-3 Hop: The Morris step is used in combination with the hop in the following manner:

Step right (count 1); step left (count 2); step right, (count 3); hop right (count 4). When repeated, step is begun with left foot.

The Jump: The jump is made from both feet with straight legs and as high as possible landing on balls of both feet again. Clap own hands together at forehead level on each jump.

The Caper: This is a Morris step with an exaggerated spring, leaving the floor as far as possible. The free leg is raised forward as in the Morris step, but no further. More time is given to the Caper than to the Morris step:—two beats for each Caper. This gives time to get way off the floor.

Arms: In the traditional Morris dances, the arms are used in a certain manner in combination with the feet. This, however, is quite difficult, therefore, for the present purpose the use of the arms is omitted, with the exception of the hand clapping which will be described below.

The Dance

Music A. (4 meas.): "Once to yourself." The side stands in column formation facing up. On the third beat of the fourth measure all jump high in place and clap hands together at forehead level. This serves as an Introduction.

Music A. (4 meas.). "Foot-up": Still in column formation facing up take 1-2-3 hop two times beginning right foot (2 meas.). Then take "step-hop" two times (1 meas.). Step right and hold (ct. 1-2); jump with clap (count 3) facing to front formation on the jump, hold (ct. 4), (1 meas.).

4 measures repeated. Face down in column formation, and repeat the above steps; jump to front formation.

Music B. "Hand-clapping"

Measure 5: Clap own hands (ct. 1).

Raise right knee and strike it with right hand (ct. 2).

272 IOWA STATE TEACHERS COLLEGE

Shepherd's Hey
→

```
       5   3   1
Bottom ⟩   ⟩   ⟩ Top
(down) ⟩   ⟩   ⟩ (up)
       6   4   2
```
Column formation facing up

```
     5   3   1
Down             Up
     6   4   2
```
Front formation

The Hey for 1-3-5
Bottom — 7 — 5 — 3 — 1 — top

Half-Hands
I.   II.

Back-to-back
I.   II.

Cross-over and Turn

Whole Rounds

Shepherd's Hey

Partners (dancers opposite) strike right hands together (ct. 3).

Hold (ct. 4).

Measure 6: Clap own hands.

Raise and strike left knee with left hand. Strike left hands across with partner.

Hold.

Measures 7 and 8: Clap own hands (1).

Raise right thigh and clap own hands under it (2).

Clap own hands (3).

Raise left thigh and clap hands under it (4).

Clap own hands (1).

Clap own hands behind back (2).

Partners strike both hands across, left with right, and right with left (3).

Hold (4).

Measures 5-8 repeated. Repeat hand-clapping.

Music A. Measures 1-4. "Half-hey": The half-hey is described for one line only; the other line executes the same thing. Nos. 1 and 5 face down, No. 3 up. Refer to diagram. No. 1 along unbroken line passes No. 3 by the right shoulder who follows the dotted line, while No. 5 moves around the loop to the left. Nos. 1 and 5 then pass left shoulders, No. 1 following heavy line and No. 5 dotted line, while No. 3 moves around the top loop to the right. Nos. 3 and 5 pass by the right, No. 3 on the heavy line, No. 5 on the dotted line, while No. 1 moves around the bottom loop to the left. This completes the Half-hey, Nos. 1 and 5 have changed places, while No. 3 is back in the middle.

The steps used are 1-2-3 hop twice, step-hop twice, step and jump. Then face to front formation on the jump.

Measures 1-4 repeated. Half-hey—returning to own place, using same steps as before Nos. 1 and 5 face up, No. 3 down. Nos. 1 and 3 pass by the left shoulder, No. 1 on the dotted line, and No. 3 on the heavy line, while No. 5 moves around the top loop to the right. Nos. 1 and 5 pass by the right shoulder, No. 1 along the dotted line, No. 5 along the unbroken line; while No. 3 moves around the bottom loop on the heavy line, to the left. Nos. 3 and 5 pass by the left shoulder. No. 3 along the dotted line, No. 5 along the heavy line, while No. 1 passes around the top loop to the right. All face to front formation on the jump, and are in original position in the line.

Music B. Measures 5-8 and repeated. Repeat hand-clapping.

Music A. "Half-hands." Front formation.

Each dancer moves forward bearing a little to his left passing his partner by the right shoulder. Use 1-2-3 hop two times (2 meas.).

Return on the same track, backward to place. Use step-hop twice then step back and jump (2 meas.) See diagram "Half-hands" I.

Each dancer now moves forward, bearing a little to his right and passing his partner by the left shoulder. Use 1-2-3 hop two times (2 meas.).

Return backward to place with 2 step hops, step and jump (2 meas.). See diagram II, "Half-hands."

Music B played twice. Same as before for this music, i. e., hand-clapping.

Music A. "Back-to-back."

2 measures. Partners advance to left passing right shoulder and pass each other back to back. Use two 1-2-3 hops.

2 measures: Partners retire backward to position. Use two step-hops, then step and jump. Diagram I, "Back-to-back."

2 measures: Partners advance to right passing left shoulders and back to back.

2 measures: They retire backward to position. Diagram II.

Music B. Played twice. Hand-clapping.

Music A. "Cross and turn."

2 measures: Partners advance to left passing right shoulders with two 1-2-3 hops.

2 measures: After having crossed over and exchanged places they turn left about in a loop to face in front formation, with 2 step-hops, a step and jump.

See diagram. No. 1 follows heavy line, No. 2 dotted line.

4 measures: Partners return to place in same manner.

Music B. Played twice. Same as before.

Music A. "Whole-rounds and caper-out, all-in."

4 measures. All turn right and around to face in a circle already to move clockwise. See diagram. Nos. 3 and 4 move outward away from center at the same time. This turn is made immediately as first step is begun and the circle moves around clockwise with two 1-2-3 hops and two step-hops, a step and jump. At the end of the 4 measures, all shall have progressed half way around and should finish in opposite corners. On the jump all face center in 2 lines.

4 measures: All turn right and around as before to face in a circle to move clockwise again, and continue on around circle to own place with two 1-2-3 hops, 3 capers and jump to

face forward in column formation. After the jump (and clap in front of forehead which comes with the jump), dancers pause a moment, holding hands erect. This is called "all-in," which means the manner of finishing the dance.

Russian Folk Dance

Arr. G. V. N.

Formation: Couples arranged in a circle, facing to move counter-clockwise. Each girl in front of her partner.

Measures 1-7: Take 7 Russian steps around circle, beginning with right foot. The Russian step is executed in one measure, as follows: Step forward on heel of right foot (1 count), bring left foot to right (count and), step forward on toe of right foot (count 2), bend trunk right; repeat left foot. Girl has both hands on hips and turns to look at boy over right shoulder when bending right, and over left shoulder when bending left. Boy has left hand at hip, and swings right arm to side right on Russian step right, and across in front of body to left on Russian step left.

Measure 8: Take 3 stamps in place, the girl turning left about to face partner. Right arms come high over head on these stamps.

Measures 9-16: Place right arm about partner's waist, left out at side; dance around partner in this position with 7 Russian steps, starting right, and finish with 3 stamps.

Measure 17: The girl faces the center of the circle and moves in while the boy faces outward and moves away from center. Each steps right on count 1, and brushes left heel across in front on count 2, clapping own hands in front of chest on 2.

Measures 18-20: Take 2 Russian steps on in same direction, then turn left to face about on third. The first Russian step begins with left foot; the left arm is at hip, the right swings across in front to left and body bends left. As the step is taken right, right swings sideways to right and across to left again on the 3d step.

Measures 21-24: Repeat the above 4 measures moving back toward partner.

Measures 17-24 repeated: Right arms about each others' waists, turn around with 7 Russian steps, finishing with 3 stamps on last measure.

American Country Dance
(Lady in the Center and Seven Hands Round)

This description is arranged to fit the Victor record of the White Cockade. Any country dance tune may be used as Old Zip Coon, page 255.

This "change", as different American country dance patterns are called, is one of the collection made by the Physcial Education Department of Iowa State Teachers College through the help of Mr. Josiah Petty, Fiddler, and Mr. M. J. Nolan, Caller, both of Perry, Iowa, to whom we are indebted. The arrangement which follows was made by Miss Grace Van Ness to definitely fit the music for teaching purposes.

Formation: Quadrille, man on left of lady.
First Figure: "Balance and Swing."
　Step to R with R foot—Ct. 1.
　Bring feet together—Ct. 2.
Repeat to left—Cts. 3 and 4.
Then take partner in regular dancing position and swing around in place—clockwise. Use 12 counts for this. Use walking step on the turn around. Buzz step may be used).
Second Figure: "Left Allemande."
Each person gives his left hand to his neighbor and they walk around in place counter-clockwise, hands joined—8 counts. Then give R hand to partner and swing around (clockwise) in place—8 counts.
Third Figure: "Promenade All."
Partners join crossed hands, R with R and L with L and walk around the set, counter-clockwise, finishing in their original places—16 counts.
Fourth Figure: First Change.
　Call: "First lady, swing by the right."
First lady who is the lady of the couple nearest the music takes her neighbor by the right hand and swings around in place with him, clockwise—8 counts.
Then she gives her partner her left hand and walks around with him counter-clockwise—8 counts.
The call for the last is "partner by the left."
　Call: "Lady in the center and seven hands around."
At the finish of her swing around with her partner, the first lady now takes her place in the center of the group who join hands and circle around her, counter-clockwise—16 counts
　Call: "Lady swing out and gent swing in.
　　Join your hands and go it again."
At the end of the previous 16 steps the lady who has been in the center of the circle gives her left hand to her partner, who takes it with his left, breaking the circle. He leaves the circle and swings into the center while his partner takes his place in the circle of seven.
This change of places takes four steps. The circle of seven continues moving as they were in the preceding and the lady as she gives her left hand to her partner reaches forward with her right hand to grasp the hand of the person who will be ahead of her in the circle. (The circle of seven remains broken after the man moves into the center, until his partner takes her place in it). During the time of the change of center people, the circle of seven keeps on moving. They finish in their original places—16 counts.
This finishes the first change. "Balance," "Left Alle-

mande," and "Promenade" follow, and then the second lady does what the first lady has just done. Same is repeated by each lady in turn. "Balance," "Left Allemande," and "Promenade" follow each change.

Method of Giving Calls.

1. Balance and swing: Given just before the first strain begins.

2. Left Allemande: Count 14 of the preceding strains and then say "Left Allemande" on counts 15 and 16.

3. Promenade all: Count 14 of preceding strains and then say "Promenade All" on counts 15 and 16.

4. First lady swing by the right: Count 12 and then give the above call on remaining 4 counts of strain.

5. Lady in center and seven hands round: Count 4 and give call on last 4 counts of the strain.

6. Lady swing out and gent swing in, join your hands and go it again: Count 12 and give call on last 4 counts of strain. The last sentence, beginning "Join your hand" is given on first 4 counts of the next strain.

These calls are given on the last counts of the strain preceding the one during which the figure described is to be executed. Sixteen counts means 2 strains.

Irish Lilt

Arr. G. V. N.

Irish.
Steps:
1. Forward Rock.
2. Kick.
3. Toe and Heel.
4. Leg Twist and Kick.
5. Side Step.
6. Kick and Change.

Break—A connecting step.
Note: Throughout the dance the music is counted two beats to a measure.

Introduction—8 measures.
Stand, hands on hips and tap the right toe in time to the music.

First Step—Forward Rock
Measure 1: On count one, leap with weight on left foot, raising right foot backward. On count two, leap on right foot and raise left foot forward.
Measures 2-6: Repeat always raising left foot forward and right foot backward.
Measures 7 and 8: By means of the "Break" (one measure) bring the right foot forward.
Measures 1-8: Repeat the step with "Break."

Break
On count one, spring and land with feet astride. On count two, spring and bring feet together again. On count three, hop and raise right leg backward. On count four, hop and kick right leg forward. Two measures.

Practise this movement thoroughly. After having learned it the "Break" is not used as a separate step but is used to connect the various steps, and to connect the first and second halves of each step. For example, when the 7th measure in the first half of "Forward Rock" is reached, the left foot is forward in the air; the feet should then be spread (count one of the Break), brought together again (count two), the right leg raised in back (count three), then brought forward (count four), ready to be placed on the ground for the first count of the second half of the "Forward Rock," which is done with the right foot forward. The same process is gone through with at the end of the step in order to bring the left leg in position to start the next step.

Second Step—Kick
Measures 9 and 10: Two counts to each foot. On count one, spring and touch left toe at the right instep. On count two, spring and kick left leg forward outward. On count three, spring to left and touch right toe at the left instep. On count four, spring and kick right leg forward outward.

Measures 11-16: Continue the same, then do "Break" for four counts (two measures).

Measures 9-16: Repeat step with "Break."

Third Step—Toe and Heel

Measures 1-8 and repeat. On count one, spring and face to right, stretching left leg backward, but to left of starting position and placing left toe on floor. On count two, spring and about face to left, rotating left leg and placing left heel where toe was. On count three, spring and face to front, placing left toe on floor near right foot. On count four, spring and kick left leg forward outward. On count five, spring and land on left leg, facing to left with right leg extended and toe on floor. On count six, seven and eight, proceed as with left leg. On counts nine to twelve, repeat with left leg. Then "Break" and start with right leg for twelve more counts (six measures) and "Break".

Fourth Step—Leg Twist and Kick

Measures 9-16 and repeat. Similar to the "Toe and Heel" except that the toe and heel of extended leg are not placed on the floor. On count one, spring and face to right, raising left leg backwards. On count two, spring and about face to left, rotating left leg, but keeping it pointed in same direction with knee slightly bent. On count three, spring and place left toe near right foot. On count four, spring and kick left leg outward. On count five, spring to left foot and face to left, raising right leg backward. On counts six, seven and eight, same as with left leg. On counts nine to twelve, with right leg. Then "Break" four counts—two measures.

Repeat starting with left leg.

Fifth Step—Side Step

Measure 1: Using four steps to a measure, cross left foot in front of right, draw right foot up to left, step left foot to right side again, draw right foot to left.

Measure 2: Continue the same, but on the last beat hop on the left foot and throw the right foot over across left.

Measures 3 and 4: Repeat above, but move to left starting with right foot.

Measures 5 and 6: Repeat moving right again.

Measures 7 and 8: Do break.

Measures 1-8 repeated. Repeat all of fifth step.

Sixth Step—Kick and Change

Measures 9-16 and repeat. On count one, spring and place left toe in front of right foot. On count two, spring and kick left leg diagonally forward. On count three, spring and place weight on left foot and raise right leg backward. On count four, hop with left leg, and still hold right leg up in back. On count five, hop with left leg, and place right toe in front of left foot. On count six, spring and kick right leg diagonally forward. On count seven, spring to right and raise left leg backward. On count eight, hop with right foot, holding right leg up in back. On counts nine to twelve, same as in first four counts. Then "Break", and repeat, starting with right toe.

Each step should start with the left and continue for twelve beats. Then the "Break" should come in for four beats bringing the right leg forward; the step then is resumed for twelve counts starting with the right, and finishing with the "Break", preferably stamping with the left leg on the fourth count instead of swinging it forward.

Folk Dances for Boys

1. Those especially suitable for boys alone included herein are:

>Seven Jumps
>Norwegian Mountain March
>Fist Polka
>Troika
>Shepherd's Hey
>Irish Lilt

2. Suggested list:

Ox-dansen, Crampton, "Folk Dance Book," A. S. Barnes and Co.; Highland Fling, Crampton, "Folk Dance Book," A. S. Barnes and Co.; Laudnum Bunches (Morris Dance), Crampton, "Folk Dance Book," A. S. Barnes and Co.; Captain Jinks Clog and Dixie Clog, Frost, "Clog Dance Book", A. S. Barnes and Co.

Folk Dance and Singing Game Bibliography

Burchenal: 1. Folk Dances and Singing Games, G. Schirmer Co., New York; 2. Dances of the People, G. Schirmer Co., New York; 3. American Country Dances, G. Schirmer Co., New York.

O'Gara: "Tap It." A. S. Barnes Co. New York, 1937.

POSTURE EDUCATION

Significance of Posture.

Posture is the manner in which we carry our bodies, and is the silent outward expression of certain physical and mental states. A bad posture bespeaks physical weakness, illness, fatigue, or some unwholesome emotional condition, as unhappiness, depression or some negative attitude toward life as lack of self-confidence, courage, hope. Good posture is the expression of a sturdy physique, and vigorous vitality, of wholesome emotions, attitudes or traits. Should you ask any of your boys and girls to express joy, sadness, strength, being tired, feeling sick, ready to play, a soldier, a thief, courage, fear,—just what changes in the position of the body would be made with each suggestion? Would this not make clear that posture is not only important as a thing in itself, but its significance also lies in that of which it is evidence. Furthermore it will be seen that posture is not purely a physical phenomenon.

Posture is sometimes cause, sometimes result of that of which it gives evidence. The individual who assumes a bad posture day after day at the school desk, in the office or factory soon finds that this habit has weakened muscles, disarranged organs, and interfered with bodily functions, so that poor circulation, respiration, digestion, and elimination, and predisposition to disease are physical results, and mentally he will find himself irritable, less happy and hopeful, and his general outlook less clear.

Good posture (correct juxtaposition of body parts in sitting, standing, and walking), as a cause, effects (in order):

Correct positions of vital organs, with consequent adequate blood and nerve supply.

Sufficient space for organs to properly function.

Adequate blood and lymph circulation without impediment.

Proper nutrition of parts, so that growth is not handicapped.

Conservation of nerve energy.

Attractive and commanding appearance.

A feeling of uplift and buoyancy.

A breeding of respect for and confidence in self.

A hopeful and courageous outlook.

Bad posture negatives all the above.

Good posture as a result comes from:

Good muscle tone, a product of much big muscle play activity.

Good food.
Plenty of rest, avoiding muscle and nerve fatigue.
Being happy.
Feeling the joy of having accomplished something.
Confidence in self, arising from the accomplishment.
Courage, honesty, hope—as character traits.
An inspiration from an ideal.

Posture is thus closely related to health and to personality. A watchful teacher can often read characters and watch development of traits in the postures of her children. The erect carriage which indicates a desirable character shows strength without assumption. A teacher can have no more satisfying reward for her work with boys and girls than to see because of what it signifies such a type of body carriage.

In this review of the significance of posture we must feel convinced (1) that bad posture must be prevented and the child protected from its development and from anything which may help to induce it as a habit: (2) that instruction leading to certain necessary phases of development must be given to secure good posture.

That this protection and instruction must be a part of the general educational process is shown by the following facts:

1st—The characteristics and environment of the school child's life are unnatural.

2d—The child's growth needs demand especial attention to right habits of carriage during the growing or school period.

3d—If good posture is to be learned it must be an organized educational activity.

4th—Good posture can be learned in and is the result of many and varied activities of the school curriculum. The physical education program is not wholly responsible for its development.

Criteria of a Good Standing Position

The following are synthetic methods of judging good posture

1. Good poise with the appearance of uplift, vigor and ease. A good posture should not be rigid.

2. The body as one flexible segment rather than three.

The axes of the three segments (1—head and neck; 2—trunk; 3—legs) when viewed from the side, should be vertical. This gives the appearance of one segment. A vertical line (imaginary or real) is the standard which helps to determine the right juxtaposition of one segment upon the other. See page 285, Fig. 2. When the axes of these seg-

Fig. 1   Fig. 2   Fig. 3

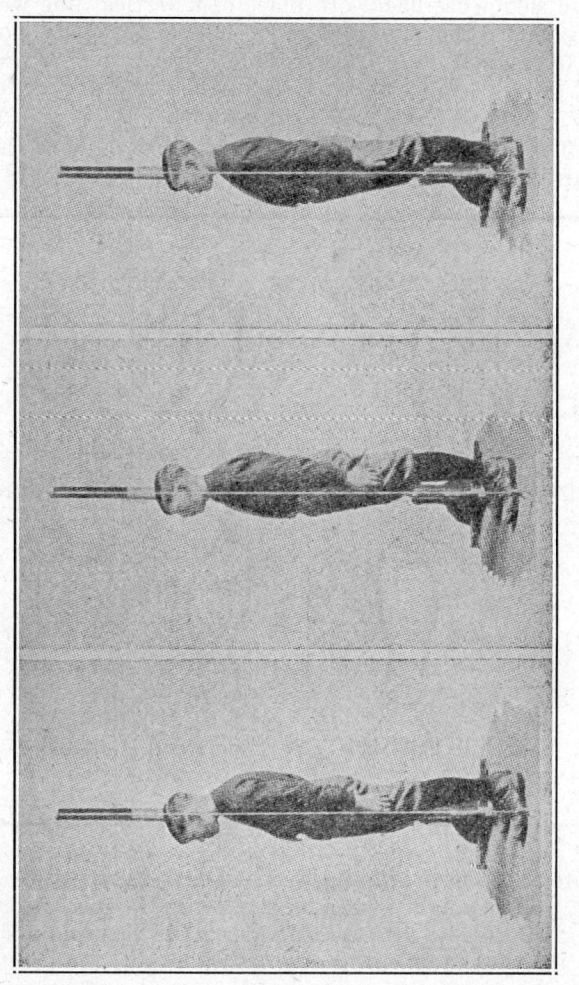

ments are not vertical, we are impressed when viewing the body from the side with the three distinct parts of the body and we find that the axis of the head and neck runs diagonally down and back, of the trunk down and forward, of the legs down and somewhat back. In place of a vertical line we have a zig-zag line. See page 285, Fig. 1. Such a body position is due to relaxation of neck, upper back, and abdominal muscles, is induced by fatigue, and can be called the fatigue posture.

3. The weight of the body poised forward onto the forward part of the feet. In the fatigue posture the weight sinks

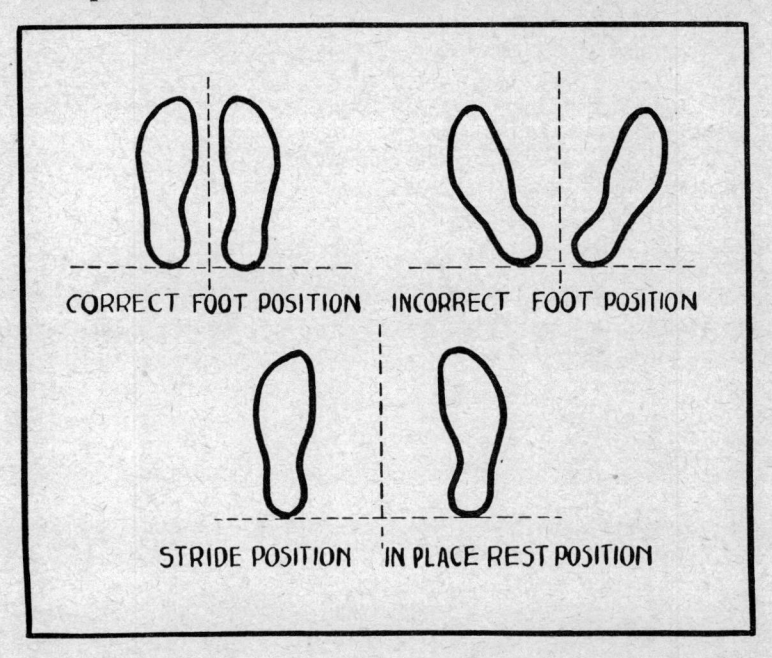

CORRECT FOOT POSITION   INCORRECT FOOT POSITION

STRIDE POSITION   IN PLACE REST POSITION

back onto the heels. In the over-exaggerated posture (page 285, Fig. 3) the weight is also on the heels. In this latter body position a spasmodic attempt is being made to stand correctly without knowledge of the proper mechanics of the erect position or without sufficient control of the muscle groups associated with the placing of the segments into right relationship to each other. It is called the "bantam" attitude because of the lifting of the chest by a distention of the ribs and a bending of the spine backward at the waist. It is undoubtedly caused by such mis-directions as, "Throw the shoulders back," "Throw the chest up."

The foregoing criteria consider the body as a whole.

This is the best way to judge good posture. Should our attention however be called to separate body parts, we would describe their position in good carriage as follows:

1. Feet parallel and straight forward, three to four inches apart. The right placing and use of the feet, our base of support, is fundamental in obtaining correct adjustment of joints above this base of support. We must emphasize the straight-ahead foot position in standing at recitation and in walking, knees easy, neither stiff nor relaxed too much.

2. Abdomen flat. A pulling in at the waist which is a contraction of the abdominal muscles associated with a contraction of the thigh extensors stretches to a correct position the spine at the waist and gives a normal tilt to the pelvis.

3. Chest high and forward, a result of having stretched up tall through the whole length of the spine.

4. Shoulders flat on back, with middle of tip of shoulder back of point of ear, if head is as described in 5. This is Bancroft's ear-test for the shoulders.

5. Head high with axis of neck vertical and chin horizontal.

Summary:

The vertical line is the standard to be used to assist in the judging of posture. The body must be viewed from the side. At first use a real plumb line as in the illustrations. According to Bancroft, this plumb line should drop from the forward border of the ear to the front (middle of the arch to the ball) part of the foot, if the body is in the correct position. The segments of the trunk will parallel this plumb line. A teacher will need but a little practise to distinguish between vertical body segments and zig-zag relations if she uses a plumb line to make comparisons. After some experience she can work without the plumb line, an imaginary line assisting her to judge the body alignment.

How to sit correctly:

The axes of head and trunk must be vertical in sitting as in standing. In order to keep them in line the following directions for sitting must be observed:

1. Push as far back into the seat as possible so that the lower back touches the back of the seat.

2. The upper back or region of the shoulders must not touch the back of the seat, unless the lower back touches it also.

3. If the trunk is to lean forward, the bend must be only in the hip joint.

4. The feet must be flat and heavy on the floor, and the knees at a right angle.

How to walk correctly:

The correct standing posture should be assumed during walking. The arms should be allowed to swing naturally and with ease. The bearing should be one of animation without

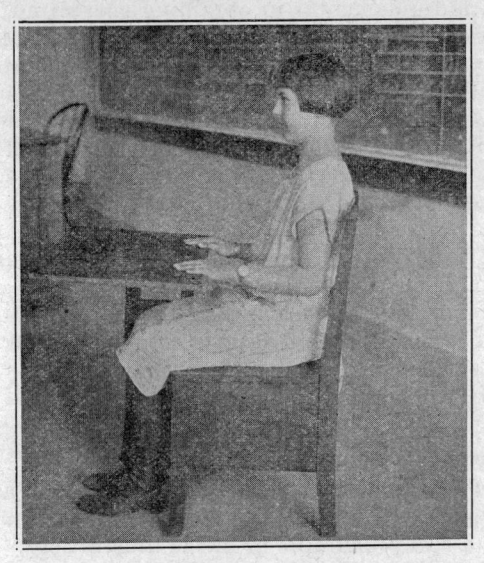

Correct Sitting Position

tenseness. The use of the feet in walking will help to insure the right relationship of the joints above and thus keep good body uplift. The feet should be always parallel and the toes moving straight ahead, the heels should first strike the ground, then the weight transferred to the ball, thus keeping the weight forward.

How to Maintain or Secure Good Posture

Two necessary phases:

1st—Methods of preventing poor posture.
2d—Methods of developing good posture.

Methods of Preventing Poor Posture

The preventive phase of the procedure of working for good posture has to do with:

1st—Sanitary **environment** of the school child.
2d—Physical **condition** of the school child.

The plan then is to recognize those situations in the environment and physical condition of the child which influence posture and to remove, modify or correct them. The following suggestions are essential.

1. The school desk and seat must fit the child.
Rules to follow in adjusting seats and desks:

(a) Height of seat: Knees at right angle and the feet flat and heavy on the floor.

(b) Depth of seat: When child sits properly the edge of the seat should strike the thigh about midway between the knee and the middle point of the thigh.

(c) Back of seat should follow the natural curves of the spine.

(d) The height of desk above seat: When seated in the correct manner and with upper back against the seat back, if the elbows are at right angles and directly at side of the body, the desk should then be in line with forearm. It is best to have a desk-top the slant of which can be changed for different types of work.

(e) Distance of desk from child. There is still difference of opinion on this rule. The following is good to follow: The child sits as in (d) with elbows in same position. The finger tips should overlap the desk edge.

If seats are not adjustable, putting children into seats which best fit them must be conscientiously tried, and foot stools should be provided.

2. Lighting must be favorable.
(a) There must be sufficient light. Provision for artificial lighting (indirect) must be made.

(b) Light must come from right direction—seats must be so faced that light will come from left and rear (with exception of left-handed pupils who must be placed where the light coming from different directions is so balanced as to eradicate shadows).

3. Weights must be properly carried. Work for right habit of carrying books. See accompanying illustration.

4. Insist upon correct manner of sitting, standing and walking.

5. The type used in textbooks, the kind of chalk used at blackboard are also matters which demand the attention of administrators in regard to right habits of body positions.

6. Defective vision and hearing must be recognized, and dealt with as to seating and as to possible correction.

7. Malnutrition. This is one of the most common and malicious enemies of good body carriage. No means of prevention or instruction of posture will bring results if the body is under-nourished. Therefore, steps must be taken to combat malnutrition.

I.   II.   III.

I. and III. illustrate common faults in weight-carrying which result in spinal deformities. II. illustrates the proper way of dividing the load.

8. Fatigue must be prevented or removed. Causes are malnutrition, lack of sufficient sleep, overwork, recent illness. Short rests should be given in the course of the session.

9. Plenty of big muscle play activity must be provided for by means of:

Relief periods, generously scattered throughout the school day.

Full use of recess and before school play periods.

The regular class period in Physical Education.

10. Parents must be influenced as to important contributing factors in home hygiene, as:

Nourishing food.
Plenty of sleep.
Carrying of loads.
Clothes that fit and allow good posture.
Children's furniture.
Posture habits.

Note: Considering posture from a physical standpoint three things are paramount in prevention:
Proper Nutrition.
Avoidance of fatigue.
Full daily quota of muscular exercise, preferably in open air.

If these three conditions exist in full measure, poor posture can be physically prevented in spite of other unfavorable conditions.

Methods of Developing Good Posture

That phase of posture training which has to do with developing good posture deals with the following two methods of procedure:

I. Learning the physical part of posture, that is, learning to properly handle the body.

II. Developing mental responses (for example, self-confidence) which are associated with good posture.

Learning the physical part of good posture includes:

1. Learning by experimentation, observation and instruction the proper manner of sitting, standing and walking.

2. Becoming acquainted with the muscular sense which accompanies a right carriage, thus being always able to recognize whether or not one is in the right position.

3. Learning and establishing the needed muscular control.

Note: A predisposing condition is: Sufficient muscle tone a result of:
Good food.
Sufficient rest.
Much big muscle play activity in the open air.

Exercises for Learning Good Posture

The following exercises will help to put the body into the right position. The child will by experimenting with these exercises learn what the right relationship is of one part of the body to another and how to secure that right relationship. He will also sense and thus learn to recognize the muscular feeling which goes with a good posture as distinguished from that which accompanies wrong postures. Then with practise of and drill in these exercises, the neuro-muscular control governing posture will be learned and established.

Note: For methods of giving signals for the following exercises, refer to page 14.

292   IOWA STATE TEACHERS COLLEGE

Fig 1.
Posture Exercise I.—Pushing palms downward at side

Fig. 2
Posture Exercise II.—Flinging arms eyes-high

Fig. 3
Posture Exercise IV.—Shelter spine stretch position.

Exercise I. Pushing palms downward at side—One!
Let go—Two!

Stand with feet four inches apart and parallel. Place the arms down at the side with palms of hands in a horizontal position. Push down hard with palms against the air. See page 292.

This pushing is accompanied by a lifting of the chest and a stretching upward of the whole body. The body parts are brought into right relation and a definite feeling of this relation is sensed. On "Two!" the body is relaxed but not to a poor posture.

Exercise II. Flinging arms eye-high—One!
Cues: Push hard; stretch far; up; up.
Still holding chest high, position—Two!

Arms are stretched diagonally upward with palms up and at the height of the eyes. See page 292. Push up against the air with the palms, until body is lifted and stretched as high as possible, even to being lifted up on to toes.

Exercise III. Arms bending forward and lift—One!
Cues: Raise chest; pull up tall, etc.
Keeping chest high, position—Two!

Arms are brought to horizontal position with elbows bent, (see Fig. 3, Page 300), palms in front of chest and down. An effort is made to raise the hands higher without changing their relative position to the chest. To do this, the chest must be raised, and body stretched its tallest.

Exercise IV. Shelter spine stretch position—One.
Cues: Push up against hands; push up hard; make yourselves as tall as possible.
Keeping body tall and chest high, position—Two!

The palms are placed on the top of the head and the head is pushed up against them as if against a weight. Push way up as high as you can. See Page 292.

Exercise V. Reaching to high shelf—One!
Cues: Reach way up; stretch far.
Position—Two!

The arms reach diagonally forward upward as far as possible with effort of touching something real high.

Exercise VI. Pretend to squeeze through a very narrow door sideways—One!
Cue: Make yourself real tall and thin.
Keeping chest high, position—Two!

This exercise needs no explanation. It is very effective in getting the right use of muscles to pull segments into correct relationships and to place the weight where it belongs.

Exercise VII. Relaxing forward—One!
Pull up—Two!

The body is relaxed forward, the whole spine rounded, with head down, arms hanging loosely, and knees relaxed. From this position, beginning at the base of the spine gradually pull body erect to an easy but perfectly upright position. Contract thigh extensors (muscles on back of thighs) with abdominal muscles (muscles in front of abdomen) as trunk is straightened on thigh, to get right position of hips and lower back.

All exercises which are explained under and used for the triple test are also exercises which should be used for the purpose of learning, sensing, and establishing control of correct posture. See page 296.

How to Use These Exercises

Since vigorous muscular activity is of first posture importance, owing to the fact that it establishes essential conditions for procuring good posture, the physical education class period must be given over almost entirely to such activity. However, every lesson should include at its beginning or end several of the above exercises, for only when such exercises are done is special attention given by the child to obtaining correct body relations, whereby he learns what good posture in himself really is. This knowledge he must have, but undue time should not be given to learning it at the expense of the constructive process coming from wide use of large muscle groups. Therefore a teacher does not need a large number of posture exercises. A few well chosen and well directed ones will supply all needs.

These exercises should be directed by using the signals as given above. These signals should be clear, definite, and stimulating to the best efforts. Cues assist in getting the effort desired but must be well-worded in order to do so. They are usually called "elevation" cues, for their purpose is to stimulate to further **uplift** of the body in performance of the exercises.

Cues

Helpful

Stand tall.	Pull in at waist.
Grow an inch.	Waist flat.
Head high.	Chest broad.
Lift chest.	Shoulder blades together.
Stretch the whole body upward.	Swing weight forward, as if to raise the heels.
Lift the head.	Feet parallel.

Incorrect

Throw shoulders back.   Stomach in.
Head back.   Hips back.
Chest out.   Heels together.

Primary Grades: Little attention is called to the body and its parts with Primary children, so whatever is learned about posture in these grades has to do with learning the right feeling of good posture. This learning should come largely indirectly and unconsciously from performing such mimetic exercises as picking fruit from a high limb, flying birds, being a tall pine tree, playing soldier, etc. It can come directly in the upper primary grades from the use of tests I and II of the Triple Test.

Preventive measures must be put into force and possible causes of poor posture controlled. The physical activities of primary children must contain from the posture standpoint:

(a) Much big muscle play activity.

(b) Much opportunity for large movements of arms and shoulders in order that at this period chest proportions and placement of shoulders will follow the normal lines of development.

(c) Much opportunity for the natural activities of hanging and climbing for the same reason as given under (b).

The Triple Test for Posture

Purpose:

To test the efficiency of the posture muscles in holding the body in good posture under varying circumstances.

To get a posture record of each child.

To get a posture rating of the class.

To thus determine progress.

To enable teacher to know to which children most attention should be given.

To offer an incentive for more earnest effort when drilling on posture exercises.

The Posture Test is often included as a factor in group competition and may be added as another "Motor Ability Test." When utilized in either of these ways its effectiveness in bringing results is increased.

Explanation of the Test

First test: Standing test.

Standard: Vertical line (class viewed from side).

Purpose: To see if child can assume correct posture at will.

Method: A row of children stand across the front of the room, facing the side of the room. Each child takes his best standing position. Those who stand incorrectly are assisted and told what is wrong. The children at the seats help in forming judgments. Those who do not pass the first test are rated "D". All take their seats. Each row is thus tested.

Second test: Walking test.

Standard: Vertical line (class viewed from the side).

Purpose: To test stability of posture, endurance of posture muscles, and establishment of correct coordinations while engaged in walking.

Method: Class walks up and down the aisles (See Diagram, page 312) in a natural manner, as if going down the street. Teacher watches each child as he passes and looks for variations of head, trunk and weight. Those whose postures lapse are so informed and are rated "C". All children walk during this test, including those who failed in the first test. These walk at the end of the line, are not tested, but have the opportunity of working for correct posture.

Third Test: Exercise test.

Standard: The vertical line (class viewed from side).

Purpose: To further test stability of posture, endurance of posture muscles and their established coordinations while the individual is busily engaged in responding to commands and executing exercises which particularly test the posture muscles.

Method: In selecting exercises for this test, those are chosen which call into use certain muscle groups whose weakness or poor coordination causes poor posture. The postures must be observed from the side and most particularly during the execution of the exercise, as well as after the position has been taken. Those who fail in this test are rated "B". All children take the exercises, but just those who passed the marching test are being tested. The others are grouped in one place. Two different sets of Triple Test exercises are given here. The second is a little more difficult than the first. All the exercises must be learned. The first set can be learned and used as test exercises in the 4th and 5th grades, the second in the 6th grade. This test is omitted in the Primary grades. When these exercises are taught the suggestions herein given must be used. When the exercises are employed as tests, these admonitions should not be given.

Note: For methods of giving signals of the following exercises, refer to page 14.

Set I. **Triple Test Exercises.**

1. **Hands on hips; change to hands at neck.**

Signals: Class—Attention! (See page 14, also Fig. I in illustration).

Hands on hips—Place!
Change to hands at neck—Change! See Fig. 1, page 300.
Change!—Change!
Arms!—Position!

Note: Shoulder blades together and elbows back. Keep head up. Do not change its position.

Fig. 1.—Class—Attention! Fig. 2.—In Place—Rest!

2. **Heels raising and knees bending** (See accompanying illustration).

Signals: Class—Attention!
Hands on hips—Place!
Raising heels—One!
Bending knees—Two!
Stretching knees—Three!
Lowering heels—Four!
Arms—Position!

Repeat several times.

In Place—Rest! (See page 14, also Fig. 2 in illustration, page 297).

Note: Knees should go outward as they bend. Trunk should remain erect. Weight should be well forward and remain the same.

Knees Bending.
See Set I.—Triple Test Exercise—No. 2.

3. **Arm Stretchings.**

(a) Signals: Class—Attention!
Arms bending upward—One! (See Fig. 2, page 300).
Stretching upward—Two! (See Figs. 4a and 4b, page 301).

Repeat this several times.

Take same commands for stretching arms sideways and to position.

Note: Keep waist flat on arms bending upward. The trunk should remain perfectly in line, with no wavering of parts. Common errors are: head forward, hips forward. In stretchings sideways, draw shoulders well back and together.

(b) Signals: Class—Attention!
Arms stretching upward in this rhythm (Clap 1-2)—Stretch!
Arms stretching sideways—Stretch!
Repeat the stretchings, especially the upward one several times.
Arms to position—Stretch!
These rhythmic stretchings are performed by combining the two movements found under (a) with one signal. The arms are bent upward on 1, and stretched upward on 2, with emphasis on 2 on the stretch.

4. **Arms flinging forward-upward and sideways-downward.**

Signals: Class—Attention!
Arms flinging forward-upward—One! (See Figs. 3a and 3b, page 301).
Arms flinging sideways-downward—Two!
Again—One! Two! Repeat several times.
Note: Same cautions and faults as in arm stretchings. Bring arms well back as they come down.

5. **Alternate knee bending upward.** (See Fig. 6, page 300).

(a) Signals: Class—Attention!
Hands on hips—Place!
Alternate knee bending upward beginning left—Go!
Class—Halt! (Stop in 2 counts)
Arms—Position!
In place—Rest!
Note: Knees must be brought up as high as possible in front. They alternate in this action in fairly brisk rhythm. Trunk must remain erect throughout exercise. Weight must remain forward.

(b) The above exercise can be made harder by placing hands at neck.

6. **Running in Place.**

Signals: Class—Attention!
Hands on hips—Place!
Beginning with left foot, running in place—Go!
Class—Halt! (1-2-3)
Class—Position!
In place—Rest!
Note: This exercise is executed just like Ex. 5—alternate knee-bending upward—except that the rhythm is faster, the feet leave the ground as in running, and the landing is on the balls of the feet. The halt is executed with two more

300   IOWA STATE TEACHERS COLLEGE

running steps (1-2) and on 3 the feet are brought together and heels lowered. Care should be taken in teaching not to allow the weight to settle backward.

7. West-Point Breathing.

Signals: Palms turning outward—One! (slowly)
              Position—Two! (slowly)
      Note: Breathe in on "one" out on "two." Signals must be given slowly to indicate deep breathing.

Fig. 1—Hands at neck place.
Fig. 2—Arms bending upward.
Fig. 3—Arms bending forward.
Fig. 4—Arms raising sideways.
Fig. 5—Hands on hips, head bending backward.
Fig. 6—Hands on hips, alternate knee bending upward.

PHYSICAL EDUCATION 301

Set II. Triple Test Exercises.
1. (a) **Arms bending forward; change to hands at neck.**
    Signals: Class—Attention!
    Arms bending forward—Bend! (See Fig. 3, page 300).
    Changing to hands at neck—Change!
    Change!—Change!
    Arms—Position!

Fig 1—Hands on hips, alternate leg raising forward.
Fig. 2—Hands on hips, trunk bending forward.
Fig. 3a—Arms flinging forward-upward.
Fig. 3b—Completion of 3a—Arms flinging sideways-downward.
Fig. 4a—Arms bending upward.
Fig. 4b—Arms stretching upward. Taken from 4a.

(b) **Same from knees deep bend position.**
   Signals: Class—Attention!
   Arms forward—Bend!
   Heels—Raise!
   Knees deep—Bend!
   Changing arms to hands on neck—Change!
   Change! Change!
   Knees—Stretch!
   Heels—Sink!
   Arms—Position!
   In place—Rest!

2. **Heels raising and knees bending in rhythm.**
   Signals: Class—Attention!
   Hands on hips (or at neck)—Place!
   Raising heels—One!
   Bending knees—Two!
   Stretching knees—Three!
   Lowering heels—Four!
   Again—One! Two! Three! Four!
   Now in this rhythm (Indicate rhythm by clapping)—Go!
   Again—Go! (Repeat several times)
   Arms—Position!

3. **Arm stretchings.**
   Signals: Class—Attention!
   (a) Arms two times upward in this rhythm
   (Clap 1-2; 1-2)—Stretch!
   Arms two times sideways—Stretch!
   Arms to position—Stretch!
   The number of rhythmic stretchings in any one direction can be increased.
   (b) Arms stretching once upward, once sideways, once downward—Stretch!
   Various combinations of (a) and (b) can be made.

4. **Arms flinging forward, upward—and sideways, downward.**
   Same as 4 under Set I.

5. **Alternate Leg Raising Forward** (See Fig. 1, page 301).
   (a) Signals: Hands on hips—Place!
   Alternate leg raising forward beginning with left—Go!
   Class—Halt! (Stop in 2 counts)
   Arms—Position!
   In Place—Rest!
   Note: Legs are raised forward from the hip with straight knee and ankle. They alternate in a fairly brisk

rhythm. Trunk must remain erect throughout the exercise and the weight forward.

(b) This exercise can be made harder by placing hands at neck.

6. **The Forward Cut-Step.**

Signals: Class—Attention!
Hands on hips—Place!
Beginning left, the forward cut-step—Go!
Class—Halt! (1-2-3)
Arms—Position!
In Place—Rest!

Note: This exercise is alternate leg raising forward (Ex. 5) in fast rhythm, and is similar to running in place with a straight knee. Land on balls of feet. The halt is taken in 3 counts; two more cut-steps on 1 and 2, and on 3, the feet are brought together and heels lowered.

Care must be taken in teaching it not to allow weight to settle back.

7. **Arm Raising sideways with breathing.**

Signals: With breathing arms raising sideways—One! (slowly) (See Fig. 4, page 300).
Position—Two (slowly)

II.

Developing Mental Responses which are associated with Good Posture

Two means at hand:
1st: Development of certain character traits.
2nd: The establishment of ideals.

First: There are certain character traits and attitudes toward life which find physical expression in good body carriage. Some of them are: Contentment, optimism, self-respect, self-confidence, fair-mindedness, courage, hope. Social adjustment and success in life depend much upon the presence of such traits and attitudes. The business of education should be to develop them. The whole school program can and must contribute. The Physical Education program can offer much opportunity for development along this line, provided the teacher plans and guides with this objective in mind. Self-testing activities and combative exercises (see section on Stunts and Contests) are of value in this respect; also do team games and track and field stand high in possibilities. Wherever a sense of accomplishment results or courage is a required factor, good posture is a by-product.

To utilize every means in the school program to make individuals look up and forward, both mentally and physically, should be a teacher's aim. The end sought is not posture, but character and personality.

Second: The second means lies in the arousing of a vital interest in an ideal or ideals of the type which stimulates good carriage. At first, ideals embodied in specific personalities, as the teacher herself, an old soldier in the community, a specific athlete, a great hero, a national leader, are of special importance in creating admiration of and desire for good posture. Here also stories of accomplishment, and pictures can be the means of conveying knowledge and incentive. Later on an ideal embodied in a principle, as honesty, bravery, good health, patriotism, etc., will have its appeal.

Establishing ideals of this kind belongs to various phases of the school program, as Hygiene, Reading, and History, especially the latter. There must then be coordinated effort in the whole school program toward posture education of this kind. Here again, posture is not the end, but evidence of the end, which is character and personality.

Special Corrective Exercises
I. **For Drooping Head and Relaxed Neck.**
1. Head backward move. (See Fig. 5, page 300).
   (a) Signals: Hands on hips—Place!
   Head moving backward—One! (slowly)
   Cues: Press back hard; pull chin in! pull in at waist.
   Head to position—Two!
   Arms—Position!

   Note: To localize this movement in the spine of neck and upper back, have class sit. The head and neck are moved backward. If class is standing, follow exercise by exercise 8 under II, below.

   (b) Signals: Hands at neck—Place! (See Fig. 1, page 300).
   Head moving backward—One!
   Two!
2. Shelter spine stretch. See page 293.
3. Flinging arms eyes high. See page 293.
4. Walk, carrying book on top of head.

   Take Ex. I, page 293 in order to put body in best posture.

   Then place the book on top of head, and walk.
5. Chinning—page 10.

PHYSICAL EDUCATION

II. **For Round Shoulders.**
1. Exercise I, on page 293.
2. Exercise III, on page 293.
3. Hands on neck—Place! (Fig. 1, page 300).
    Arms—Position!
4. Arms bending upward—Bend! (Fig. 2, page 300).
    Cues: Pull shoulder blades together; elbows close to side; pull in at waist.
    Arms—Position!
    Note: This exercise is preferably taken from the sitting position especially if there is evidence of hollow back. If taken standing, it should be followed by Ex. 8, below.
5. Arm stretchings.
    See Triple Test Exercises: Set I, Ex. 3, page 298. Set II, Ex. 3, page 302.
6. Arms flinging forward upward and sideways downward, Triple Test Exercises; Set I, Ex. 4, page 299.
7. Swimming Movement.
    Signals: Arms bending forward—Bend! (Fig. 3, Page 300).
    Arms stretching forward—One!
    Arms flinging sideways—Two!
    Arms bending forward again—Three!
    In this rhythm (Clap 1-2—3)—Go!
    Arms—Position!
    Emphasis should be on 2 as arms are flung sideways. Bring them well back and shoulder blades together.
8. Trunk Bending Forward.
    (a) Signals: Hands on hips—Place!
    Cue: Stretch trunk as tall as possible.
    Trunk bending forward—One! (Fig. 2, page 301).
    Cues: Bend only at hips; keep backs flat; head in line with trunk; shoulder blades together.
    Raising trunk—Two!
    Arms—Position!
    (b) Take same with arms in following positions:
    Arms bending upward.
    Arms bending forward.
    Hands on neck place.
    (c) Trunk bending forward with swimming movement.

Signals: Arms forward—Bend!
Trunk forward—Bend!
The Swimming Movement in this rhythm (1-2—3)—Go!
Again—Go!
Trunk—Raise!
Arms—Position!

9. With hands on shoulders, arms circumduction. Arms are forward on shoulder level, elbows are bent so as to bring hands on top of shoulders, elbows pointing forward. From this position, lift elbows upward, backward, and downward finishing with them close at sides, shoulder blades flat on back.

Take this exercise, **sitting,** or follow it with Ex. 8, above.
10. Chinning, page 110.
11. Climbing, page 111.
12. Swinging from arms on horizontal bar.

III. For Protruding Abdomen and Hollow Back.

1. Ex. I; II; III; etc., page 293. All of these, call for hard contraction of abdominal muscles (muscles in front wall of abdomen).
2. Alternate knee bending upward.
Triple Test Exercise, Set I, Ex. 5.
3. Running in place, Triple Test Exercises, Set I, Ex. 6.
4. Alternate leg raising forward. Triple Test Exercises, Set II, Ex. 5.
5. Sitting, trunk backward fall.

Class is commanded to sit on desks facing rear of room, feet on seats.

Signals: Hands on hips—Place!
Cues: Sit as tall as possible, Lift chest.
Trunk falling backward—One!
Cues: Move just in the hip joint; keep head in line with trunk.
Trunk raising—Two!
Arms—Position!

6. Climbing, page 111.
7. Trunk lifting, page 110.
8. Hanging, knees raising, page 119.
9. Leg exercises to teach sprinting, under the Dash, page 339.

IV. For Weak Feet.

1. Marching, with especial emphasis on correct use of feet. Follow boards of floor to help keep the straight foot position. See Marching, page 308, III, 3, also page 286.

2. Alternate regular marching with tip-toe marching, page 309.

3. Alternate regular marching with toes down first, page 310.

4. Leg exercises to teach form of sprinting, under the dash, page 339.

5. Sitting, feet on floor, about four inches apart and parallel. Draw toes in, lifting inner edge of foot, keeping outer edge pressed against floor.

6. Walking, toeing in, and lifting inner edge of foot; alternate with walking, toeing ahead.

MARCHING

I. Purposes.

Children should learn and drill to a limited extent upon simple marching evolutions for the following reasons:

1. The possibility of organizing with ease large groups of children becomes a necessity for various school and community situations as fire drills, grand marches, and parades.
2. To facilitate class organization for physical training work, marching and open orders (see page 313) are necessary.
3. Children must be given opportunity for paying attention to and practice in (a) the right use of the foot in walking, (b) the right carriage of the body in walking.

II. Definitions:

Alignment: A straight line (single or double) along the length of the room or on the school yard by which pupils are formed or assembled for purposes of organization.

Column or File: Children standing in line one behind the other.

Front Rank: Children standing side by side.

Take distance: To take a specified distance between lines or individuals in the rank.

III. Suggestions:

1. The following marching commands constitute very nearly the minimum for purposes given. No others will be included.
2. Marching should always be begun with class in best posture.
3. Marching should be executed in a natural manner, heels striking ground first, and feet moving forward parallel to each other, toes straight ahead. Allow children to follow boards of floor while marching across one end of room. Arms must be allowed to swing naturally. The strides should be free, brisk, light, and elastic, without noise or haste.
4. Do not allow one foot to strike the ground with greater emphasis than the other. Therefore do not emphasize rhythm by saying, "Left—left—left," etc. Rather say, "Left-right-left-right," etc.
5. For methods of giving signals see page 14. In a number of signals given below it is indicated upon which foot in marching the various parts of the signal should come.

IV. Marching Signals and Their Execution.

A. For open space, as gymnasium or playground.

1. Class—two lines! or Class—one line!

To get class gathered together into a definite formation or at a definite place. There may be one line or two, along the side of the room or down the middle. The tallest are at the right end and the children line up according to height.

2. Class—Attention! See illustration, page 297.

This signal always follows the first one. Each pupil assumes the correct standing position.

3. In place—Rest! See illustration, page 297.

4. Class Right (left)—dress! Front!

All pupils place left hands upon the hip and turn the head to the right (except one at right end who looks to the front). Each pupil by taking short steps, places himself so that his right arm rests lightly against the elbow of the one on his right, and so that his eyes and shoulders are in line with those to his right. The head should be kept erect. On command "Front" the head is turned front and the left arm is dropped to the side.

5. Right (left)—Face!

Raise slightly the left heel and right toe, face to right, turning 90° on right heel, assisted by a slight push of left toe (count one); place the left foot quickly parallel to the right (count two). The left face is executed on the left heel and right toe. About facings (180°) are done in the same manner.

6. Mark time—March!

This is marching in place. Starting with left foot, raise feet alternately about two inches from floor, ankles stretched, knees up in front. The rhythm may be set by the teacher calling "left, right," etc.

Class—Halt!

This is executed in 2 counts by taking two more mark time steps after the word "Halt", and finishing with feet parallel on the second step.

7. Forward—March!

Beginning with left foot march forward in manner described under III.

8. Class—Halt! (from marching)

This is executed in two counts—After the word "Halt", one more step forward is taken (count 1); then the other foot is brought up parallel and placed on the ground (count 2). In order to assist children in stopping in 2 counts they may be allowed to count "1—2" aloud, after the word, "Halt".

9. Tip-toe—March!

The class is marching forward, and upon this command they rise on the balls of their feet and continue marching. This kind of marching aids in getting the weight forward and the body in better alignment. To return to normal marching give following command:

| Normal | (pause) | March! | 1 | 2 |
| 1 foot | r foot | 1 foot | r | 1 |

After the signal "March," which comes on left foot as indicated, one more tip toe march step is taken on right foot (count 1); then next step with the left foot (count 2) is a normal march step and is slightly emphasized, after which, without change of rhythm, normal marching is continued.

10. Toes down first—March!

After the signal "March" the class changes from the natural form of marching with heels striking first, to a full stretch of ankle with each step bringing the toes in contact with floor first. This is an arch exercise, and also assists in learning to toe straight ahead.

To return to normal marching:

| Normal | (pause) | March! | 1 | 2 |
| 1 | r | 1 | r | 1 |

Execution same as for normal from tip-toe.

11. Quick Time—March!

This is taken either from tip-toe or from normal marching. Immediately upon the command (which may come on right foot) the class breaks into an easy run, the rhythm of which is determined by the age of the class. The run should be natural, a jogging stride with knees raised forward. The arms are bent at elbows, and swing naturally forward and back at side of body.

To resume normal marching:

| Normal | (pause) | March! | 1 | 2 | 3 | 4 | 5 |
| r | 1 | r | 1 | r | 1 | r | 1 |

The signal "March" comes on right foot, after which take four more running steps gradually slowing down, and on count five take the first normal march step with left foot, slightly emphasizing it, and continue marching.

12. About | (pause) | March! | 1 | 2 | 3 |
    1 | r | 1 | r | 1 | r |

This is turning left about and marching in opposite direction, and is executed in 3 counts after the signal "March" which comes on the left foot. On count 1, advance right foot in old direction with slightly emphasized step. On count 2, rise on both toes and turn left about. On count 3, advance right foot with a slightly emphasized step in the new direction and continue marching. There has been no change of rhythm.

13. (a) Face left | (pause) | March! | 1 | 2 |
        1 | r | 1 | r | 1 |

To change direction while marching in any formation. On count 1, after the word "March," which comes on left foot, take one more step with right foot in old direction. On count 2, take a slightly emphasized step with left foot, to the left making a quarter turn in that direction and continue marching.

(b) Face right | (pause) | March! | 1 | 2 |
r | 1 | r | 1 | r |

Executed as (a) above except that "March" comes on right foot as noted, and facing is made to right.

These signals are sometimes given thus:
by the left (right) flank—March!

By these commands the line changes its formation from front to file, or vice versa. All face at same time.

14. (a) Column left (right)—March!

To change direction while marching in a column or file, yet retain this formation. The signal is given when the leader reaches the place where the teacher wishes the line to change directions. The leader faces and marches in designated direction. The rest march to this spot, face, and follow him.

If the column is marching in double file, this is retained.

(b) If column is marching in single file, and double file is desired at the change of direction, command "Form twos—column right—March!" The first two turn at same time, swing in abreast and march in new direction together. Following twos do likewise at same spot.

(c) Same procedure, to form fours from single file, or from double file. The first four face at same time and swing in abreast, etc. Any number desired can be thus commanded.

(d) Also, the column can be reduced from 4's to 2's, 4's to 1's, 2's to 1's, etc. by commanding.

Fours forming 2's—column r (1)—March!
Fours forming 1's—column r (1)—March!
Twos forming 1's—column r (1)—March!

In case of 4's forming 2's the rank of 4's marching abreast split at the given spot one couple going ahead, the other dropping in behind. Each succeeding rank of 4's does the same.

The procedure is the same for whatever division is desired.

15. Backward | (pause) | March! | 1 | 2 |
    1 | r | 1 | r | 1 |

To change direction without facing when marching in flank formation. After word "March," on count 1 take one more step forward with right foot; on count 2 step backward with left foot slightly emphasized, and march backward with short steps.

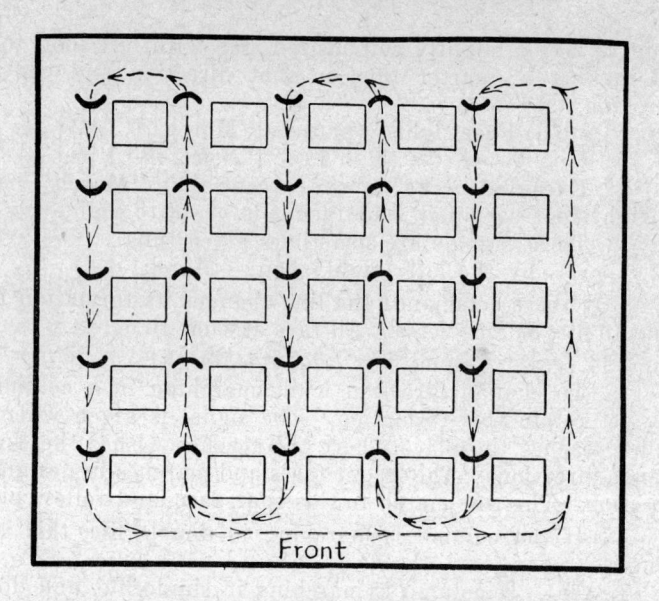

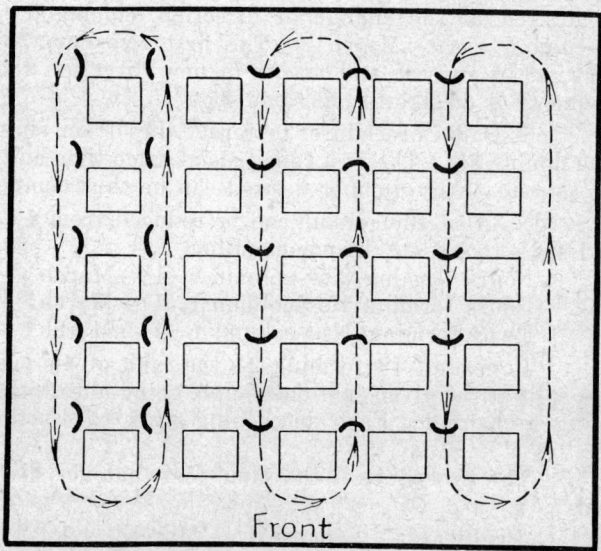

Schoolroom formations for marching and folk dancing evolutions. First diagram shows usual formation for marching. First scheme shown in second diagram illustrates formation used in sliding sideways as in a circle; the second scheme illustrates formation for skipping, running or marching forward as in a circle.

From marching backward to marching forward command:

| Forward | (pause) | March! | 1 | 2 |
| 1 | r | 1 | r | 1 |

Count 1—One more step backward with right foot.
Count 2—Step forward with left foot slightly emphasized, and march forward.

16. March steps.
   (a) One step forward—March! (count 1-2).

From stand, step forward with left foot (1); place right foot parallel with it (2).

   (b) One step backward—March! (1-2).

From stand, step backward with left foot (1); place right foot parallel with it (2).

   (c) Two steps forward (backward)—March! (1-2-3).

Feet close on count 3.
Any number of steps may be commanded.
   (d) One step to right—March! (1-2).
Step to right (1); bring left foot to right (2).
Same to left.
   (e) Two steps to right (left)—March! (1-2; 1-2).
Two counts for each step as in (d).

B.—For Schoolroom.

1. The commands possible of execution in the schoolroom are:

March steps as in "16" above.
Tip-toe—March!
About—March!
Quick time—March!
Toes down first—March!

2. All must be in single file formation.
3. For marching evolutions in schoolrooms see schemes shown in diagrams on page 312.

To execute successfully counter-marching, which is illustrated in the top figure of the diagram, the following rule must be observed: the leader who is at the head of the first line, must arrange to march around so that he will fall in behind and follow the last child in the last line. For an uneven number of rows, the path of the leader will be across the front and down the outside aisle of the opposite side of the room in order to fall in behind this last child. The diagram illustrates this situation. Should there be an even number of rows the leader marches across the front of the room until he comes to the last row of children, who face the rear, and follows them down their aisle. The path can be worked out on the diagram by considering the first four rows only.

4. For attention at desks and rising from seats, see pages 14 and 15.

Methods of Opening Order

The following two simple methods of open order are given to provide an easy way of organizing the class into open order formation in the gymnasium or out-doors, for general class instruction in posture exercises and natural gymnastics, and for group practice in games technique.

1. Line class up in two straight lines along one side of room. Commands used are:

Class—Two lines!
Class—Attention!
Right—Dress!
Front!
Right—Face!
Forward—March!

The manner in which these commands are executed is given under "Marching." The class marches down one side of the room around the corner to the middle of one end, where the command "Form fours, column left and open order—March!" is given. The first two couples then turn left, swing in abreast and march down the middle of the room in fours side by side. As they proceed they gradually spread apart diverging outward until their arms stretched sideways do not touch. When they reach the place designated by the teacher, they mark time. The fours which follow them march down in the same manner, taking distance of about 6 feet back of line in front. This taking of spaces is continued by each line of fours abreast, until all are in open order. The result is four files.

2. Line class up in two lines down middle of room. Commands:

Class—Two lines!
Class—Attention!
Right—Dress!
Front!

(These commands are explained under "Marching.")
From the right by two's—Count!

The front row counts off by 2's beginning at the right end. As each counts he turns his head left and then turns it immediately forward. The rear line takes the numbers of those standing directly in front of them. Care must first be taken that the two lines are paired off and arranged so that each individual in the rear line is standing directly behind partner.

Facing left—Face! (This puts class in 2 files).

Opening lines sideways—March! Each line takes two sidesteps away from the other line. The right file moves right and left file moves left. A side-step right is done by taking a step sideways with right foot and then bringing left foot to it. Each side-step is counted 1-2 and the opening of ranks is done in rhythm counted 1-2, 1-2.

Opening spaces sideways—March!

Each No. 1 in either file takes one side-step right, each No. 2 in either file takes one side-step left. The rhythm is counted 1-2.

This arranges the class into four files. There is sufficient distance between individuals in the file from front to rear; and every one is opposite a space.

When the above method is well understood, time may be saved by giving just one command.

Open order sideways—March!

The lines open sideways first with two side-steps and then the 1's and 2's open spaces sideways one side-step. The rhythm for the open order can be counted 1-2, 1-2, 1-2.

MOVEMENT FUNDAMENTALS

The term "Movement Fundamentals" is used to include practice in technique of all motor movements that relate to play, occupation, and dance forms. The various types of activity that come under this head are:

1. Games Fundamentals: The learning of and drill in the correct form used in the different athletic sports, in order to increase skill in these sports.

2. Mimetic Exercises: Exercises similating various movements occurring in every-day life in our work or play. They differ from Games Fundamentals in that they are imitative in character, and their purpose is activity rather than development of correct form.

3. Practice in such natural activities as climbing, hanging, jumping and vaulting. This discussion will not go into detail on these activities. The "Motor Ability Test" under the section on "Trak and Field" takes up a number of forms of the first three mentioned. Vaulting requires considerable and expensive apparatus, and though valuable is not as practical for use in the grades as the other material herein included. It will therefore not be emphasized. Should the school playground be equipped with the usual hanging and climbing apparatus, the children of that school are very fortunate, since such exercises are of much developmental importance, first from the standpoint of the development of fundamental body co-ordinations, second, because of the fact that normal development follows the course of the recapitulation of racial movements, third because of normal development of contours and posture made possible as emphasized under the section on "Posture Training." However, if the simple and small amount of apparatus is provided which is called for in the "Motor Ability Tests" already referred to, some opportunity can be afforded for this type of activity.

4. Story Plays or Action Stories: Similar to Mimetic Exercises, but follow a story and are therefore more dramatic in character. Their use is found in the Primary Grades.

5. Drill in Dance Steps: This may or may not be separated from the teaching of the dances where the steps are employed.

Significance and Value of Movement Fundamentals

The significance and resulting value of movement fundamentals lie in:

1st. Character of the appeal. Because the activity is a natural racial activity, or related to the perfection of such an activity, there is a directness of appeal, the interest is inherent in the activity, the performance of the activity gives much satisfaction, and the results obtained are along the lines of natural development.

2nd. Its naturalness. Again because the activity is a natural one, there are no devised strained movements or positions of joints. The joint-muscular mechanism is thus used along natural and normal lines, and the neuro-muscular control developed is that which can find adjustment and practical use in daily life. If the lesson is well planned, some of the movements included may have excellent postural effects.

3rd. Big muscle activity involved. Being associated with work and play forms, practice in movement fundamentals affords much activity of the large muscle groups of the body.

4th. Its association with play forms. It offers an opportunity for mass instruction in the fundamentals of games and sports which should comprise so large and important a part of the play life and motor education of boys and girls.

Games Fundamentals

1. Their Importance.

By Games Fundamentals we mean the learning of and drill in the correct form used in different athletic games in order to increase skill in these sports. In this division of Movement Fundamentals we particularly find a large measure of the significance and values as stated above, i. e., the character of the appeal, the naturalness of the movement (with a few exceptions), the degree of muscle activity involved, the association with play forms. The fact that it offers a well organized method of mass instruction in games technique gives it particular significance. Further, its importance lies in the fact that much of the material lends itself well to adaptability to poor conditions of space, as in the schoolroom.

2. Planning a Lesson and Method of Instruction.

First Step: In planning to teach technique of a certain game it becomes necessary to pick out isolated movements which are fundamental to the game because in playing these movements are employed a great deal. One of these isolated movements is taken at a time, as throwing, for example. This movement is demonstrated and explained, then the class which is in open order formation (see page 313) is asked to take this movement by command in the correct form described. For methods of giving commands refer to page 14. The apparatus is not used. All the class are working at the same time. The teacher can correct and assist until movements are done in fairly good form, or at least until a good idea of correct form and the kinesthetic sense of doing the movement right are gained. This gives something to build on in the practise-work which follows:

Second Step: Practise work with the equipment. A plan for practise and drill is devised by the teacher, and the class is organized for this practise according to the amount of available equipment. This practise, supposing it to be practise in throwing and catching a softball, is carried on for a short time.

Third Step: Then a contest game based on the practise plan is played which uses the fundamental of throwing and catching, thus giving more drill in it, yet having the added interest afforded by the competition. The lesson must always include the game, even at the expense of cutting short the time used in the previous steps.

The Type Lessons given in the various sections which follow demonstrate this method of presentation.

The fundamentals in the standard sports, Basket Ball, Softball, Soccer, Track and Field are included below. These sports are selected because it is believed that during the elementary grades the basis for these sports should be laid with the large mass of children, hoping that in the Junior and Senior High Schools, general skill in the general group of students will be evidenced so that a continuation of growth in this skill will be demanded for the large number. Such a plan may play the largest part in getting athletics for all into the Senior High School.

A. GAME FUNDAMENTALS LEADING TO SOFTBALL

Fundamentals to be worked on:
  I. Catching.
  II. Throwing, including Pitching.
  III. Batting.
  IV. Base-Running.

I and II. Catching and Throwing

Catching.

1. All balls caught above the waist are caught in the following manner: Thumbs together and parallel, fingers pointing upward and somewhat spread yet relaxed. Hands and arms give as catch is made. See Fig. 1, 319.
    (1) In front of body above waist.
    (2) Above waist to right or left.
    (3) Above head.
2. All balls caught below the waist are caught in the following manner: Little fingers together and parallel, fingers pointing downward, somewhat spread, yet relaxed. Hands and arms give as ball is caught. See Fig. 1, page 319.
    (1) Below waist in front of body.
    (2) Below waist to right or left.

Fig. 1: Position of hands in catching a Softball above and below the waist.

Fig. 2: Position of hands in catching a fly in Softball.

Fig. 3: Preliminary position for throwing—weight on right foot—body twisted to the right.

Fig. 4: Finish of the throw—weight transferred to left foot—body twisted to left. There should be an extension backward of left arm not shown here.

(3) Grounder.
(4) Pick-up.

3. Flies: Fly-balls, balls received from above are usually received in a nest position. The hands are placed in front of chest close to body, little fingers together, palms up, and hands cupped. See Fig. 2, page 319. Arms give as ball is received, and body is hunched over ball to prevent its spinning out of the hands.

The method of developing proper catching is described below under Type Lesson I.

Throwing.
1. Overhand Throw. Fielder's throw.
2. Underhand Throw. Pitcher's throw.

These are described in the Type Lesson which follows immediately.

Type Lesson I. in Fundamentals of Softball: (Throwing and Catching).

Formation: Four lines facing forward.

1. (a) Demonstrate and explain methods of catching an indoor baseball (without ball).
   (b) Commands for catching:
   Catch a ball above the waist—One!
   Position—Two!
   Catch a ball below the waist—One!
   Position—Two!
   Jump to catch above the head—One!
   Position—Two!

Command all of various catching positions in the same manner.

2. (a) Demonstrate and explain fielders throw (without ball).

Right arm is drawn back as body turns right with weight on right foot. Right arm is bent then thrust forward as the weight is transferred forward to the left foot. Left foot is always forward in the direction of the throw. See Figs. 3 and 4, page 319.
   (b) Commands for Throw:
   Draw back arm and twist body—One!
   Transfer weight and throw ball—Two!
   Position—Three!

3. Demonstrate and command pitcher's throw (without ball.)
   Starting position—heels together.
   Draw right arm back parallel with the body—One!
   Swing the right arm forward parallel with the body,

at the same time take a step forward with the left foot—Two!
Position—Three!
4. Catching and throwing in pitcher's position (without ball).
Command rapidly the following:
1. Catch a ball above the head—One!
Throw (overhand) to first base—Two!
2. Catch a ball below the waist to the right side—One!
Throw to second base—Two!
3. Catch a ball low front—One!
Pitch (underhand) it to the catcher—Two!
Etc.
5. Catching and throwing (with the ball).
Formation: Lines two and three stand back to back and close together. Lines one and four move back 15 or 20 feet from lines two and three.

A ball is passed between lines one and two and another between lines three and four, care being taken that catches and throws are made correctly.

After a degree of proficiency has been gained, contest between the teams (1 and 2, 3 and 4) to see which will make the fewest errors in passing down and back. Then play "Zig Zag Pass," p. 72.
6. Play "Ten Trips," No. 5, p. 73.

Formation: Line one stands in file formation at one side of one end of the gymnasium. Line two faces line one but at the opposite end of the room. Line three stands at same end of gymnasium as line one but on other side of room. Line four stands opposite line three.
7. Repeat 5 and 6 using Pitcher's Throw.

Additional Games for Catching and Throwing.
Teacher and Class, p. 27.
Leader Spry, p. 32.
Line ball, p. 32.
Baseball Pivot and Throw, p. 85.
Fongo, p. 85.

Practise in Catching Flies.
1. Commands for the catching position without the ball are the same as for other modes of catching. See Lesson I. above.
2. Class in formation as for "Ten Trips," No. 5, p. 73, described in Lesson I. Play without contesting using a fly throw instead of a straight throw, thus giving opportunity to catch flies.
3. Ring Call Ball, p. 50.

Practise in Stopping Grounders.

Class in shuttle formation. As many groups as desired. Play "Grounders Shuttle Relay," p. 84.

At first play slowly for form without competition. Then follow with the game for competition in speed. It can be played through a number of times without stopping as Ten Trips, before the competition is at an end.

Target Practise.

The following practise in aiming is good. Either throw can be used. When the underhand throw is used, the thrower stands the distance away from the target that the pitcher's box is from home-plate (23 feet on a 27 foot diamond and 30 feet on a 35 foot diamond. The practise is then called pitching for strikes.

1. A basket ball is placed on a chair or higher (at a height between knee and shoulder). Use several targets if there are several balls. Each thrower from each team gets five pitches or throws. If the basket ball is hit, one point is scored. The pitching average of each player is recorded and scores of the teams are compared.

2. Another method is to suspend a board 15 by 24 inches about two feet from the ground. This represents the space between a boy's knee and shoulder and across the home-plate. The same procedure as in 1 is followed.

III. Batting.

The manner of batting and how to teach it is described in the following type lesson.

Type Lesson II.

1. Review Exercises of Lesson I, that need more drill.

2. Demonstrate and command the batter's position and swing (without bat). Face right with weight on right foot. Both arms drawn back to right shoulder, hands together with right hand high. Left elbow held high—One!

Transfer weight to left foot and swing arms in full swing from right to left keeping them in a horizontal plane—Two!

Position—Three!

3. Batter's position and swing (with bat).

Do same as 2 only give out as many bats as are available. Give them first to the leaders of each line. The rest of class do movements without bat while those with bats use them. After one or two swings the bats are passed back to the next in line until all have had a turn.

4. Batting Practise (with bat and ball).

Four bases are marked at one end of the room or at various places on the playground. Line one takes one of these bases. The first player in this line is the batter, the second player the catcher, the third the pitcher, the next fielder one, etc. The pitcher pitches the batter four strikes and the number of these the batter is able to hit fair count as his score. The batter then goes to the lowest fielding position and each player works up one place thus: catcher goes to bat, pitcher to catch, first fielder to pitch, etc.

Each other line does as described for line one. At the end the total score for each line is added and the winning line is declared.

Other games which develop Batting.
1. Circle strike, p. 90.
2. Box Ball, p. 88.
3. Long Ball, p. 88.
4. One-old-cat, p. 83.
5. Work-up, p. 83.

IV. Base-running

1. Form of presentation: Class in four lines. Nos. 1 in each line take the commands first, and then go to end of line. Each one thus gets a turn. Do not drill long.
    a. Run at top speed forward—One!
       Stop short—Two!
       Turn right and return to line—Three!
    b. Run at top speed forward—One!
       Slide—Two!
       Stand and return—Three!

The slide when done on the right leg is performed as follows: From the run, jump into slide relaxing body, feet toward bag. Body is on back and right side, slide being made on outside of right leg, thigh and hip. The right leg is slightly flexed, that is, relaxed. Left leg is flexed, left foot hooking base as runner slides around outside of base. To stand, bend at waist, flex right leg and thigh, bringing right foot under body and come to stand.

If the slide is made on the left leg, the above is reversed, and the body passes the base within the diamond.

Sliding is useful in that it acts as a brake to stop short in the run, and that it is a means of evading being tagged out.

2. The above presentation should be followed immediately in the lesson by a game with base-running in which the teacher can insist upon the application of the slide. "Work-up" (page 83) can be used in this way; or the regular game, Softball, can be played with insistence of the use of the slide. This can be adapted for the sake of practise by having all of one team bat before changing sides. All the outs the fielding team are able to make on the other team score as points for the

fielding team. Every player must be tagged out. No scores are made by the batting.

3. Games which can be used at other times to teach base-running and stopping and speed in getting around the diamond are:

    Box Ball, p. 88.
    Punch Ball, p. 86.

Bibliography

For official rules of Softball, refer to Sports Library—"Official Softball-Volley Ball Guide," A. S. Barnes, New York.

For Coaching, refer to "Softball"—A. T. Noren, 1940, A. S. Barnes, New York.

B. MOVEMENT FUNDAMENTALS LEADING TO BASKET BALL

Fundamentals to be worked on:

I. Catching.
II. Passing.
III. Goal Shooting.
IV. Pivoting.
V. Dribbling.
VI. Guarding.
VII. Jumping.
VIII. Dodging and Feinting.

I. and II. Catching and Passing

Catching:
1. Above the waist.
2. Below the waist.
3. Above the head.
4. At the sides, above and below waist.

Passing:
1. Chest.
2. Underarm.
3. Underhand.
4. Over-head.
5. Side arm to side.
6. Backward underhand.
7. Bounce.
8. Shoulder.
9. Overarm or hook.

The following is a type lesson showing how fundamentals in catching and passing may be taught. An exercise to develop Dodging and Feinting is included in this lesson in order to give more general activity.

Type Lesson I.

Formation: Class in four equal lines facing forward (see methods of opening order, page 313), or in the aisles of a schoolroom.

I. Demonstrate methods of catching a basket ball. See Fig. 1, page 327.

    1. Above the waist—thumbs parallel and pointing upward about 4 inches apart. Fingers well spread and slightly cupped.

2. Below the waist—little fingers parallel and pointing down about 4 inches apart.
II. Commands for Catching.
 1. Catch a ball above the waist—One!
    Position—Two!
 2. Catch a ball below the waist—One!
    Position—Two!
 3. Catch a ball above the head—One!
    Position—Two!
III. Demonstrate and command throws.
 1. (a) Chest—hands at chest in catching position—stretch both arms straight out from the chest.
    (b) Commands.
        Catch ball above waist—One!
        Throw with chest throw—Two!
        Position—Three!
 2. (a) Demonstrate over-head pass—both arms above head in catching position, bring both arms forward bending trunk forward somewhat.
    (b) (1) Catch ball above head—One!
            Throw ball with over-head throw—Two!
        (2) Catch ball at feet—One!
            Bring over-head—Two!
            Throw—Three!
            Position—Four!
        Repeat the above several times by using just the counts as commands, thus; 1-2-3-4.
IV. Demonstrate and command the dodge.
    Catch the ball at the right with the trunk bent far to the right—One!
    Bend the trunk to the left and move the hands to the left as if to throw—Two!
    Bend back right and throw right—Three!
    Position—Four!
    Repeat several times with counts as commands, thus; 1-2-3-4.
V.—With the ball.
 1. Lines 1 and 2 face each other. Lines 3 and 4 face each other. A ball is given to each two lines and they are told to pass it between them using the chest pass and the proper manner of catching.
 2. After this has been done several times play "Zig Zag Pass," p. 72. The same procedure is then used with the overhead pass.
    Note: The same method as used in this Lesson can be carried out employing the different catches and passes enumer-

ated above. The passes not already described are executed as follows:

Underarm Pass.

The ball is held in the right hand, fingers outspread. The hand and arm are carried slightly to low rear. The pass is made by swinging the hand and arm to the front and at the same time stepping forward with the left foot.

Underhand Pass.

The ball is held low in front by both hands and the body is bent forward. The ball is passed by a full arm swing or a wrist snap either to the right or left or to the front.

Overarm or Hook Pass.

The body is turned to the right as the right arm swings back. The ball is held in the right hand. The pass is made by a full arm swing upward transferring the weight from the right to the left foot and delivering the ball above the head.

Shoulder Pass. See Fig. 2, page 327.

The ball is held in both hands over the right or left shoulder and is delivered by an extension of the forearms across the body to the left, or right.

Bounce Pass.

The ball is passed to a colleague by bouncing it on the floor so that it will strike three or four feet in front of him. When bounced past an opponent it should strike the floor just beyond his feet. See game "Bounce Pass Keep Away".

Sidearm to Side Pass. See Fig. 3, page 327.

Ball in both hands at right side of body. Swing both arms across the body with the right arm underneath and the left on top and deliver the ball to left under left arm. When delivering ball to right reverse the above. See Type Lesson II.

Backward Underhand Pass.

Same as side arm to side except that the ball is delivered backward, rather than sideways. See Type Lesson II.

Additional Games for Passing.

    Center Catch Ball, p. 52.
    Pass for Points, p. 78.
    Basket Ball Shuttle Relay, p. 75.
    Zig Zag Goal Ball, p. 75.
    Keepaway, p. 77.
    Goal Keepaway, p. 78.
    Ten Trips—all varieties—especially No. 2, p. 73.
    Newcomb, p. 79.
    End Ball, p. 80.

PHYSICAL EDUCATION 327

Fig. 1: Position of hands in catching a Basket Ball above and below the waist.

Fig. 2: Shoulder Pass.

Fig. 3: Side arm to side pass

Fig. 4: Chest loop shot.

III. Shooting.

Two styles of shooting only are included here, and described simply as sufficient for grade use.

1. Chest loop shot. See Fig. 4, page 327.

Ball in both hands at chest, elbows close at side. Lower the arms to near the waist line and draw them toward the body. Raise the hands chest high and extend the arms upward, releasing the ball.

The method of developing this shot is given in Type Lesson II below.

2. Underhand loop shot.

Ball in both hands at waist level or below, with elbows bent and close to sides. The ball is raised forward and upward, usually with full swing and extension of arms until hands are about at level of and far out from face, at which point the ball is released.

This shot can be developed in a similar manner to the Chest Loop Shot. See Type Lesson II.

Games which will aid in developing Goal Shooting are:
    Bounce Goal Relay, p. 74.
    Zig Zag Goal Ball.
    Basket Ball Goal Games, p. 72.

IV. Pivoting.

Boys and girls of the 6th grade can learn the fundamental form of Pivoting.

1. The Front Pivot.
    Turn to the right on the right foot.
    Turn to the left on the left foot.

The method of developing this pivot is given in Type Lesson II, which immediately follows.

2. The Reverse Turn.
    Turn to the right on the left foot.
    Turn to the left on the right foot.

The Reverse Turn can be developed in the same manner as the Front Pivot. See Type Lesson II.

Type Lesson II.

This lesson follows a logical progression from and sequence upon Lesson I. Therefore two passes are introduced not given in Lesson I.

Formation: Four lines in a gymnasium.

1. Review any exercises in previous lesson that need repeating.
2. Chest loop Shot (without ball).
    Catch ball at chest—One!

Lower the arms to near the waist line and draw them toward the body—Two!

Raise the hands chest high and extend the arms upward —Three!

Position—Four!

Repeat with counts as commands: 1-2-3-4.

3. Pivot and Pass (without ball).

Catch ball at waist—One!

Pivot to the left on the left foot—Two!

Throw the ball—Three!

Position—Four!

Repeat with counts as commands: 1-2-3-4.

Repeat turning right on the right foot.

4. Side Arm to Side Pass (without ball).

Catch ball in both hands at right—One!

Swinging both arms across the body with the right arm underneath and the left on top—Two!

Position—Three!

Repeat with counts as commands.

Repeat catching ball at left.

5. Chest Loop Shot (with ball).

Lines 2 and 3 face each other. Lines 1 and 4 face center as 2 and 3 have done. Ball is given to lines 1 and 2.

Line 1 shoots the ball using a high loop to line 3.

Line 2 does same to line 4.

6. Pivot and Pass (with ball).

(1) All four lines face forward.

A ball is given to the first person in each line. This person pivots on left foot to left (or right foot to right) and passes ball to person back of him. This person catches the ball, pivots and passes it to next person and so on. All remain facing as they were after the pivot and then the ball is started from the other end of the line without a second signal.

Repeat this until all have reached a reasonable amount of proficiency.

(2). Play "Pivot and Pass Relay," p. 74.

7. Side Arm to Side (with ball).

(1) Lines 1 and 2 face each other and close in the ends of the two lines making an elongated circle. Lines 3 and 4 do the same. A ball is then passed from right to left using side arm to side pass.

Repeat, throwing ball from left to right.

(2). Play "Ten Trips," No. 2, p. 73.

8. Backward Underhand Pass (with ball).

(1). Lines 1 and 3 face the back of the room. Lines 2 and 4 face forward. Lines 1 and 2 are one circle, 3 and 4 another.

The ball is passed backward under the arm of the passer to the player directly behind.

(2). Repeat the above but have the circle in motion. The "running with the ball" rule must not be violated. The ball either must be passed before a step is taken or the passer must stop until ball is passed.

9. Goal Shooting Contest.

Lines 1 and 2 go to one basket. Lines 3 and 4 to the other basket. Standing about ten feet from the basket and using the chest loop shot each line takes its turn at shooting for goal and counts each goal shot as a score. The winning lines then compete and losing lines compete.

V. Dribbling.

Technique in dribbling is taught only to boys of the elementary grades, since dribbling is used only in boys' basket ball.

Description of Dribbling:

With body slightly bent forward, the ball is pushed (not slapped) to the floor by the curved fingers and the action of the wrist and forearm of one hand. The ball should not rise above the waist line. The correct use of the hand in relation to the ball must be emphasized.

Drill in Dribbling:

1. (a) Class in four lines formation. A ball is given to the first player in each line. He dribbles it in place, paying especial attention to the hand action in relation to the ball and to the height of the bounce. When he has dribbled it the number of times designated by the teacher he catches it in both hands, and at the same time pivots, then passes it to the boy, behind him in line. This is repeated by the second boy, and continued down the line until all have had opportunity to practice.

(b) The above is repeated as a game for competition between lines in good dribbling form.

2. (a) Ball is given to the first person in each line. He dribbles progressing forward about 40 feet, pivots, and passes to the second in line. He then returns to the rear of his line. This continues until all players have dribbled and passed.

(b) After proficiency has been gained in this, a game is played to see which line can complete this first.

3. Refer to "Dribble and Take Away," p. 77.

Note: For girls, the same process as 1 (a) and (b), making but one bounce, can be used. For further drill in the bounce for girls, see "Dribble and Bounce Pass Shuttle Relay," p. 75.

VI. Guarding.
Drill in Guarding for Boys.
1. Dribble and Take Away, p. 77.
2. Keep Away, p. 77.
3. Goal Keep Away, p. 78.

Drill in Guarding for Girls.
1. Class in four lines. Lines 2 and 3 close in close together and face each other. Lines 1 and 4 face in and may move out a little. See accompanying diagram. Lines of fours across the class work as one unit. Balls are given to as many units as there are balls. The ball is given to either No. 2 or 3 in the unit. Two passes it to 4, 3 trying to intercept, violating no guarding rules; 4 passes it back to 2, 3 again trying to

Formation for Guarding Practice (Girls)

intercept, but always guarding 2. If 3 is successful, she throws it to 1, and 2 guards 3. This passing and intercepting continues for a short period, for it is quite strenuous. Then 2 exchanges places with 1, and 3 with 4. Practice is continued for a short time. These groups are then allowed to rest, while other groups work.

2. The above practice can be converted into a game similar to "Bounce Pass Keep-away," p. 78.

VII. Jumping.
1. Class in four lines.
Left hand behind the back—One!
Bending the knees—Two!
Jump and reach high over head with right arm—Three!
Position—Four!
Repeat with counts as commands: 1-2-3-4.

2. Classes in four lines. Lines 1 and 2 line up according to height to compete against each other in jumping. Lines 3 and 4 do the same. A ball is tossed up between two players of equal height and the player who gets the toss-up wins a point for his team. The competition continues until each member of the team has jumped. The team scoring the highest number of points wins.

Bibliography

For rules refer to Sports Library, A. S. Barnes, New York.
"Official NCAA Basket Ball Guide for Men."
"Official Basket Ball Guide for Women."
For Coaching refer to:
    1. "Basket Ball for Girls"—Meissner and Meyers, A. S. Barnes, New York, 1939.
    2. "Basket Ball"—Charles Murphy, A. S. Barnes, New York.

C. MOVEMENT FUNDAMENTALS LEADING TO SOCCER

(Rules for Simplified Soccer, an adaptation for Elementary Grades, are found in this bulletin. See Index).

Fundamentals to be worked on.
    I. Dribbling
    II. Passing
    III. Stopping the Ball
    IV. Kicking

I. Dribbling:

Description of Dribbling.

Dribbling is advancing the ball by a series of taps with the foot, keeping the ball always under control by following it up so that it is always near or between the feet. The advance forward is made by short running steps, occasionally hopping on one foot, the other foot giving the series of short taps.

Drill in Dribbling.

1. Class in four lines formation. The class on signal moves down the field trying the above method of advancing forward. No ball is used.

2. A ball is given to the first person in each line. This player dribbles the ball down the field around a goal and back to the next person in line.

3. Play "Soccer Dribble Relay," p. 65.

II. and III. Passing and Stopping.
Passing.
A pass is a directed kick to a team-mate, the ball remaining close to the ground. Different ways of passing are:
1. Passing to left with inside of right foot.
2. Passing to left with outside of left foot.
3. Passing to right with inside of left foot.
4. Passing to right with outside of right foot.

Stopping the Ball.
Manners of stopping are:
With sole of foot.
With inside of foot.
With inside of leg.
With both feet.
With thighs, knees, chest, top of shoulder, back, head.
Never with hands and arms.

Methods of developing passing and stopping.
Class in four lines.
1. Describe and demonstrate use of foot in above passes.
2. Command class.
Swing right foot diagonally to left—One!
Position—Two!
Repeat using other passes.
3. Demonstrate and describe the ways of stopping the ball.
4. Lines 1 and 2 face each other. Lines 3 and 4 face each other. Each two lines work together. A ball is given to each group. The ball is passed between these lines until some skill is developed in passing and stopping and then the game "Soccer Pass," p. 67, is played in both of its forms.
5. All lines face forward again but each two lines continue to work together. The first players in lines 1 and 2 carry the ball to a designated spot and back again by the use of the passing forms learned above. This continues until all couples in each line have carried the ball. Lines 3 and 4 do likewise. When sufficient skill is developed the game "Soccer Pass and Shoot," p. 67, is played in both its forms.

IV. Kicking.
By kicking, as differentiated from passing, is meant a long kick to gain distance, usually used by the full-backs or goal-keeper in getting the ball out of their own territory, and by the forwards in shooting goals.

Forms of Kicking:
1. Forward kick. This is done in two ways, either by kicking it from the ground, or before it hits the ground called

a volley kick. In either case the ball is kicked by the instep and not by the toe. It is lifted above the heads of the opponents.

2. Backward Kick. This kick is used when the player has allowed the ball to go beyond him. He runs to overtake it and without turning kicks it back. It is used most frequently in preventing the ball from going out of bounds.

Methods of Developing Kicking:
1. Without the ball.
   a. The Forward Kick.
      Draw the leg back from the hip—One!
      Kick forward and follow through—Two!
      (By follow through is meant that the leg continues to swing forward upward after it has kicked the ball).
      Position—Three!
   b. The Backward Kick.
      Run forward—One!
      Swing leg forward from hip preparatory for kick—Two!
      Kick backward—Three!
      Position—Four!
2. With the Ball.
   a. The players are lined up in different groups. A ball is thrown in to each group by a leader throwing to each player in rotation. This player tries to kick it out with a volley kick.
   b. For stationary long kicks see "Shuttle Kicking Contest," p. 68.

Practice schemes and games which develop the various combinations of technique:
1. Soccer Dribble and Shoot, p. 66.
2. Simple Soccer Keep-away, p. 64.
3. Double Soccer Keep-away, p. 65.
4. Square Football, p. 68.
5. Corner Kick-ball, p. 68.
6. Soccer Drive, p. 67.
7. Soccer Target Kicking Relay, p. 66.
8. Forward Practise. The five forwards take the ball down the field dribbling and passing. After some practise in this, the opposing two full-backs and goal-keeper are put against the forwards and try to take the ball away from them. If they are successful and get the ball back past the middle they win. If the forwards succeed in keeping the ball and get it through the goal, the forwards win. Later the three half-backs are added to the opposition, and the play is carried on as above.

Bibliography

"The Coaching of Soccer," H. E. Coyer, W. B. Saunders Co., Philadelphia, 1937.

D. MOVEMENT FUNDAMENTALS LEADING TO TRACK AND FIELD EVENTS (See pages 98-112).

Organization of Class for Work in Track and Field.

1. For class instruction, the class should be organized into the four line formation, by an open order, see page 313. This formation keeps the class compact, yet with sufficient spacing to carry on activity. The class can see the teacher, the teacher can get about the class and give individual help, thus all can receive instruction at same time. Then, too, this formation lends itself well to group practise and line contests which always follow the practise in fundamentals. The class thus remains organized throughout the lesson.

2. Squad Organization. After the fundamentals of a number of events have been taught by class instruction, practise in the events in order to measure accomplishment must be given. This can best be done by organizing the class into squads with squad leaders. If there is no provided basis for squad organization the leaders are selected by the class and these leaders take turns in choosing up their squads. If there is a natural basis of organization, such as age classification, or grade-age-height-weight classification, the class should be divided if possible into squads according to their classification. Each squad then selects a leader. Two systems of classification are given in the section on Track and Field.

When squad organization has been effected the teacher conducts the class by stating at the beginning of the lesson the order of events for each squad. The squad leaders then take their squads to the place for their first event. A definite and permanent place for each event has been arranged on the gymnasium floor or play field.

When the teacher blows the whistle, each squad rotates to its next event. The squad leader is held responsible for keeping his squad busy; he assists its members in doing their best, and keeps records of accomplishment.

This system effects a most desirable method of organization, and gives opportunity for development in leadership and initiative. It also makes for good followership and earnest co-operation.

Events used in Motor Ability Tests included in this Bulletin for which practise in fundamentals should be used:

(See section on Track and Field, p. 98)
I.   Basket Ball Far Throw (Overhead).

II. Basket Ball Far Throw (Single Arm).
III. Play ground Ball Throw.
IV. Standing and Running Broad Jumps.
V. Running Hop, Step and Jump.
VI. Running High Jump.
VII. Goal Shooting (See "Shooting" under "Movement Fundamentals for Basket Ball" for work on goal shooting).
VIII. Dash: (a) Sprinting, (b) The Start.

Note: Most of the time spent on Track and Field should be used in acquiring correct form.

I. Basket Ball Far Throw (Overhead).

Class in 4 lines.
1. Description and demonstration by teacher.
2. Commands: (Without use of ball)

Stepping to the side stride position, throwing arms above head—One!

Bending the trunk forward, and forcibly swinging the arms forward—Two!

Position—Three!

Repeat—One! Two! Three!

3. Lines 1 and 2 face each other, and lines 3 and 4 face each other. A ball is passed between the members of lines 1 and 2 (similarly lines 3 and 4), in the manner just described, but easily, with attention to form. Ball should be released from the hands in the forward swing of the arms so that it will move upward at an angle of about 45 degrees with the horizontal.

4. Spread lines farther apart. Work for more distance by using a harder throw. Give attention to rules.

5. After form has been taught, subsequent lessons should be conducted on the basis of squad formation, each squad taking its turn at working on this particular event.

6. Conduct "Shuttle Basket Ball Throw," p. 111.

II. Basket Ball Far Throw (Single Arm).

Class in 4 lines.
1. Description and demonstration by teacher.
2. Commands: (Without use of ball)

Step back with right foot turning body right draw right slightly curved arm back, palm up, weight on right foot, bend right knee slightly—One!

Swing around on left foot, bring right foot forward, and swing full arm forward and up—Two!

Position—Three!

Repeat—One! Two! Three!

Note: If difficulty is experienced in changing feet, the feet should be worked on separately by command.

3. Lines 1 and 2 face each other; also lines 3 and 4. A ball is thrown between members of lines 1 and 2 (similarly, lines 3 and 4) in the manner described, but without force, paying attention only to form. Ball should be released from the arm as it swings forward upward, so that ball will move upward at an angle of about 45 degrees with the horizontal.

4. Take more distance between lines. Add more force but still pay attention principally to form.

5. Draw four six-foot circles, one in each corner of room. Lines 1 and 2 take places at circles across from each other at either end of room. Lines 3 and 4 are similarly placed. Members of lines 1 and 2 throw back and forth to each other, using the circles. Pay attention to rules. Lines 3 and 4 do likewise.

6. Work in squads.

7. Conduct "Shuttle Basket Ball Throw," p. 111 (no circle used)

III. Playground Ball Throw.
Class in 4 lines.
1. Demonstration and description by teacher.
2. Commands: (Without ball).
   Step forward, right foot—One!
   Hop forward on right foot, twist and bend body right, with right arm back—Two!
   Pivot on left foot, swing right foot forward, and bend and stretch right arm forward—Three!
   Position—Four!
   Repeat—One! Two! Three! Four!
3. With the run.
   Run forward—One!
   Hop on right, etc.—Two!
   Pivot and throw (as above)—Three!
   Position—Four!
   Repeat—One! Two! Three Four!
4. Lines 1 and 2 opposite each other at either end of room. Draw a line in front of each. Lines 3 and 4 are similarly placed.
   Members of lines 1 and 2 throw back and forth to each other, using the run, and being careful not to step over line. Pay attention to form.
5. Work in squads.
6. Conduct Shuttle Baseball Throw as "Shuttle Basket Ball Throw," p. 111, is conducted.

IV. (a) Standing Broad Jump.
Class in 4 lines.
1. Demonstration and description by teacher.
2. Commands:

Rise on toes, swing arms forward upward above head
—One!

Bend knees and bend body forward and swing arms forward downward to behind body—Two!

Jump up bringing knees up in front and arms forward landing with knees bent—Three-Four!

Position—Five!

Repeat—One! Two! Three-Four! Five!

3. Repeat same jumping forward.
4. Work in squads.
5. Conduct "Shuttle Broad Jump," p. 111.

(b) Running Broad Jump.

1. Demonstration and description by teacher.
2. Commands:

Step forward left (or right, if right is natural take-off foot)—One!

Swing right leg forward, bringing knee up in front left knee following, swing arms forward, and jump forward, landing on both feet—Two-Three!

Position—Four!

Repeat—One! Two-Three! Four!

3. With three running steps beginning with left—Go!
(Count 1-2-3 or Left-right-left)—Jump!

Repeat, increasing speed of running steps.

4. To increase the run, yet not fail to take off with the take-off foot, give commands thus: Run! Jump!

On "Run" the class runs an indefinite number of steps forward. When the signal "Jump" comes, each pupil steps on his take-off foot (the one which leaves the ground last) and jumps forward as described in 1.

5. Squad work. Work for form, not distance.

V. Running Hop Step and Jump.

Class in 4 lines.

1. Description and demonstration by teacher.
2. Commands:

(a) Removing the right foot from the floor hop forward on the left foot—One!

Step forward onto the right foot—Two!

Taking off with the right foot jump and land on both feet—Three!

Back to starting position—Four!

Repeat—One! Two! Three! Four!

(b) With three running steps beginning with the left —Go! (count 1-2-3 or left-right-left)—Hop! (land on left foot).

(c) With three running steps as above—Go!

Hop! Step! (This time the step should be more of a leap and the landing should be on the right foot).

    (d) With three running steps—Go!

Hop! Step! Jump! (Land on both feet).

Repeat, increasing the run but working only on form.

  3. Divide into squads and work for form, then distance.

VI. Running High Jump.

There are a number of forms for the High Jump. The one which grade boys usually desire to use is the scissor style. For an immature class, it might be well to take up the jump with mass instruction.

    (a) For the scissors style this may be done in the following manner:

Class in four lines.

  1. Demonstration and explanation by teacher.

  2. Springing from left foot, swing right foot high in air, following it with left foot, which passes it as it comes down, landing on right foot, then on left—Jump! Repeat using other foot.

  3. With three running steps forward, beginning left—Go! (count 1-2-3 or Left-right-left)—Jump! (Swing right leg up, springing from left, which took last step, and jump as in 1).

Repeat starting right foot.

Repeat using favorite foot.

  4. Divide into squads and use low jumping standards for form. The run should then be made from either side of the standards and the spring taken from the foot farther from the cross bar.

    (b) The Straight Jump. This style is next in difficulty, and will be more effective in giving height if it can be mastered, and children should be encouraged to work on it.

Class in 4 lines.

  1. Three running steps forward beginning left—Go! (Left-right-left)—Jump! (Spring from left foot, swing right foot up hard and make half turn left, as left leg comes up and kicks back. Land on one or both feet).

Repeat starting right foot.

Repeat using favorite foot.

  2. Divide into squads and use low bar on jumping standards for form. The preliminary run should be short and straight at the bar.

VII. Dash.

  A. Sprinting Form.

Class in four lines.

1. Demonstration by teacher.
2. Commands:
(1). Bringing knees high in front, run in place beginning with the left foot—Go!
Class—Halt!
(2). Repeat above and add the motion of the arms, i. e., with a 90-degree bend in the elbows swing the arms from the shoulders in opposition to the bending of the knees. The running is done wholly on the toes and the balls of the feet.
(3). Class runs forward and around the room paying especial attention to high knee action, toeing straight ahead and swinging the arms parallel with the body.

B. Start of Sprint.
Class in four lines.
1. Demonstration by teacher.
2. Commands:
(1). On your marks—One!
On this command each member of the class kneels on right knee even with or slightly ahead of the left instep. The fingers are placed on the floor about 2 to 6 inches in front of the left toe so the arms make a straight line from the shoulders to the floor. Head is up and eyes are fixed about 20 feet ahead. See figures on page 105.
Get set—Two!
The right knee is lifted from the ground and the weight of the body is shifted over the arms. The back is flat but the head looks straight forward as before.
Back on your marks—Three!
Stand in position—Four!
Repeat above using just counts as commands—One! Two! Three! Four!

(2). Repeat commands "One!" (on your marks) and "Two!" (get set) but on "Three!" or the command "Go!" the right leg is brought forward and the left arm is swung sharply forward while the right arm is swung back.
Return to position—Four!

(3). Repeat commands "One!" and "Two!" but on "Three!" or "Go!" bring the right foot up as before and continue to run for four or five steps gradually raising the body to an upright position of about 15 degrees from the vertical. The first step should be short and choppy and the arm action should be as described above. The head is kept in line with the body and looking straight ahead.
Return to position—Four!

(4). Repeat above, except after command "Go!" run for ten or fifteen feet then gradually slow down for this same distance and on "Four!" turn around and jog back to place, keeping knees high in front, toes straight ahead and pointed down, arms swinging from the shoulder in opposition to the feet, elbows bent.

    3. Divide into squads and continue to work on form, only occasionally working for speed.

E. MIMETIC EXERCISES

I. Mimetic Exercises are those simulating various movements occurring in every-day life in work or play.

II. Sources
    1. Imitation of natural movements as climbing, throwing, etc.
    2. Imitation of occupational movements as chopping, paddling, etc.
    3. Imitation of things observed in nature or environment as screw-driver.

III. Types
    1. Arms stretchings or flingings.
    2. Trunk exercises, bending forward or sideways, or twisting sideways.
    3. Leg exercises.

IV. Purposes
    1. For general activity with large physiological value (trunk and leg exercises).
    2. For body elevation and natural posture (arm stretchings and flingings).
    3. For relief work. Adaptable to schoolroom.
    4. To fill a need formerly supplied by formal devised gymnastic movements without tenseness or unnatural joint positions, and with the presence of a natural appeal commonly lacking in regular gymnastics.

V. How given

By signal (see page 14) in a fairly uniform, yet natural manner. Desirable body positions should be secured. When first presented they must be explained and demonstrated and likened to the movements they are to imitate; when learned, the name of the exercise can be stated, signals following immediately.

VI. Sample Exercises

  A. Arm exercises
    1. **The Windmill**
      Signals: Starting position. Right arm forward-upward—Fling! (See Fig. 3a, page 301).

Flinging left arm forward upward and right arm sideways downward—One! Left arm sideways downward, right arm forward upward—Two!
Change again—One! Two!
Take rhythmically and continuously—Go!
Halt!

2. **Stretching** (as one does upon getting up in the morning)
Signals: Stretching hard—One! (slowly).
Position—Two!

3. **Throwing a Lasso.**
Signals: To the stride position (feet apart) with right arm overhead—Jump!
Swinging right arm 8 times and then throw, ready—Go! (count).
Again—Go!
Arms—Change!
Repeat signals for left arm.
Class to position—Jump!

4. **Shaking a High Limb.**
Signals: Jump to grasp limb high above head—One!
Shake the limb hard—Go!
Halt!

B. **Trunk Exercises.**

1. **Paddling a Canoe.**
  (a) In standing position.
Signals: Hands in position for paddling on right side—Place!
(Both arms are placed sideways forward to right side, left arm above right).
Push paddle back—One!
Bring it forward—Two!
In rhythm—Go! Halt!
Arms—Position!
Repeat signals for left side.
  (b) In kneeling position.
Signals: In 2 counts, right knee first, Class—Kneel! (1-2). (On count 1, right knee is brought to floor, on count 2, left knee).
Use signals for paddling as given above.
Standing in 2 counts, right foot up first—Position! 1-2).

2. **Rowing.**
This may be taken either in sitting or standing position.

Signals:
    Arms and trunk in position for rowing—Place!
    (Trunk is bent forward and arms stretched forward from chest).
    Pull oars back—One!
    Reach forward—Two!
    In rhythm—Go! Halt!
    Arms—Position!

3. **Swimming Movement.**
    The signals for this exercise are given on page 305.

4. **Chopping.**
    Signals: Feet to stride—Jump!
    Raising axe over right shoulder—One!
    Chop—Two!
    In rhythm—Go! Halt!
    Repeat for left-handed chopper.
    To position—Jump!

5. **Throwing.**
    Signals: Left foot forward—Place!
    Swing right arm back ready to throw—One!
    Throw—Two!
    In rhythm—Go! Halt!
    With a jump changing feet—Change!
    Repeat for left-handed thrower.
    Foot—Position!

6. **Screw driver.**
    Signals: Arms bending forward (Fig. 3, page 300) and jumping to stride position—Jump!
    Turning screw in—Go! Stop!
    (This is executed by twisting trunk hard to right and immediately forward in a fairly brisk rhythm; emphasize the twist right).
    Taking screw out—Go! Stop!
    (As before, except twisting hard to left).
    To position—Jump!

C. Leg Exercises.

1. **Climbing a ladder.**
    Signals: Alternate arm reaching upward with opposite alternate knee bending upward beginning right arm, left knee—Go! Class—Halt! (1-2).
    (Executed like alternate knee bending upward—see Triple Test Exercise, Set I, Ex. 5, except that the opposite arm reaches above head each time).

2. **Pumping up Bicycle Tire.**
    Signals: Jumping to stride position—Jump!

Bending knees to pump up tire—in rhythm—Go! Halt!
To position—Jump!
(This exercise is executed by quick knee bendings and stretchings with hands held in front of body and elbows bending with each bend of the knee).

3. **Riding a Bicycle.**
Signals: Hands on handle-bars—Place!
Alternate knee bending upward beginning with left —Go! Class—Halt! (1-2).
Hands at neck—Place!
(Riding without hands on bars).
Beginning with left again—Go!
Class—Halt!
Arms—Position!

4. **Jumping Jack.**
Signals: Jumping Jack Exercise—Go!
Class—Halt! (1-2-3).
(Jump bringing feet astride, then together, at the same time flinging arms sideways upward clapping hands overhead, then flinging them down to side. On "Halt", jump to stride on 1, jump together on 2, and lower hands on 3).

5. **Teamster Warming Up.**
Signals: Jumping to stride and flinging arms sideways—Jump!
Bringing feet together and slapping arms across chest, then repeat in rhythm—Go! Class—Halt!

F. STORY PLAY (Primary Grades)

A story Play is physical activity which accompanies the telling of a story, the activity dramatizing the action suggested by the story.

The story itself must be:

First: Consistent, simple, short and to the point, in season.

Second: a. Either related to things within the child's environment, as occupations and activities of daily life, for example:—"On the Farm," "Going Nutting," or

b. Related to some other activity of the schools as "The Garden," "On the Play Ground," "The Pilgrims," or

c. An abbreviated version of some story which has been told to or read by the children as "Goldilocks."

Third: a. Contain many action words that can be expressed by large vigorous movements as "run," "jump," "row," "chop," etc.

b. Also contain phrases which make for an increasing amount of such large vigorous movements as "hurry," "ran faster," "worked as hard as he could," etc.

c. Contain (1) also action words or descriptive phrases which suggest lifting the body and stretching the spine, as "reach," "look up," "very tall," etc., (2) or phrases which represent an ideal as "straight tall soldier," "stand like big strong trees," " he was not afraid," etc.

The Purpose of the Story Play

1. To give equal opportunity to all for dramatization through big muscle activity. Since the story is usually acted out in the aisles of the schoolroom, all the children can participate at the same time.

2. To give activity of the big muscles variety for the sake of the physical benefits of the activity. The story play then is a good relief period activity.

3. To counteract bad postures assumed at the school desk.

Planning the Story

(a) Plan wording of the story so as to use words expressing desirable and vigorous movements.

(b) Plan for some of or all of the following types of movement.

Types	Application
1. Running, skipping, walking, etc., as—	Hurrying home.
2. Stretching head and spine upward, lifting chest, as—	Watching an aeroplane.
3. Stooping, as—	Picking up apples.
4. Stretching arms overhead, as—	Reaching for wraps on high hook.
5. Trunk exercises:	
(a) Bending trunk forward, as—	Rowing a boat.
(b) Bending or twisting trunk sideways, as—	Chopping a tree.
6. Leg exercises which bring knees up in front, as—	Climbing or running.
7. Jumping exercise, as—	Playing jack in the box. Jumping over a brook.
8. Breathing exercise, as—	Smelling a flower.

The above need not be given in any definite order, except that a breathing exercise should conclude the activity. Types can be repeated or omitted if desired, but sufficient activity must be procured.

Telling the Story

1. The story must be told briefly, be of few words, most of which can be converted into action.

2. The story must be told interestingly and with expression, so that the imagination will be strongly appealed to. It must not as a rule contain commands for the actions. The actions must come spontaneously, although the manner of telling the story can suggest or stimulate increased vigor in the movements. Yet care should be taken not to overstimulate or unduly excite.

3. The story must be the children's—to express in their own manner. An exception to this rule may be in regard to body positions which are poor from the standpoint of posture, in which case the teacher can suggest or show the body position most desirable. Another exception may be to utilize a particular manner of expression used by some one child which is of especial value, all children then executing the movements in that manner. This may often bring more desirable movements and postures. However, to insure uniformity is not the purpose of using such a method and it must be remembered that freedom and spontaneity of expression are paramount and that care should be exercised in regard to the manner and amount of using these suggestions. The teacher will find that her main method of reaching the purposes of the story play is the manner of telling the story.

Suggestions as to Manner of Execution:

When walking, running, skipping, etc., two rows can move around one row of seats (Diagram on page 312), and stop when they again reach own seats. After the rows have learned how to face and follow each other around the row of seats between them, this can be indicated in the story by saying, "Rows face. Around your row of seats." Then if it is desired to go around again, it can be indicated again. For slower movements they can move forward in the aisle, then turn around and move back to place. Fast running and jumping can also be done in place.

A Sample Story Play: Getting the Christmas Tree.

I. Outline of Story Play.

Types	Application
1. Running	Walk fast to woods. Then turn to keep warm. Spark, the dog, runs on ahead.
2. Spine Stretching	Smell cedar trees.
3. Stooping	Stoop to push away snow.

4. Arm stretching
Look for bird's nest.
Birds flying.
Different sized trees.

5. Leg Exercise (bringing knees up)
Walking through deep snow.

6. Trunk Exercise (bending sideways)
Trees blowing from side to side and twisting around.

Trunk Exercise (twisting sideways)
Chopping tree down.

Trunk Exercise (bending forward)
Pulling it home on sled.

7. Leg Exercise (bringing knees up)
Hurry through deep snow.

8. Jumping
Sisters jump up and down and clap hands.

9. Breathing
Sisters smell of cedar.

II. The Story.

(Words important to the action are in bold face type).

Two boys and their father had made plans to go to the woods after school to get their Christmas tree. It was a cold night and they had **to walk fast** to keep warm. (Rows face. Around your rows of seats). Finally they just had to **run** to keep warm. (Again, around your row of seats). Spark, the dog, **ran** away ahead. **Gallop fast,** as Spark did. Soon they came to the woods where the cedars grow. John said to his father, "**How** good the cedars **smell**. Do you **smell** them, Frank?" And Frank answered, "Yes, they surely do smell good."

They selected a tree, but the snow was so deep that in order to get to the tree trunk to chop it down, they had to **stoop** to **push** away the snow—first on **one side,** then **on another side,** then on **another.** But just as they were going to cut down the tree, John **saw a** nest **away up high in it.** Frank **tried to see** the nest too. Then they **both looked again.** And then they thought of the little birds that would come back in the spring, and look for their nest, and they would **fly around** here and there and **fly,** and **fly,** trying to find their nest. So the boys decided to look for another tree.

They saw so many, all **straight and tall**—one just **this tall;** another was **this tall** (put arms out from shoulder); then there was one taller still **like this** (hands at neck, stretch up tall); and still another **real tall** one (arms stretched way above head). But they decided the one which was **this tall** (any of the above positions) was the one they wanted.

It was quite a ways over and the snow was **deep**. They had to take **great big high steps** to get through the **deep** snow. (Face, around your row of seats). The wind was blowing **hard** and the trees **bent from side to side**, and **were twisted around** first **one way** and then **the other**. Finally their father began to **chop** the tree, and soon the tree was on their sled and through the **deep snow** they **pulled** it home. (Face. Around your row of seats). When their sisters saw them coming, they **jumped** up and down and **clapped** their hands, for they were very happy to see the Christmas tree. The boys said, "**Smell** of the Christmas tree." And the girls **smelled** of it, and said, "Oh, doesn't it **smell** good?"

Outlines of More Story Plays
On the Farm

Reach up to harness horse.
Horses trot to field.
Pitch hay into wagon.
Horses trot home.
Feed the chickens.
Pump water.
Climb up into hay mow.
Stoop to look for eggs.
Jump down on to hay.
Smell of hay.

The Circus

The band marching in the parade. (Each row plays a different instrument).
The shetland ponies.
Looking up at the elephant.
The elephant swinging his trunk.
Tall as the giraffe.
The monkeys climbing up the wall of the cage.
The lady standing on one foot and turning around.
The trapeze performer swinging and pulling himself up.
Jumping through hoops.
Smelling the popcorn.

Jack and the Bean Stalk

Runs home after having sold the cow.
Tired from running. Looks up at sky; decides to plant seeds.
Stoops to plant beans.
The bean stalk growing. It grows very high.
Jack climbs the bean stalk.
The Giant. He is very tall. Has large strong arms.
The Giant takes long strides.
The Giant looks here and there for Jack.

Jack hides first here, then there.
Jack runs home as fast as ever he can.
Jack breaths heavily.

In the Woods
Walk rapidly but softly through the quiet woods.
Hear a bird's call. Look up to find it. Look for another.
Stoop to see reflection in the brook. Pick up stones from its edge.
Jump to catch low branches of trees. Swing on these branches.
Push thicket aside to find way through.
Climb over fallen logs, and walk carefully along one, one foot placed just ahead of the other.
Jumping over the brook.
Whistle to companions, for it is time to go home.

The Garden
Run out to the school garden.
Stretch up tall, so glad to be out doors.
Stoop to see if plants are coming up.
Hoe the rows.
Spade new ground.
Rake it over.
Plant the seeds.
Skip back to the door.
Walk in slowly.

Jack o' Lantern
Drive horses out to field.
The horses are tired and breathe heavily.
Jump down out of wagon.
Lift big pumpkins up into wagon.
After the Jack o' Lantern is made, hurry from house to house, lifting Jack o'Lantern high up to windows.
Hide behind a tree. Look out from one side, then the other.
Climb up steps of own porch, and try to scare Father and Mother.
Run around house to back door.
Come in laughing, because of having frightened them.

Going Nutting
Run to woods.
Look for nut trees.
Reach up to grasp branches above head and shake them hard.
Pick up nuts from ground.
Climb the tree.

Reach way out and shake branches real hard at one side, then on the other.
Stamp the limb you are standing on hard with one foot, then with another.
Jump down from tree.
Knock off nuts with long sticks. Gather all the nuts.
Blow a dandelion to see if Mother wants us to come home.
Go home slowly with nuts and put them in the garage.

The Farmyard

The young colt.
Stand on tiptoes to look through gate. Reach up to unhook gate.
Ducks waddling.
The rooster flopping his wings and raising his chest to crow.
The weather vane on the barn turning right, then left.
The turkey strutting (bring knees up high).
The geese running (lean trunk forward, arms back, and run).
The calves frisking about.
The mother cow says, "Moo-oo-ooooooo."

Building a House

Horses bringing a load of lumber.
Reach up and lift boards from wagon placing them on ground.
Saw the boards.
Climb up the ladder.
Pound the nails. Reach out at one side, then at the other, first one board, then another.
Climb down the ladder.
Walk home.
Smell supper.

Going Fishing

Run to garage to get fishing tackle.
Reach up high to get poles off of nails.
Row up the river. (Sit on desk with feet on seat).
Throw out line and pull in fish.
Row to shore.
Run home.
Mother surprised, says "Oh, Oh!"

Birds Learning to Fly

Mother bird flies to nest.
The tree is very tall.
The little birds look over edge of nest to see how far down the ground is.

They hop onto the edge of the nest, and hop on down the limb.
They spread their wings to feel them and to see if they are strong enough.
Then they fly away.
Mother bird stands on one foot as she watches them.
They fly this way, and that way, and finally fly back to nest.
Mother bird is very proud. The little birds are tired and go to sleep.

Coasting

Hurry home from school to get ready to go coasting.
Look for warm mittens and mufflers on top shelf of closet.
Stoop to put on boots.
The snow is falling (lift arms overhead and lower them, moving fingers).
The wind bends the trees this way and that, and swoops them around.
Walk up hill through deep snow pulling sled.
Break sticks over knee for fire. Lean forward to warm hands at fire.
Jump to knock icicles off of low limbs.
Skip around fire. Jump up and down to warm toes.
Blow breath out to see it in the cold air, as you walk home.

The Leaves' Party

A gentle breeze comes softly to invite leaves to party.
The leaves are high up on trees.
One leaf is blown off and flutters way to ground. Another away up high on a branch drops and comes to ground. Another (etc.)
As the wind picks them up, they seem to hop, and hop again, and again.
Finally they all come together at the party.
They whirl (in place) as they play, then dance together (skip around row). Then whirl again, and dance.
The wind is so happy that he blows and blows, and the mother trees bend and bend.
Finally the party is over, and the leaves drop to the ground (sit in seats) and go to sleep (heads on desks).

On the Playground

Skip out to play.
Hang on the bar and chin.
Play on the See-saw.
Throw and catch.
Push the swing.

Climb the steps to slide, then slide (suddenly bend knees and swoop down).
Jump rope.
Walk on stilts.
Tired (sigh).

Hiawatha's First Hunt

Goes into forest.
Listens to birds, looks for them and talks with them.
Creeps forward to look for deer.
Lifts arms high to pass through a thicket, to keep bow-string dry.
Jumps over logs as he hastens along.
Sees deer, aims, and shoots.
Runs forward, picks it up and carries it home.
The feast Nokomis makes smells so good.

Brownies

Brownies come out softly at night.
They stand on tiptoes to see if all people have gone away and if the moon is up.
They hide.
They creep out again, and do good deeds.
They make the shoes for the shoemaker.
They chop wood for the poor woman.
They carry in fuel and food.
They sweep the house.
They climb the trees to gather nuts and fruit.
They are very happy and dance in a circle.
They steal away home, saying, "Sh-h-h—"

The Snow Man

Snow falls softly.
Run out to play in it and to make a Snow man.
Roll the snow into big balls.
Put the big heavy balls on top of each other.
Reach up to put in eyes and mouth.
Wade back to house through deep snow to get a hat for snow man.
Reach up to put hat on head. Straighten it.
Skip around the snow man.
Make small snowballs to throw at him.
Throw (one child stands in front as snow man; his head drops first, then a hand, an arm, etc.).
Jump up and down with glee.
Blow out long breaths into the frosty air.

Goldilocks

She hurries along path to woods.

She picks flowers. Reaches to get blossoms from trees. Stoops to gather them from ground.
She comes to bears' house and reaches up to table to eat soup.
She sits down on each chair.
She climbs the stairs and goes to bed.
The bears come home and finally go upstairs.
Goldilocks runs home very fast.
She is all out of breath, but so glad to be at home.

In the Orchard

Run to the orchard.
Pick apples from lower branches and put them in basket.
Crawl under fence to get apples that have rolled away.
Jump up and grasp a lower limb. Chin yourself.
Lift ladder and place it at tree.
Climb the ladder.
Hold on to one limb and reach down to other side to get an apple. Then reach the other way.
Climb down.
Chase butterfly.
Sit down on soft grass and listen to bees "buzz."

The Pilgrims

The waves sweep along, first high, then low.
The Mayflower rocks from side to side.
The Pilgrims row to shore from the ship.
The forest is dark and tall.
The Pilgrims cut down many trees for fire and homes.
They go into the woods to hunt game.
They joyfully return home.
The wind makes a soft sound through the pine trees.

Christmas Toys

Run down stairs to look at toys.
See the tall tree. Reach up to light candles.
Stoop to pick up and distribute gifts.
Tin soldiers marching.
On the rocking horse.
Riding the tricycle.
The jumping jack.
Smell the Christmas dinner.

Bibliography

Wright: "Story Plays"—A. S. Barnes and Co., New York.
Clark: "Physical Training for the Elementary Schools"—Benjamin H. Sanborn and Co., Chicago.

G. DANCE STEPS AND RHYTHMICAL JUMPING EXERCISES

A. Dance Steps. The simplest ones and those used in the folk dances are found on page 115 in the section on Rhythmical Activities.

B. Rhythmical Jumping Exercises.

(1) These are included because:
1. They have a natural appeal, being combinations of the natural activities of jumping and hopping.
2. They have a natural appeal, being done in rhythm.
3. They are vigorous big muscle activity.
4. They can be done in the aisles of the schoolroom and are easily organized.
5. They are good relief period activities.

(2) How presented:
a. With music.

The exercise is first presented by signal, as below, then done to music.

b. Without music, and by signal. This is more practical especially for relief period purposes, where time is a determining factor. For methods of giving signals, refer to page 14.

(3) Exercises.

1. **Stride spring jump on both toes.**

Signals: Stride spring jump in this rhythm:
(Say "out, in, out, in")—Go!
(1 2 1 2)
Class—Halt! (1-2-3).

Jump to stride (feet apart) on count 1, and together on count 2, continuing this in natural rhythm. On "Halt!" feet go apart on count 1, together on count 2, and heels down on count 3. Hands can be at hips. Always land on toes.

2. **Stride spring jump with arms flinging sideways.**

Signals: (Name exercise as above)—Go!
Class—Halt! (1-2-3).

Execute the exercise as in Ex. 1, flinging the straight arms sideways to height of shoulder on count 1, and down to sides on count 2.

3. **Jumping Jack Exercise.** (See mimetic ex., page 344).

Signals: Jumping Jack Exercise—Go!
Class—Halt! (1-2-3).

Execute the exercise as Ex. 2, flinging the arms sideways upward to clap over heads on count 1, and sideways

downward to sides on count 2.
>Caution: Keep chest and head high.

4. **Stride to Crossed Spring jump.**
>Signal: Jump to stride position—One!
>Jump bringing feet together and left crossed in front of right—Two!
>Jump to stride again—One!
>Jump bringing right foot across—Two!
>In this rhythm (clap rhythm), continuously—Go!
>Class—Halt! (1 — 2 — 3)
>>(out—together—down)
>
>Hands can be at hips.

5. **Zig-Zag Spring Jump.**
>Signals: Jump from both feet landing with left crossed in front of right—One!
>Jump, changing feet—Two!
>In rhythm—Go!
>Class—Halt! (1 — 2 — 3)
>>(cross—together—down)

6. **Forward Cut-Step.** (See Triple Test Ex. Set. II, Ex. 6).
>Signals: Raising left leg forward—One!
>Changing feet quickly, right forward—Two!
>Forward cut-step—Go!
>Class—Halt! (1 — 2 — 3)
>>(change—together—down)
>
>Knees and ankles stretched.
>Weight not allowed to sink back.

7. **Side Cut-Step.**
>Signals: Raising left leg sideways—One!
>Changing quickly to right leg sideways—Two!
>(The left is brought back to place and instantaneously the right is raised sideways to right)
>Changing continuously—Go!
>Class—Halt! (1 — 2 — 3)
>>(change—together—down)

8. **Simple Rocking Step.**
>(a) Signal: Raising right leg forward—One!
>Changing quickly to raising left leg backward—Two!
>(Right is brought back to place and instantly the left is raised in the rear)
>Changing to right leg forward—One!

Changing to left leg backward—Two!
Continuously—Go!
Class—Halt! (1 — 2 — 3)
(change—together—down)
(b) Same as (a) but with left forward and right back.

9. **Rocking Step (with swing).**
(a) Cut back, swing forward.
Signals: Raising right leg forward—Raise!
Change to left leg backward—One!
Swing left leg forward and hop on right foot—Two!
Change to right leg backward—One!
Swing right leg forward and hop on left foot—Two!
Cut and swing continuously—Go!
Class—Halt! (1-2-3).
(b) Cut formed, swing back.
Signals: Raising right leg backward—Raise!
Change to left leg forward—One!
Swing left leg backward and hop on right foot—Two!

Change to right leg forward—One!
Swing right leg backward and hop on left foot—Two!

Cut and swing in rhythm—Go!
Class—Halt! (1 — 2 — 3)

10. **The "Break"** (Irish Lilt, page 279).
Signals: Jumping to stride—One!
Jumping together—Two!
Swing left foot back and hop on right foot—Three!
Swing left foot forward and hop on right foot—Four!

Jump to stride again—One!
Jump together—Two!
Swing right foot back and hop on left—Three!
Swing right foot forward hop on left—Four!
In rhythm, swinging left first—Go!
Class—Halt!
(On Halt, finish break on 3—4 by bringing feet together and down).

11. **Leaping in place,** bringing feet up behind.
Leaping in place—Go!
Class—Halt! (1 — 2 — 3)
(Leap—together—down)
This exercise is running in place, but feet are raised behind in the run.

12. **Leaping** to turn in place.

Four leaping steps turning right (4 counts)—Go!
Four leaping steps turning left (4 counts)—Go!
Turning right, then left (8 counts)—Go!
Four in place, 4 turning right, then four in place, and 4 turning left (16 counts)—Go!

13. **Hopping on one foot;** change feet.

(a) Slide forward right and hop 3 times, change to left and hop 3 times, continue until "stop"—Go! Stop!

Teacher demonstrates and explains first, then class takes exercise on signal.

Slide right	hop. r.	hop. r.	hop. r.
ct. 1	ct. 2	ct. 3	ct. 4
slide left	hop. 1.	hop. 1.	hop. 1.
ct. 1	ct. 2	ct. 3	ct. 4

The free foot is lifted to the rear.

(b) Hop on one foot, at same time turn in place; change feet.

Slide hop, hop, hop beginning right foot, and turning right about, then left—Go! Stop!

14. **Toe touch,—in, out.**

Signals: Hop on left, and touch right toe to left toe —One!

Hop on left, and extend right leg outward—Two!

Change to right foot, and touch left toe to right—Three!

Hop on right, and extend left leg outward—Four!
In rhythm beginning with right toe—Go!
Stop!

15. **Reverse toe and heel touch.**

Signals: Hop on left, and touch right toe to right side with heel turned out—One!

Hop on left and touch right heel to right side—Two!

Change to right foot and touch left toe to side, heel up—Three!

Hop on right and touch heel—Four!
In rhythm, beginning with right toe—Go!
Stop!

16. **Toe touch in, out; Reverse toe and heel.**

Combine Ex. 15 and 14 thus:

Count 1—Hop left—touch right toe to right side, heel up.

Count 2—Hop left—touch right heel to right side.
Count 3—Hop left—touch right toe to left toe.
Count 4—Hop left—swing right leg outward.
Repeat, hopping on right foot.

17. **Slide hop.**

Review 13 (a).

Slide hop forward beginning right—Go! Stop!

Slide forward right (count 1); hop on right, left leg raised rear (count 2).

Slide forward left (count 1); hop on left (count 2).

STUNTS AND CONTESTS

Stunts, individual, couple, and group are included here. They are self-testing activities, and thus have a strong natural instinctive appeal. They give satisfaction and sense of accomplishment, which engender self-confidence and respect, which in turn lead into initiative and leadership.

Contests, herein included are simple personal combative exercises, and have for their appeal personal contact, self-testing and rivalry. They lead into the same emotional responses and character traits as mentioned above.

These types of activity offer a great range of events. They can be planned for almost any condition of space. By means of organization into groups, many events can be carried on in the schoolroom. Some of the stunts included in the following pages are suitable for girls, even with dress limitations.

Stunts and contests lend especially well to group organization according to capacities and give opportunity for student leadership. These activities will also carry over into home play periods.

Bibliography

Cotteral and Cotteral, Teaching of Stunts and Tumbling, A. S. Barnes Co., New York, 1936.

LaPorte and Renner, The Tumbling Manual, Prentice Hall Co., Chicago.

Rodgers, A Handbook of Stunts, MacMillan Co., New York, 1940.

Individual Stunts

Knee Dip.
Stand on the right foot, reach behind you and grasp the left foot with the right hand. Go down and touch the left knee to the floor and rise again. Do the stunt on each foot.

Chair Creeper.
Sit on a chair so that its back is at your right shoulder. Grasping the top of back, lie on your right side, and keeping your legs on the seat, crawl around the back of the chair head first, until you can pick up with your teeth some object such as a piece of paper from the edge of the seat at the farther corner.

Crane Dive.
Fold a piece of paper a foot long and stand it upright on the floor. Extend the arms sideways and raise one foot backward and bend the knee of the supporting leg. Bend down and pick up the paper with the teeth without losing the balance or touching the floor with any part of the body except the one supporting foot.

Frog Dance.

Squat on one heel with the other foot extended straight sidewise. Draw the extended foot under the body and shoot the other out to the opposite side. Change back and forth rapidly keeping the upper part of the body as upright as possible. This and the Jumping Jack are Russian dance steps.

Jumping Jack.

Drop to a full squat with knees bent and spread, arms crossed in front of the body, upper part of the body erect, and weight resting on toes. From this position spring immediately to a standing position with the knees straight, weight resting on heels, toes pointing up, feet about 18 inches apart, hands extended sidewise. Repeat the squatting and rising motion several times rapidly, without losing the balance.

Cart Wheel.

Stand erect with left hand at the side, fingers spread, palm down, and right hand raised over the head. Incline the body directly to the left side, throw the right foot in the air, the left hand striking the ground. Follow immediately by the right hand and then by the right foot, the left foot striking last. When done correctly, the body has the appearance of a wheel; the arms and legs are the spokes. The more rigid the body is kept, the better is the appearance of the stunt; feet must travel straight up in the air over the head.

Take a Chair from Under.

Arrange three chairs in a line and place the heels on one and the head on the other, the middle one being under the back. Now, sustaining the weight of the body by the heels and the head, take the middle chair from under you with your hands (or have someone else take it away) without falling.

Balancing Exercise.

Place a light book on the crown of the head; place the hands on the hips; place the heels together with the feet at an angle of 90 degrees; rise on the toes; from this position bend the knees until the body touches the heels; return to standing position. The knees should be turned outward over the toes and the trunk should be erect throughout. Continue a number of times or until book falls.

Stiff Leg Bend.

Stand with both heels together and the arms perpendicular. Bend body forward downward, sweeping the arms downward, and touch the floor with the finger tips. Keep the knees stiff.

Bicycling.

Lie on the floor and then with an upward throw of the legs

stand on the shoulders, legs above head. Maintaining the balance in this position move the legs as if pedalling a bicycle.

Back Spring.

Boy No. 1 gets down on hands and knees, No. 2 with a little run places his hands on the ground close up to No. 1 and turns a somersault over his back. Make it as much of a handspring as possible, that is, don't use the back of No. 1 any more than is necessary.

Forward Roll (Somersault).

This is done by putting the hands on the floor, tucking the head between the knees, pushing off with the feet, rolling over on the back, and coming up on the feet again. To make a good finish, grasp the ankles with the hands just before coming up on the feet, or raise the arms forward, then straighten the body up to its full height.

Double Forward Roll.

This is done the same as the forward roll except two complete turns are made without a break before coming to an erect position. You must go in a straight line.

Ankle Throw.

This feat consists in tossing some object over the head from behind with the feet. A beanbag, book or basket ball is held firmly between the feet. With a sudden jump the feet are kicked backward so as to jerk the object into an upward throw, which should end in its curving forward over the head. It should be caught as it comes down.

Leap Frog and Forward Roll.

No. 1 squats and No. 2 leap-frogs over him, places his hands on floor in front and executes a forward roll.

Hand Stand.

Place hands on floor, spring from feet to lift them upward gradually and raise them to a perpendicular position. Head is held back.

Hand Walk.

This stunt needs very little description as its name tells what must be done. Go to a hand stand with the feet above the head and used as a balance. Attempt to walk on the hands. If the head is used in connection with the first method of balance, this stunt may be learned very easily, i. e., keep the head bent far back.

Heel Click.

(A) Stand with feet apart.

Jump from both feet high into the air, hitting heels before landing.

(B) Swing right leg sideways and jump from both feet sideways right. Make left foot meet right in the air, and click heels, before landing. Repeat left.

Tip Up.

Squat down with hands flat on floor, elbows inside of and hard against the knees, and arms tight against the ribs. Lean forward slowly, placing the weight of the body on the hands and elbows, until the feet swing clear of the floor. Attempt to pick up a handkerchief from the floor with the teeth and regain the original position. This is a good exercise to lead up to one form of the head stand. Instead of attempting to pick up anything, simply rest the head on the floor six or eight inches in advance of the hands and push the feet up in the air. This head stand comes easy to some boys.

Through the Stick. (A broomstick may be used).

Grasp the stick with both hands behind the back, palms forward. Bring the stick over the head to a position in front of the body, arms straight, hands still grasping the stick. Lift up the right foot, swing it around the right arm and

Through the Stick (Individual stunt). Each boy shows one stage in the stunt.

through between the hands from the front over the stick. See illustration, first boy. Crawl through head first, by raising the stick with the left hand over the head, skinning the stick over the right knee and the back. See illustration, second boy. Come to an upright position and step back over the stick with the left foot finishing with the stick still grasped in the hands in front of the body. At no time let go of the stick.

Top.

Stand with both feet firmly planted on the ground. Spring upward into the air and attempt to make a complete turn in the air before landing without losing the balance at the finish. Use the arms to pull one's self around. Learn to turn both right and left. The turn is a 360-degree turn; face the same wall at the finish as at the beginning.

Head Stand.

One form of the Head Stand is described under "Tip Up." This is probably the simplest way of learning. Another form of Head Stand is done by kneeling and placing both elbows on the floor and the head in both hands. From this position push the feet to a vertical position and hold for at least ten seconds.

Still another form is done by kneeling with arms folded and placing the elbows on the floor, the head several inches in front of them, and pushing the feet up as before.

Prostrate and Perpendicular.

Fold the arms across the chest, lie down on the back and get up to a standing position again without using the elbows or hands.

Jump Stick.

The performer holds a stick horizontally between the forefingers of his hands, pressing with the fingers to keep it from falling. Keep the stick in this position and jump over it forward and backward. This same feat may be performed by pressing the middle fingers of the two hands without a stick and jumping over them forward and backward, as a dog jumps through curved arms. Draw knees well in as you jump.

Couple Stunts

Stomach Stand.

One player lies on his back with his feet and hands in the air. His partner lies forward onto his feet and grasps his hands. The lying player lifts his partner into the air and the partner straightens his legs so that they are pointing almost straight up as in a head stand. Upon a second signal the lying player drops his feet and the partner springs down onto his own feet at the same time pulling the lying player to a standing position.

Chinese Get Up.

Two persons sit on the floor back to back with arms locked, and retaining such relative positions they try to stand upright.

Flopper.

Two boys stand facing each other. Boy No. 1 grasps the right hand of boy No. 2 with his left, and the left hand of boy No. 2 with his right. A third boy, with a short running start, thrusts his head over the first barrier of arms and under the second; that is, he starts to dive through the opening made by the two sets of arms. Boys No. 1 and 2 lift up on set of arms No. 1 and force boy No. 3 to turn a somersault in the air, landing him on his feet on the opposite side from which he started. He may be flipped completely clear of the arms or he may be held with his head still in the opening and flipped back to his original position. Try lining up a group of boys and flipping one through after another as fast as they come.

Twister (couple stunt)

Twister. See illustration, page 364.

Two boys stand facing each other about three feet apart, with their right hands clasped. Boy No. 1 throws his right leg over locked hands and head to a straddle position, with his back to boy No. 2. Boy No. 2 follows with his left leg to same position, so that they are back to back. Boy No. 1 follows with his left leg, returning to his original position. Boy No. 2 follows with his right leg. This should be continued indefinitely and very rapidly. It may be done on the same spot or may have a rolling motion. The hands must be clasped throughout.

Bobbin Ahead.

No. 1 stands with his back to No. 2 who stands on his hands close up to heels of No. 1, and throws his feet up over the shoulders of No. 1. The first boy catches the feet of No. 2 as they come over, and bends forward pulling him up so that he sits on his shoulders. No. 2 goes on over, landing on his feet, and No. 1 then stands on his hands, throws his feet over the other boy's shoulders and they go on over and over.

Eskimo Roll.

Boy No. 1 lies on his back while boy No. 2 stands with one foot on either side of his head. Each takes hold of the other's ankles, and the boy standing, dives forward between the legs of No. 1, turning a somersault, at the same time pulling No. 1 on his feet. The positions are thus reversed and No. 1 dives over No. 2 and they go over and over several times, always holding tightly to each other's ankles.

Group Stunts

Merry-Go-Round.

Six or eight boys stand in a circle with hands firmly clasped. Upon a signal every other boy with a slight spring and holding his body stiff thrusts his feet into the center of the circle touching the feet of the others, who have done likewise. As soon as this is done the standing boys run in a circle giving the lying boys a fast ride. The lying boys should hold their bodies up so that they will not sag onto the ground.

Pendulum.

Two players face each other, with one foot forward to steady their position. A third boy stands between them, no more than 2 feet from the other players, and faces one of them. He keeps his body very straight and stiff and allows himself to fall backward; the player behind him catches him with his hands and pushes him forward. He thus swings way forward and is caught by the other player, who pushes him back. This swinging back and forward is continued. The center boy must be of a little lighter weight than the two who catch him, and must keep his body rigid throughout, rocking back and forward from heel to toe.

Pyramid No. I. See diagram, page 367.

One stunt that all children like is to build up a structure and then suddenly knock it down. This pyramid is built on that principle. Four boys kneel on hands and knees on a mat or the grass, the hands and knees of one player almost touching those of the players next to him. Then three more boys crawl onto the backs of these boys, each boy placing his hands on the shoulders of the two boys directly under him and his knees on their hips. Then two more boys crawl on these three boys in a similar manner and the tenth boy takes his place on top of all. When all are placed the leader claps his hands and all the boys at exactly the same moment stretch their arms straight out in front and their feet straight out behind and the pyramid collapses. No boy falls directly on any other boy nor directly onto the ground so there is little difficulty of anyone experiencing any discomfort if the directions are carried out as given.

Pyramid No. II. See diagram, page 367.

Another pyramid for ten people is formed as follows: Two of the largest boys put two smaller boys on their shoulders and stand side by side. To do this quickly the large boy takes a partial kneeling position with his right knee, his left knee being bent out in front. The smaller boy approaches him from the left side and places his right hand in the larger boy's right hand and his left in his left. He then steps onto the larger boy's left knee with his own left foot and by aid of an upward pull from the larger boy's hands places his right foot on this boy's right shoulder. His left foot then is placed on the left shoulder. After they are well balanced one couple releases right hands and the other couple releases left hands. The boys on top join their inside hands and raise them above their heads, while the larger boys join their inside hands but keep them low.

On either side of these standing boys, two boys take a head stand, facing the center group. On either side of the head standers two boys kneel facing as the central group. Outside of all, two boys placing their toes on the knees of the kneeling boys and their hands on the ground, head pointing away from the group, do a prone fall. When the leader gives a signal all the players perform the following movements simultaneously. The boys who are standing take both hands of the boys on their shoulders and by a resisting movement assist them in turning a flip between their hands landing

PYRAMID I

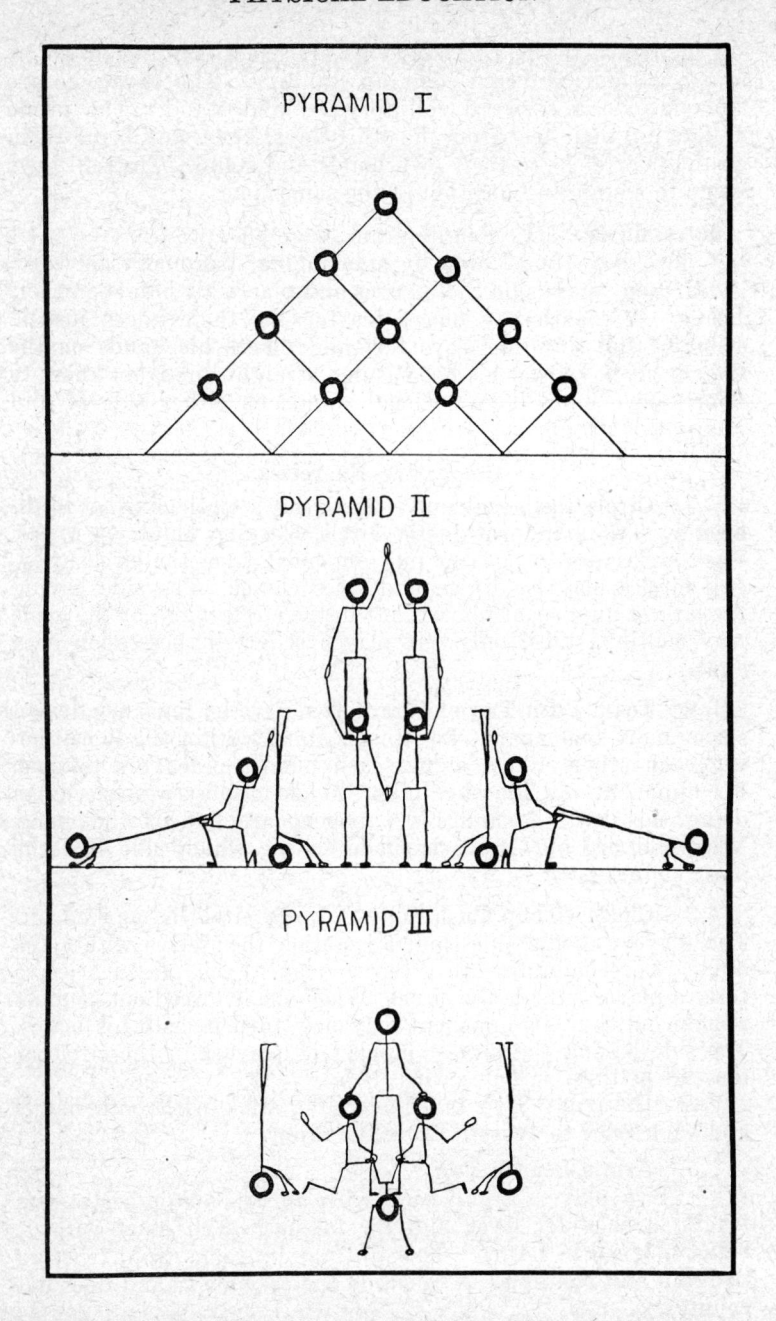

PYRAMID II

PYRAMID III

on their own feet. The boys who are head standing do a forward roll outward and come up standing. The boys who are kneeling do a forward roll forward and stand. The prone fallers flip their feet from the other boys' knees and bring them to the floor close to their own hands and stand. Thus all boys come to a standing position at the same time.

Pyramid No. III. See diagram, page 367.

Two boys kneel side by side facing diagonally forward. A third boy stands on their knees and places his hands on their heads. A fourth boy places his toes on their knees just in front of the standing boys feet and places his hands on the floor in front so that his body is in a straight line from knees to floor. Two more boys do head stands on either side of and facing this group.

Combative Exercises.

1. **Circle Push and Pull.** Mark out a circle six feet in diameter. Two stand within the circle, clasping hands or wrists. Each endeavors to push or pull opponent from the circle. Several circles may be drawn and sides chosen. The side having the largest number of players left in the circle wins; or the game may continue until only one player is left in possession of a circle.

2. **Team Push Tug of War.** Two parallel lines are drawn six or more feet apart. Two teams stand within the lines, facing each other. At a signal each player endeavors to push his opponent outside the lines. When a player succeeds in doing this both he and his opponent are out of the game. When all are out count is made to see which side had the most victories.

3. **Circle Group Push Out.** A large circle is marked off. The players choose sides and all station themselves within the circle. Three minutes are given to play. Each player tries to force a player outside the circle. When one is forced out he must remain out, but his opponent may now turn to help his mates. The side having the largest number of players in the circle at the end of three minutes wins.

4. **Dis-arm.** Two take hold of a stick with both hands and each tries to twist it from the other.

5. **Arm's Length Tag.**

Two players stand each with an arm extended at full length at shoulder level, and try to touch each other without being touched in return. This will require some rapid twisting dodging and bending. A touch on the extended hand does not count.

6. **Eskimo Jumping Race.**

Fold the arms across the chest with the knees rigid and the feet close together. Jump forward with short jumps. Pupil who reaches the finishing line first wins.

7. **Hand Wrestle.**

The wrestlers stand with the right foot advanced clasping right hands. The object is to make one's opponent move a foot from its position on the ground. This constitutes a throw. This may also be done by placing palms together shoulder height and pushing.

8. **Pulling Sticks.**

Two sit upon the floor, toes against toes. A broom handle is grasped by the players and at the signal each tries to pull the other up off the floor.

9. **Indian Wrestle.**

Two boys lie side by side on their backs, with heads pointing in opposite directions, their arms securely locked. On the signal "go" each raises leg nearest opponent once, twice and on the third time locks leg with other fellow and attempts to turn him over.

10. **Toe Wrestling.**

The wrestlers are seated on the ground facing each other with hands clasped about the knees. A stick is placed between the arms and knees while in this position. The object is to get the toes under those of the opponent and roll him over backwards. If either wrestler breaks his hand clasp about the knees it constitutes a victory for his opponent.

11. **Line Tug of War.**

Class is divided into equal lines facing each other with a line drawn on the floor half way between. Upon a signal each man tries to pull the man opposite him over the line and avoid being pulled over himself. A score is counted for the puller's side whenever he succeeds in pulling a man over the line. The side having the most scores wins.

12. **Push Tug of War.**

Played the same as the above only that each player tries to cross the line into his opponent's territory but is restrained by the opposite player who pushes him back. Then those succeeding in getting across the line count one point for their side.

13. **Rooster Fight (a).**

A circle is drawn upon the floor. Two players squat within it and place a stick under their knees, the arms under the stick and hands clasped in front of the knees. Each endeavors to tip his opponent over.

14. **Rooster Fight (b).**

Each contestant must stand on one foot and fold his arms then hop on one foot and bunt the other with the shoulder and try to make his opponent touch the other foot to the floor. As soon as one contestant touches the foot he is not hopping on to the floor, he loses.

15. **Settings Pegs.**

Use three sharpened pegs about the size of a lead pencil. Three spikes will do. Use a mark or starting board as with the broad jump. The boy hops on one foot as far as he can, sets one of the pegs, takes a second hop and sets the second peg, takes a third hop and sets the third peg. During the three hops he must not touch the ground with any part of the body other than the foot from which he started. If he loses his balance or hops out of place to retain it, he may hop back and place his heel in the same place and continue his trials. The pegs are left in the ground and each boy has three trials to set them further out. Indoors this can be carried out by making a chalk mark on the floor in place of setting the pegs.

16. **Elbow Wrestling.**

A table or some flat surface is necessary for this event. The opponents stand on opposite sides of the table placing the right elbows together on same. They clasp hands and endeavor to push the back of the hand of the opponent down on the table without lifting the elbow.

17. **The Finger Feat.**

Place your hands horizontally across and close to your breast, and put the tips of your forefingers together; another player should then endeavor to separate them by pulling at each arm; but if you hold them firmly in the manner described, he will be unable to achieve it, although he may be much bigger and stronger than you. It is not proper for the second player to use sudden or violent jerks in his attempts; he must employ only a steady, regular pull straight sideways.

Group Stunt Contests

Speed Stunt Series Relay.

Any series of stunts may be used. Players are arranged in files behind a starting line. At the signal the first player in each file runs forward and performs each stunt in succession, returns and touches off next player. This continues until all have run. The line finishing first wins. A good series of stunts is the following: Through the Stick, Chair Creeper, Forward Roll. The stick is placed on the starting line, a mat or mark is placed at the far end of the running space, and a chair is placed half way between. Through the Stick is first performed and the stick replaced on the starting line. The player runs forward to the chair, and after doing the Chair Creeper, runs on to the mat or mark and performs the Forward Roll. Then he returns at full speed to starting line.

Eskimo Race on All Fours.

The players stand with hands and feet on the floor, the knees and elbows should be stiff. In this position the race is run, or rather "hitched" over a course about fifty feet in length.

Tunnel Race.

Any number of players may compose a team. They are placed in lines, one behind the other, with feet spread far apart. The last player stoops and crawls forward, between the legs of the players, through the tunnel. Each player follows in order. When they reach the front of the tunnel they stand in position. The team wins whose players first return to their original position.

Leap Frog Relay.

Contestants are arranged in files, down in position for leap frog. Last man leap frogs over all in front of him, runs and touches wall, returns to his place touching off man directly in front of him. Second man leap frogs over all in front, touches wall, returns and leap frogs over last man, gets to his own place and touches off next man. In this way each man goes over every man in his own line. The line finishing first wins.

Bibliography

Staley, S. C. "Games, Contests and Relays," A. S. Barnes Co., New York, 1924.

APPENDIX I
PAGEANT

Because many requests are received for pageants that can be given out of doors by public school children, the following pageant for May Day which was given by the grades and high school of the Teachers College Training School is included herein. It is expected that changes will be necessitated to meet local conditions, and substitutions made in the case of the three dances for which permission to reprint was not granted. However, the following pageant has been found to be well adapted to public school use, and its form is given almost in its entirety.

THE CONFLICT OF THE SEASONS

Program

Processional in honor of the Queen—Whole School
   The May Queen . . . . Beulah Fletcher
     Pageant in Honor of the Queen

The Conflict of 1923

1. The Struggle of the Four Winds—Senior Girls.
2. Winter and his Snowflakes—Marjorie Huber and Kindergarten.
3. Spring—Dorothy Egbert.
4. Raindrops—Kindergarten.
5. Icicles and Snow—Third Grade.
6. Overtures of the May Queen and the summons to the Nations.
7. Italy: Trantella—Fresh. and Soph. Girls.
8. Ireland: Irish Lilt—Seventh and Eighth Grade Girls.
9. England: Shepherd's Hey—Fresh. and Soph. Girls.
10. Switzerland: Swiss May Dance—Seventh Grade Girls.
11. Sweden: Weaving Dance—Eighth Grade Girls.
12. Germany: Seven Jumps—Third Grade.
13. Denmark: Dance of Greeting—First Grade.
14. Finland: Fist Polka—Second Grade.
15. Japan: Cherry Blossoms—Sixth Grade Girls.
16. Norway: Mountain March—Fourth Grade.
17. Scotland: Highland Fling—Sixth Grade Boys.
18. Russia: Russian Dance—Fresh. and Soph. Girls.
19. Spain: Spanish Baby—Jun. and Sen. Girls.
20. Holland: Villagers—Jun. and Sen. Girls.
21. American Group
    Uncle Sam—Eugene Mueller.
    Goddess of Liberty—Anna Dorrell.

PHYSICAL EDUCATION

   Easterners: Virginia Reel—Fifth and Sixth Grades.
   Mid-Westerners: Pop Goes the Weasel—Fifth and Sixth Grades.
    Westerners—Fifth Grade.
    Southerners: Dixie—Sixth Grade Boys.
 22. Crowning of the May Queen.
 23. Gavotte in honor of the Queen—A Group of Seniors.

Synopsis

King Winter has ruled the world mildly during his allotted time thinking that by so doing the people of the world will be satisfied and he will not be forced to give up his throne to any other season. So confident is he that he is the favorite in the eyes of the world that when Spring comes to claim the throne he drives her back with his Snowflakes and his North Wind. Spring, however, is not so easily rebuffed and struggles hard to keep her position. Winter rises up in all his cold fury. The icy, penetrating North Wind drives against poor Spring and the snow and sleet beat her relentlessly until finally she is overpowered. King Winter then orders that she be hidden away in a large cocoon. His orders having been executed he dances for joy laughing with fiendish glee to think that he is ruler of the world.

 The May Queen knowing that May Day cannot be successful in any country without Spring requests that King Winter release her. But he tells the May Queen that the countries of the world are satisfied and do not want Spring. The Queen of the May suggests that they have a contest and let the nations decide which they would rather have, Spring or Winter. King Winter confident that all of the nations will choose him agrees. The May Queen then sends out word for the nations to assemble.

 The nations come all dancing a characteristic dance to prove their identity. After each nation has danced King Winter sends forth a symbol to represent himself, and the Queen of the May to represent the season she is championing. The nations make their selection and go to the side of their choice. King Winter soon realizes that his popularity was mostly in his own mind as one nation after another chooses Spring's symbol.

 The last to enter the contest is America, headed by Uncle Sam and the Goddess of Liberty, with the Easterners, the Farmers of the Mid-West, and the Cowboys and Indians of the Far-West and some Southerners with their negroes. After all groups have danced the usual symbols are sent out from Winter and the May Queen. But Uncle Sam, who is unaccustomed to being bribed into making his choice of rulers and who believes that those who have ruled their legitimate time should graciously withdraw in favor of the rightful successors, drives away the Tokens and calls upon his cowboys to frighten Winter from the throne. Then at Uncle Sam's command the cowboys release poor cramped Spring from the cocoon. She is then permitted to ascend the throne vacated by King Winter, unmolested. Uncle Sam, satisfied with the results of his effort bids the Queen's attendants crown her and do her homage.

Action of the Pageant

The prelude of the pageant consists of a processional of all the children of the school who take part. The order of march conforms to the appearance of the various characters on the program to follow. The line of march is from the school building to the pageant grounds and once around the grounds, then down through the center of the space toward the Queen's throne where the various groups break off to their allotted spaces near the boundaries of the performing space. The May Queen accompanied by her attendants is carried in a flower-covered carriage at the head of the procession. While the dancers take their places around the performing space the Queen alights from her carriage. This carriage is then placed on a high platform where she takes her place to view the pageant. Another throne covered with cotton to represent ice and snow is occupied by King Winter at a distance of about 20 yds. from the May Queen.

1. When all the characters have taken their places the four winds enter from the four corners of the performing space and dance.

"The Struggle of the Four Winds"—"Fanfare."

At the close of the dance the North and West winds drive the South and East winds back to their original places.

2. Winter descends from his throne and with a proud and haughty stride walks into the center of the stage and dances.

"Winter and His Snow Flakes." ("Boyar Dance").

During the last half of Winter's dance many little snowflakes (Kindergarten children) run in and about Winter as he dances. After Winter dances he strides back to the throne with his snowflakes following him.

3 and 4. During the playing of the music used by the Raindrops, Spring enters and takes her place in front of the Queen's throne where she beckons to the Raindrops (more kindergarten children) to enter. They run in and run about the field and off again while Spring watches and encourages them. Spring then dances over the field and without looking toward Winter gradually walks back toward his throne where

she finishes her dance with one foot on the first step of the throne.

See Spring's first dance and music for it on page 385.

5. Winter watching Spring's advance, slowly but angrily descends the throne and beckons to his icicles and snow to attack her. This they do by throwing confetti, paper strings, and cotton at her and by dancing about her in such a way as to entangle her in the paper coils. Spring momentarily falls to her knees but recovers her step again and makes a final attempt to advance toward the throne. This is impossible so she retires to a place near the Queen's throne and falls exhausted on the ground. The icicles and snow then run out and carry in a large oblong wooden frame covered with light brown cambric to represent a cocoon, and cover her over. After this is accomplished winter turns back toward his throne and with head high and high step hops he returns to it followed by his icicles and snow who imitate his actions.

6. During the playing of "To a Toy Soldier"—Robert Warner—the May Queen rises, summons her messenger and sends a scroll to King Winter. King Winter reads the scroll, shakes his head and pretends to write upon it, then hands it back to the messenger and assumes a determined and haughty attitude. The May Queen receives the scroll again and after some thought, pretends to write upon it and resends it to the King. This time the King nods his head and returns the scroll. When the Queen reads his answer she beckons to her bugler to blow three blasts to summon the peoples of the world.

7 to 20—In answer to this bugle call the first nation, Italy, comes in and dances Tarantella. When the dance is finished the dancers stand still, and to the first phrases of "To a Toy Soldier," a kindergarten child, representing some activity of spring, such as tennis, canoeing, etc., runs out from the May Queen's throne and holds up some symbol such as a tennis racket. At the same time a child dressed to represent an activity of winter such as coasting, skating, etc., comes out from Winter's throne and holds up a sled or a pair of skates. Italy having come from a country where the weather is balmy, of course, chooses Spring's token and when the music starts again with the second strain of "To a Toy Soldier," the Tokens run off and Italy follows Spring's Token to a place behind her throne.

This action is repeated for each country's dance except America's and all countries choose to accept Spring except Russia. When Russia goes to Winter's side the "Song of Sorrow" is played.

21. (a) Music, "Columbia the Gem of the Ocean."

The American Group led by Uncle Sam, the Goddess of Liberty and the Flag Bearer enter in double file from the north east, south and west. The Easterners come first then the Southerners, Mid-westerners and Westerners. They come up the center of the field toward the thrones and when near the southern boundary of the performing space the Goddess of Liberty, Uncle Sam and the Flag Bearer stop and review the rest while they march past them and around to their left going back to the north boundary of the field and coming up center again toward south end where they spread out, forming two wider lines reaching across the field from north to south. The marchers now hold up small American flags forming the sides to an arch, and Uncle Sam, the Goddess of Liberty and the Flag Bearer march through this arch and take their places at the north end of the field. Then the Westerners (Cowboys and Indians) lead off to the northwest, the Mid-Westerners to the west, the Southerners to the southwest while the Easterners remain in the center of the field for their dance.

(b) "The Virginia Reel," by Easterners. During this dance the children pretend to be very "high brow" and superior and all their actions are very disdainful and haughty. The girls take little running steps in their high heeled pumps and instead of the usual hand clasp they raise their right hand in the air with the hand bent downward and touch hands in typical "society" manner. After the dance the Easterners go off to their original places to the same music as the dance.

(c) As soon as the Easterners are off the Mid-Westerners come in to the music of "Pop Goes the Weasel," and form two sets for their dance. Their dance is rollicking but somewhat awkward. After the dance they retire to their places.

(d) To the music of "Dixie" the Southerners enter. This group consists of a Kentucky Colonel, his wife and a group of negroes. The negroes dance a few clog steps to this music, then they all retire to their places.

(e) To the music "Trot de Cavalier," by James H. Rogers, pub. by Theodore Presser Co., 1712 Chestnut St., Philadelphia, the Cowboys gallop on to the field in single file and form a circle for their dance.

(f) After the Cowboys have finished and retired the music for the Indian Dance is played and the Indian Squaws come in with small waddling steps and form a small circle and around them the Indian Braves form a large circle using the step hop with high knee bend.

When the Indians have finished, the usual strains of music are played and the Tokens are sent out to Uncle Sam from the May Queen and King Winter. When Uncle Sam sees them coming, he strides toward them and motions them off with big gestures of his arms. Then he turns to the cowboys and motions to them to arise and attack King Winter. This they do while the music "Trot de Cavalier" is played again. Each cowboy is armed with a toy repeating pistol which he draws from his holster and flourishes in the air while he rides wildly about upon his wooden horse. At an appropriate time in the music these pistols are fired off and at this time winter slinks down from his throne and escapes behind a big tree in the background.

Uncle Sam then strides across the field and motions to his Cowboys to follow and with appropriate gestures tells them to remove the cocoon from Spring. This they do and then gallop back to their original places. Uncle Sam then bids Spring arise and dance. Spring, rubbing her eyes and stretching as though having been long asleep arises and dances.

"Spring's Dance," Music: page 385; Sorrentina—Lack. After the dance she ascends the throne vacated by winter.

Uncle Sam then motions to the May Queen to commence her festivities. Whereupon her attendants lead her forth and crown her and then dance in her honor.

"Attendants' Dance"—Gavotte-Menzeli.

Description of Dances

1. **The Struggle of the Four Winds**—Music "Fanfare."

Measures 1 and 2: Two polka steps (hop step together step) with trunk low and right arms forward, left at side. Winds coming in from the four corners of the stage.

Measures 3 and 4: Four skip steps, trunk held high and arms raised high.

Measures 5 and 6: Repeat step for measures 1 and 2.

Measures 7 and 8: Repeat skip of measures 3 and 4.

Measures 9-12: All four winds having reached the center of the stage run around in one large circle lowering the trunk forward as they run and reaching forward with the right arm, following the pitch of the music.

Measures 13 and 14: Whirl around in place using many little steps.

Measures 15-18: (First ending). North Wind and West Wind stamp forward then bring feet together and move arms as though driving the South and East winds away. This is

Fanfare

Fanfare *(Continued)*

repeated three times. The South and East winds step backward with a motion of protecting themselves each time the other winds come toward them.

Music repeated.

Measures 1-8: The same steps are done as the first time through only that the winds turn in place during the skip steps. The South and East winds return toward the center of the stage while the North and West winds go back toward the place from which they came originally.

Measures 9-14: All run around in a circle again as at first and whirl in place on last two measures.

Second Ending.

The same pantomime as for first ending excepting that on the last measure the North and West winds chase the other two winds clear off of the stage.

Music repeated again.

North and West winds use same steps as before but whirl more vigorously on the skip steps. They run around in the circle as at first and then on the second ending stamp vigorously with a gesture of a conqueror and then run off.

Boyar Dance

Andante

Arr. G. V. N.

Boyar Dance *(Continued)*

Boyar Dance *(Concluded)*

2. **Winter and his Snowflakes—Boyar Dance.**

Boyar Dance (Russian Solo)

I. Slow Dance.

1 measure: Step right (1) close left (and) step right (2), brush left forward (and). Extend right arm forward, palm down, and pantomime drawing up right sleeve with left hand. Body leans toward right with a good bend; bend also in knee. Slowly change arms on the "brush" of feet.

1 measure: Same left.

4 measures: Repeat 2 times, completing a small circle.

2 measures: Step right, right hand to left shoulder, (1) close left, bow low, sweeping right arm out to side (2), slowly rise, arms still extended, head high (1-2), bring hands to hips.

II. (Music of Fig. I).

1 measure: Low leap (jete) diagonally forward right, left toe at right heel. Arms from hips in a semi-circle outward to second position (1). Low leap back left, hands return to hips (2).

1 measure: Same forward left (1), back right (2), changing weight quickly before leap to left.

1 measure: Swing heels out, toes together (1); swing heels together, toes out (2).

1 measure: 3 stamps, rather haughty but with stamps subdued.

4 measures: Repeat whole starting left. Pull handkerchief from belt, right hand.

III.

1 measure: Right heel touch at right side, sweep handkerchief toward right foot, bending R (1). Cross step right back, step side left (2), at the same time bend left and sweep handkerchief across body. Arm movement follows a figure 8.

3 measures: Repeat three times, right heel always touching on count 1.

4 measures: Turning right, step right (1), push with left toe, raising right heel (2), lower right heel (1), raise and push left (2). Continue pivoting thus. Slow strong movement. Arms sideways, body swaying slightly. Arms slowly raised until handkerchief is held in both hands above head.

4 measures: Repeat 1st four measures to left—put handkerchief in belt.

2 measures: Pivot, turning left.

2 measures: Step left, right hand to left shoulder, deep bow, hold, sweeping right arm out sideways.

Fast Dance.

I.

16 measures: High pas de basques beginning with right —arms low, swinging from side to side, lateral movement, with the swing of the shoulders. Large circle, forward right, and circle left to place. Pas de basque is performed as follows: leap on to right foot, bringing knee high in front (ct. 1); step on to left foot in front of right (and); step on right (ct. 2). This is done high upon toes and knees well raised.

II.

1 measure: Hop on left with right toe at left foot (1), extend right sideways, hopping on left (2). Move sideways left on the hops, right hand on hip, left at head.

2 measures: Repeat two times.

1 measure: Stamp right, left, right, at the same time 3 claps with a vertical movement of hands.

4 measures: Repeat left.

III.

2 measures: Hands on hips, bend knees (1), extend right leg forward (2), bend (1), extend left (2).

1 measure: Cut right back (1), cut left forward (2), swinging both arms backward at right side, then forward left.

1 measure: Leap left, swinging right foot forward (1). On leap, big upward outward circle with arms. Feet together, hands on hips (2).

4 measures: Repeat.

IV.

1 measure: Jump to feet apart, toes in (1); slide weight to heels, toes up and out (and). Heels together, knees bent (2).

1 measure: Stretch knees, sliding heels apart, toes up and out (1). Slide heels together, knees bent (2).

6 measures: Repeat three times. Arms fling out sideways when on heels, feet apart, knees straight. Arms swing low in front, crossed palms in and straight, when knees are bent.

V.

3 measures: Stamp right, at same time clap hands vertically, bringing right high, with palm straight; turn right with push of left toe as in III of slow part (pivot step). One turn—right arm up, left sideways.

1 measure: Three stamps, three claps.

3 measures: Repeat three measures (no stamps) to left. Last count of second ending, brush right foot out to side, brush in.

VI. (a)

1 measure: Step right behind left (1), step on left in front of right with accent (and), step on right (2), brush left out and in (and). When left foot is forward, left hand is on hip, right at head (when brush is right). Change arms on the "brush."

3 measures: Repeat three times alternating left and right.

Note: This step is like the "three" in Clogging, followed by 2 steps.

VI. (b)

4 measures: Stamp right and turn right as in V. increasing speed, but not rhythm.

1 measure: Step left, right hand at left shoulder. Sweeping bow and pose.

Note: The Snowflakes run in on the beginning of the fast part of Winter's dance and run about him.

3. **Raindrops**—Music "Raindrops," page 129. Description under 3 and 4 of "Action of Pageant" is sufficient.

Spring's First Dance

4. **Spring's First Dance.**

Fig. I.

Waltz step—3 measures.

Hold—1 measure.

(Waltz—going forward—step right—1; rise on toes as you step forward with left—2; and down on right—3. Alternate feet. Arms, starting at the side, slowly move forward).

Repeat all—8 measures.

Pas de basque—1 measure.

3 tiny steps turning right—1 measure.

Repeat last two measures—2 measures.

(Pas de basque—small leap on rt. foot (ct. 1); bring left across in front, starting turn (ct. 2); step right (ct. 3). The 3 tiny steps finish the turn to face forward. Trunk is well bent to left—head high—arms high and hands crossed over head).

Repeat from beginning—16 measures.

Fig. II.

Pas de basque (4) rt. l. rt. l.—4 measures.

(Go straight forward. Right arm on right pas de basque at side shoulder-high and left arm forward).

Pas de basque back (3) rt. l. rt.—3 measures.

Tiny running steps around a large circle—8 measures.

(Arms and body high and gradually slowly lower until last note—head low and relaxed body, facing forward).

Pose—Arms crossed tightly on chest; high on toes—1 measure.

Pose—Body turned slightly to side weight on rt. ft. (rt. ft. on step of throne), arms brought down to side—much abandon—1 measure.

Here Spring is ready to go on throne, but does not see Winter.

In Greenland

5. **Icicles and Snow**—Music "In Greenland."
Description under 5 of "Action of Pageant," sufficient.
6. See "Action of Pageant."

7. **Tarantella**—Music: Folk Dances and Singing Games by Burchenal.

Formation: Two lines in couples, then in fours. Boys on left, girls on right. Each girl carries a tambourine.

1 A—Introduction: Beginning with the right foot, and taking two steps to a measure, all run onto the stage and up the center in a straight column, facing each other and making courtesy on the last two measures.

2 A—16 measures: Lines separate and run once around stage and return to place.

1 B—2 measures: Beginning with right foot, all run past partners four steps keeping to right.

2 measures: With four running steps turn around in place facing partner.

2 measures: Run back to place.

2 measures: Same as 3 and 4.

1 C—1 measure: Hop on left foot twice, at the same time touching the right toe in front and to the side.

3 measures: Continue the above.

4 measures: Repeat the same as the 4 measures above but hop on the right foot.

8 measures: With shoulders and head inclined slightly toward partner, and arms lowered and held in line with the trunk, partners slide around each other twice, keeping face to face and moving sideways for 16 slide steps. At end of this they should be in their own places again.

3 A—1 measure: Hop on the right foot and at the same time touch the left toe forward. Hop and change the position of the feet.

7 measures: Continue the same.

8 measures: Slide twice around partner as in last 8 measures of preceding figure.

2 B—1 measure: Jump and make a quarter-turn to the right and touch the left toe forward, rise on both toes and sink.

1 measure: Repeat same jumping to left.

6 measures: Continue turning alternately to right and left.

2 C—8 measures: Continue turning as above.

8 measures: Cross right arm under partner's right arm, and placing left hand behind own waist grasp partner's right

hand with it. With left foot raised backward, hop on the right foot, making two hops to each measure, and move forward and around, at same time swinging partner. Finish on the last note with partners side by side in original formation.

    4 A—16 measures: Same as 2A.

    3 B—8 measures: Same as 1B.

    3 C—8 measures: The first two couples now form one set; the third and fourth couples form another set, etc. All face toward the center of their square, so that the boy of one couple faces the girl of the other couple. In this formation they do the same steps as in 1C.

    8 measures: With heads and shoulders inclined toward the center of their set slide around to the left as described in last 8 measures of 1C.

    5 A—8 measures: Same as first 8 measures of 3A.

    8 measures. Same as last 8 measures of 3C.

    4 B—8 measures: Same as first 8 measures of 3B but in sets of four.

    4 C—8 measures: With arms raised slightly higher than shoulder-level first boy and second girl, and second boy and first girl, join right hands across center of square (the girls shifting tambourine to left hand). Raise the left foot backward, and hop on the right foot forward and around in a circle making two hops to one measure, the whole set swinging twice around and the girls shaking their tambourines vigorously.

    8 measures. All face other way joining left hands and repeat above in other direction.

    6 A—16 measures: In double column all run forward around the room and off, girls shaking tambourines overhead and boys snapping fingers high overhead.

    8. **Irish Lilt**   Victor: 21616
        See page 279 of bulletin for description of this dance.

    9. **Shepherd's Hey**   Victor: 20641
        See page 270 of bulletin for description of this dance.

    10. **Swiss May Dance**—Columbia Record No. A-3153.
        See page 242 of bulletin for description of this dance.

    11. **Weaving Dance**
        See page 264 of bulletin for description of this dance.

    12. **Seven Jumps**   Victor: 21617
        See page 213 of bulletin for description of this dance.

    13. **Dance of Greeting**—Victor Record No. 20432.
        See page 172 of bulletin for description of this dance.

14. **Fist Polka**
    See page 253 of bulletin for description of this dance.

15. **Cherry Blossoms**—Purchase from Vestoff-Serova School of Dancing, 47 West 72 St., New York City.

16. **Mountain March**—Victor Record No. 20151.
    See page 243 of bulletin for description of this dance.

17. **Highland Fling**   Victor: 21616
    May be found in "Folk Dances and Singing Games" or "Dances of the People" by Elizabeth Burchenal—G. Shirmer, 3 East 43 St., N. Y. The Highland Schottische may be substituted for this.
    See page 261 of bulletin for description of this dance.

18. **Russian Dance**—Music and description found on page 275.

19. **Spanish Baby**—Purchase from Vestoff-Serova School of Dancing or substitute any other Spanish Dance.

20. **Villagers**—Purchase from Louis H. Chalif, 163 West 67 St., New York or substitute any Dutch Dance.

21. (a) **Virginia Reel**—Music "Old Zip Coon."
                                                       Victor: 20592
    See page 256 of this bulletin for description of this dance.

    (b) **Pop Goes the Weasel**—Victor Record No. 20151.
    See page 238 of this bulletin for description of this dance.

    (c) **Cowboy Dance**—Music "Trot de Cavalier."
    Measures 1 and 2: Uncle Sam signals for Cowboys to arise and dance.
    Measures 3-18: Cowboys gallop in on wooden horses and form a single circle facing forward and continue galloping around.
    Measures 19-22: Stop and swing lariat around head.
    Measure 23: Throw lariat.
    Measures 24-31: Swing lariat again.
    Measure 32: Throw lariat forward as if roping a steer.
    Measures 34 and 35: Wind rope around imaginary pommel in front of saddle.
    Measures 36-52: Gallop around circle holding rope as if dragging steer behind.
    Measures 53 to end: Leader of Cowboys leads rest off and back to original places.

Indian War Dance

Indian War Dance (Continued)

(d) Indian Dance—Music "Indian War Dance."

During the playing of the first strains of the music the squaws waddle on to the stage and make a small circle facing in. The braves follow with a high step hop and form a big circle around the squaws but facing forward. Throughout the dance the squaws move sideways around the circle with slow steps thus: Step sideways right and bend the trunk right. Draw the left foot up to the right foot and bend the trunk to the left. The braves use the same step hop throughout the dance but observe the pitch of the music, and when this is low they bend over sharply and when it is high they raise their trunk high and throw back their heads. After the music is played through once the first strains are repeated again for the Indians to go off.

(e) Southerners' Clog—Music—Chorus of "Dixie."

1st Step

A. Measures 1-4: Step on right foot behind left, step left foot to the side, step on right foot in front of left and step to the left again. Repeat all of this again moving straight to the left side, and ending with right foot in front and weight on it.

Measures 5-8: Same as above only starting with left foot and moving to the right.

B. On last note of 8th measure and first note of 9th measure, rise on toes and pull the heels apart. On last note of 9th measure and first note of 10th measure, draw both heels in and at the same time draw the left foot behind the right with the left toe touching the right heel.

Measures 11 and 12: Make six quick changes with the same step as described above.

Measures 13-16: Repeat all.

Chorus repeated.

2nd Step

A. Measures 1 and 2: Draw the right foot straight back then draw the left foot back to it. Step forward with right foot and draw the left foot up to it.

B. Measure 3: Stand still.

Measure 4: Leap into the air from the right foot, throwing the left foot high into the air to be followed by the right. The landing is made on the left foot and then the right foot is crossed over in front of the left. All this resembles the scissors high jump.

Measures 5 and 6: Repeat A of 2nd Step.

Measures 7 and 8: Take three step hops backward kicking the heels up behind and outward.

Measures 9-16: From last of 8th measure to end of chorus do clog steps using six "threes" and one "seven," then that repeated.

3rd Step

A. Measure 1: Leap into air and land with both knees bent outward and hands on thighs, elbows out.

Measure 2: Leap again and land with weight on left foot and right foot extended to the side with the heel down.

B. Measures 3 and 4: Spin around to the left on the left foot, pushing with the right in time to the music. Arms are extended to the side.

Measures 5 and 6: Repeat A of 3rd Step.
Measures 7 and 8: Repeat B of 3rd Step.
Measures 9-16: Repeat B of first Step.

22. **Spring's Second Dance:** Music, page 385; and Lack; "Sorrentina."

Cocoon is taken off from Spring.

She slowly awakens and looks about her—8 measures.

Waltz step—4 measures. For explanation of these steps see "Springs First Dance".

Pas de basque—1 measure.
3 steps turning—1 measure.
Repeat last two measures—2 measures.
Repeat above steps twice—16 measures.
Pas de basque forward—4 measures.
Pas de basque backward—3 measures.
Running steps forming circle but ending in center of stage—8 measures.

Pose as in Spring's first dance, on measure 16 of Fig. 2—1 measure.

Pose as in Spring's first dance on measure 17 of Fig. 2—1 measure.

(Music "Sorrentina") Introduction—2 measures.

Fig. 1: Step rt. leap l. step rt. step l. step rt. step left—1 measure.

(Leap is executed by bringing knees bent high up in front).

Repeat rt. again—1 measure.

(Arms are high above head with backs of wrists brought together on leaps).

Step rt., slide together left (cts. 1-3), slide hop rt. (cts. 4-6) (left foot raised in rear)—1 measure.

Repeat last measure with left foot—1 measure.

Repeat as for first 3 measures—3 measures.

Hold—1 measure.

(Arms parallel and high as in arabesque position).

Run away to left as if not quite sure—2 measures.

Same way run back to right—2 measures.

With 3 or 4 tiny steps and stepping high on toes on each measure going in different direction as in dismay or questioning—3 measures.

With much abandonment and small running steps whirl—1 measure.

Fig. 2: Step rt.—cut left—step rt. step left—1 measure.

Repeat rt. ft.—1 measure.

Repeat measures 3 and 4 of Fig. 1—2 measures.

Repeat all—4 measures.

Fig. 3: Slide on rt. ft. (left up in rear) with enough force to make a complete turn on ball of right foot—Step 1.—step rt.—1 measure.

Tour Jete left—1 measure.

(Tour Jete: Step 1.—throw rt. foot over left and leap into it. Step 1. again making complete turn).

Repeat left, but do Tour Jete right—2 measures.

Small running steps toward l.—kneel on rt. knee—2 measures.

Dancing back to right 2 step hops, high knee in front—1 measure.

Tour de Basque rt.—1 measure.

(Hands back of head—trunk well bent back and to side. Tour de Basque—step rt.—step l. across in front of rt. and turn on toes—arms are high).

Repeat last 2 measures—2 measures.

Small running steps off to left—2 measures.

Kneel on right knee and beckon—1 measure.

Up and run toward center of stage (arms extended)—1 measure.

Omit music from middle of measures 42 to 73 using following 8 measures.

Two skips left and right and cross polka with left (turning about)—2 measures.

(Cross polka:—Hop right swinging left foot across right to step and turn right; step right, step left to finish the turn). Repeat 2 more times—4 measures.

Six cut steps beginning right foot, arms at side, finishing center stage—1 measure.

Saute right foot—1 measure.

(Saute:—Step on right foot and hop on it, left leg high in rear, head back. Right arm high, left diagonally upward).

The music is brought to an end in the last measure used by playing a high chord for the last half of the measure.

23. Dance by Queen's Attendants: Music Gavotte Menzeli —MacDonald & Steiner Co., 52 Bradhurst Ave. ,N. Y.

Formation: A double circle of four couples facing forward. Gentleman on the lady's left and a little behind her, holds her right hand in his right and her left in his left. His right arm lies across behind but does not touch her shoulder.

The Gavotte Step used in the dance is done to Gavotte or 4/4 time music as follows: Step forward right, left, right (counts 1, 2, 3). Swing left foot forward and across in front of right, with a little lift of the right heel on this swing (count 4). Repeat, starting with left foot.

Introduction: Partners find each other and come forward into position.

Step 1

Measures 1 and 2: Two gavotte steps forward with dancers beginning with right foot.

Measure 3: With one gavotte step lady moves sideways to cross in front of man to his left side while he does a gavotte step in place.

Measure 4: Lady returns in front of gentleman to place.

Measures 5 and 6: Two gavotte steps forward.

Measure 7: Release left hands. Lady turns with three steps and faces man. Both point left foot.

Measure 8: Lady does deep courtesy and gentleman bows.

Step 2

Measures 9 and 10: Join right hands and beginning with right foot take two gavotte steps around partner.

Measure 11: Lady turns left under gentleman's right arm, both taking one gavotte step to place.

Measure 12: Couples face, join both hands high and balance forward on left foot. Right in rear raised (2 counts). Step back on right foot; point left forward (2 counts).

Measure 13: Beginning with the left foot and moving to the right partners standing side by side in original position, take bourre' change' and point (step across behind with left count 1, step sideways with the right count 2, step across in front with left count 3, point count 4).

Measure 14: Repeat bourre' change' beginning right and moving left.

Measure 15: Gentleman walks diagonally backward while lady turns four steps left under his right hand. Left hands disengaged.

Measure 16: Step apart, courtesy and bow.

Step 3

Measure 17: Balance forward toward partner, right foot (2 counts). Step back left (2 counts). Arms are raised sideways not joined.

Measure 18: Swing right foot behind and step on it, step left with left foot (count 1). Step right across in front (count 2). Step left with left foot (count 3). Point right forward (count 4). During the above the man takes very short steps and both turn so as to finish in the original position, hands joined.

Measure 19: Balance forward on right foot, step back on left.

Measure 20: Three canters (gallop) forward with right foot leading and step forward right.

Measure 21: Balance forward left, step back right.

Measure 22: Three canters forward left and step left.

Measure 23: Facing partner both hands held high, balance forward right and step back left.

Measure 24: Lady holding gentleman's right hand with both of hers turns under gentleman's right arm with four canter steps while man walks backward.

Step 4

Measure 25: Beginning left foot take one gavotte step, the gentleman sideways left to center of circle to join hands with other men, the lady in place. Partner's inside hands joined.

Measures 26-32: Do seven more gavotte steps forward around circle in this wheel formation.

Omit the next four measures.

Step 5

Measures 37 and 38: With two gavotte steps the couples turn around in place to the left, the men going backward and the ladies forward placing the ladies in the center who join right hands.

Measures 39-44. The wheel now moves in the reverse direction with six gavotte steps.

Step 6

Measures 45 and 46: Beginning left foot turn around with

the gavotte steps swinging the lady out into the original position, with right hands joined and left hands joined.

Measures 47-52: Finish the dance using the same steps as the last six measures of Step 1.

Finish the music with measure 52 with a retard.

Description of Costumes (Main Characters)

The costumes worn by the different countries consist of caps, aprons, bodices or boleros that are characteristic of that country.

King Winter: White smock with white cotton around bottom, white bloomers, white cotton whiskers, white cap covered with cotton.

Snowflakes: White cheesecloth dresses similar to that of raindrops except trimmed in cotton.

Spring: White cheesecloth costume, Grecian style; garland of flowers around head and also a garland draped around shoulders crossed in front, and brought around waist.

Raindrops: Gray cheesecloth dresses, with skirt slit up from bottom in about 2 inch strips with silver balls of tin-foil at end of each strip and a rainbow colored underskirt under all.

Uncle Sam: Red and white striped trousers, long, dark blue swallow-tailed coat, high hat with red and white striped crown, stars around bottom of crown.

Goddess of Liberty: White Grecian draped dress and gold crown with long points in front.

Easterners (Boys): Tall stiff hats made of black paper, eyeglasses cut out of black paper. Long Prince Albert coats made of black cambric, long trousers, white gloves.

(Girls): Long skirts, white waists with high collars, long black gloves. Hair drawn back tight and knotted, stiff sailor hats, preferably black.

Midwesterners (Boys): Farmer costumes, overalls, straw hats, red bandanas knotted around neck.

(Girls): Aprons and sunbonnets.

Westerners (Cowboys): Khaki colored long trousers, wide brimmed hats, khaki shirts, red handkerchiefs around necks. Holsters carrying repeating cap pistols around waist, wooden horses (sticks with heads carved to represent horses' heads).

Indians (Braves): Long khaki colored trousers with fringe along outside seams of legs. Smocks with fringe along bottom, short sleeves and bright colored pieces of cloth cut in shape of stars, moon or sun or other decorative designs sewed on the front. These costumes can be made of brown or tan cambric. Headbands with feathers, tomahawks, bows and arrows, etc. The Big Chief has a more elaborate headdress with many feathers that go around his head and hang down the back.

(Squaws): Colored Indian blankets, hair parted in middle and braided in two braids. Headbands with one feather up the back.

Southerners (Negroes): Negro makeup, long trousers and bright colored shirts, colored stockings, red handkerchiefs around neck, caps on head.

Colonel: Prince Albert coat, white waistcoat, long trousers, gray felt hat.

Colonel's wife: Colonial costume, full skirt with drapes of flowered material at sides. A hat tipped up in back and covered with ruffles of tissue paper.

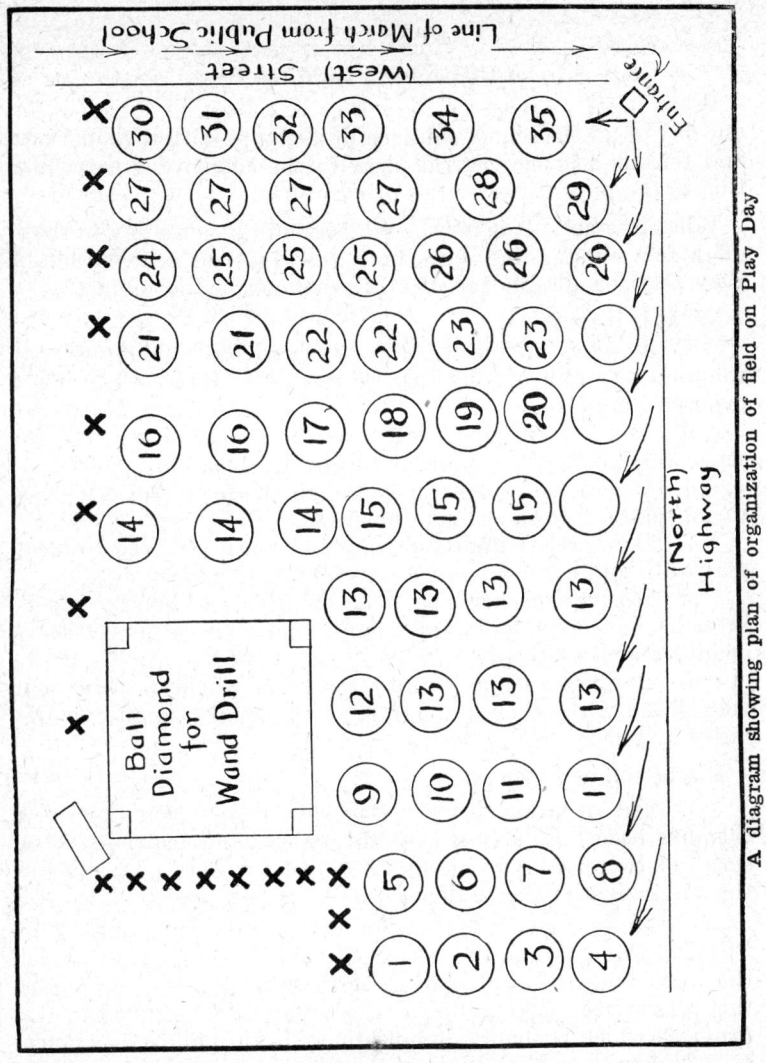

A diagram showing plan of organization of field on Play Day

Key to Numbers
1. Peru Twp.
2. Center Twp.
3. Dubuque Twp.
4. Jefferson Twp.
5. Balltown Twp.
6. Sherrill's Par.
7. Concord Twp.
8. Liberty Twp.
9. Iowa Twp.
10. New Wine Twp.
11. Holy Cross
12. Dyersville Public
13. Dyersville Par.
14. New Vienna
15. Luxemburg
16. Bankston Par.
17. J dge Twp.
18. Cascade Twp.
19. Taylor Twp.
20. Whitewater Twp.
21. Epworth
22. Farley
23. Farley Par.
24. East Cascade
25. St. Mary's
26. St. Martin's
27. Worthington
28. Vernon Twp.
29. Mosalem Twp.
30. Prairie Creek Twp.
31. Table Mound Twp.
32. Washington
33. Bernard
34. Filmore
35. Zwingle

APPENDIX II.
A COUNTY PLAY DAY

What is it? A County Play Day is a meeting together for one day of all the school children of a county with their parents and friends at some central place in the county for participation in the physical activities of child life.

What it is not. It is not an exhibition day, not a day to show off a few outstanding stars or a few superior schools, but a Play Day for all children of all the schools of the county.

What is it for?

1. It gives an incentive to teachers for teaching a well rounded program of Physical Education in their own schools prior to Play Day.
2. It gives an opportunity for the people of a county to see a well rounded program of Physical Education.
3. It gives an opportunity for all the people of a county to get together for a common purpose.
4. It broadens the opportunity of rural children to meet play with and contest against children of their own age.
5. It gives teachers, patrons, children and county superintendent an opportunity of seeing what a large institution a county school system is.
6. It gives an opportunity for rural teachers to become acquainted with other teachers in their vicinity because of the unifying scheme of township organization.

Discussion of Purposes.

1. The program of Play Day should represent the work that has been regularly taught throughout the year and not a series of exercises that are planned just for Play Day and for the amusement of the audience.
2. Many times people who think they are opposed to Physical Education in the schools are able to see its value when the work is demonstrated to them in an attractive way. For this reason some spectacular drills are usually included in the program which probably do not appeal to the children as much as, nor give them the physical or moral training that some less spectacular things would.
3. It has been demonstrated many times that the most successful way of unifying any body of people is to give them a common task to perform. A county is a unit of our government and yet it often feels its unity less than a state or a city. It is a common testimony that the County Play Day has given the rural population their first big opportunity of thinking in terms of county and township.

4. One of the conditions most favorable to play is a group of children of the same age and sex. It is not uncommon in a rural school for some boy or girl to go through the elementary grades with no other boy or girl of corresponding age to match himself against. Then too, the school offers the greatest opportunity for making friendships and therefore such a boy or girl must pass through the friendship forming period with little opportunity for making satisfying friendships.

The Play Day gives occasion for many nearby schools to come together for group practises and in this way children meet other children and become their friends where they otherwise would probably not meet at all. On Play Day they come in contact with large numbers of children of their own age and interests.

5. A common expression on Play Day is "I didn't suppose there were so many children in our county." The collective statement of the school taxes of a county do not seem so large if the occasion for these taxes are seen collectively.

6. Industries and corporations make an effort to further the acquaintance of their employees, as acquaintance tends toward understanding and unity, and common understanding and unity of a group of people working for a common cause tend to further that cause. The cause of education is likewise furthered by the acquaintance and unity of educators. Many teachers have admitted that they did not even know the names of the teachers teaching nearest them until the Play Day gave the occasion for this acquaintance.

Suggestion for Further Organization.

Because the county wide organization of a Play Day is such a big undertaking and means so much work for a few individuals it is better, after the above aims have been reached, to carry on the same activities with a smaller unit of organization such as a Township Play Day or a Sectional Play Day where several Townships unite. In this way there can be a more intensive realization of some of the aims. This plan is more possible of organization and realization and, therefore, can occur more frequently with a larger percentage of attendance.

Plans for a County Play Day

I. Nature of activities for the program.
  A. General Characteristics.
    1. Should be those that make a fairly all round course in Physical Education.
    2. Those which make the organization of large numbers of people possible and easy without previous practise.

3. Those which are enjoyable to participate in and interesting to witness and yet which reach the main objectives of Physical Education.

B. Types of Activities and their specific characteristics.
1. Rhythmical Activities: Folk Games.
  (a) Essential Characteristics.
    (1) Such that children may participate in together without previous practise of the group. This makes it possible for children from a small rural school to join a larger group such as a township circle without previously having participated with them.
    (2) Should be of the circle variety, not dependent upon a definite number of participants and where all taking part perform in about the same manner.
    (3) Should contain steps that carry the performers around the circle as this is more spectacular to watch, from a distance when many circles are performing at one time.
    (4) Should preferably be those, the music of which is found on a phonograph record as this standardizes the use of the music.
    (5) The selection should contain some games that allow hand clapping as the sound gives a pleasing variety.
    (6) Must contain steps that are simple enough for primary children to perform and yet interesting enough for the upper grade children.
  (b) Some Folk Games that have most of the above characteristics and have been proved by use to be satisfactory Play Day Material.
    1. Danish Dance of Greeting.
    2. Shoemaker's Dance.
    3. Looby Loo.
    4. How D'ye Do My Partner.
    5. Swedish Ring Dance.
    6. Chimes of Dunkirk.
    7. Cshebogar.
    8. Ace of Diamonds.
    9. German Hopping Dance.
    10. Seven Jumps.
    11. Swedish Klapp Dance.
    12. Hansel and Gretel.
    13. Tantoli.
2. May Pole Dance.
  (a) Essential Characteristics.
    1. Simple steps with much movement of the circle as a whole.

2. Streamers must be held from the start of the dance because a windy day makes the picking up of streamers to a given strain of music difficult if not wholly impossible.

3. The dance is best performed by High School or Junior High girls.

(b) A May Pole Dance that has been used is found on Page 415.

3. Wand Drill.

(a) Essential Characteristics.

1. Wands should be decorated in patriotic or other bright colors.

2. The drill should be simple but give some general physical activity.

3. Should be done by 7th and 8th grades of city or consolidated schools.

(b) A Wand Drill that has been used is found on page 419.

4. Flag Drill.

(a) Essential Characteristics.

1. Should include large movements of the arms as flags in motion are more spectacular to watch.

2. Must include simple yet interesting movements so that the small children may participate along with the large.

(b) Two flag drills that have been used are found on pages 416 and 418.

Note: These drills are added to the program 1st because they are of a patriotic nature—2nd because they are spectacular and will thus please the eyes of the audience—3rd because they are simple of organization and thus allow large numbers to take part. They are not recommended as the best type of physical activity.

5. Contest Games.

(a) Essential Characteristics.

1. These must be of simple organization requiring a minimum of interdependence of team members since in most cases the teams will be composed of players from different schools who have not played together before.

2. They must require a minimum of skill in fundamentals since in the rural schools where the games must be worked up children of varying ages and skills must play together.

3. They should require a minimum of equipment so that no school will be prohibited from participating because of the expense involved.

4. There should be a varied selection of games so that children, teachers and parents may see and thus become interested in a fuller games program.

(b) Some contest games that have been used and proved satisfactory according to the above essentials are:
1. Newcomb.
2. End Ball.
3. Bat Ball.
4. Long Ball.
5. Circle Dodge Ball.
6. Progressive Dodge Ball.
   (Less desirable because it requires three teams)
7. Punch Ball.
8. Box Ball.

6. Track Meet (Motor Ability Tests).
  (a) Essential Characteristics.
1. Must be simple to teach and require a minimum of apparatus.
2. Must be events for which there are established standards since rural children will have only this to measure themselves by before the Play Day in many instances.
3. Should contain a variety of activities so those participating will receive all round physical development with no over-developing of any one part of the body.
4. A fair basis for competition must be worked out so that varying ages of children will feel justified in entering the meet on Play Day.
5. If a High School boys' meet is conducted at the same time as the grade meet events must be chosen that will not endanger the lives of the children contesting on the same ground.
  (b) Events and Methods of classification that may be used in meets at Play Days are found on page 98.

II. General Plan of Participation.
  A. Some of the plans for division of the county for participation in the various events follow.

First Scheme: All the townships of a county are grouped into four divisions according to geographical relationship and density of population. To each of these divisions are taught two folk dances, one team game, and to all are taught the Flag Drill and Athletic Tests. To all high schools the May Pole Dance is given and to all 7th and 8th grades the wand drill is given.

Second Scheme: The county is divided as above for everything excepting the folk dances. For these two of the above divisions are united and are given the same three dances making six in all for the Play Day program.

Third Scheme: Divided as above for all but the folk dances and for these no division is made and the same four folk dances are taught to all the teachers and children of the county. This scheme is much to be preferred so far as the audience is concerned as it makes a much more spectacular sight to have all circles moving at once than for some to be standing still while a few dance. The only difficulty with this scheme is that of music. If it is a windy day or there is not a very strong band to play, the music might not carry to all parts of the field. In one county, however, this problem was very successfully solved by the use of a magnavox with three horns stationed at various parts of the field. In this way all dancers heard the music at the same time and were, therefore, all moving in unison.

B. In order that the smallest rural schools may have a part in the activities of Play Day the circles for the folk games and the teams for the contest games are formed on the township basis, i.e., all the rural schools of one township form one or more township circles instead of individual school circles. For the township team each rural school submits the name of its best and second best players to the township leader and this leader forms a township team from all of the first choice players and as many drawn names of second choice players as are necessary to complete the team. The separate grades or a combination of grades from the city schools form circles for the folk dances, and a round robin tournament held in each city school system determines the city team that will compete against other city teams. A round robin tournament is one where each grade from the 4th to the 8th, inclusive, plays every other grade and the grade winning the greatest number of games wins the tournament.

C. The above organization necessitates the appointment early in the year of township and town leaders. The township leaders may either be appointed by the county superintendent or elected by the teachers from the township. The town leaders are usually appointed. It is the office of these leaders to keep the other teachers interested and working and report back to the County Superintendent the progress made. Other duties falling upon these leaders as outlined for them by the county superintendent or Play Day Director will be found later in this discussion.

III. **Detailed Plan of Organization and Participation on Play Day.**

1. The day before Play Day the field where the organized program is to be given should be staked off with stakes bearing numbers and marking the centers of all circles. These numbers correspond to a diagram previously given out to all the teachers of the county showing them where on the field

their school or township will form its circles and showing what number on the field will stand for their school. Stakes must also mark the lines for the flag drill and wand drill and line should outline the boundaries of the games to be played. The field should be prepared for the track meet by digging pits for the jump and staking off dashes and throws. On the morning of the Play Day pasteboard placards bearing large numbers corresponding to the numbers on the stakes are placed on these stakes so that they are easily visible from some distance.

2. At 9 oclock on Play Day, children and teachers begin lining up for the parade. This is done either in double file or four abreast and with or without floats. Spaces are designated where each of the four divisions is to form and these divisions line up as previously indicated on the sheet of instructors by towns, townships, schools and grades. A previously appointed division leader is responsible for the proper arrangement of towns and townships in his division and the township and town leaders are responsible for the proper arrangement within their respective groups. They report to the division leader when their sections are ready to march and he in turn reports to the director of the Play Day when his division is ready.

The order of lining up for the parade of course must correspond to the arrangement of placards on the performing field. If floats are used these line up with the town or township which they represent. There are usually prizes given for the best three floats counting originality of idea and cleverness of thought as the main basis for decision.

If all the children wear bright colored tissue paper caps the general appearance of the parade and the program as a whole is greatly improved. The children may make these caps themselves.

A good band is a big factor in a successful parade and program. The band usually marches at the head of the parade, and then takes its place on the band stand in a central position to play for the flag and wand drills and the may pole dance.

3. The following is the procedure after the parade.

(1). Children and teachers form circles for first folk dance.

(2). First and second dances are done in immediate succession.

(3). Dancers sit and seventh and eighth grades do wand drill.

(4). Dancers rise and do other two dances in order.

(5). Circles stretch back into lines for flag drill while High School girls come onto field for their May pole dance.

(6). Following May pole dance the lines move up for flag drill.

(7). After the flag drill and before lines disband the teams for the contest games are collected.

(8). Contests in the various games are held under the direct supervision of the division leader. A sample schedule follows:

Contest Games 11:30
Division I—Bat Ball

- Peru Twp.
- Center Twp.
- Dubuque Twp.
- Jefferson Twp.

Division II—Newcomb

- Concord Twp.
- Liberty Twp.
- Iowa Twp.
- New Wine Twp.
- Dyersville Par.
- Luxemburg
- New Vienna
- Holy Cross

Division III—Long Ball

- Dodge Twp.
- Cascade Twp.
- Taylor Twp.
- Whitewater
- Epworth
- Farley Pub.
- Farley Par.
- East Cascade
- Worthington

Division IV—End Ball

- Vernon Twp.
- Mosalem Twp.
- Prairie Creek Twp.
- Table Mound Twp.
- **Washington Twp.**

4. Picnic dinner by families by schools or by townships.

5. 1:30 meeting of officials of Track Meet for final instructions. 1:45 meeting of various age classes at designated spots for organization under ushers.

Note: The Motor Ability tests on page 98 are suggested for use in connection with Play Day. They should have been carried on in all the schools before Play Day and a badge of merit given by the county superintendent to each boy and girl who attains the age aim (25 points) in all of the events. On Play Day two age classes are united into one thus making 4 classes of grade girls and 4 of grade boys. Each of these classes is given a letter or a number which they wear in a conspicuous place on Play Day. Thus:

Girls	Tag	Boys	Tag
8-9 years	A	8-9 years	1
10-11 years	B	10-11 years	2
12-13 years	C	12-13 years	3
14-15 years	D	14-15 years	4
High School Girls	E		

Each class has an usher who takes it from event to event and awards all ribbons after each event is finished. The order of events for the various classes are:

Girls—(Rural and Town Grades)

8-9 year class
Playground ball Throw
Standing Broad Jump
50 yd. Dash

10-11 year class
Standing Broad Jump
50 yd. Dash
Playground Ball Throw

12-13 year class
50 yd. Dash
Playground Ball Throw
Potato Race
Standing Broad Jump

14-15 year class
Potato Race
Standing Broad Jump
50 yd. Dash
Playground Ball Throw

High School Girls
Basket Ball Far Throw
50 yd. Dash
Standing Broad Jump
Potato Race

Boys—(Rural and Town Grades)

8-9 year class
50 yd. Dash
Standing Broad Jump
Playground Ball Throw

10-11 year class
Running Broad Jump
Playground Ball Throw
75 yd. Dash
Running High Jump

12-13 year class
Playground Ball Throw
100 yd. Dash
Running High Jump
Running Broad Jump

14-15 year class
Running High Jump
Running Broad Jump
Playground Ball Throw
100 yd. Dash

High School Boys

These events are usually decided upon by the High School coaches. The same track and the same running officials are used for these as for the grade girls' and boys' dashes.

Officials for Track Meet

For all classes:
  Official scorer.
  Starter of Dashes.
  Clerk of Dashes.
  4 Judges of finish.
For Girls' Events:
Clerk and judge of broad jump.
  2 Measurers.
Clerk and Judge of Playground Ball Throw.
  5 Measurers.
Managers of girls' potato race.
  4 Assistants.
High School Girls:
Judge and Clerk of Basket Ball Throw.
  2 Measurers.
For Boys' Events.
Judge of running and standing broad jump.
Clerk of running and standing broad jump.
  2 Measurers.
Clerk and judge of playground ball throw.
  5 Measurers.
Ushers.

Class A	Class 1
Class B	Class 2
Class C	Class 3
Class D	Class 4
Class E	

Equipment Needed in Track Events
Girls

Potato Race
  6 or 10 boxes about 12x12x8.
  12 to 20 blocks of wood (1 to 2 inch cubes).
  Lime and tape for marching ground.
Broad Jump (standing)
  16x8x2 take-off board set into the ground.
  A tape.
  Pit.
Dash
  50 yard track.

Playground Ball Throw
    3 14-inch playground balls.
    Long tape (75 ft.).
    Lime for marking line to throw from.

Basket Ball Throw
    Basket Ball.
    Tape.
    Lime to make a mark.

Boys

Playground Ball Throw
    Same as for the girls' events except that arcs are drawn 50 ft., 75 ft., 100 ft., from throwing line.

High Jump
    Pit
    Two pairs of jumping standards.
    Two cross bars.

Broad Jump (running)
    Pit
    Take-off board as in girls' events.
    Tape.
    Rake and spade.

Dash
    50-75-100 yds. marked on same track as used for girls.

6. Added Organization Suggestions:

(a) A detailed plan of organization containing diagrams (see sample diagram, page 399) should be prepared by the county superintendent and given out to each teacher well in advance of Play Day. These plans should be carefully gone over with the teachers at a meeting held near the Play Day date. If the meeting can be held at the grounds where the performance is to be it is well to have the teachers practise going onto the grounds where circles will be formed and run through the whole scheme of organization.

(b) Samples of instruction sheets that have been given out to Township, Town and Division leaders follow.

Instructions To Township Leaders—Play Day

Things to do before Play Day.

1. See that there is a township float if possible and a township banner.

2. Get from your teachers the number of children coming to Play Day. This will help you in deciding whether your township will need more than one circle for the folk dancing, counting 40 or 50 children to a circle.

3. Select with your teachers the township team for the contest game. Keep a list of these players and have a few

PHYSICAL EDUCATION 411

substitutes in case some children do not come. 15 constitutes a Newcomb and End Ball team and 12 a Long Ball and Bat Ball team. Both boys and girls may be on the team.

4. Appoint an assistant who will help in making the lines for the flag drill. See that she wears a large number, the number of your line in the drill. Your line will be the same number as your circle was.

5. Get results of motor ability test work from teachers in your township. These blanks (form 3) filled out by the teachers should be sent by them not later than May 1. You must then compile the results on form 4, the Township Record Sheet, which should be sent to the County Superintendent not later than May 6.

Things to do on Play Day.

1. Parade.

(1) Line up your townships in double file ready for the parade. Have your own school in the lead so that they can be with you as you lead the township.

(2) Take the place in the parade assigned to you by the division leader. This will be the same as given in the last bulletin handed to you.

(3) Make divisions of your township if more than one circle is needed. Do this before the parade. Place a teacher in charge of each division who will lead that division to its place on the field.

2. Circles and Folk Dances.

(1) Lead your township to the place for its circle on the field. Should more circles be needed for your township than that arranged for on the field, you designate to the extra division where on the field they can form the circle.

(2) Take charge of your township circles for the folk dancing. Get them up and ready in time and remind them as to the number of times each dance is to be done.

3. Flag Drill.

After folk dances are over form your children into one line for the flag drill. When the may pole dance is over, lead your line up to your assistant who is holding your number. See that there is plenty of room between pupils for movement of arms and flags. If you have too many children for one line (about 75 will be as many as can be in one line) break the line in two and form two lines by bringing last half up to the front beside the first half.

Contest Games.

Be able to referee the game your township is playing if the Division Leader calls on you to do it.

Instruction Sheet for Town Leaders

Things to do before Play Day.

1. Know who your Division leader is and be willing to cooperate under his direction.
2. See that there is a town float if possible and a town banner.
3. See that each grade is provided with some sort of banner or placard so that spectators may tell who they are.
4. Get from your schools the number of children coming on Play Day. This will help in determining if enough circles have been provided for your schools, counting 40 or 50 children to a circle.
5. See if possible that a round robin tournament is carried on in your schools to determine the team that will play the contest game on Play Day.
6. Secure a list of names of those on the school teams for the contest game. Fifteen constitute an End Ball and Newcomb team and 12 constitute a Long Ball and Bat Ball team. Both boys and girls may be on the team. Half and half is desirable.

Things to do on Play Day.

1. Be sure you know (from outline handed out) where your school comes in parade and on performing space.
2. **The parade** (1) make the divisions of your town groups for the folk dancing before the parade begins. Place a teacher in charge of each division who will lead that division to its place on the field. (2) Line up your town school in double file ready for the parade. (3) Lead your school in the parade or see that a good leader is in charge.
3. **Circles and Folk Dances:** See that your town gets to the proper place for its circle on the field. Should more circles be needed for your school than arranged for on the field, you designate to the extra division where they can form the circle. Have this be near your other circle.
4. As soon as the folk dances are over, form your schools into one or more lines each and after the may pole dance is over, lead your lines or appoint some teacher to lead them down to an assistant who is holding a number to indicate where your line is to be. This assistant is to be appointed by you before Play Day and he will hold the same number as is used to indicate your circles on the field. See that there is plenty of room between pupils for movement of arms and flags. If you have too many children for one line (about 75 will be as many as can be in one line) break the line in two and form two lines by bringing last half up to the front beside the first half.

5. **The Contest Game:** (1) Report after the flag drill to your Division Leader at the place your game will be played and have your team ready to play. (2) Be ready to officiate in any way if the Division Leader calls on you for help.

6. **The Track Meet:** (1) See that the boys and girls from your schools are properly instructed in the events they may enter on Play Day. (2) See that they understand what their first event is and when it comes. (3) See that all boys and girls are properly supplied with letters or numbers to indicate to the officials to which class they belong.

7. **May Pole Dance.** See that there is a group of May Pole dancers from your school. A May Pole will stand 15 ft. above the ground and streamers of your school colors 24 ft. long and 1 ft. wide should be furnished by your school. You should oversee or appoint someone to oversee the fastening of your streamers to the May Pole before the parade starts in the morning.

8. **Wand Drill.** See that the 7th and 8th grade pupils from your school know the wand drill and that there is someone appointed to lead them to their proper place on the baseball diamond on Play Day. (See Diagram.)

Instructions To Division Leaders

First: The Division Leader is to be in charge of his division for the parade and morning program. His duties in this regard are as follows:

1. Besides lining up your own township or school, see that your whole Division is lined up in double file in the proper place for the parade, ready to start on time. Report to the parade director when your division is ready to march.

2. See that your division or its separate parts stay in proper order in line of march and break off on the infield of the race track at the proper place to form circles. Help township and town leaders and teachers of your division to find the places for their circles and see that all are placed ready to dance.

3. See that your division is forming with dispatch the lines for the flag drill in the manner described in the bulletin of instructions. If extra lines are needed, help in bringing children up from rear to form these extra lines.

Second: The Division Leader is to be in charge of the Contest Games of that Division.

1. Before Play Day appoint the necessary officials for your game. In Divisions I, II, and III, two contests will occur simultaneously; therefore two sets of officials will be

necessary. Appoint these officials from township or town leaders or teachers. Be sure to appoint someone you can depend upon. The officials must be there, so there is no delay in running off the contests. Give officials instructions listed below. Also secure the necessary apparatus for the two contests. Bring this apparatus or see that it is brought and take it to the Judges' Stand. Someone will be in charge there all day, so that you can leave it there in safety until needed. The necessary officials and equipment for each game are as follows:

Division I. End Ball.
   2 referees
   2 score keepers   One of each for each contest.
   2 time keepers
   2 Basket Balls
   2 score cards
   2 pencils.

Division II. Newcomb.
   2 referees
   2 score keepers   One of each for each contest.
   2 time keepers
   2 Basket Balls or Volley Balls
   2 score cards
   2 pencils.

Division III. Long Ball.
   2 umpires
   2 score keepers   One of each for each contest.
   2 Indoor Baseballs
   2 Indoor Baseball Bats
   2 score cards
   2 pencils.

Division IV. Bat Ball.
   1 umpire
   1 score keeper
   1 Volley Ball
   1 stake
   1 score card
   1 pencil.
2. Place and Order of Playing:

    (a) Find out at Judges' stand just after the Flag Drill where your contests will occur. At this time assign officials. Take teams and officials to courts. See that courts have all been satisfactorily marked out. If lines need remarking, see that it is done.

(b) The competition will be carried on as follows:
(A program of games similar to that found on page 407 of this bulletin would be inserted here in the Division Leaders' instructions).

3. Get reports of all the games of your division from the score keeper and report these in writing to the secretary at the Judges' Stand.

4. Give the following instructions to your officials:
(1) Report at Judges' Stand at 11:30.
(2) Find out from Division Leader what contest you are to judge.
(3) Secure your apparatus at Judges' Stand from Divison Leader.
(4) Go with Division Leader and teams to place where contest is held.
(5) Referee should bring his own whistle, and should be sure of the rules governing the game to be officiated.
(6) The time keeper must have a watch.
(7) The **time** for playing End Ball and Newcomb will be **ten minute halves.**
(8) The number of **innings** for Long Ball and Bat Ball will be **four.**
(9) The score keeper will report results to Division Leader who in turn will report to Secretary at Judges' Stand.

May Pole Dance

May pole: 4 inch pipe 15 feet high.

Streamers: High School colors—12 of each color. Each streamer should be one foot wide and 24 feet long.

Formation: 12 couples in single circle facing pole. Left hand partner is No. 1, right hand partner is No. 2. Each dancer holds streamer in her right hand throughout the dance.

Music: Introduction and four strains of 16 measures each. Play this all through twice as written. Streamers are taken before music begins.

Introduction: Measures 1-4.
(Meas. 1-2) Courtesy to partner.
(Meas. 3-4) Courtesy to pole.

First strain: Measures 1-16.
(Meas. 1-4) All join hands and walk to the right 8 steps.
(Meas. 5-8) Skip to the right 8 steps.
(Meas. 9-12) Turn and walk to left 8 steps.
(Meas. 13-16) Skip to left 8 steps.

Second strain: Measures 1-16 and repeated.
(Meas. 1-2) All take 3 steps toward center of circle and finish on fourth count with feet together.

(Meas. 3-4) All take 3 steps out and finish on fourth count with feet together.
(Meas. 5-8) All slide right 8 slides.
(Meas. 9-10) Repeat steps done to Meas. 1-2.
(Meas. 11-12) Repeat steps done to Meas. 3-4.
(Meas. 13-16) All slide to left 8 slides.
(Meas. 1-16 repeated) Repeat all of above steps.
First Strain (Meas. 1-16)
(Meas. 1-8) Break hands and partners face each other in a single circle, each holding streamer in her right hand. Each skips in the direction she is facing for 16 skip steps. (This makes a double circle with number ones on outside skipping counter-clockwise, and number twos on the inside skipping clockwise).
(Meas. 9-16) Without changing streamers to other hand, all face in opposite direction and skip back to starting place by partner 16 steps.
Introduction: Measures 1-4.
(Meas. 1-2) Courtesy to partner.
(Meas. 3-4) Courtesy to pole.
First and second strains with second strain repeated, 48 measures in all.
Partners face each other and starting to the left weave streamers throughout the 48 measures, using the skip step. In weaving No. 1 goes to the left of her partner ducking under her partner's streamer and to the right of the next one she meets holding her streamer high so this person may pass under it. All the number ones are circling around counter-clockwise, while the number twos circle clockwise; and by this alternate ducking under the passing over around the circle, the streamers are braided.
First Strain: Measures 1-16.
Drop streamers and skip off with partner, inside hands joined. This music should be finished with a chord.
Note: Any good skipping rhythm may be used which can be played by the band, or which is on a phonograph record. The above steps may need to be adapted in accordance with the music used.

Flag Drill No. 1

Four figures and interlude. Music—Any march.
Starting position, arms bent upward, flags vertical.

Fig. 1.

Stretch arms upward raising heels—Counts 1 and 2.
Arms part sideways to shoulder height, bending knees halfway—Counts 3 and 4.

Raise arms upward stretching knee—Counts 5 and 6.
Arms bend and heels sink—Counts 7 and 8.
Do four times in all.

Fig 2.
Lunge obliquely forward left, crossing flags obliquely upward left, without twisting trunk—Counts 1 and 2.
Arms part sideways, shoulder height, and change to lunge with right—Counts 3 and 4.
Arms upward to first position and lunge left—Counts 5 and 6.
Arms and feet return to position—Counts 7 and 8.
Feet are not removed from floor in change of lunge.
Do four times in all, left, right, left, right.

Fig. 3.
Jump to stride, stretching arms sideways—Counts 1 and 2.
Twist trunk until facing side of room—Counts 3 and 4.
Twist trunk forward again—Counts 5 and 6.
Feet to position and arms bend—Counts 7 and 8.
Do four times in all, left, right, left, right.

Fig. 4.
Raise left arms obliquely sideways upward and right obliquely sideways downward, touching left foot sideways looking up at flag at left—Counts 1 and 2.
Cross arms in front, left flag pointing down right and right up to left, touching left foot in back of right foot—Counts 3 and 4.
Unwind arms, and touch foot sideways as in first position—Counts 5 and 6.
Bend arms upward, and feet to position—Counts 7 and 8.
Do four times in all, left, right, left, right.

Interlude, done before and after every exercise.
Three steps forward, feet together on 4th count, with arms flinging forward, crossing arms in front on 1st and 3rd counts (arms being sideways on 2nd and 4th counts)—Counts 1 to 4.
Standing in place, fling arms upward, crossing arms over head on 5th and 7th counts (arms being sideways on 6th and 8th counts)—Counts 5 to 8.
Repeat arms, walking backward 3 steps, feet together on 4th count—Counts 1 to 4.
Arms flinging upward as before, standing still—Counts 5 to 8.
Repeat this again—Counts 1 to 8.
Note: The interlude is done twice in succession each time. As it is finished the first time, the arms can remain sideways, but as it is completed the second time, that is, just

before starting on the next exercise, the arms should return to the fundamental arm position—arms bent upward.

Flag Drill No. 2

Three Figures and interlude. Music: "Columbia the Gem of the Ocean."

Starting Position: Arms bent at elbows, hands near shoulders. Flags held vertically at either side of the face. Each figure begins and ends this way.

Fig. 1.
    A. One full outward circle—4 cts.

Flags are thrust straight upward from the starting position until arms are fully extended. Arms then part to sides, the left going down left, the right going down right until they are fully extended at low front. Here they cross and return to starting position. The right arm crosses over the left.

    Repeat A—4 cts.
    B. One full inward circle—4 cts.

Flags are thrust straight upward as above, but this time when at highest point the right arm crosses over the left and travels down the left side of the body while the left goes down the right side. After they cross at low front they return to starting position with a full swing at the sides of the body.

    Repeat B—4 cts.
    C. Point both flags to left horizontal—2 cts.
        Point both flags to front horizontal—2 cts.
        Point both flags to right horizontal—2 cts.
        Return flags to starting position—2 cts.
        Repeat all of C starting to right side—8 cts.

Do whole figure two times in all, using all of music for the 1st stanza—64 cts.

Interlude.
    A. Walk 3 steps forward with arms stretched sideways horizontal, bringing feet together on 4th count—4 cts.
    B. Jump to the stride with arms stretched diagonally upward—4 cts.

Stand in place and cross and uncross flags overhead—4 cts, i. e., flags are crossed on count 1, uncrossed on count 2, etc.

    Jump to starting position—4 cts.
    C. Walk backward 3 steps with arms stretched sideways horizontal bringing feet together on 4th count—4 cts.
    Repeat B—12 cts.
    Use all of chorus music. 32 counts in all.

Fig. 2.
Step backward left, stretching the arms above the head, keeping flags parallel—4 cts.
Kneel, bringing flags through forward to sideways horizontal—4 cts.
Stretch knees and fling the flags forward upward above the head as in first movement of this figure—4 cts.
Replace the foot forward and bring the arms to starting position—4 cts.
Do all four times left, right, left, right—64 cts.

Interlude.

Fig. 3.
A. Step to the side with the left foot and stretch arms to forward horizontal—2 cts.
Bend trunk forward and fling arms sideways, keeping them shoulder height—2 cts.
Straighten trunk and fling arms back to forward horizontal again—2 cts.
Replace left foot and bring flags to starting position—2 cts.
Repeat A but begin with right foot—8 cts.
B. Point both flags to left horizontal—2 cts.
Point both flags to front horizontal—2 cts.
Point both flags to right horizontal—2 cts.
Bring flags to starting position—2 cts.
Repeat all of B but start to right—8 cts.
Do whole figure two times in all—64 cts.

Interlude.

Wand Drill

Music—March rhythm. 8 strains of 8 measures each of 4/4 time needed. If 2/4 or 6/8 time is used, each of these strains should be repeated. The interlude requires 1 count for each movement. The figures require two counts for each movement. If a short interlude occurs in the music leave it out or let children stand in place during it.

Size of Wand: Take a broom-stick and saw it off to be 42 inches long.

How to decorate Wand: Cover the wand with white cloth. Tack to each end a tuft of red, white and blue streamers made from crepe paper, 6 inches long and ¾ inches wide. Use ten of each color on each end.

Starting Position of Drill: Wands low in front horizontal.

Fig. I.
Raise wands forward, arm length from chest, and raise heels (ct. 1-2). Knees bend, and turn wand to a vertical position,

right hand high (3-4). Knees stretch and return wand forward to horizontal position (5-6). Position (7-8).
Repeat 3 times 24 cts. 32 cts. in all.

Interlude—Follows each figure.

Wand swing forward upward and behind shoulders on ct. 1 and hold 3 cts. taking at the same time four hops in place (4 cts.); 3 walking steps forward, starting with left foot, feet together on ct. 4, wand brought arms length over head on first step, and held for 3 cts. (4 cts·); 4 hops in place bringing wands behind shoulders on ct. 1 (4 cts.); 3 walking steps back beginning with left foot, feet together on 4th ct., wands stretched over head on first step and hold 3 counts (4 cts.) 16 cts. Repeat all—16 cts. bringing wand to starting position on last count—32 cts. for whole interlude.

Fig. II.

Wands raising forward sideways right, (ct. 1-2).
Wand moving to position, forward downward (3-4).
Wand raising forward sideways left (ct. 5-6).
Wand moving to position forward downward (ct· 7-8).
Wand raising forward shoulder height and crossing the right arm over left.—(Ct. 1-2). Unwind and bring wands to position (3-4). Wand raising forward, and crossing the left over the right (5-6). Position (7-8).
Repeat all—16 cts. 32 cts. in all.

Fig. III.

Jump to stride position and bring wand to chest (1-2).
Stretch wand over head and look up at wand (3-4).
Bring wand back to chest (5-6).
Jump to position, bringing wands to starting position (7-8).
Repeat 3 times—24 cts. 32 cts. in all.

Fig. IV.

Wand raising forward sideways right and right foot placing sideways (1-2).
Wand moving forward downward and foot replace (3-4).
Wand raising forward sideways left and left foot placing sideways (5-6).
Wands moving forward downward and foot replace (7-8).
Wand raising forward and crossing the right arm over the left and right foot placing forward (1-2).
Unwind and bring arms and foot to position (3-4).
Arms raising forward and crossing the left arm over the right and the left foot placing forward (5-6).
Unwind and bring arms and foot to position (7-8).
Repeat—16 cts. 32 cts. in all.

SUPPLEMENT
COURSE OF STUDY IN PHYSICAL EDUCATION FOR ELEMENTARY GRADES

FIRST GRADE

Fall

Games
- A. Playground
  1. Hot Ball
  2. Slap Jack
  3. Squirrels in Trees
  4. Cat and Rat
  5. Midnight
  6. Brownies and Fairies
  7. Farmer in the Dell
  8. Kitty White
  9. Sally Go Round the Sun
- B. Schoolroom Games
  1. Lost Child
  2. Huckle Buckle Bean Stalk
  3. Street Car
  4. Squirrel and Nut

Folk Dances and Rhythms
1. Marching to Music
2. Skipping
3. See Saw
4. King of France
5. Here We Go Round the Mulberry Bush
6. Pussy Cat

For further suggestions see pages 139 and 204.

Story Plays (Page 344-353)
1. Circus
2. In the Orchard
3. On the Playground
4. Goldilocks

Posture Work

This should be accomplished by climbing and hanging on apparatus, by plenty of big muscle activity in the open air and by care as to diet and sleep, avoiding over fatigue.
See pages 288 and 295.

Stunts
1. Forward Roll, Page 361
2. Cart Wheel, Page 360

Winter (First Grade)

Games
- A. Playground or Gymnasium
  1. Midnight
  2. Brownies and Fairies
  3. Squat Tag
  4. Pom Pom Pullaway
  5. Tucker
  6. Farmer in the Dell
- B. Schoolroom
  1. Kaleidoscope
  2. Have you Seen My Sheep
  3. Do This, Do That
  4. Squirrel and Nut
  5. Partner Tag

Folk Dances and Rhythms
1. The Train
2. Elephants
3. Looby Loo
4. Shoemaker's Dance
5. Here We Go Round the Christmas Tree
6. The Thread Follows the Needle
7. Hickory, Dickory, Dock

Story Plays (Pages 344-353)
1. The Farmyard
2. The Snow Man
3. Brownies
4. Christmas Toys

Posture Work—Same as for Fall

Stunts—Same as for Fall

Spring (First Grade)

Games
A. Playground
1. Big Black Bear
2. Run for your Supper
3. Animal Chase
4. London Bridge
5. I want to go to London
6. Farmer in the Dell
7. Kitty White

B. Schoolroom
1. Partner Tag
2. Line Bounce Ball
3. Do This, Do That
4. Street Car

Folk Dances and Rhythms
1. Raindrops
2. Rolling Hoop
3. Birds Flying
4. The Snail
5. Let us Wash our Dolly's Clothes
6. To Market, To Market
7. I See You

Story Plays (Pages 344-353)
1. In the Woods
2. The Garden
3. Building a House
4. Birds Learning to Fly

Posture Work—Same as for Fall

Stunts
Same as for Fall
Top, page 363
Other stunts on apparatus where this is available, i. e., skinning a cat, hanging by knees, etc.

SECOND GRADE
Fall

Games
A. Playground
1. Black and White
2. Wood Tag
3. Tag the Line Relay
4. Aeroplane Relay
5. Slap Jack
6. Cat and Rat
7. Animal Chase
8. Ring Call Ball

B. Schoolroom
1. Tag the Wall Relay
2. Indian File Relay
3. Do This, Do That
4. Beanbag Circle Carry
5. Lost Child
6. Huckle Buckle Bean Stalk
7. Line Bounce Ball

Folk Dances and Rhythms
1. Playing Soldier
2. See Saw
3. Yankee Doodle
4. I am Very Very Small
5. A'Hunting We Will Go
6. Roman Soldiers
7. Carrousel

Story Plays (Pages 344-353)
1. Going Nutting
2. Jack o'Lantern
3. Pilgrims
4. The Leaves' Party

Posture Work
1. Same as in First Grade and also the 1st and 2nd tests of the Triple Test, page 295. A study is made of pictures of heroes in good posture and efforts are made to stand like them.

Good sitting position is encouraged and efforts made to walk like soldiers.

Stunts
1. Same as for 1st grade
2. Double Forward Roll (Page 361)
3. Leap Frog and Forward Roll (Page 361)

Contests
1. Adaptations of Combative Exercises 1, 2, 3, Page 368
2. Rooster Fight (b), Page 370.

Winter (Second Grade)

Games
A. Playground or Gymnasium
1. Indian File Relay
2. Midnight
3. Rabbit in the Hollow
4. Tucker
5. Cats and Rats
6. Snow Ball Game
7. Pom Pom Pullaway

B. Schoolroom
1. Have you seen My Sheep
2. Indian File Relay
3. Tag the Wall Relay
4. Kaleidoscope
5. Teacher and Class
6. Auto Race
7. Meet Me at the Switch
8. Circle Bounce Ball

Folk Dances and Rhythms
1. The Swing I
2. The Snow Storm, Page 139
3. Christmas Rhythms, Page 139
4. The Gallant Ship
5. Muffin Man
6. Snowball Game
7. Three Little Kittens

Story Plays (Pages 344-353)
1. Getting the Christmas tree
2. Coasting
3. Hiawatha's First Hunt

Posture Work Stunts and Contests—Same as for Fall.

Spring (Second Grade)

Games
A. Playground
  1. Sidewalk Tag
  2. Old Roger is Dead
  3. Thorn Rosa
  4. Roman Soldiers
  5. Round and Round the Village
  6. Pom Pom Pullaway
  7. Animal Chase
  8. Black and White
B. Schoolroom
  1. Teacher and Class
  2. Indian File Relay
  3. Tag the Wall Relay
  4. Line Ball
  5. Schoolroom Basket Ball Relay
  6. Circle Bounce Ball

Folk Dances and Rhythms
1. The Butterfly
2. Cock-a-doodle-doo
3. How D'ye Do, My Partner
4. Three Little Mice
5. My Son John
6. Draw a Bucket of Water
7. Playing Ball

Story Plays (Pages 344-353)
1. On the Farm
2. Jack and the Bean Stalk
3. Going Fishing

Posture Work, Stunts and Contests—Same as for Fall.

THIRD GRADE
Fall

Games
A. Playground
  1. Center Base
  2. Dodge Ball (Simple)
  3. Bull in Pen
  4. Ghosts and Witches
  5. Hang Tag
  6. Stores
  7. Ring Call Ball
  8. Snatch
  9. Red Light

B. Schoolroom
1. Tag the Wall Relay
2. Indian File Relay
3. Auto Race
4. Beanbag Circle Carry
5. Meet Me at the Switch
6. Lost Child
7. Huckle Buckle Bean Stalk
8. Wall Ball Bounce

Folk Dances and Rhythms
1. Kinder Polka
2. Indian Dance
3. Ride a Cock-horse
4. Otto and the Crow
5. Gustaf's Skoal
6. Hallowe'en is Here

Gymnastics (The following work to be used throughout the year)
  A. Posture Work
   1. Class-attention; class-position; in place rest, page 14.
   2. Formal rising from seats, page 14.
   3. Marching, tiptoe and marking time, page 309. See diagram page 312.
   4. Hands on hips and change to hands at neck-place, page 296.
   5. Arm stretchings, Exercise 3 (a), page 298.
   6. Alternate knee bending upward (a), page 299
   7. West Point breathing, page 300
   8. Posture Exercises IV and V, page 293
   9. Triple Test, page 295
  B. Mimetic Exercises, page 341
   1. Shaking a high limb
   2. Stretching
   3. Throwing
   4. Chopping
   5. Climbing a ladder
   6. Pumping up a bicycle tire
  C. Jumping Exercises, page 354
   1. Stride Spring Jump
  D. Movement Fundamentals
   1. Catching and throwing with a baseball and basket ball leading to games of this grade where these balls are used. Refer to Type Lesson I, pages 320 and 324.

Stunts and Contests (The following work to be used throughout the year)
1. Repeat those done in 1st and 2nd grade
2. Balancing Exercise, p. 360
3. Prostrate and Perpendicular, p. 363
4. Tip up, p. 362
5. Knee Dip, p. 359
6. Eskimo Jumping Race, p. 369
7. Disarm, p. 368
8. Rooster Fight (a), p. 369
9. Eskimo race on all fours, p. 371

Motor Ability Exercises
1. Short Informal Races
2. Chinning
3. Standing Broad Jump
4. Playground Ball Throw
5. Knee Raising
6. Trunk Lifting
7. Climbing

Note—All these are to be done informally.

Winter (Third Grade)

Games
- A. Playground or Gymnasium
  1. Crows and Cranes
  2. Midnight
  3. Tucker
  4. Pom Pom Pullaway
  5. Indian File Relay
  6. Red Light
- B. Schoolroom
  1. Kaleidoscope
  2. Indian File Relay
  3. Tag the Wall Relay
  4. Teacher and Class
  5. Partner Tag
  6. Auto Relay
  7. Last Man
  8. Beanbag Ring Toss
  9. Beanbag Board
  10. Schoolroom Basket Ball Relay
  11. Schoolroom Snatch
  12. Wall Ball Bounce

Folk Dances and Rhythms
1. Bean Porridge Hot
2. Danish Dance of Greeting
3. Away We All Go
4. Santa Claus and Reindeer
5. Hobby Horse
6. Jumping Jack
7. Heads, Shoulders, Knees and Toes

Gymnastics—Refer to Fall Term

Stunts and Contests—Refer to Fall Term

Spring (Third Grade)

Games
- A. Playground
  1. Poison Snake
  2. Snatch
  3. New York
  4. Hound and Rabbit
  5. Nuts in May
  6. Ring Call Ball
  7. Triangle Ball
  8. One Old Cat
  9. Punch Ball
- B. Schoolroom
  1. Tag the Wall Relay
  2. Beanbag Circle Carry
  3. Auto Race
  4. Line Ball
  5. Teacher and Class
  6. Leader Spry
  7. Hoop Relay
  8. Wall Ball Bounce

PHYSICAL EDUCATION

Folk Dances and Rhythms
1. Swing Song II
2. The Farmer Plants the Corn
3. Little Miss Muffet
4. Chimes of Dunkirk
5. Three Crows
6. Nest Making
7. Playing Ball
8. Jumping Rope

Gymnastics—Refer to Fall Term
Stunts and Contests—Refer to Fall Term

FOURTH GRADE
Fall

Games
A. Playground
  1. Soccer Dribble Relay
  2. Soccer Dribble and Shoot
  3. Soccer Pass
  4. Soccer Drive
  5. Shuttle Kicking Contest
  6. Simple Soccer Keep Away
  7. Soccer Pass and Shoot
  8. Simplified Soccer
  9. Hop Scotch
  10. Ring Call Ball
  11. Three Deep
  12. Last Couple Out
  13. Red Light
  14. Shuttle Relay
  15. Snatch
  16. Tag the Line Relay
  17. Indian File Relay
  18. Hound and Rabbit
  19. Bat Ball

B. Schoolroom
  1. Last Man
  2. Posture Tag
  3. Indian File Relay
  4. Auto Race
  5. Tag the Wall Relay
  6. Hoop Relay
  7. Partner Tag

Folk Dancing
  1. Bleking
  2. Reap the Flax
  3. Heads, Shoulders, Knees and Toes
  4. Swedish Clap Dance
  5. Hallowe'en is Here

Gymnastics (A, B, and C include work for the whole year)
A. Posture Work
  Note: See discussion on Posture (pages 283 to 307)
  1. Review work given in Third Grade
  2. Toes down first march (310)
  3. Quick time march (310)
  4. Posture Exercise I (293)
  5. Arms stretching (b) (299)
  6. Alternate knee bending upward (b) (299)
  7. Running in place (299)
  8. Arms bending forward changing to hands at neck (a) (301)
  9. Heels raising, knees bending (297)

       10. Head backward move (a) (304)
       11. Trunk bending forward (a) (305)
       12. Sitting trunk backward fall (306)
       13. Arms raising sideways with breathing (303)
  B. Mimetic Exercises (pp. 341-344)
       1. Windmill (341)
       2. Throwing lasso (342)
       3. Paddling a canoe (342)
       4. Rowing (342)
       5. Screwdriver (343)
       6. Riding a bicycle (344)
       7. Jumping Jack (344)
       8. Teamster warming up (344)
  C. Jumping Exercises
       1. Stride spring jump with arms flinging sideways (354)
       2. Leaping in place (356)
       3. Leaping to turn in place (357)
  D. Movement Fundamentals
       1. Movement Fundamentals leading to Soccer (pp. 332-334)

Stunts and Contests (pp. 359-371)
       1. Chair Creeper
       2. Through the Stick
       3. Hand Wrestle
       4. Eskimo Race on all Fours

Motor Ability Tests—See Spring

Winter (Fourth Grade)

Games
  A. Playground or Gymnasium
       1. Hen and Chickens
       2. Pom Pom Pullaway
       3. Midnight
       4. Black and White
       5. Jack Be Quick
       6. Musical Indian Clubs
       7. Push Ball Relay
       8. All Up Relay
       9. Ten Pin Contest
      10. Beanbag Board
      11. Zig Zag Pass
      12. Catch Ball
      13. Newcomb
  B. Schoolroom
    Review Schoolroom Games of Fall
       1. Zig Zag Pass
       2. All-over Relay
       3. Going to Jerusalem
       4. Schoolroom Snatch
       5. Teacher and Class (Use Basket balls)
       6. Leader Spry
       7. Newcomb
       8. Potato Race Relay
       9. Beanbag and Basket Relay
      10. Overhead Beanbag Relay
      11. Arch Ball
      12. Meet Me at the Switch
      13. Beanbag Ring Toss
      14. Potato Race Relay (Simplest Way)

Folk Dancing
       1. Pop Goes the Weasel
       2. Norwegian Mountain March
       3. Three Little Girls
       4. Christmas Dance

Gymnastics
A, B, C,—refer to Fall Term
D. Movement Fundamentals
  (a) Catching a basket ball (324)
  (b) Passing a basket ball (324-326)
    1. Chest   3. Underhand
    2. Underarm   4. Overhead

Stunts and Contests (pp. 359-371)
1. Bicycling   4. Line Tug of War
2. Jump the Stick   5. Finger Feat
3. Merry-go-round

Motor Ability Tests—See Spring

Spring (Fourth Grade)

Games
A. Playground
  1. Touch Off   7. Red Light
  2. One Old Cat   8. Hang Tag
  3. Long Ball   9. Black and White
  4. Work-up   10. Center Base
  5. Grounders Shuttle 11. Streets and Alleys
     Relay   12. Partner Shuttle Relay
  6. Punch Ball
B. Schoolroom Games
  1. Teacher and Class (Use Indoor Baseballs)
  2. Potato Race Relay (Simplest Way)
  3. Leader Spry   4. Line Ball
  Review all good schoolroom games from previous seasons.

Folk Dancing
1. Fist Polka   3. Come Let Us Be Joyful
2. The First of May 4. Seven Jumps

Gymnastics
A, B, C,—refer to Fall Term
D. Movement Fundamentals
  1. Movement Fundamentals leading to indoor baseball as needed in games in this grade such as One Old Cat, Long Ball, Work-up, and Punch Ball.
  2. Movement Fundamentals leading to Track and Field as taught in this grade. Refer to Motor Ability Tests.

Stunts and Contests (pp. 359-371)
1. Head Stand   3. Pulling Sticks
2. Chinese Get Up 4. Leap Frog Relay

Motor Ability Tests
Use Plan I, page 98, or Plan II, page 101. The vari-

ous activities making up these tests may be worked on throughout the year as follows:

Fall: Boys. 1. Chinning or Climbing
2. Ball Throw
Girls. 1. Knee Raising or Trunk Lifting
2. Ball Throw

Winter: Boys. 1. Standing Broad Jump
2. Goal Shooting
Girls: 1. Standing Broad Jump
2. Goal Shooting

Spring: Classify and test on all activities after all have been worked on.

FIFTH GRADE

Games   **Fall**

A. Playground
  1. Same games leading to Soccer as given in Fourth Grade
  2. Double Soccer Keep Away
  3. Soccer Target Kicking Relay
  4. Simplified Soccer Football
  5. Circle Dodge Ball
  6. Whip Tag
  7. Snatch
  8. Indian File Relay
  9. Stealing Sticks
  10. Figure Eight Relay
  11. Partner Shuttle Relay
  12. Hop Scotch
  13. Three Broad

B. Schoolroom
  1. Beanbag Circle Carry
  2. Posture Tag
  3. Overhead Beanbag Relay
  4. Tag the Wall Relay
  5. Indian File Relay
  6. Auto Race
  7. Last Man
  8. Partner Tag

Folk Dancing
  1. Swedish Ring Dance
  2. Sellenger's Round
  3. Pig in the Parlor

Gymnastics (A, B and C include work for the whole year)
A. Posture Work
  Note: See discussion on posture (pp. 283-307)
  1. Review work given in Third and Fourth Grades
  2. March steps (p. 313)
  3. Posture Exercises II and VI (p. 293)
  4. Arms bending forward, change to hands at neck (b), (p. 302)
  5. Heels raising and knees bending in rhythm (p. 302)
  6. Arm stretchings (a), (p. 302)
  7. Alternate leg raising forward (a) (p. 302)
  8. Head backward move (b) (p. 305)

PHYSICAL EDUCATION

    9. Trunk bending forward (b) (p. 306)
   10. Swimming movement (p. 305)
   11. Forward cut step (p. 303)
 B. Relief Period Drills (p. 16-17)
    Nos. I., II, IV, V and X.
 C. Jumping Exercises
    1. Stride to crossed spring jump (p. 355)
    2. Simple rocking step (p. 355)
    3. Hopping on one foot (p. 357)
    4. Slide hop (p. 358)
 D. Movement Fundamentals
    1. Movement Fundamentals leading to soccer (pp. 332-334)

Stunts and Contests (pp. 359-371)
   1. Crane Dive   3. Twister
   2. Hand Stand   4. Indian Wrestle

Motor Ability Tests—See Spring.

Winter (Fifth Grade)

Games
 A. Playground or Gymnasium
    1. Jump the Shot   10. Bombardment
    2. Hen and Chickens 11. Zig Zag Pass
    3. Jack be Quick   12. Basket Ball Goal Games
    4. Musical Indian Clubs   Nos. 1-2-3
    5. Driving a Pig to Market 13. Ten Trips 2 and 3
                           14. Arch Goal Ball
    6. Jump the Wand Relay 15. Pivot and Pass
                           16. Newcomb
    7. All Up Relay   17. End Ball
    8. Ten Pin Contest   18. Crows and Cranes
    9. Fifty or Burst   19. Captain Ball
 B. Schoolroom
    Review Schoolroom Games for Fall
    1. Zig Zag Pass   8. Simplified Volley Ball
    2. Run and Pass Relay 9. Newcomb
    3. Pursuit Relay   10. End Ball
    4. All-over Relay   11. Potato Race Relay
    5. Going to Jerusalem 12. Beanbag and Basket Relay
    6. Bird, Beast or Fish 13. Arch Ball
    7. Schoolroom Snatch

Folk Dancing
   1. Strasak   4. Christmas Dance
   2. Cshebogar   5. French Reel
   3. Captain Jinks

Gymnastics
   A, B and C,—refer to Fall Term

D. Movement Fundamentals
  1. Movement Fundamentals leading to Basket Ball (pp. 324-332)
  Note: The fundamentals of Basket Ball are taught in this grade because these skills are used in the games played in this grade, namely Newcomb, End Ball and Captain Ball.

Stunts and Contests (pp. 359-371)
  1. Jumping Jack
  2. Heel Click (a)
  3. Pendulum
  4. Pyramid No. III
  5. Push Tug of War
  6. Tunnel Race

Motor Ability Tests—See Spring

Spring (Fifth Grade)

Games
  A. Playground
   1. Streets and Alleys
   2. Touch Off
   3. Ball Stand
   4. Hindoo Tag
   5. Bronco Tag
   6. Partner Shuttle Relay
   7. Ten Trips Nos. 1, 4, 5,
   8. Grounders Shuttle Relay
   9. Fongo
   10. Baseball Pivot and Throw
   11. Work-up
   12. Circle Strike
   13. Long Ball
   14. Punch Ball
   15. Indoor Baseball
  B. Schoolroom Games
   1. Zig Zag Pass (Use Indoor Baseball)
   2. Leader Spry
   3. Ten Trips No. 1
   4. Potato Race Relay
   Review old schoolroom games

Folk Dancing
  1. Hansel and Gretel
  2. Ace of Diamonds
  3. Nixie Polka

Gymnastics
  A, B, C,—refer to Fall Term
  D. Natural Gymnastics
   1. Natural Gymnastics leading to Indoor Baseball (pp. 318-324) and Track and Field (pp. 335-341)

Stunts and Contests (pp. 359-371)
  1. Back Spring
  2. Flopper
  3. Eskimo Roll
  4. Indian Wrestle
  5. Setting Pegs

Motor Ability Tests
  1. Use Plan I, p. 98, or Plan II, p. 101. The various activities making up these tests may be worked on throughout the year, especially the form of the exercises.

SIXTH GRADE
Note: Boys and Girls should be divided in this grade though most of their work is the same.

Fall
Games
- A. Playground
  1. Same games leading to Soccer as given in Fourth and Fifth Grades
  2. Simplified Soccer
  3. Every man in His Own Den
  4. Circle Dodge Ball
  5. Whip Tag
  6. Ball Stand
  7. Third Man
  8. Progressive Dodge Ball
- B. Schoolroom
  1. Pursuit Relay
  2. Run and Pass Relay
  3. Last Man
  4. Leader Spry
  5. Indian File Relay
  6. Hoop Relay
  7. Beanbag Circle Carry

Folk Dancing
Girls:
  1. Highland Schottische
  2. Bounding Heart
  3. German Hopping Dance
  4. Rufty Tufty
Boys:
  1. Irish Lilt

Gymnastics (A, B, and C include work for the whole year)
- A. Posture Work
  Note: See discussion on Posture (pp. 283-307)
  1. Review work given in Third, Fourth and Fifth Grades.
  2. About march (p. 310)
  3. Face left march, face right march, backward march and column left and right march (pp. 310-311). This marching must be done in a gymnasium or on a playground.
  4. Posture Exercises III and VII (pp. 293-294)
  5. Arm stretchings (b) (p. 302)
  6. Alternate leg raising forward (b) (p. 303)
  7. Trunk bending forward (c) (p. 306)
  8. Exercise 9 (p. 306)
- B. Relief Period Drills (pp. 16-17)
  Nos. III, VI, VII, VIII and IX.
- C. Jumping Exercises
  1. Zig Zag Spring Jump (p. 355)
  2. Side Cut Step (p. 355)
  3. Rocking Step with Swing (p. 356)
  4. The "Break" (p. 356)
  5. Toe Touch-in, out (p. 357)

      6. Reverse Toe and Heel Touch (p. 357)
      7. Toe Touch-in, out; reverse toe and heel (p. 357)
  D. Movement Fundamentals
      1. Movement Fundamentals leading to Soccer (pp. 322-334)

Stunts and Contests (pp. 359-371)
    1. Frog Dance   4. Stomach Stand
    2. Ankle Throw   5. Arm's Length Tag
    3. Heel Click (b)

Motor Ability Tests—See Spring

Games   Winter (Sixth Grade)
  A. Playground or Gymnasium
     1. Center Catch Ball   18. Basket Ball Shuttle Relay
     2. Bronco Tag   19. Zig Zag Goal Ball
     3. Jump the Shot   20. Dribble and Bounce Pass Shuttle Relay
     4. Hen and Chickens
     5. Musical Indian Clubs   21. Dribble and Take Away (Boys)
     6. Push Club Relay
     7. Jump the Wand Relay   22. Keep Away (Boys)
                                      23. Goal Keep Away
     8. All Up Relay   24. Pass for Points
     9. Ten Pin Contest   25. Bounce Pass Keep Away
    10. Fifty or Burst   26. End Ball (Girls)
    11. Bombardment   27. Captain Ball
    12. Zig Zag Pass   28. Basket Ball (Boys)
    13. Basket Ball Goal Games Nos. 1, 2, 3   29. Serve and Return
                                       30. Simplified Volley Ball
    14. Ten Trips, 2 and 3   31. Volley Ball
    15 Arch Goal Ball   32. Crows and Cranes
    16. Pivot and Pass   33. Midnight
    17. Bounce Goal Relay
  B. Schoolroom
     1. Zig Zag Pass   7. Bird, Beast or Fish
     2. Run and Pass Relay   8. Schoolroom Snatch
     3. Newcomb   9. Simplified Volley Ball
     4. Pursuit Relay   10. End Ball
     5. All-over Relay   11. Potato Race Relay
     6. Going to Jerusalem

Folk Dancing
  Girls:
    1. Snow Storm   3. Tantoli
    2. American Country Dance   4. Virginia Reel
                               5. Russian Folk Dance
  Boys: 3. Czardas (From Burchenal —Folk Dances and Singing Games)
    1. Crested Hen
    2. Troika

Gymnastics
  A, B, and C,—refer to Fall Term
  D. Movement Fundamentals
   1. Movement Fundamentalls leading to Basket Ball (pp. 324-332)
Stunts and Contests (pp. 359-371)
   1. Take a Chair from Under
   2. Pyramid No. I
   3. Pyramid No. II
   4. Elbow Nestle
Motor Ability Tests—See Spring

Spring (Sixth Grade)

Games
  A. Playground
   1. Partner Tag
   2. Ostrich Tag (Boys)
   3. Bronco Tag
   4. Partner Shuttle Relay
   5. Streets and Alleys
   6. Ten Trips, Nos. 1, 4, 5
   7. Grounders Shuttle Relay
   8. Fongo
   9. Baseball Pivot and Throw
   10. Work-up
   11. Circle Strike
   12. Long Ball
   13. Punch Ball
   14. Indoor Baseball
  B. Schoolroom
   1. Ten Trips No. 1
   2. Leader Spry
   3. Potato Race Relay
   Review old schoolroom games

Folk Dancing
  Girls:
   1. Swiss May Dance
   2. Minuet
   3. Weaving Dance
  Boys:
   1. Shepherd's Hey
   2. Ox-dansen (Crampton's "Folk Dance Book")

Gymnastics
  A, B, C,—refer to Fall Term
  D. Movement Fundamentals
   1. Movement Fundamentals leading to Indoor Baseball pp. 318-324) and Track and Field (pp. 335-341)
Stunts and Contests (pp. 359-371)
   1. Stiff Leg Bend
   2. Hand Walk
   3. Bobbin Ahead
   4. Toe Wrestling
   5. Speed Stunt Series Relay
Motor Ability Tests
   Use Plan I, page 98 or Plan II, page 101. The various activities making up these tests may be worked on throughout the year, especially the form of the exercises.

Ball Bouncing Skills (O'Leary)

The child sings to the tune of "One Little, Two Little, Three Little Indians" the following words: "1—2—3 O'Leary; 4—5—6 O'Leary; 7—8—9 O'Leary; 10 O'Leary Postman."

The player bats the ball with the flat of the hand to 1—2—3 during the prescribed movement, each time at the word "O'Leary" letting the ball bounce higher by hitting it harder. To "10 O'Leary Postman" he gives one bounce and catches on "postman." The ball is never caught until the last.

Exercise 1—Swing right leg outward over ball on saying, "O'Leary."

Exercise 2—Swing left leg outward over ball on saying, "O'Leary."

Exercise 3—Swing right leg inward over ball on saying, "O'Leary."

Exercise 4—Swing left leg inward over ball on saying, "O'Leary."

Exercise 5—Grasp edge of skirt with left hand and upon saying, "O'Leary," make the ball pass upward between the arm and skirt.

Exercise 6—Same as Exercise 5, but let ball pass through from above.

Exercise 7—Grasp right wrist with left hand forming circle with arms, and make the ball pass through from below saying, "O'Leary."

Exercise 8—Same as Exercise 7, letting the ball drop over from above.

Exercise 9—Touch forefingers and thumbs together when saying, "O'Leary," and through circle formed let ball drop from above.

Exercise 10—To the words "1 O'Leary, 2 O'Leary, 3 O'Leary," and so on to "10 O'Leary Postman," bounce ball alternately to right and left of right foot. (The foot may be moved from side to side.)

Exercise 11—Bounce ball to same words as in Exercise 10, standing absolutely still.

Exercise 12—To same words as in Exercise 10, bounce ball throwing right leg over ball at every bounce.

Exercise 13—Same as Exercise 12, throwing right leg inward over ball.

Exercise 14—Same as Exercise 13, throwing left leg outward at every bounce.

Exercise 15—Same as Exercise 14, throwing left leg inward at every bounce.

Exercise 16—To the words, "Jack, Jack, pump the water; Jack, Jack, pump the water; Jack, Jack, pump the water; So early in the morning," go through the same movements of bouncing ball three times, then giving it a stronger bat on the word "water," make a complete turn left.

Exercise 17—Same as Exercise 16, making a complete turn right.

In the tournament a player is permitted to play as far as he can without a miss. The one able in a given number of trials to go furtherest wins the tournament.

ROPE JUMPING SKILLS

In these stunts emphasis should be on skill and variety. Endurance jumping should be discouraged.

Rope jumping may be done with a short single rope, long single rope, long double ropes, long single and short single ropes. The short single rope is turned by the jumper himself. The long single rope is swung by two turners. The long double ropes may be turned in two ways (1) by two persons each holding the ends of two ropes, one in each hand (2) by four persons standing at the corners of a square, each two turning a long rope across and perpendicular to the long rope turned by the other two persons. When the long single and short single ropes are turned together the long rope is swung by two people while the jumper swings his own rope and jumps it as well as the long rope.

Rope jumping may be divided into three types according to the length of time or number of beats used to swing the rope. Thus there is the two-count rope swing which takes two beats of time; the one-count rope swing which takes one beat of time; the two half-count rope swing which takes one half beat of time. Beats must be counted evenly.

The word "jumping" refers to a variety of foot movements as jumping on both feet, hopping on one foot, running or leaping, step-hops, gallop, skip in any direction and many combinations made with these. A variety of rope movements may also be done.

A. SHORT SINGLE ROPE

I. FOOT MOVEMENTS

a. Rope Jumping with Two-Count Rope Swing

These foot movements are done in even rhythm, two movements to a rope swing; the first movement, which is the one that "jumps" over the rope, is accented.

1. Leaps. The so-called "skip" is really a leap from the back foot to the forward foot (count 1) accented, and back onto the back foot again (count 2) if the rope is turning forward. Or if the rope is turning backward, leap from the front foot to the back foot on count 1 accented and return to front foot (count 2). Also a leap to the side may be taken from one foot to the other with the rope turning from side to side.

This step is used in place or to travel forward, backward or sideways.

2. Jumping in place. This is done on both feet taking two jumps to one rope swing (2 counts). The second jump is not as high as the first and may be only a slight stretching of the knees or raising of the heels as a rebound from the jump. This may be done swinging the rope forward, backward or sideways or while doing foot or head circles, slips or figure of eights.

3. Hopping on one foot. This is done by taking off from one foot and landing on that foot again. It may be done continuously on one foot for a given time, two hops to a rope swing (2 counts) then changing to the other foot. Changes may be made every eight hops (8 counts to each foot) or every four hops (4 counts to each foot) or every two counts. See No. 4.

4. Step Hop to one rope swing. This is done by leaping onto one foot (1 count), then hopping on that foot (1 count), then repeating with the other foot (2 counts), continue. This step is used standing in place, turning in place or traveling forward or backward with the rope turning forward or backward or sideways.

5. Hopping and jumping. This combines No. 2 and No. 3 above in series such as the following.

a. Hop four times on right foot with two rope swings (4 counts), jump on both feet four times with two rope swings (4 counts), hop on left foot 4 times with two rope swings (4 counts), and jump on both feet four times with two rope swings (4 counts).

b. Hop on right foot four times with two rope swings. Hop on left foot four times with two rope swings and then on both feet eight times with four rope swings.

Note—Children should be encouraged to originate their own series.

6. **Rocker.** This is the same leaping step as described in No. 1 except that the legs are kept straight and are alternately raised high forward and backward or sideways.

7. **Grapevine.** This is done by leaping sideways from one foot to the other (count 1), then bringing the free foot behind the supporting foot and leaping on to it (count 2), all with one swing of the rope; leaping again to the same side on the first foot (count 1), then leaping onto the second foot in front of the first (count 2). Continue moving sideways.

The grapevine may be combined with jumping in place and then repeating to opposite side as follows: grapevine to right with two rope swings as described above (4 counts), four jumps in place (4 counts), grapevine to left (4 counts), four jumps in place (4 counts). The rope swings continuously.

8. **Crossed spring jump.** Jump and land with feet crossed, first the right foot in front (count 1), then take a litle jump with feet still in this position (count 2); then jump and land with the left foot in front (count 1) and take a little jump again (count 2).

9. **Forward and backward spring jump.** Jump and land with feet in forward backward stride position with first the right and then the left foot forward. Make a small jump in stride position between each change. Each change takes two counts and one rope swing.

10. **Step swing.** Step swing is like Step hop (see No. 4) except that on the leap (count 1) the free foot is cut backward and on the hop (count 2) the free foot is swung forward.

11. **Rocking chair.** This is done as No. 6 except that after the leap forward (count 1) a small hop is taken on the forward foot (count 2) as in No. 4 but with the rear foot kicked well up behind as the body leans forward; then after the leap backward (count 1) the rear foot hops (count 2) with forward knee lifted high in front, body leaning back.

12. Deep knee bend jump. Same timing and form as jumping in place is used (see No. 2) except that it is done in squat position.

13. Lilt kick. With one rope swing, hop on one foot touching the other toe in front and near hopping foot (count 1); hop again on same foot and kick free foot forward (count 2). Alternate feet with each rope swing.

Try any of the Irish Lilt steps with rope swinging. See page 279.

14. Tap threes. Brush floor forward, backward and step. The step or change of weight must be taken as a leap in order to clear the rope on the accented beat. Start with a leap (count 1) and then go into the first "brush strike leap" (count 2 and 1 and continue). Both the plain threes and the hop threes may be taken.

Try other tap steps with rope swinging, as the fives and sevens. Be sure to make each accented step or change of weight which comes on count one, a leap over the rope.

b. Rope Jumping with a One-Count Rope Swing

1. Running. Move forward or backward, one leap to each swing of the rope. Each leap is accented.

2. "Salt and pepper". Jump on one or both feet in place or while turning around, one jump to each rope swing, each jump accented.

3. Skip. A real rope skip step is done in its usual uneven rhythm, in contrast with what we commonly call "rope skipping" which is a succession of leaps in even rhythm or the "step hop" which is also in even rhythm. Do the skip in the following manner: hop step, hop step, one count for each hop step, counted unevenly as "and-1 and-2". The rope slips under on the hop.

4. Gallop. The regular gallop is done in its uneven rhythm as follows: leap step, leap step, one count for each leap step, counted unevenly as "and-1, and -2". The rope slips under on the leap.

c. Rope Jumping with Two Half-Count Rope Swings

1. Doubles. Take one jump on both feet in place, swinging rope very fast either forward or backward, making two revolutions to one jump. This is most easily done by waiting for the jump until the rope has swung completely over the body and is about to touch the feet in its first revolution. The second revolution follows rapidly slipping under the feet again before they land.

II. ROPE MOVEMENTS FOR SHORT SINGLE ROPE

a. Straight Forward and Backward

The rope is swung forward or backward while jumping in place, or traveling forward or backward. Use wrist movements mostly.

b. Slips

As the rope is turning forward or backward the hands are brought together on one side of the body so that both strands of the rope swing together along the side. This movement is used as a step to go from one rope movement into another. The foot movements are usually continued during these.

c. Figure of 8

Combination of slips in which the rope is swung on both sides of the body alternately describing a figure of 8 motion in the air. Continue foot movements.

d. Head Circles

As the hands come together for a slip both ends are grasped in one hand and the rope is brought in a circle or several circles over the head by one hand, then returned to the side and re-grasped in two hands. Continue foot movements.

e. Foot Circle

Same as head circle, but done near the floor under the feet and the rope is jumped or leaped on each circle.

f. Crosses

As the rope is turning, the arms are crossed in front of the body, the rope continuing to be turned by a wrist motion for jumping as usual. Done both forward and backward, and alternated with open swing.

g. Sideways

The hands are both on one side of the body and the rope goes from side to side across the body as it turns.

h. Cradle

The rope swings back and forth like a pendulum, but must go at least waist high front and back.

III. TWO JUMPERS WITH SHORT SINGLE ROPE

a. Jumpers stand side by side, each grasping one end of the rope with the outside hand. Do any of steps described in I above in unison.

b. Jumpers stand one in front of the other. The back jumper swings the rope. The front jumper may face away from the rope swinger or they may face each other. The free person may turn from one position to the other during jumps or may run in and out of the swinging rope.

B. LONG SINGLE ROPE

I. COMMON MOVEMENTS

The rope should be at least 15 feet long. Two people each take an end and turn the rope.

There may be one or more persons jumping at one time. The most common steps used are the leap, the step hop, the jump on both feet and the hop on one foot; all of these are done with a two-count rope swing as in A I a. However, some of these steps may be done in "salt and pepper" time which gives one count to a rope swing. Running in and out of the swinging rope or running in and jumping the rope for a time and running out again are favorite stunts. If the runner enters the rope when it swings toward him from above it is called entering the "front door"; if when it swings toward him from below it is called entering the "back door". A series of stunts that may be done by a line of children taking turns follows.

a. Run through front door and out without touching rope.

b. Do same from back door.

c. Run in front door and jump three times on both feet with a little jump in between each jump, do three "hot peppers" (one jump to a swing of the rope speeded up), three high waters (rope swinging off of ground not higher than the knees) three slow jumps on both feet without a little jump in between. Run out.

d. Run in front door, do one big jump and one small jump on both feet, one step hop on right foot, one step hop on left foot, then leap from right to left and run out.

e. Run in front door, climb the ladder (leap across the rope moving to one end of rope and back) and run out.

f. Run in front door, turn completely around on three jumps and run out.

g. Run in and jump on both feet suiting the action to the following jingle as follows:

Words—Butterfly, butterfly,   turn a-   round

Action—jump, jump, jump, jump, turn jump-jump, jump-jump

Words—Butterfly, butterfly,   touch the ground

Action—jump, jump, jump, jump, jump to squat and touch floor and stand to do three more jumps

Words—Butterfly, butterfly,   show your shoe

Action—jump, jump, jump, jump, jump raise leg in front showing bottom of shoe, continue jumping three more times

Words—Butterfly, butterfly,   now ski-doo

Action—jump, jump, jump, jump, run out

The above series may be done as a contest. The children jump in turn. They follow the order of stunts given in the series above. If a child misses a step he gives way to the next jumper and waits for his next turn to try the step again. If successful this time he may continue from here as far as he can go. The child who finishes the series first wins the contest.

C. **LONG DOUBLE ROPES**

I. TWO ROPES WITH TWO TURNERS

Two persons each holding the ends of two ropes, one in each hand, turn the ropes toward each other alternately. One rope is started revolving on count one by each swinger moving his hand which holds this rope outward and upward and when this rope is on its downward course the other rope is started outward and upward and outside of the first rope count two. Each rope swing takes 2 counts but because the second rope starts one count late the jumper must jump in "salt and pepper" time in order to take both ropes.

a. Run in, jump on both feet for 10 jumps, run out.

b. Run in, turn on first two jumps, (4 counts) leap onto right foot, hop right, leap onto left foot, hop left, jump on both feet twice and run out.

II. TWO ROPES WITH FOUR TURNERS

Four turners stand on the four corners of a square each holding the end of a long single rope. These ropes swing across and perpendicular to each other. At a given signal each pair of turners swing their rope. The jumper runs in between two turners and jumps over the ropes where the two cross below. The jumper should watch to see at which point the ropes are turning "front or back door". Most of the steps used with single long ropes can be done.

D. LONG SINGLE ROPE—SHORT SINGLE ROPE

I. BOTH ROPES SWINGING FORWARD

a. The long rope is swung by two people while the jumper swings his own rope and jumps it as well as the long rope. Each rope swing takes two counts.

b. Stand in long rope and begin the swing of the short rope at same time the long rope starts. Jump the two ropes and run out still skipping short rope.

c. Swinging and leaping own rope run through long rope while it is swinging.

II. ONE ROPE SWINGING FORWARD, ONE BACKWARD

a. Run into long rope while it is swinging; start short rope backward and jump both ropes three times, with small jumps between each jump, then run out.

PHYSICAL EDUCATION

INDEX

Ace of Diamonds 233
Aeroplane Relay 43
A'Hunting We Will Go 174
Aims of Physical Education 5
All-over Relay 31
All-up Relay 58
American Country Dance 276
Animal Chase 37
Ankle Throw 361
Ante-over 50
Arch Ball 48
Arch Goal Ball 73
Arm's Length Tag 368
Auto Race 30
Away We All Go 178
Back Spring 361
Ball Bouncing Skills (O'Leary) 436
Ball Stand 55
Baseball Pivot and Throw 85
Basket Ball Far Throw (Overhead) 110
Basket Ball Far Throw (Single Arm) 109
Basket Ball: Games leading to 24
Basket Ball Goal Games 72
Basket Ball: Games Fundamentals leading to 324
Basket Ball Shuttle Relay 75
Bat Ball 61
Beanbag and Basket Relay 45
Beanbag Board 33
Beanbag Circle Carry 31
Beanbag Ring Toss 32
Bean Porridge Hot 151
Beast, Bird or Fish 45
Balancing Exercise 360
Bibliographies:
    Softball 324
    Basket Ball 332
    Corrective Exercises 307
    Folk Dances 282
    Games Books 97
    Marching 313
    Posture Helps, for 304
    Rhythms 140
    Soccer 335
    Stunts and Contests 359
    Track Athletics 112
Bicycling 360
Big Black Bear 40
Birds Flying 127
Black and White 38
Bleking 117, 122, 236
Bleking: Type Lesson in Folk Dancing for Schoolroom 122
Bobbing Ahead 365
Bombardment 59
Bounce Goal Relay 75

Bounce Pass Keep Away	78
Bounding Heart	262
Box Ball	88
Boyar Dance (Russian)	380
Broad Jump: Running	107
Standing	108
Bronco Tag	52
Brownies and Fairies	40
Bull in the Pen	37
Butterflies and Daisies	43
Butterfly, The	138
Captain Ball	81
Captain Jinks	224
Cat and Rat	36
Carrousel	192
Cart Wheel	360
Catch Ball	80
Cats and Rats	177
Center Base	37
Center Catch Ball	52
Chair Creeper	359
Chimes of Dunkirk	191
Chinese Get Up	364
Chinning	110
Christmas Dance	217
Christmas Rhythms	139, 143, 184, 217
Circle Bounce Ball	28
Circle Dodge Ball	59
Circle Strike	90
Class Athletics	111
Climbing	111
Cock-a-doodle-doo	159
Come Let Us Be Joyful	210
Conflict of the Seasons, The: A Pageant	372
Contests (Group Stunts)	370
Contests (Personal Combative)	368
Corner Kick Ball	68
Corrective Exercises	304
County Play Day	400
Course of Study in Physical Education for Elementary Schools	421
Crane Dive	359
Crested Hen	247
Crows and Cranes	39
Cshebogar	229
Cshebogar: Type Lesson in Folk Dancing for Gymnasium	123
Dance of Queen's Attendants (Gavotte)	395
Dance Steps	114, 115, 354
Danish Dance of Greeting	172
Dash	106
Dis-Arm	368
Dodge Ball: Simple	37
Circle	59
Progressive	63
Do This, Do That	27
Double Soccer Keep Away	65
Draw a Bucket of Water	181
Dribble and Bounce Pass Shuttle Relay	75

PHYSICAL EDUCATION 447

Dribble and Take Away	77
Driving the Pig to Market	56
Elbow Wrestling	370
Elephants	137
End Ball	80
Equipment:	
Minimal, for rural school	20
Minimal, for town school	12
Eskimo Jumping Race	369
Eskimo Race on All Fours	371
Eskimo Roll	365
Every Man in His Own Den	54
Fanfare (Struggle of the Four Winds)	377
Farmer in the Dell	145
Farmer Plants the Corn, The	146
Fifty or Burst	59
Figure Eight Relay	58
Finger Feet	370
First of May, The	206
Fist Polka	253
Flag Drills	416, 418
Flopper	282
Folk Dances for Boys	282
Folk Dancing Formations: Diagrams	119-121
Folk Dancing: Teaching of	119
Fongo	85
Foot Ball Baseball	85
Forward Roll, Single & Double	361
Fox and Geese	50
French Reel	249
Frog Dance	360
Gallant Ship, The	140
Games (Fundamentals)	317
Games: General Classification	21
Athletic Games	23
How to teach	21
Hunting Games	23
Intermediate Games	44
Primary Games	26
German Hopping Dance	231
Ghosts and Witches	39
Goal Keep Away	78
Going to Jerusalem	44
Grounders Shuttle Relay	84
Guard Pin Ball	36
Gustaf's Skoal	195
Hallowe'en Is Here	215
Hand Walk	361
Hand Wrestle	369
Hand Stand	361
Hang Tag	39
Hansel and Gretel	220
Have You Seen My Sheep	26
Head Stand	363
Head, Shoulders, Knees, Toes	215
Heel Click	361
Heel-toe Polka	116

Hen and Chickens (Fox and Geese) ... 50
Here We Go Round the Christmas Tree ... 157
Here We Go Round the Mulberry Bush ... 156
Hickory Dickory Dock ... 173
High Jump ... 107
Highland Schottische ... 261
Hindoo Tag ... 39
Hobby Horse, The ... 203
Hoop Relay ... 34
Hop Scotch ... 49
Hop, Step and Jump ... 111
Hop Waltz ... 117
Hot Ball ... 36
Hound and Rabbit ... 42
How D'ye Do, My Partner ... 165
Huckle, Buckle, Bean Stalk ... 26
I Am Very, Very Small ... 154
Indian Dance ... 197, 392
Indian File Relay ... 43
Indian File Relay (Schoolroom) ... 34
Indian War Dance ... 391
Indian Wrestle ... 369
In Greenland ... 387
Intermediate Games:
    Schoolroom ... 44
    Playground ... 49
Irish Lilt ... 279
I See You ... 193
I Want to Go to London ... 159
Jack Be Quick ... 51
Jumping Jack ... 132
Jumping Jack (Stunt) ... 360
Jumping Rope ... 131
Jump Stick ... 363
Jump the Shot ... 54
Jump Wand Relay ... 57
Kaleidoscope ... 26
Keep Away ... 77
Kinderpolka ... 186
King of France, The ... 141
Kitty White ... 153
Knee Dip ... 359
Knee Raising ... 110
Last Couple Out ... 53
Last Man ... 30
Leader Spry ... 32
Leap Frog and Forward Roll ... 361
Leap Frog Relay ... 371
Let Us Wash Our Dolly's Clothes ... 158
Line Ball ... 32
Line Bounce Ball ... 28
Line Tug of War ... 369
Little Miss Muffet ... 189
London Bridge ... 150
Long Ball ... 88
Looby Loo ... 147
Lost Child ... 26
March ... 125

PHYSICAL EDUCATION

Marching	308
Mass Potato Race	112
Mass Running	111
May Pole Dance	415
Mazurka	118
Meet Me at the Switch	33
Merry-Go-Round	365
Midnight	37
Mimetic Exercises	341
Minuet	259
Motor Ability Tests	98
Plan One	98
Plan Two	101
Movement Fundamentals	316
Leading to Softball	318
Leading to Basket Ball	324
Leading to Soccer	332
Leading to Track and Field Events	335
Significance and Value of	316
Muffin Man, The	142
Mulberry Bush, The	156
Musical Indian Clubs	51
My Son John	180
Nest Making	201
Newcomb	79
New York	41
Nixie Polka (Nigarepolska)	208
Norwegian Mountain March	243
Nuts in May	157
Old Roger Is Dead	166
Old Zip Coon (Turkey in the Straw)	255
O'Leary (Ball Bouncing Skills)	436
One Old Cat	83
Open Orders	314
Ostrich Tag	39
Otto and the Crow	188
Overhead Beanbag Relay	48
Pageant: The Conflict of the Seasons	372
Partner Shuttle Relay	57
Partner Tag	53
Partner Tag (Schoolroom)	29
Pass for Points	78
Pendulum	365
Personal Combative Exercises	368
Physical Education: Aims and General Considerations	5
Pig in the Parlor	226
Pin Ball	36
Pivot and Pass	74
Play Day: Plan of Organization	400
Playground Ball Throw	109
Playing Ball	133
Playing Soldier	133
Poison Snake	39
Polka	115
Pom Pom Pull Away	41
Pop Goes the Weasel	238

Posture Education:
  Criteria of Good Standing Position 284
  Developing Mental Responses Associated with Good Posture 303
  Methods of Preventing Poor Posture 288
  Posture Exercises 291, 296, 301
  Significance of Posture 283
Posture Tag 44
Posture: Triple Test 295
Potato Race 106
Potato Race Relay 47
Primary Games:
  Playground 36
  Schoolroom 26
Progressive Dodge Ball 63
Prostrate and Perpendicular 363
Pulling Sticks 369
Punch Ball 86
Pursuit Relay 46
Push Ball Relay 56
Push Club Relay 56
Push Tug of War 369
Pussy Cat 163
Pyramid No. I, II and III 366
Rabbit in the Hollow 144
Raindrops 129
Reap the Flax 245
Red Light 55
Relief Period: Activities for 15
Rhythmical Activities 113
Rhythmical Activities for Intermediate Grades 205
Rhythmical Activities for Primary Grades 125
Rhythmical Interpretations, Examples of 139
Rhythmical Jumping Exercises 354
Ride a Cock Horse 187
Ring Call Ball 50
Rocking Dolly 128
Rolling Hoop 131
Roman Soldiers, The 182
Rooster Fight (a) 369
Rooster Fight (b) 370
Rope Jumping Skills 437
Round and Round the Village 164
Rufty Tufty 268
Run and Pass Relay 64
Run for Your Supper 42
Running Broad Jump 107
Running High Jump 107
Rural School: Activities for 17
  Minimal Equipment 20
  Organization of Children 19
Russian Folk Dance 275
Sally Go Round the Sun 141
Santa Claus and Reindeer 184
Schoolroom Basket Ball Relay 35
Schoolroom Snatch 35
Schottische 117
See-Saw 136
Sellenger's Round 251

Serve and Return	91
Setting Pegs	370
Seven Jumps	213
Shepherd's Hey	270
Shoemaker's Dance	149
Shuttle Basket Ball Throw	111
Shuttle Broad Jump	111
Shuttle Kicking Contest	68
Shuttle Relay	56
Sidewalk Tag	39
Signals	14
Simple Soccer Keep-away	64
Skip	126
Slap Jack	36
Snail, The	152
Snatch	40
Snatch (Schoolroom)	35
Snow-ball Game	167
Snow Storm	212
Snow Storm, The	139
Soccer Dribble Relay	65
Soccer Dribble and Shoot Relay	66
Soccer Drive	67
Soccer Football (Simplified)	69
Soccer: Games Leading to	25
Movement Fundamentals of	332
Soccer Pass	67
Soccer Pass and Shoot	67
Soccer Target Kicking Relay	66
Softball	91
Games leading to	24
Movement Fundamentals of	318
Speed Stunt Series Relay	370
Spring's First Dance	385
Square Football	68
Squat Tag	39
Squirrel and Nut	27
Squirrels in Trees	36
Standing Broad Jump	108
Stealing Sticks	60
Step-hop	116
Stiff Leg Bend	360
Stomach Stand	363
Stores	41
Story Plays	344-354
Story Plays	344
A Sample Story Play	346
Planning a Story Play	345
Story Play Outlines	348
Street-car	27
Streets and Alleys	53
Strasak	228
Stunts: Individual	359
Couple	363
Group	365
Swedish Klappdans	240
Swedish Ring Dance	222
Swing, The	134, 135

Swing Song	135
Swiss May Dance	242
Tag Games	39
Tag the Line Relay	43
Tag the Wall Relay	30
Take a Chair from Under	360
Tantoli	235
Tarantella	388
Teacher and Class	27
Teaching a Folk Dance	119
Ten Pin Contest	59
Ten Trips	73
Third Man	52
Thorn Rosa	160
Thread Follows the Needle, The	161
Three Broad	51
Three Crows	200
Three Deep	51
Three Little Girls	207
Three Little Kittens	175
Three Little Mice	169
Through the Stick	362
Time Allotment for Physical Education Program	10
Tip Up	362
Toe Wrestling	369
To Market, To Market	171
Top	363
Touch Off	55
Tower Ball	36
Track and Field Athletics	98
Track and Field: Movement Fundamentals Leading to	335
Train, The	130
Triangle Ball	82
Triple Test Exercises	296, 301
Triple Test for Posture	295
Troika	258
Trunk Lifting	110
Tucker	155
Tunnel Race	371
Turkey in the Straw (Old Zip Coon)	255
Twister	365
Type Lessons in Folk Dancing for the Schoolroom	122
Type Lesson in Folk Dancing for the Gymnasium	123
Type Lessons in Fundamentals of Softball	320, 322
Type Lessons in Fundamentals of Basket Ball	324, 328
Virginia Reel	255
Volley Ball	92
Volley Ball (Simplified)	92
Volley Ball: Games leading to	25
Wall Ball Bounce	29
Wand Drill	419
Weaving Dance	264
Whip Tag	52
Wood Tag	39
Work-up	83
Yankee Doodle	179
Zig Zag Goal Ball	75
Zig Zag Pass	72